DESIGN
PORTFOLIOS
*Moving From Traditional to **Digital***

DESIGN
PORTFOLIOS

*Moving From Traditional to **Digital***

DIANE M. BENDER

ARIZONA STATE UNIVERSITY

FAIRCHILD BOOKS, INC.
NEW YORK

Director of Sales and Acquisitions: Dana Meltzer-Berkowitz

Executive Editor: Olga T. Kontzias

Acquisitions Editor: Joseph Miranda

Associate Acquisitions Editor: Jaclyn Bergeron

Senior Development Editor: Jennifer Crane

Development Editor: Michelle Levy

Art Director: Adam B. Bohannon

Production Manager: Ginger Hillman

Associate Production Editor: Jessica Rozler

Interior Design: Renato Stanisic Design

Cover Design: Adam B. Bohannon

Library of Congress Catalog Card Number: 2007930694

ISBN: 978-1-56367-483-9

GST R 133004424

Printed in the China

TP15

Contents

Extended Contents

Acknowledgments

This book would not have been possible without the support and encouragement of many individuals. I would like to recognize those friends and colleagues who have been so supportive. I am quite grateful for the support I received from Olga Kontzias, Executive Editor, Joseph Miranda, Acquisitions Editor, Michelle Levy, Development Editor, and the entire art department at Fairchild Publications. I would like to thank the two anonymous reviewers for their insightful comments and recommendations. In the following pages, you will see projects by many talented design students and quotes from respected educators and practitioners. A big "thank you" to all of them!

I also extend special thanks to my colleagues at Arizona State University: Jose Bernardi, Beverly Brandt, Lorraine Cutler, Connie Thibeau-Catsis, and Tom Witt. In addition, my former colleagues, Jon D. Vredevoogd, Linda Nelson Johnson, and Janetta M. McCoy, have been most helpful to me while working on this manuscript. Aaron Kulik also deserves kudos for the talents shown in many diagrams and illustrations. Thank you to my friends Alissa Bails and Brigid Rot, who both endlessly listened to my occasional manuscript traumas. Thank you to Lisa Broome, Joanie Liebelt, and my parents, Janet and Donnell Bender, for reviewing and editing initial drafts of this manuscript. And last but certainly not least, to my best friend and husband, Brian Twet, who always knew when to hug me, when to give me peace and quiet, and when to bring me a big stack of chocolate chip cookies!

Introduction

This book is written for anyone preparing for a career in architecture, interior design, or landscape architecture. It is not intended exclusively for college graduates, as a portfolio is important in many design programs for admission into upper division classes and even into graduate school. This book is also essential for those of you who are currently working in the design field and may need to update your portfolio, particularly if you're transitioning from a traditional portfolio to a digital one. Knowing how to properly organize your work and present it in the best context can help you sell yourself when you change jobs or seek a promotion from your current employer.

This book provides insight into both the traditional printed portfolio and the newer format of the digital portfolio. More than a collection of your work, your portfolio is a marketing tool. It is a sales kit for the most important project you'll ever sell—yourself! In its pages (whether printed or electronic), the portfolio is a reflection of your artistry, vision, technical skill, and resourcefulness. Your portfolio is the single most important record of your design education and professional experience. It records your ideas and thinking processes, and the end results of your design efforts.

Competition is tough in the professions of architecture, interior design, and landscape architecture. Competition for schooling, jobs, and clients often hinges on your design skills and abilities. The artifacts you produce as evidence of these skills and abilities must be carefully gathered and impressively presented in a design portfolio. A portfolio is an evolving collection of design problems and creative solutions. It is an assumption in our fields that you will have a portfolio of your work. It's an expectation and a part of life as a designer. The work in your portfolio must stand on its own and speak for itself yet be an integral component of your overall design philosophy and intent. A successful portfolio indicates that you can visually relay a message to others.

Various types of portfolios and different ways to present them are discussed in this book. The appearance of your portfolio will differ depending on the situation in which you need to present it. A portfolio is an important component of a job interview. The portfolio will be displayed at that critical moment in the interview when the interviewer, already impressed with your personality, intelligence, and wit, is ready to see your work. At that point you will take out your portfolio for him or her to review. Will your portfolio position you head and shoulders above the other applicants?

Today's generation of incoming professionals is expected to display their work in a digital format, either on CD-ROM or on the Internet. In organizing, creating, and presenting your digital portfolio, you'll use the same classic design principles as in a printed portfolio. You'll just use them digitally. Instead of paper, marker, and presentation boards, you'll use computer software, scanners, and web sites. Throughout the book, various computer components, software programs, and digital presentation methods are discussed. I offer guidelines on which ones to choose to meet your needs.

Your portfolio is often the determining factor for success when interviewing for a job, applying to school, or securing a project with the most sought-after client in town. The goal is to demonstrate through your portfolio that you are a creative and thought-provoking designer, with evidence of excellent time-management, communication, and presentation skills. A superb portfolio won't ensure that you will get the job of your dreams or be accepted into the top school in your field. Part of that responsibility lies with you, your credentials, and how you express yourself in writing or verbally during an interview. But a bad portfolio will certainly ruin your chances for success. This book provides insight into features that can make your portfolio better, as well as advice on what *not* to do.

I cannot stress enough that the creation of your portfolio is cyclical. In other words, its development is unlikely to occur in a simple linear sequence. The procedures in this book are set up in a somewhat chronological manner so you can clearly understand the meaning of the process. When working on your portfolio, you will experience moments of reflection that spur you to rethink a project in your portfolio. So you'll go back and redo a page or two. This is a cyclical process. Also, keep in mind that a portfolio is only a snapshot of your abilities at one point in time. It will continually evolve as your design skills increase and your design philosophy comes together over the coming years.

INTENDED AUDIENCE AMONG THE DESIGN DISCIPLINES

Although a portfolio is useful in many careers, the focus in this book is shifted toward the design disciplines of the built environment: architecture, interior design, and landscape architecture. Professionals in these three disciplines work closely to design and build the spaces in which we live, work, rest, and play. The term *design* is being used now more frequently in business and commerce, but the focus of this text is on the constructed, human-made environment. The title *designer* will be used frequently in this text. It broadly refers to an architect, an interior designer, a landscape architect, and other types of designers as well, such as an industrial designer, a graphic designer, and of course an artist. All of these professionals design, and they all will develop a portfolio. Obviously, the contents will differ, as the scale of design differs from discipline to discipline. For example, an architect may include the work of a 20-story building in her portfolio, whereas an interior designer may include a custom carpet design in his portfolio. Practitioners in each discipline expect to see certain items as evidence of skill in a portfolio. These skill sets and typical contents are discussed in this book.

What you put in your individual portfolio may differ slightly from the examples provided in this book. But how these portfolio items are gathered and presented will be similar among the design disciplines. Whether designing the building itself, the interior, or the exterior, professionals in these related fields tend to use similar visual elements and artifacts when working with clients. However, these artifacts are unlike artifacts produced in other design professions. Artifacts such as rough sketches, oversized two-dimensional (2-D) drawings and presentation boards, three-dimensional (3-D) scale models, and computer-generated animated walk-throughs are typically used in presentations to our clients. The focus of this book is therefore on the content and multiple formats of your portfolio. It will help designers organize items and present them in a coherent manner that also piques the interest of reviewers.

PRACTITIONER ADVICE

Practitioners and the firms they represent vary in their assessment of portfolios. So do educators and the schools they represent. Who hasn't shown their work to someone and gotten rave reviews, only to show it to someone else who reacts with an earful of negative criticism? Different practitioners and educators like to see different things. After all, these are people with personal opinions. Sometimes the requirements are made clear to you prior to application; sometimes the requirements are less concrete.

The comments from respected educators and practitioners provided in the sidebars of this text expand on basic concepts and offer alternative viewpoints of the topic. These are practitioners who make hiring decisions and educators who judge admissions to academic program. You will learn what turns them on and what turns them off. These comments provide a wide variety of opinions and guidelines to assist you in portfolio creation and presentation.

The information and advice presented here are only suggestions. The insightful comments elicited from practitioners and educators are included to provide a broader perspective on portfolio design and review. Some of these comments are in contrast to one another. This is a clear indication that not everyone agrees on what makes a portfolio a brilliant success.

EXAMPLES OF STUDENT WORK

Examples of outstanding student projects and portfolio pages are provided whenever possible. They are scattered throughout the book to highlight important concepts. Many examples are from exit and graduate school portfolios, representing a mastery of knowledge at the senior and graduate level. Some are included from admissions portfolios, to show a good example of a basic design skill or presentation. These illustrations present a variety of portfolio techniques, content, and formats specific to the design disciplines of architecture, interior design, and landscape architecture. Portfolio pages from traditional printed media, as well as digital portfolios from CD-ROMs and web site presentations, are included.

OVERVIEW OF EACH SECTION

Following this introduction, the book is divided into four sections. Section I introduces the design portfolio in its two primary formats, traditional and digital. The diversity of portfolios is presented in the context of the design disciplines, taking into account the differences between residential and commercial design. The section concludes with some insights into how practitioners in these firms will evaluate your portfolio and what types of career choices are available to you.

Section II focuses on a four-step process of gathering and organizing the contents of your portfolio. Regardless of its presentation format, your portfolio will need to represent your skills and abilities as they relate to those necessary in the design professions. Descriptions of common skill sets required by college accrediting boards, and examples of career skills are provided to help you ascertain what types of materials you have (or don't have) to include in your portfolio. Based on these guidelines, typical portfolio contents are listed along with comments on how best to present them. Different strategies are discussed for organizing and storyboarding your work. This section concludes with a chapter on the visual layout and construction of your printed portfolio and packaging materials.

Section III, a detailed discussion of the digital portfolio, begins with an overview of how designers typically use computers. A brief description is provided of technologies you'll need in your digital portfolio production, including the computer, scanner, printer, digital camera, and digital storage devices. Important considerations of digital presentation are discussed next, such as color systems, image formats, and resolution. Working digitally raises unique portfolio challenges, such as photographing 3-D work, scanning material, and enhancing drawings with image-editing software. This section ends with guidelines for putting your digital portfolio together with navigation, audio, video, PDF files, and web pages.

Section IV concludes the book with chapters that focus on presenting your digital portfolio via laptop, web site, or CD-ROM. Each presentation format has benefits and drawbacks. All the information you've gathered in the previous sections will help you determine the best presentation method for your end goal, whether it's admission into a school or securing a position in a design firm. A vast amount of information is provided on finding and securing a job, including guidelines for creating a personal promotion package that includes a resume, cover letter, marketing sampler, thank-you letter, and leave-behind piece. Guidelines and tips are offered for successfully presenting your portfolio in an interview and for securing a job. And finally, an explanation is given of how to evaluate your portfolio, get feedback from others, and update your portfolio for future needs.

SECTION I

THE PORTFOLIO

The Design Portfolio

To begin our exploration of the design portfolio, we will discuss the context of creating and presenting a portfolio. It is important to understand not only your profession but also those related to it in order to converse intelligently with other practitioners. A brief overview of architecture, interior design, and landscape architecture is provided. The chapter concludes with an explanation of both the traditional and digital formats of a portfolio and the benefits of both.

OVERVIEW OF DESIGN DISCIPLINES

When going to school part or full time, or working in the profession a little bit here and there, it is easy to become so engrossed in your own design discipline that you miss the forest for the trees. You don't see the interrelationship that exists between all the design disciplines of the built environment. Three disciplines are typically involved in the design and construction of our environment: architecture, interior design, and landscape architecture. One profession unto itself does not construct our built environment. It takes the knowledge, experience, and expertise of a team of practitioners to construct a house, office building, campus, or city. As designers, we work in close collaboration with others. An architect cannot do it all, nor can an interior designer, engineer, landscape architect, graphic designer, urban planner, industrial designer, or artist. Each profession brings to the table a slightly different perspective on the place of humans in our environment. Most projects in the real world are completed in multidisciplinary teams, with representatives from each design discipline contributing to the project's outcome.

You are a designer: a person who creates things. You solve problems. You create alternative solutions to meet the needs of a client, and you communicate these solutions in appropriate ways. You are not an artist. Art is a personal

It is critical that the student or young professional not mistake the portfolio for something it is not—i.e., a work of art. In my opinion, a portfolio should be akin to a beautifully assembled art catalogue wherein the quality of the reproductions comes first rather than an artist's book, which places a premium on the artifact itself. The best portfolios are indicators of future potential as much as they are demonstrations of past accomplishment.

Wellington Reiter
Dean
College of Design
Arizona State University
Tempe, AZ

Box 1.1

expression of the artist's idea and beliefs (Tain 2003). Design is a logical problem-solving activity that ends in a plan with anticipated outcomes. It is not haphazard or accidental. A person or a firm hires you to create designs that function and solve a problem, and are pleasing to the eye. Designers use both deductive reasoning (from general to specific) and inductive reasoning (from specific to general) in the creative process. You are not hired to make pretty pictures. Design is not art but, rather, creative problem solving. Your portfolio should reflect this focus (see Box 1.1).

Designers need to be disciplined, organized, and skilled businesspeople. What's more, they need to be creative, imaginative, and artistic. Combining aesthetic vision with practical skills and knowledge, designers work with clients to develop solutions that actually function in addition to being visually appealing. All graduates of design programs have acquired a broad foundation of education and have applied this education in solving complex design problems. You should be a technically accomplished and conceptually sophisticated designer by the time you approach graduation. You should know something about each of these fields and how they relate to the other fields. Become familiar with the hot issues in them and some of the leaders, the movers and shakers in each field. This additional knowledge will only make you more salable in an interview setting. After all, regardless of your stated design field, you'll be working with professionals in these other disciplines once hired. If you are unfamiliar with the fields of architecture, interior design, and landscape architecture, some information is provided next.

Architecture

Architecture is a profession that deals with the construction and ornamentation of buildings and environments. Design principles and aesthetic considerations are taken into account, along with the structural integrity of the building itself. Architecture often includes a broader scope of design for the built environment, from the larger context of urban planning to the smaller context of furniture design.

1.1
Architecture often
involves the creation of
large-scale buildings.
Design work courtesy
of Michael J. Barnsfield.

In general, an architect is a person who provides the vision for a project's design, creates construction documents and drawings like those shown in Figure 1.1, and coordinates the actual construction of a building and its site.

Part of the architect's responsibility includes observing the progress of construction and processing any changes that might alter the building or its site. An architect is a person qualified and skilled to design, certify, direct, and oversee all aspects of design and construction.

Interior Design

Interior design is a recognized profession that involves the creation of functional and aesthetically attractive interiors within a building or structure. Because the designs are typically created within a building's shell, the practice of interior design involves knowledge of regulatory requirements, construction codes and practices, structural components, and building systems (this is in contrast to interior decorating, which focuses exclusively on selecting and placing fixtures, furnishings, and decorative elements in an interior space).

Interior designers focus on the intimate relationship between the user and the built environment. Interior designers are aware that decisions they make in the design of the interior environment can have an impact on human interaction and the users' emotional response (see Figure 1.2).

Designers experiment with space, form, texture, and color in light of historical, environmental, global, and cultural references. Both two-dimensional (2-D)

connection

1.2
Interior design focuses on the interaction of humans with an intimate interior environment.
Design work courtesy of Alexandra C. Ayres, Sally Azer, and Kelly Robinson.

and three-dimensional (3-D) thinking are part of the profession, represented in both simple residential dwellings and more complex commercial projects.

Landscape Architecture

While an interior designer concentrates on interior spaces, a landscape architect focuses on exterior spaces. Landscape architecture can be considered the practice of effectively arranging land, walkways, and buildings for human use and enjoyment. Landscape architects design exterior rooms and spaces with not only plants, but hardscapes as well. Projects can range from a small garden, to a large city park, to a river area revitalization project like the one in Figure 1.3.

The profession encompasses the external planning of large commercial urban areas as well as intimate residential garden sites. In addition, it includes the design of a building site, selection and installation of horticulture on the site, environmental restoration, and historic preservation.

A landscape architect is a professional who has training in horticulture, landscape design, irrigation systems, construction, and site design. He has a working knowledge of the principles of architecture, urban planning, and civil engineering. The landscape architect contributes to the design of a master site plan, from which construction and detail drawings are prepared. The goal of the landscape architect is to make meaningful connections between the indoors and outdoors.

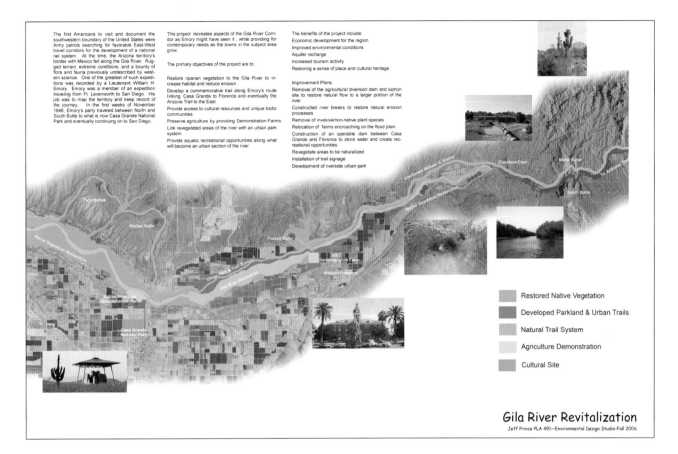

The first Americans to visit and document the southwestern boundary of the United States were Army patrols searching for favorable East-West travel corridors for the development of a national rail system. At the time, the Arizona territory's border with Mexico fell along the Gila River. Rugged terrain, extreme conditions, and a bounty of flora and fauna previously undescribed by western science. One of the greatest of such expeditions was recorded by a Lieutenant William H. Emory. Emory was a member of an expedition traveling from Ft. Leavenworth to San Diego. His job was to map the territory and keep record of the journey. In the first weeks of November 1846, Emory's party traveled between North and South Butte to what is now Casa Grande National Park and eventually continuing on to San Diego.

This project recreates aspects of the Gila River Corridor as Emory might have seen it , while providing for contemporary needs as the towns in the subject area grow.

The primary objectives of the project are to:

Restore riparian vegetation to the Gila River to increase habitat and reduce erosion

Develop a commemorative trail along Emory's route linking Casa Grande to Florence and eventually the Arizona Trail to the East

Provide access to cultural resources and unique biotic communities

Preserve agriculture by providing Demonstration Farms

Link revegetated areas of the river with an urban park system

Provide aquatic recreational opportunities along what will become an urban section of the river

The benefits of the project include:
Economic development for the region
Improved environmental conditions
Aquifer recharge
Increased tourism activity
Restoring a sense of place and cultural heritage

Improvement Plans:
Removal of the agricultural diversion dam and siphon site to restore natural flow to a larger portion of the river
Constructed river breaks to restore natural erosion processes
Removal of invasive/non-native plant species
Relocation of farms encroaching on the flood plain
Construction of an operable dam between Casa Grande and Florence to store water and create recreational opportunities
Revegetate areas to be naturalized
Installation of trail signage
Development of riverside urban park

Restored Native Vegetation

Developed Parkland & Urban Trails

Natural Trail System

Agriculture Demonstration

Cultural Site

Gila River Revitalization
Jeff Prince PLA 491—Environmental Design Studio-Fall 2006

COMMON GROUND

The professional architect, interior designer, and landscape architect create and enhance the function and quality of interior and exterior spaces for the purpose of improving the quality of life, increasing productivity, and protecting the health, welfare, and safety of the public. These three disciplines have their own approaches to the design process and presentation materials. Another obvious difference between the three disciplines is evident in the scale within which each profession works. The scales of projects can vary from discipline to discipline. Interior design is usually conceived on an intimate scale, landscape architecture tends to include much larger projects, and architecture covers the range in-between. This is not a law, but a general rule of thumb.

Yet the three disciplines collaborate and overlap each other in the parameters of the project. Where does one profession end and another begin? Take the exterior door in Figure 1.4 as an example. This illustrates one of the innumerable instances in which the disciplines have an impact on each other. Which profession "owns" the door? Does the architect own it because it's part of the building? Does the interior designer own it because its location will influence the design of the interior space? What about the landscape architect, who must provide an exterior entryway leading to this door? Everyone has a vested interest in the size, location, and appearance of the door. If the loading dock for the building must be relocated because of street access, the door will be moved. This will affect the location of

1.3
Landscape architecture centers on the exterior environment.
Design work courtesy of Jeffrey Prince.

1.4
An exterior door is a good example of the overlapping of professional responsibility for architecture, interior design, and landscape architecture.

interior corridors, stairs, and other aspects of the circulation pattern. It may have an impact on the structural integrity of the building if the new location of the door is in the middle of a load-bearing wall. As you can see, these and other decisions made by one member of the team will influence the decisions made by the rest of the team members.

The Four Es

To be considered a professional in your chosen field, you must meet four criteria: education, experience, examination, and more education. Each discipline has specific requirements, which may vary from state to state. For the most part, all of them require entering professionals to be deemed qualified both by peer evaluation and government regulation. Professionals must also continue their education throughout their careers.

Educational Accreditation

Educational accreditation is a voluntary system of self-regulation that is overseen not by the government, but by professionals in the field. All three professions have accrediting bodies that oversee the educational standards of their programs. The Landscape Architectural Accreditation Board (LAAB), the Council for Interior Design Accreditation (CIDA), and the National Architecture Accreditation Board (NAAB) all accredit hundreds of bachelor's and master's level programs. Each board has established a list of competencies that must be exhibited by each graduating class. See each exam board's web site for more details (www.asla.org; www.accredit-id.org; www.naab.org).

Supervised Experience

The second component of becoming a professional architect, interior designer, or landscape architect involves gaining experience in the field upon graduation. Each discipline requires a specific number of years of design experience, to be supervised by an experienced professional in the field. If the state in which you work has licensure legislation in place, you would be required to work under a licensed professional in your firm. In architecture, the three years after your education is completed but before the registration examination has been passed is referred to as the internship period. In interior design and landscape architecture, the term *internship* refers to work experience gained while completing formal education. The goal of supervised postgraduate experience is to obtain a diverse understanding of the profession and to gain familiarity with as many facets of the discipline during this period as possible.

Registration Examination

All three professions require practitioners to successfully pass one or more registration examinations. These examinations provide an authoritative measure of proficiency that is specifically designed to protect the health, safety, and welfare of the public. If you can't pass this test, you are not eligible to be a professional designer. The examinations are the same across the United States, but each state issues its own certificate or license. Landscape architects must pass the Landscape Architect Registration Examination (LARE) issued by the Council of Landscape Architectural Registration Boards (www.clarb.org). Interior designers must pass the National Council for Interior Design Qualification Examination (NCIDQ) administered by the organization of the same name (www.ncidq.org). Architects must pass the Architectural Registration Examination (ARE) prepared by the National Council for Architectural Registration Boards (www.ncarb.org). For more information on these specific examinations, please refer to the web site for each registration board.

Continuing Education

To retain status in a professional design organization and to maintain registration, certification, or licensure in the profession, you may be required to participate in annual education and training. This ensures that you are continually learning about new developments in your discipline. Each training course is assigned a certain number of continuing education units (CEUs). The exact number of CEUs and contact hours required by each profession varies from state to state. See the web site of your professional organization for more details (www.aia.org; www.asid.org; www.asla.org; www.iida.org).

Regulation

All three professions have commonalities in regulation and professional preparedness. They all strive for the strictest regulations in order to maintain the rigor of the profession and to protect the public's well being. Professional design organizations lobby government officials to support and pass laws that elevate the status of the practitioner, separating them from unskilled individuals who practice the discipline without the knowledge, familiarity, or testing required to ensure competency. Professional regulation is important to our design professions. It can take one of two forms: a title act or a practice act.

Title Act

A title act prohibits anyone not certified or registered by the state from representing or identifying himself or herself as a certified or registered professional. She cannot call herself an architect, landscape architect, or interior designer. It does not prohibit her from practicing or performing that profession.

Practice Act

A practice act prohibits someone from calling himself an architect, landscape architect, or interior designer. It also prohibits the actual practice of the profession by anyone not licensed by that state. This is the most stringent form of regulation and is in effect for the protection of the public from unqualified individuals.

Furthermore, there are three categories of regulation: registration, certification, and licensure. Most people use these terms interchangeably and some states even use more than one of these terms. All design professions face this confusion.

Registration

State registration requires that anyone wishing to practice a specific profession must have his or her name and contact information on file with the state. Simply stated, it is no more than a state roster of practitioners. This is the weakest form of regulation and is only relied upon for confirmation of a professional's credentials when the threat to the public is minimal.

Certification

Regulation under a title act means the individual is certified to do the job. The individual can use the title of the profession but is not licensed. Although certain standards and criteria must be met for certification, it is not the highest level of regulation.

Licensure

A licensed landscape architect, interior designer, or architect is regulated under a practice act. This is the highest and most rigorous form of regulation. In the United States, licensure refers to the giving of a license by the state government to an individual in order to work in a specific profession. Licensure ensures that practitioners are competent in their field and will not harm the public. It requires the candidate for licensure to have a determined amount of accredited education, a certain length of experience in the field, and have successfully passed one or more regulated professional examinations. It is granted to a practitioner after requirements have been met for education, examination, and experience. Licensure law varies from state to state (you'll need to check with your state to see if these are required). It allows you to work in an area that would otherwise be legally prohibited, but it also holds you legally responsible and accountable for that work.

Design professions seek licensure to protect the public. If an untrained, uneducated, and untested individual carried out the tasks of your discipline, the results could be devastating. Negligence can harm the people using a space, building, or site. It can result in physical harm to occupants, damage to the property, and higher construction costs (which no client really likes), and can even harm the environment.

Let's consider a few examples of negligence. An incompetent landscape architect has designed a residence without grading the land properly. Instead of the rain draining away from the house, water pools around the entryway. In a cold climate, this water freezes. The occupant comes home one day, slips, falls on the ice, and is seriously injured. The landscape architect is at fault. In a similar cold climate, an architect must calculate the load of a rooftop to account for seasonal snow and ice. If this is not calculated correctly, the roof could collapse on all who reside inside. The architect is at fault. Likewise, an interior designer must be knowledgeable of all materials specified in an interior. The carpet in the commercial office building must meet building codes. If the wrong carpet is specified and a fire occurs in the space, the occupants could die from the fumes emitted by the burning carpet (rather than the fire itself). The interior designer is at fault. What you do as a professional designer can positively or negatively affect those who use your designs.

WHAT IS A PORTFOLIO?

Practitioners of architecture, interior design, and landscape architecture recognize portfolios as a part of the professional culture. Designers are unique and require special communication methods. We communicate visually and graphically, with most of our work described in two- and three-dimensional media. Every designer has created a portfolio. Every designer owns one. And every designer is continually updating one.

You may have heard the word *portfolio* being used in education to refer to evidence of learning and progress, or in finance as a collection of investments and securities. Design portfolios are different. Dictionary definitions of portfolio are not very helpful. They tend to categorize a portfolio as the case that surrounds a person's work. For example, Merriam-Webster defines a portfolio as "a hinged cover or flexible case for carrying loose papers, pictures, or pamphlets" (Merriam-Webster OnLine 2006). Dictionary.com (2006) describes it as both a portable case for holding material and the materials collected in such a case. This gets closer to what a design portfolio is: a collection of your work presented together in a cohesive whole.

A portfolio is more than just a repository of past work; it is a unique object of work in itself. It is an organized collection of artifacts that demonstrates your skills and abilities as a designer. What you put in the portfolio and how it is presented will vary depending on its intent and audience. As seen in Figure 1.5, there is no standard format for a portfolio.

In the same way that a resume or cover letter is a unique statement about you, so is your portfolio. Some portfolios are entirely consistent in graphics and presentation format, while others are diverse in format, size, and style (Mitton 2004). Like the portfolio books in Figure 1.6, the format becomes an extension of the individual and a reflection of a unique personality (Hall 2001).

Being a successful designer means having vision, imagination, and judgment. To be able to detect an idea, use it effectively, and then assess its value is the mark

RIGHT: 1.5
**There are different
varieties and formats
of portfolio
presentations.**

BELOW: 1.6
**The presentation book
is a popular format to
reproduce your work
and express your
individual personality.**

of a good designer. All this is evidence of your ability to communicate a design to others, which can be shown in a design portfolio. The portfolio is generally accepted as an artistic, intellectual, and comprehensive assessment of your design capabilities. Its main purpose is to document your knowledge, skills, and accomplishments.

There are several uses for a portfolio. Portfolios can be used for learning and self-evaluation; many designers use their portfolio as a means to review, critique, and reflect on their own work. A portfolio offers a way to identify your strengths and weaknesses, by allowing you to review your work in one consolidated format. Portfolios are also used for assessment and evaluation in educational programs. They are used for career advancement, and you will need to present your portfolio in job interviews when seeking an internship or full-time employment.

Portfolios rely on a variety of pieces or artifacts that provide evidence of your competence. These artifacts can range from written materials, models, photographs, and images, to large drawings and presentation boards. You have complete control and ownership of your portfolio because items included in a portfolio are self-selected. You will decide what is to be included, excluded, emphasized, and ignored. Unfortunately, there is no magic formula or checklist for what goes into your portfolio (although some suggestions are given in Chapter

1.7
Your portfolio pages should relate to each other and represent one "whole." Design work courtesy of Yang Peng.

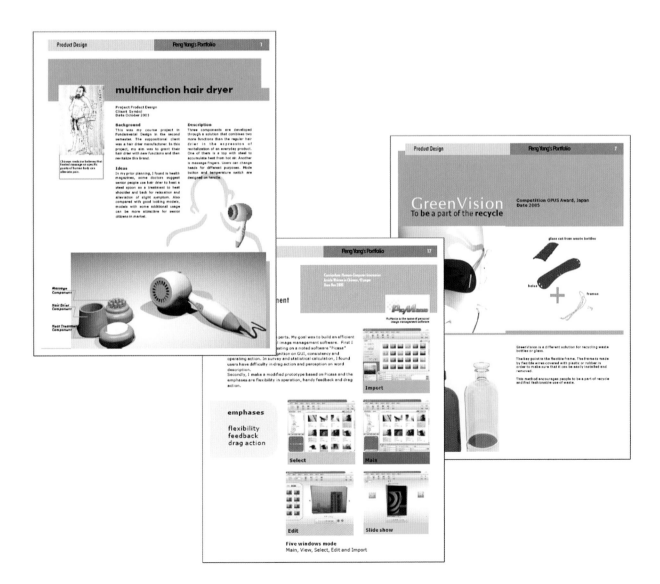

4). You need to determine the exact contents yourself. What most designers create is a cross between a showcase portfolio, which shows the best work across the entire educational experience, and an employment skills portfolio, which includes projects that demonstrate readiness to enter the workforce (Lankes 1995).

Know that your portfolio is more than a stack of projects crammed together in the same book or case. As Figure 1.7 demonstrates, it has to be well designed and cohesive as a whole.

Creative designers tend to be eloquent, expressive, and critical of their own work. They also tend to be critical of the work of others. These are talented, busy professionals who know how to successfully communicate both verbally and visually. The expectations for you in an interview are high. An adequate portfolio that includes all the components but lacks cohesiveness and a uniqueness factor will not impress these creative individuals. Something must spark their interest; something must jump off the page that says you are the creative talent they are seeking. In addition to your work, *how* you present your work can mean the difference between an adequate portfolio and *one that really impresses*. Two forms of portfolio are generally used today: a traditional portfolio and a digital portfolio. The style of presentation you choose depends on the purpose of your portfolio, your audience, and your personal preference and style.

THE TRADITIONAL PORTFOLIO

A traditional portfolio is a collection of your work in printed format, such as drawings, sketchbooks, presentation boards, matted projects, sample and material boards, and bound illustrations (see Figure 1.8). They can have a wide variety of formats, appearances, and carrying cases. All this will be discussed in detail in Chapter 7.

Traditional portfolios allow reviewers to see either original or reproduced work right in front of their eyes. Most practitioners still like to hold your work in their hands when reviewing it. With a traditional portfolio, there is no need for technology to review the work. You don't have to worry that the technology will fail during an interview or that your work will appear differently on someone else's computer monitor. The practitioner needs no special technical

1.8
The numerous items you can present in your traditional portfolio range from line drawings to images of models. Design work courtesy of Jeremy Gates.

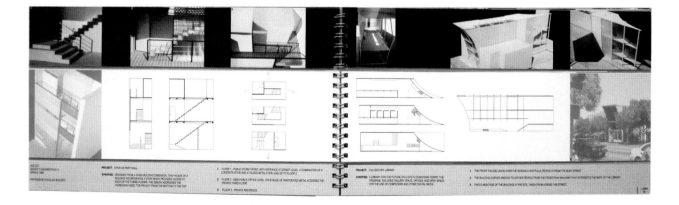

knowledge and computer applications to access your portfolio when reviewing printed material.

A disadvantage of the traditional portfolio can be its cumbersome size and weight. Multiple presentation boards are often large and bulky, making them difficult to transport. Using more than one portfolio case can solve this problem, but this is still not an ideal solution. The more popular book format and reduced reproduction costs are making the smaller traditional portfolio more advantageous. Yet even with this format, you cannot easily (and inexpensively) make 40 copies of your entire traditional portfolio and mail it to schools or firms around the world. You may need to consider another format for your portfolio, known as the digital portfolio.

THE DIGITAL PORTFOLIO

For many years, the presentation of a portfolio has been an intimate experience occurring face-to-face between designer and client, or designer and employer. Things have changed with the advent of advanced technology and the increased globalization of the marketplace. The designer's job description has been comprehensively transformed. We no longer work *only* with print media, but in a world of multiple media. Designers are now complementing their traditional portfolio with an electronic version known as a digital portfolio. As the disciplines of the built environment use more and more digital media to address the relationship between actual and virtual environments, the same digital media should be used to communicate your work to others. The ways in which we connect, communicate, network, and control the flow of information have changed forever.

What is a digital portfolio? A digital portfolio has been broadly defined as a collection of information, work, and achievement in electronic format (Univ. of Wisconsin–Madison 2003). Barrett (2000, 14) defines it as a portfolio that "includes the use of electronic technologies that allow the portfolio developer to collect and organize artifacts in many formats (audio, video, graphics, and text)." A digital portfolio is also known as an electronic portfolio, an e-portfolio, an e-folio, a computer-based portfolio, or a multimedia portfolio. To keep things simple, we'll continue to call it a digital portfolio.

A digital portfolio is a collection of your work that uses multimedia to present it to others, such as on CD-ROM or on a web site (see Figure 1.9). Multimedia simply means the practice of combining multiple elements from various artistic and communications media. The efficiency of digital portfolios cannot be underestimated. Your work presented in an electronic medium illustrates that you are enlightened about today's technology and its potential. It's also much easier to put together a digital portfolio today than it was years ago because the technical barriers for producing one have eroded in recent years.

Although you may be hearing more and more about digital portfolios and how important they are in securing employment, the digital portfolio has yet to replace a traditional one. A digital portfolio is generally considered an introduction to

1.9
A digital portfolio presents your work in a newer medium by showcasing your work in a dynamic way. Design work courtesy of Amol Surve.

you and your work, and a preview to your printed portfolio; however, the quality of a finely printed design piece is still needed. Electronic media cannot replicate the tactile experience of actually holding an object in your hands. Consider the example of the e-book. While their popularity has increased in recent years, the concept of reading digitally is not closing libraries and putting booksellers out of business. The use of a digital portfolio is still limited in today's society.

Instead, a digital portfolio augments a traditional printed portfolio and is useful in demonstrating technology skills in addition to your existing mastery of traditional techniques.

The need to create a digital portfolio depends largely on the amount of data to be presented. If the amount of data is large, it's not always possible to carry oversized design sheets and other materials from place to place, thus exposing them to all kinds of risks (like humidity, rain, dust, and so on). Smaller quantities of materials are easy to carry and may not need to be converted into digital format. So even in our society, with its reliance on advanced computers, the digital portfolio has yet to replace the traditional one.

Benefits of the Digital Portfolio

Because digital portfolios are considered a new form of communication, it's important to understand the benefits to various groups: students, educators, and practitioners. Digital portfolios are quickly becoming necessary for any design student entering a profession so heavily influenced by digital media.

First, more and more design work is being created on the computer. With more work begun and completed, all in digital format (like the drawings in Figure 1.10), why would you take computer-generated work and reduce its quality by printing to paper? A digital portfolio seems a logical approach to selling your work to others.

Second, a digital portfolio can enable you to communicate with potential employers and clients who live in other states and even other countries. You can broaden your reach to others through a web-based portfolio or being able to inexpensively mail a portfolio on CD-ROM (or just CD).

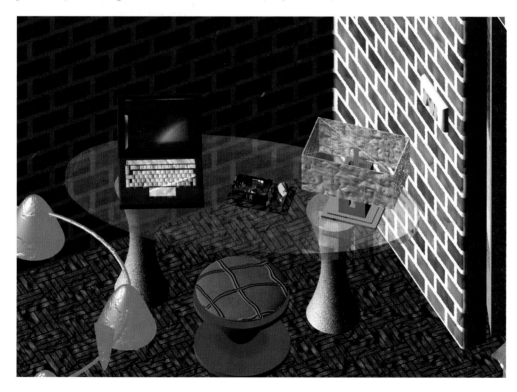

1.10
The transition from digitally created work like this FormZ model to a digital portfolio is an obvious progression. Design work courtesy of Mat Wingate.

Third, the portfolio is often the key to getting an internship or entry-level job. Think of it as an employment-generating tool. You wouldn't think about interviewing for an internship or a job without a digital portfolio because using multimedia can suggest to a reviewer that you have an understanding of this technology and could do the same for the firm's professional portfolio. On the other hand, complex audio and video technology may require specialized skills that you do not possess but must seek out.

Finally, the skills acquired while preparing and presenting the digital portfolio are yet another benefit. The process of converting work into digital format provides novel ways to categorize, peruse, and transport portfolios. And you'll probably learn some new technology skills in the process.

Educators and their institutions can benefit from encouraging students to create digital portfolios. First, the process of creating any form of portfolio involves multiple activities in which students can collect, select, and reflect on their professional competencies as they relate to industry standards. This allows students to enlarge their capacity to reflect on and direct their own professional growth. Second, the portfolio process helps students with their organizational skills, as they cannot put every item they've ever created in their portfolio. Projects must be "weeded," keeping the good and deleting the bad. Third, technological strategies are being incorporated into design curricula today and will only increase as better technology is developed. Although none of the accrediting organizations (CIDA, LAAB, or NAAB) yet require digital portfolios in their accreditation processes, it is helpful for students to organize their materials in a digital format. This seems logical because computers and other technologies are having an impact on every stage of the design process, from ideation to construction. Yet how much more advanced is a senior studio project if the final presentation includes a multimedia presentation? This presentation is then just one step away from being put into the student's digital portfolio. How great is that?

There are benefits for practitioners as well. The portfolio is all about assessment of your skills and knowledge. Assessment systems are judged on the value of the provided information. A portfolio provides a practitioner with proof of your qualifications. Without a portfolio, all you have as evidence of your greatness is your resume and a few letters of recommendation. A portfolio makes it possible to demonstrate professional competency in more depth and breadth. In addition to reviewing your traditional portfolio, a practitioner can determine to some extent your abilities with multimedia by reviewing your digital portfolio. Many practitioners are relying on students currently in higher education to bring an increased sophistication of technology skills into their workplace. A digital portfolio demonstrates your understanding of technology, electronic communication, and presentation medium (see Figure 1.11).

Knowing the benefits of digital portfolios from these three different perspectives can help you decide to what extent you use one.

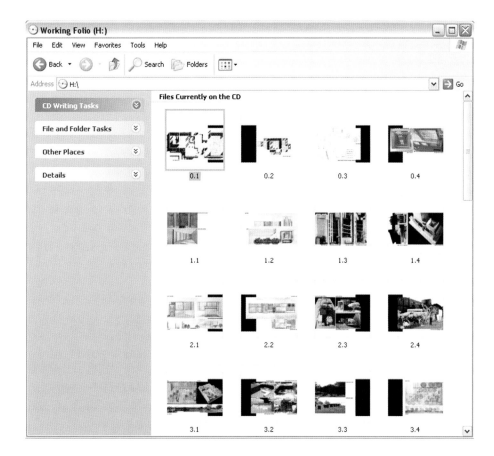

1.11
A portfolio on CD-ROM can showcase your hand drawing and physical models, as well as your ability to use today's technology.
Design work courtesy of Daniel Childers.

CONCLUSION

Your profession of architecture, interior design, or landscape architecture will influence the way you create and present your portfolio to practitioners in these fields. Both traditional and digital portfolios have benefits, and they should be created in unison. Each should complement the other, yet be independent and specific to its medium. In the next chapter, you will become familiar with the different types of portfolios. These include two forms of academic portfolios, the admission and graduate school portfolios, and the two forms of professional portfolios, the internship and exit portfolios.

2

Diversity of Portfolios

An organized and professionally designed portfolio can be a determining factor in getting into upper division or graduate school, getting that first internship or job, or even getting promoted. It can be what sets you apart from the competition (see Box 2.1). In this chapter, you will be introduced to several different types of portfolios, which all follow the same principles for organization, format, and presentation. It's the audience that is dissimilar for each one.

You will probably have a portfolio at the end of your second year in school. You will need a portfolio when you interview for part-time work or an internship while you are still in school. You will need a more advanced form of your portfolio when you graduate and apply for entry-level positions in architecture and design firms. You may decide to pursue more education, and you'll need a different type of portfolio when you apply for graduate school. Finally, you'll need to continually update your portfolio throughout your career. It will evolve into something totally new whenever you want your professional career to change.

Most likely, you will be creating and submitting a traditional portfolio, printed on paper and presented in a book or case like the one in Figure 2.1. Most educators

---

The portfolio should be distinct and creative, stand out from the crowd. There should also be a level of polish to the portfolio that shows attention to detail and pride in the work. We understand that an applicant may not have access to the best technology or equipment but attention to detail can be a deciding factor.

Lia Dileonardo, M.Arch, AIA Assoc.
Principal
DiLeonardo International, Inc.
Warwick, RI

Box 2.1

and practitioners are comfortable evaluating this form of your work. As technology becomes more entwined in the design professions, digital portfolios will become much more common. Your use of digital tools may help you get ahead. But the person with the best looking and most creative digital portfolio may not be the best candidate for graduate school or for the job. That person may just have mastered the skills needed to create a really good electronic presentation.

ACADEMIC PORTFOLIOS

Institutions of higher education may require you to submit a portfolio as a criterion for admission into their design programs. Many of these programs have a limited enrollment, partly because the foundation of education is based on studio education. This method of instruction is based on the traditional instructional methods of the École des Beaux-Arts schools established in France in the eighteenth century. Students in studios are grouped into smaller classes in which the instructor teaches and gives demonstrations, and students work on projects together. These small classes ensure a low faculty-to-student ratio and a high level of interaction in intimate group settings. These small classes sometimes influence the number of students that can be admitted into an upper division (junior and senior year) or a graduate program. There are two forms of academic portfolio: the admission portfolio and the graduate school portfolio.

The Admission Portfolio

Your first portfolio will most likely be created while completing your undergraduate degree. In a program with limited enrollment in the junior and senior years, students compete for spots at the end of their sophomore year. An admission portfolio is a portfolio used in this process. This review process may also include

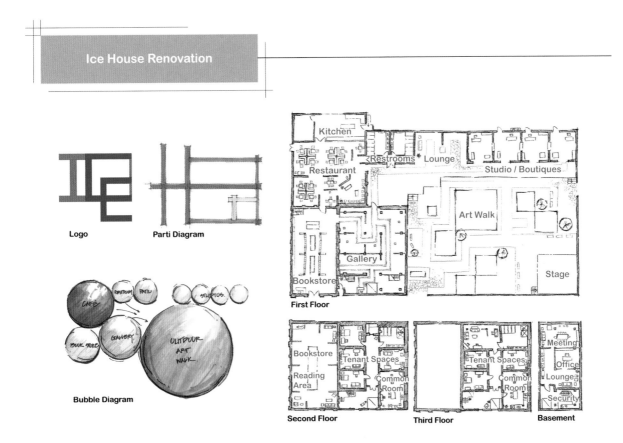

Ice House Renovation

Logo

Parti Diagram

Bubble Diagram

Kitchen

Restrooms * Lounge

Restaurant

Studio / Boutiques

Art Walk

Gallery

Bookstore

Stage

First Floor

Bookstore

Tenant Spaces

Reading Area

Common Room

Second Floor

Tenant Spaces

Common Room

Third Floor

Meeting

Office

Lounge

Security

Basement

an evaluation of your grade point average and some type of written requirement, such as an essay or design philosophy statement. This portfolio will consist of work from your previous classes. Your portfolio is not a resume in chronological order. It should not show examples of work from every class you've ever taken. Most of these classes tend to be technical courses in which you are learning technical skills, such as drawing, sketching, drafting, computer-aided design, computer modeling, basic construction, presentation, and visualization projects (see Figure 2.2). These classes usually focus on small projects that illustrate your ability to use and understand the medium. For example, you may be asked to reproduce a drafted construction drawing but you probably didn't design the construction detail yourself. You copied it from what was provided. Ideally, you understood the components of the detail you drew, too.

Your portfolio provides documented evidence that you have learned skills necessary to succeed in the profession. It is a qualitative assessment of work that shows a variety of work and skill. The guidelines and requirements for an admission portfolio are likely to be dictated to you and vary from school to school. Check your school's guidelines for acceptable portfolio contents and formats. The portfolio review for admission into an upper division program may require you to reformat your work into an 8½" × 11" booklet, like the one shown in Figure 2.3. (Check out the section in Chapter 10 on reducing your oversized work to this smaller format.)

2.2
The skills evident in your portfolio will range from your design process work to more finalized drawings and images. Design work courtesy of Elaine Hu.

2.3
An undergraduate admission portfolio book may have a regulated format. Check your school's admission guidelines before compiling your work.
Design work courtesy of Jennifer Walls.

Some schools allow you to be present at the review while others do not. You may be told what categories of work to show and in what type of portfolio case to present this work. Pay close attention to what is requested. Digital work may not be a submission medium, even though much of your work may be computer based. The admissions committee will have standards for reviewing your work, and a digital format may not currently fit their procedures. Ask for clarification on digital submissions if the school's guidelines are unclear.

Not sure what is best to include? Ask some of the higher level students. They will have some great advice for you. You may wish to rework some of your projects for inclusion in your portfolio (you'll find more on this in Chapter 4). There is debate on this topic. One negative aspect of reworking some of your projects is that the time component involved can be difficult for others to assess. As a student, it is common to work on your portfolio longer than practitioners would work on their portfolios. Evaluating your work in comparison with that of your peers can be challenging for your instructors, as your project may have taken 10 hours to complete whereas your peer's reworked project may have taken 30 hours. The instructor is no longer comparing apples with apples but instead, apples with oranges.

Most instructors understand that you may rework some of your projects. They will review an admission portfolio by looking at your potential, promise, and possibilities. How you arrived at a project solution is important and is represented by rough sketches and preliminary drawings, such as those in Figure 2.4. Don't forget to include some of these alongside your more finished work. Creativity is scrutinized most closely in an admission portfolio. Work that displays solid visual thinking is very desirable. Craftsmanship and technique can be taught or improved upon once you are admitted into the program, but an individual's sense of creativity is innate and can rarely be taught.

The Graduate School Portfolio

Competition to get into the top-rated graduate schools for architecture, interior design, and landscape architecture is fierce. There will definitely be more applicants than the faculty can realistically handle so cuts will need to be made. A portfolio submitted for admission into a graduate program must be first-rate (see Figure 2.5).

Graduate programs vary in focus from research based to studio based. Know which program you are applying for before you apply. A research-based program will certainly require you to produce either a thesis or an applied project, both of which are based on learned theory and quantitative or qualitative research methods (see Figure 2.6). Your research interests should match those of the faculty and program. It is important to have something in common with the strengths of the program.

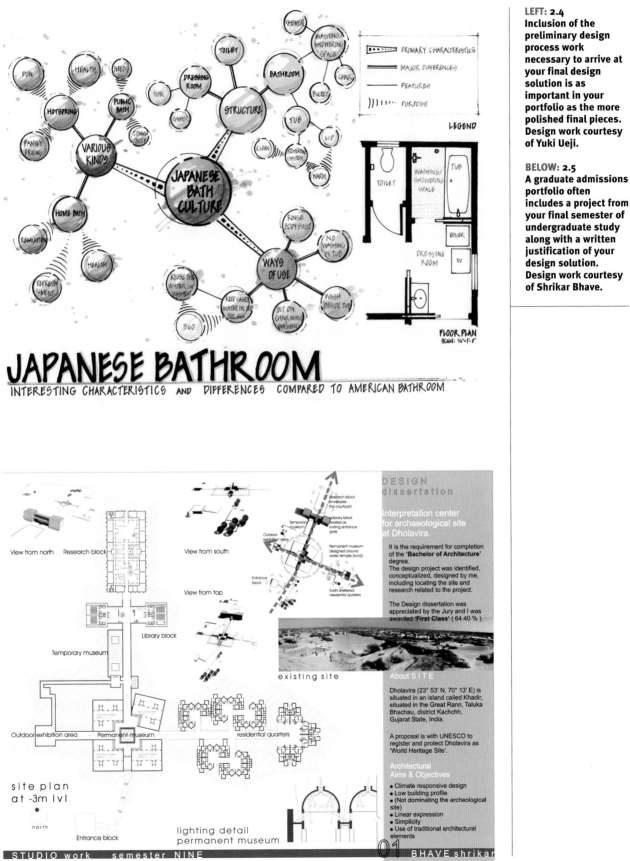

JAPANESE BATHROOM
INTERESTING CHARACTERISTICS AND DIFFERENCES COMPARED TO AMERICAN BATHROOM

LEGEND

▭▭▭◦◦◦ PRIMARY CHARACTERISTICS

▬▬▬ MAJOR DIFFERENCES

──── FEATURES

)))|||||| PURPOSE

FLOOR PLAN
SCALE: 1/2"=1'-1"

LEFT: 2.4
Inclusion of the preliminary design process work necessary to arrive at your final design solution is as important in your portfolio as the more polished final pieces. Design work courtesy of Yuki Ueji.

BELOW: 2.5
A graduate admissions portfolio often includes a project from your final semester of undergraduate study along with a written justification of your design solution. Design work courtesy of Shrikar Bhave.

DESIGN
dissertation

Interpretation center for archaeological site at Dholavira.

It is the requirement for completion of the **'Bachelor of Architecture'** degree.
The design project was identified, conceptualized, designed by me, including locating the site and research related to the project.

The Design dissertation was appreciated by the Jury and I was awarded **'First Class'** (64.40 %).

existing site

About S I T E

Dholavira (23° 53' N, 70° 13' E) is situated in an island called Khadir, situated in the Great Rann, Taluka Bhachau, district Kachchh, Gujarat State, India.

A proposal is with UNESCO to register and protect Dholavira as 'World Heritage Site'.

Architectural
Aims & Objectives

● Climate responsive design
● Low building profile
● (Not dominating the archeological site)
● Linear expression
● Simplicity
● Use of traditional architectural elements

site plan
at -3m lvl

north

Entrance block

lighting detail
permanent museum

STUDIO work   semester NINE   01   BHAVE shrikar

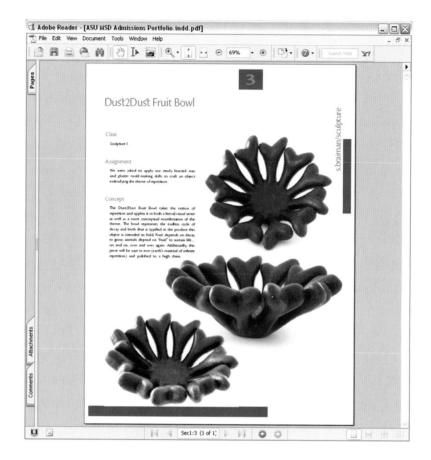

Research the directive of the school, and the research and creative scholarship of the faculty. Do you have any interest in working with these professors? Do you agree with the direction of the college and its educational focus? For example, it would make little sense for you to apply to a studio-based graduate school with a focus on building acoustics when you are interested in pursuing a research-based degree with a focus on sustainability. This would be a horrible mismatch and a waste of your time and money. I'm amazed when I review applications for graduate school at my college. It's easy to see which students simply mass mailed their applications to all large universities with design programs. For example, an applicant might state that he wants to study a certain topic, yet it's clear from our college web site that the scholarly activities of our faculty don't include this topic. There would be no one available to guide the applicant through his studies. Before submitting an application to a graduate program, do some research and match your interests to those of the school and faculty. Ask yourself, "Will I fit into this environment? Are these the professors who can help me achieve my greatest potential?"

Application requirements vary from program to program. Check and double-check these before mailing your application packet, which could be as extensive as the one shown in Figure 2.7.

An explanation of the admission process should be available on the school's web site, along with a contact name and phone number. Call this person to ask

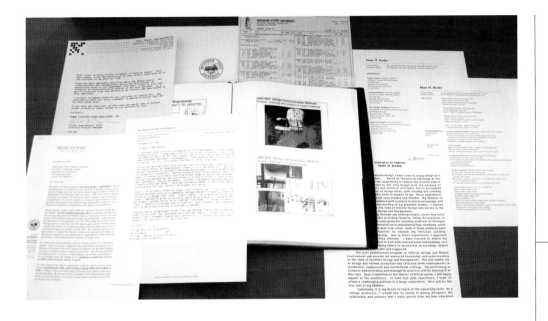

LEFT: 2.7
A graduate admission packet can be extensive, consisting of a portfolio, letters of recommendation, resume, design philosophy, and more.

BELOW: 2.8
A graduate statement of intent is very important in degree programs that culminate in a written thesis project. Design work courtesy of Emily K. Callaghan.

Discuss your proposed research topic.

I propose to research the importance of interdisciplinary efforts as a means of problem solving in Design and how this teaching and learning experience transcends the student's academic experience, evolving throughout their career, producing leaders of their industry. I see this process as a strong evolution of thought and innovation, an element missing in many classrooms and offices. I am interested in the product of an interdisciplinary educational approach. I am particularly interested in studying the development of leadership skills, critical creative thinking and an awareness of elements beyond one's field of expertise—including the important role these elements must play in decision-making. The efforts of Innovation Space speak directly to this cause and I would like to be a part of the program, its research efforts, and its successful integration of disciplinary knowledge.

Why is this research important to you, the design community, and the general population?

This research will study, ultimately, the production of leaders in Design. The Design community would reap benefits from a curricular agenda that emphasizes leadership amongst educators and students. Students will become the catalysts of evolution and change; forging alliances as leaders and idea-makers in the industry and perpetuating the cycle of innovation leadership. The professional world will benefit from a strong group of new graduates who are eager to lead, and not simply follow. The general public may be the most unknowing, although not unaffected, recipients of these benefits. Their interaction with products—be they editorial, functional or promotional—will improve, becoming more efficient and requiring less time. Furthermore, persons involved in non-Design industries will have greater opportunities to be a part of interdisciplinary forums, as a result of the Design leaders.

any questions. It's better to ask than to send an incomplete application packet. Besides the portfolio, your application may include any or all of the following: transcripts of previous education, indication of a high grade point average, letters of recommendation, a high GRE or TOEFL score, a statement of design philosophy, and essay answers to specific stated questions (Marjanovic, Ruedi, and Lokko 2003). This sample of your writing is usually in the form of an essay, like the one in Figure 2.8, that explains your interest in the program and how you see your goals matching that of the program.

The admissions committee is composed of some or all of the school's instructing faculty. In some schools, professors review each portfolio individually and assign a score based on their own personal criteria or criteria established by the entire faculty. All of the scores are then totaled and averaged to provide a ranking of candidates. At others, professors spend an afternoon together with their colleagues viewing and discussing the merits of each candidate, and then they make a decision as a group to accept or reject the candidate. Be aware of the review procedures, as you may need to submit multiple copies of application material.

As for the portfolio, tailor it to meet the school's requirements. Find out what format is requested and how it will be reviewed. Is a specific size and layout required? Are a minimum and maximum number of pages specified? Does the school require printed portfolio pages, or can you submit slides or a digital portfolio on CD? It's tempting to show only your best, completed design work, but what about the evidence of your thinking process? To demonstrate this aspect of your skills, you might want to include a short written description of the design problem, as in Figure 2.9.

Don't forget to include conceptual diagrams, sketches, and drawings that explain how you developed the idea. Instructors who want to see how you think and develop your ideas will review your portfolio. The ability to carry your original thoughts to fruition is desirable. They will look for evidence of originality, the ability to develop an idea from initial concept to final design schemes, and the increasing complexity of your ideas.

2.9
It is helpful to include some context in writing to indicate why you are showing an element in your portfolio.
Design work courtesy of David M. Solnick.

Sending and Retrieving Your Academic Portfolio

Never mail or drop off your original portfolio! You may never get it back. Nine times out of ten, the school will request a portfolio to be reviewed when you are not present. Give them a copy. This is not to say the copy must be inferior to the original. Clear, color copies of all portfolio pages can be quite good. When I interviewed for teaching positions a few years ago, I mailed to each university a 12-page mini-portfolio. I knew I would not get these back. I purchased relatively inexpensive books in which to showcase my work.

When using the postal service or an independent carrier, take advantage of their package tracking option. Insure your application packet and request a delivery confirmation so you know when it has arrived. This way, you can call the school to confirm that they did receive it. If the packet never arrives, contact the carrier to track it down. Also contact the school to negotiate an extension to resend everything. This is another reason why it's so important to send only copies.

After the admissions committee has finished reviewing all portfolios, the portfolios are no longer needed. Check with the school about retrieving your portfolio. Because you will invest a lot of time and money into the portfolio (even if it's only a copy), you may want it back. If so, the school will have a procedure to return your portfolio, probably in a self-addressed, stamped envelope that you provide.

PROFESSIONAL PORTFOLIOS

There is another type of portfolio, called a professional portfolio. This includes both an internship portfolio and an exit portfolio. An admission portfolio is often the beginning of your portfolio journey, one you will continue as you practice in your field. Most academic programs in interior design, landscape architecture, or architecture require an internship in the field before granting you your degree. To interview, you will need a professional-quality portfolio. A similar yet more accomplished version of this portfolio is necessary when you interview for full-time employment. The exit portfolio is a reflection of your accumulated education and experience up to this point in your career. Specific information about interviewing with your portfolio is provided in Chapter 14. For now, let's discuss the two versions of the professional portfolio: the internship portfolio and the exit portfolio.

The Internship Portfolio

A portfolio will be necessary when you interview for an internship (see Figure 2.10). An internship is a practical learning experience outside the school setting in a professional design firm. Its goal is to fill the gap between the academic and professional worlds.

The internship offers you a means to maximize the undergraduate educational experience by expanding your professional training and developing strength in areas of special interest. For interior design and landscape architecture, the internship is a part of the undergraduate curriculum. For architecture, the internship is the period after graduation during which you train under a seasoned licensed practitioner in preparation for taking the registration examination. Architecture students also have the opportunity to work in firms during their

2.10
These three wire-bound portfolio books can be used together or separately for interviewing. Design work courtesy of Zubin Shroff.

undergraduate education. We'll focus on this period of learning and refer to it as the internship for all three disciplines.

By serving as a vehicle to facilitate learning, the internship will offer you the opportunity to further develop your abilities in design-relevant competency areas. It will assist you in focusing on a career choice and enhancing your awareness of theory and practice before making the transition from campus life to professional life. Usually, you will be given minor tasks to accomplish and will be allowed to observe and participate in various operations of the firm. You will be encouraged to contribute ideas that will assist the firm. Daily association with all the professionals in the firm allows you to learn first-hand about client expectations and the professional skills required to meet those expectations. It also helps acquaint you with all of the professional roles and with the organizational structure in the firm.

Because the internship in most academic programs is completed after admission into the upper division, the best way to start this type of portfolio is by using your admission portfolio as a foundation (see Figure 2.11). This should give you a good base on which to build.

The time required to complete this new version of your portfolio will be less than when you began from scratch. Review your admission portfolio. Seek feedback from your instructors on what was good and bad about it. Determine which projects are your best and keep those. Remove all others. (Do not discard them because you may need them again someday. Instead, place them in a safe place for temporary storage.)

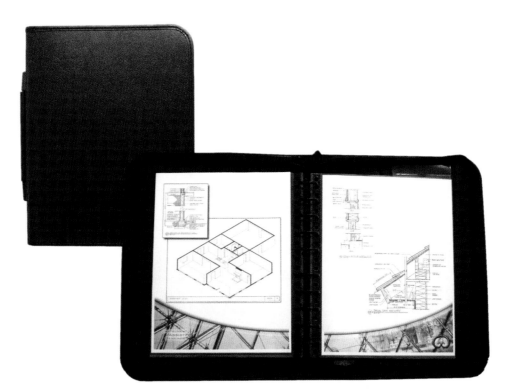

LEFT: **2.11**
The admissions portfolio is a good place to start when creating your first professional portfolio. Putting it inside a professional-looking case is helpful, too. Design work courtesy of Shelby Bogaard.

BELOW: **2.12**
This smaller book could complement a larger selection of design work. Design work courtesy of Amy Oditt.

If your internship is completed in the summer months between your junior and senior years, you will have an entire year of additional design work to include in your portfolio. Select the best projects and add them to your previous work, either in the same format or in a supplemental book like the one in Figure 2.12. (If you feel your previous work is better than your more recent work, you have a problem.) Practitioners will recognize that you are still in school and may not have fully completed projects to show (i.e., from concept sketches all the way to a full set of construction documents). Most of your work will still represent your mastery of technical skills. It's not until your final year in school that you'll begin to synthesize all aspects of your design training.

The Exit Portfolio

The main focus of this book is on the portfolio you will use when you complete your education and are stepping into the workforce full time (see Figure 2.13). This is known as the exit portfolio because you are exiting the educational phase of your life as an architect, interior designer, or landscape architect. This

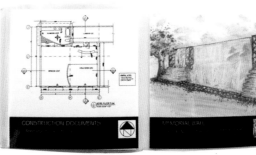

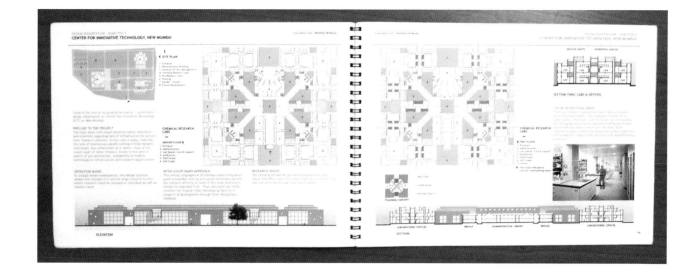

2.13
An exit portfolio demonstrates your readiness to step into the workforce. Design work courtesy of Charudatta Joshi.

is when your portfolio will receive the most scrutiny by several, if not many, practitioners (see Box 2.2).

Your work should be fresh, creative, and individual. It is imperative for you to recognize that you will be competing against other recent graduates. The competition for jobs can be fierce. More importantly, you might be competing against practitioners who have a professional portfolio.

Continue with the portfolio you created when interviewing for your internship. Putting this portfolio together should be easy if you've been continually collecting your work, in both traditional and digital formats. Concentrate only on your best work! As this will be a reflection of your entire educational experience, include a capstone or thesis project if you have one. Or include all or most of your last complete studio project (see Figure 2.14 on page 33).

Reviewers are expecting you to have the skills to walk into their office on Monday and start being profitable to the firm on Friday. They will be looking for your skills to be comparable to those of their current designer staff, just at a slightly lower level. Show your most advanced work (see Box 2.3). Show work that

---

The **purpose of** a portfolio is to generate a discussion with the practitioner, who is trying to evaluate the character of the interviewee. The content of the portfolio allows you to speak about your work. It's the words that reflect who you are and what you believe. Ultimately, these words will tell the practitioner if you can fit into the culture of that office.

Jon D. Vredevoogd
Associate Professor
School of Planning, Design & Construction
Michigan State University
East Lansing, MI

Box 2.2

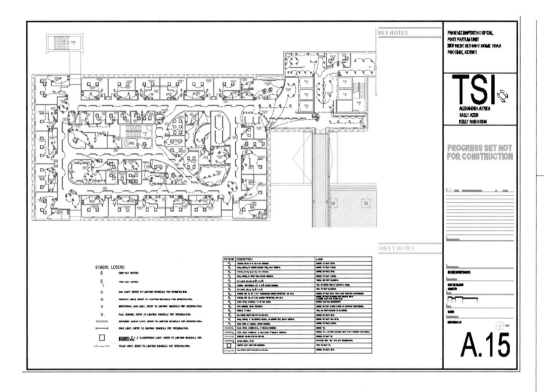

2.14
A portion of your
entire final senior
project is a good
choice for your
portfolio as it
represents the breadth
of your skills.
Design work courtesy
of Alexandra C. Ayres,
Sally Azer, and Kelly
Robinson.

says, "I have the skills and creativity to be a benefit to your firm." This is your chance to demonstrate to the reviewer that you are ready to leave the confines of the university and enter the workforce.

CONCLUSION

Throughout your career as a landscape architect, architect, or interior designer, you will create a series of portfolios to showcase your talents both in school and for the profession. The first portfolio you create is likely to be an admissions portfolio. Modify this to form the other types of portfolios when you need them. In the next chapter, we'll discuss an element of your portfolio that will have a significant impact on its design—the evaluation process.

If you are just out of school, two thirds of the work can be class work, and the last third can be your thesis assignment. Each year or so, add two pages of commercial work, and remove a page or two of older work. Your thesis and other class work should totally go away about two to three years out of school. As your career continues, cultivate "greatest hits" and let some of the smaller ones go.

Mike Davin
Director of Hospitality Studio
FRCH Design Worldwide
Cincinnati, OH

Box 2.3

3

Knowing Your Audience

Who will assess and evaluate your work? This may be the most important consideration when deciding what work should be presented in the portfolio and in what format it would be most successfully accepted and evaluated. This chapter discusses how both an admissions portfolio and an exit portfolio are reviewed. Even more important is to understand the audience who will be reviewing your work and to know that you may view things differently because of your age and background. The chapter concludes with an explanation of potential job markets and a series of questions that can help you determine whether you are leaning more toward residential or commercial design in your profession. Knowing what career opportunities are available to you will ultimately help you tailor your portfolio for that market and audience.

PORTFOLIO REVIEW

There is a saying, "If you want to get somewhere, you first must know where you are going." This is why it is so important to know your audience and to recognize *who* will be reviewing your portfolio. It makes sense to determine your goal (such as getting a job) and how to reach that goal. To reach it, establish a process (such as sending out resumes and getting an interview with a firm) and stick with it. Impressing a practitioner with your portfolio and interviewing skills may be how you get a job. Ask yourself, "Why am I doing this?" Examine your objectives. Keep your goal at the center of your attention.

The audience reviewing your portfolio will influence how it is organized and presented (see Box 3.1). Different audiences will review different types of portfolios. Are you doing this to get into a school program or to get a job? A portfolio created for admission into your school's upper division will be very different than one created for an entry-level job. The audience for admission into upper division or graduate school consists of professors who are interested in your potential as a student of higher learning. Work that shows your development is valuable in this type of portfolio (see Box 3.2).

The audience for an internship or a part- or full-time job consists of employers who are looking to see if you could be an asset to their team. In a firm, the people who are the most likely to review your work are design directors, senior designers, managing directors, and directors of the human resources department. They want to know if you can make money for their firm. Your work must emphasize your competence and ability to hit the ground running, making a profit for the firm soon after you start working for it. Depending on the type of audience, you will insert and remove parts of your portfolio as needed to match its content to their needs. In essence, you must know your audience, use their vocabulary, and create a portfolio they will *want* to see.

How a Portfolio Is Reviewed

Besides understanding who will be reviewing your portfolio, you may want to consider *how* it will be reviewed. This may influence what you include and how it is presented (see Box 3.3).

As you leaf though the pages of any great portfolio, seeing new ideas and endless possibilities, you become curiously inspired. You realize that you are not only reviewing an individual's ongoing learning and achievements, but you are sharing in an intimate conversation with them about how they perceive, question, visualize, and ultimately speak in their own distinctive creative voice.

Max Underwood
Professor
School of Architecture and Landscape Architecture
Arizona State University
Tempe, AZ

Box 3.1

Always show examples of your design process. To some extent, the final design product demonstrates a skill set: an ability to use digital technology, lay out a floor plan, produce wall sections and details, and build physical models. However, the design process demonstrates how you think about architecture: your ability to conceptualize, analyze, and synthesize information, and have a graphic dialogue about design ideas. Including examples of your design process will insure your position in a firm as someone who can both initiate and produce design solutions as opposed to someone who produces architecture from the ideas of others.

Jane Britt Greenwood, AIA
Associate Dean
College of Architecture, Art, and Design
Mississippi State University
Starkville, MS

Box 3.2

Each designer is unique and so is his or her portfolio. Remember there are no "magic balances" or "correct percentages" of the types of images, drawings, models, or simulations. My advice is take a moment, pause, and ask yourself two questions, "What is unique about my own creative voice?" and "How can I best communicate how I see, think, visualize, and materialize my creative voice?"

Max Underwood
Professor
School of Architecture and Landscape Architecture
Arizona State University
Tempe, AZ

Box 3.3

A portfolio is recognized as a valid form of assessment of your skills as a designer (Testerman and Hall 2000–2001). There is an assumption that a reviewer assesses work using predetermined criteria and that these criteria are equally considered. This is not always the case. In a formal study (Karpati et al. 1998), researchers found reviewers of art portfolios to have one favorite criterion, such as technical skill, originality, or quality of design solution. If the criterion is not present in the work being reviewed, the project is evaluated lower, even if all other project requirements are met. Personally, when I review admission portfolios for students wishing to enter the upper division at my college, I view the entire portfolio as a design project. That's what I focus on when I evaluate the portfolio—the design and layout of the portfolio itself. Other faculty members focus on certain projects or are looking to see a certain skill (such as sketching, construction drawings, or computer work) represented in the projects (see Figure 3.1). If that skill isn't there, that portfolio is evaluated lower. As long as I or the other faculty members are evaluating *all* the portfolios with the same criteria, our evaluation is valid and reliable. We all evaluate differently.

Each practitioner also reviews material in his or her own special way. In essence, it is extremely *subjective*. One person's partly cloudy day is someone else's partly sunny day. In other words, one person's view of your portfolio will not sufficiently characterize the next person's view. What is being evaluated is usually based on slanted definitions of creativity and successful aesthetic, rather than objective criteria. I wish I could give you a list of the "Top 10 Criteria" for portfolio review but it's not possible. There is no definitive approach to evaluating a portfolio and no clear agreement on the format and content of it. There is no common thread among all practitioners because every designer values different parts of the profession.

Some practitioners highly value sketches, like the chair in Figure 3.2, while others value technical skills, as shown in the space plan in Figure 3.3. Still others will see your creativity as something more important than how you technically communicate a project. The fact is, there is no right or wrong when evaluating your portfolio—there is only opinion.

RIGHT: 3.1
Items or artifacts in your portfolio can range from historical sketches to 3-D computer-generated renderings.
Design work courtesy of Cindy Louie.

BELOW: 3.2
Your ability to quickly sketch anything from interior elements to trees and structural components is essential in design disciplines.
Design work courtesy of Erin Dinno.

The furniture sketches are pieces that reflect the influence of historic references and technology known to the people during that time. They are important because design comes from recollections of the past merged with integration of new ideas. The basic forms and motifs used in these pieces are repeated in some of the furniture used in later times and are still manufactured designs of today. This is essential to any design because sucessful designs are ones that last.

Hepplwhite Shield Back Chair
18th Century Style

Brewster Chair
American 17th Century Style

Wingback Chair
Queen Anne Style

Bedstead
Elizabethan style

APH 314/446 + INT 412
Historic Subject Sketching

What practitioners prefer to see in your portfolio is somewhat of a mystery. Some information on this topic has been gathered from practitioners in the design disciplines. (One source is the practitioner comments found in this book.) In interviews with practicing interior designers, the optimum portfolio for a job applicant varied widely and demonstrated a range of skills, from freehand concept drawings to material boards and finished construction documents (Pitrowski 2004). There is some debate about whether it is better to include the actual work or a reproduction of that work. In a study of 395 interior design practitioners with an average of 6.65 years of reviewing experience, the majority preferred reviewing the actual projects, rather than reproductions. Over half of them believed the most important consideration was the presentation itself (Matthews and Gritzmacher 1984). This group also felt an important factor when considering a recent graduate's portfolio was seeing complete projects that included all aspects of a design project. Comprehensive and complete projects that included 2-D plans, working drawings, sample boards, and visual presentations were preferable to showing a variety of work, with a little of this and a little of that. In addition, the majority of respondents in this survey believed the most important considerations were the layout and presentation of the work (Matthews and Gritzmacher 1984) (see Figure 3.4).

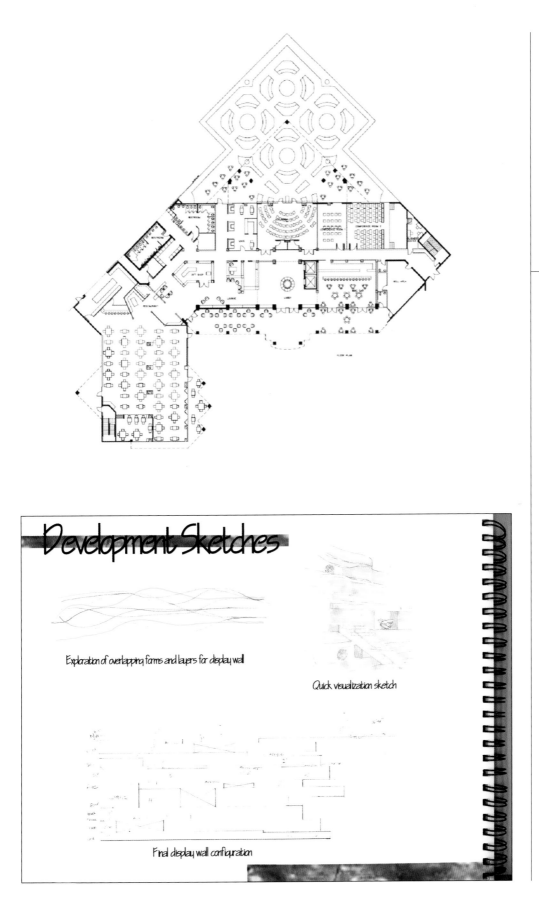

Development Sketches

Exploration of overlapping forms and layers for display wall

Quick visualization sketch

Final display wall configuration

The Generation Gap and the Digital Portfolio

You, the reader, are most likely a member of the new generation of designers known as Generation Y. Also referred to as Gen Y or the millennial generation, this group of individuals was born in the late 1970s to the late 1990s, spanning approximately 17 years (Nayyar 2001). Most members of this group are currently in school pursuing their education. Additional characteristics of Generation Y are provided in Box 3.4.

Most people in today's workforce represent other generations, such as Generation X or the baby boomers. *Generation X* is a demographic term used to categorize individuals born between the 1960s and 1970s, after the baby boom. Members of the baby boom generation are those persons born after World War II (1946–1964). There are approximately 78 million baby boomers in the United States. They can be grouped into three distinct subgroups by the years in which they were born: Leading Edge (1946–1950), Core (1951–1959), and Trailing boomers (1960–1964) (Paul 2001). Every year, our society grows older and more people over the age of 65 remain in the workforce.

What makes Generation Y so different from Generation X and the baby boom population is a readiness to embrace technology. If you are a member of Gen Y, you probably feel right at home working with computers and digital media. You are likely at ease with computer technology and know how to experiment with it when designing your projects. As illustrated in Figure 3.5, you view the computer as an essential tool (Oblinger 2003). You are more of an expert at multitasking than those who are older than you. This age of digital media rewards a different type of designer, one who is comfortable with technology. This is not necessarily the same type of designer who would have done extremely well in the past (Wood 2004).

You use technology every day to communicate, socialize, collaborate, compile, and research. You email, text message, surf the web, instant message, and chat on a cell phone all the time. As evidence of this phenomenon, research has found 46 percent of Generation Y use instant messaging even more frequently than email. This figure is significantly higher than users in the other generations. This indi-

---

MEMBERS OF GENERATION Y ARE:

- Highly influenced by information technology
- Fascinated by new technologies
- Extremely familiar with technology so it's not a novelty to them but a part of everyday life
- Fluent in the use of the Internet for schoolwork and for leisure
- Communicating via email and instant messaging as a means of socialization
- Recognizing better ways to use technology than their college instructors
- Quite intolerant with delays, expecting service and quick responses 24/7 in multiple modes such as telephone, email, or in person

Box 3.4

3.5
A computer-generated rendering is more representative of today's generation of designers than those of yesterday, when this medium was not available.
Design work courtesy of Charudatta Joshi.

cates the ubiquitous nature of technology for Gen Y. In addition, this group takes technology for granted, seeing it as an invisible and seamless part of everyday life (Talarico 2003).

Most likely, you have much experience with computers and know more about technology in general than those older than you. But keep in mind that those are the people who will be reviewing your portfolio. Whether a practitioner in the field or an educator at your school, it is likely that someone older than you will be evaluating your work. According to the National Center for Education Statistics, the average age of postsecondary faculty is between 45 and 54 years of age, and most of them graduated in the 1970s (NCES 2002). While you may be able to razzle-dazzle them with your digital prowess, ultimately it is your design work that will be scrutinized the most. An animation like the one shown in Figure 3.6 will be analyzed not only to determine your abilities with technology, but for its design merit as well.

In theory, digital portfolios should be evaluated with the same standards, proficiencies, and competencies as a traditional portfolio because the medium should make little difference. Yet in reality, a digital portfolio has an additional layer of complexity because the reviewer is also required to know, understand, and evaluate digital skill. Some practitioners may not yet have the capability of evaluating your digital portfolio for what it is: a representation of both your design work and a sampling of your capabilities with technology (see Figure 3.7).

RIGHT: 3.6
This still image, taken from an animated movie, is representative of the technology skills expected in today's Generation Y designers.
Design work courtesy of Jeffrey Prince.

BELOW: 3.7
The 3-D modeling shown on this web page required skill not only to create the model but also to develop the layout and web site.
Design work courtesy of Mat Wingate.

Introductory Computer Modeling Project
The purpose of this project was to create a small freestanding space and to develop the interior elements with detail. The final deliverable was a short animated walkthrough.

The reviewer must be comfortable with technology and must be able to evaluate this type of portfolio differently than a traditional portfolio. With this in mind, your digital portfolio (whether on CD or on the web) must be simple enough to view. Ensuring that your digital portfolio is available to a large audience may rule out using the latest and greatest technology tools. (Remember, the

Internet is so full of information that it's popularly referred to as the information superhighway.) You should stick with a simple format that will allow any user (irrelevant of technology skill level) to access and view your portfolio.

POTENTIAL MARKETS

Part of knowing your audience is recognizing your interest in an area of study. You will have a diverse background of skills when you complete your education, and more skills after you have completed an internship or your first entry-level job. As a designer, you will most likely start your design career by joining an existing design firm. The inspiration for entering your chosen field of design may be the dream of designing awesome skyscrapers, public parks, or elaborate interior spaces. There is more to architecture, landscape architecture, and interior design than what is seen on television design shows.

Many potential markets with awesome design possibilities exist. Designers work in a wide range of settings, both public commercial and private residential. Surveys indicate that a majority of designers practice at least part of the time in both the residential and commercial areas, although they tend to favor one or the other. There are a variety of specializations in each category. Residential designers can focus on remodeling, development, or new construction (see Figure 3.8).

Because commercial designers must be knowledgeable about their clients' business needs, most concentrate within design specialties, such as designing for the hospitality or health care industries (see Figure 3.9). Some designers restrict themselves to particular subspecialties, for example, designing restaurants or residential kitchens and baths. Some work in highly specialized fields, designing interiors for airplanes or yachts, creating houses of worship, or doing historic preservation

3.8
The residential model shown in this illustration has a sense of intimacy not found in a larger commercial project. Design work courtesy of Daniel Childers.

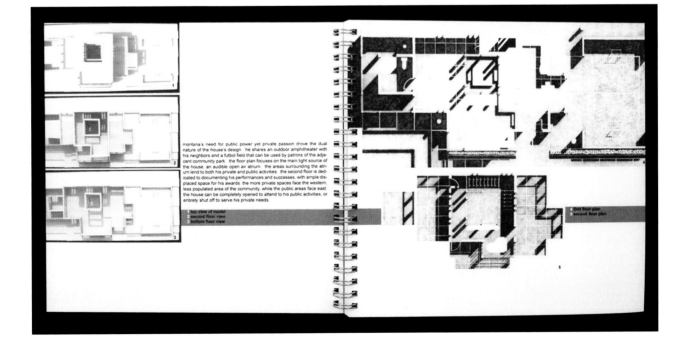

ABOVE: 3.9
If the work in your portfolio addresses a specific area of design, call attention to it. This is especially advantageous when interviewing with a firm that specializes in the same area. Design work courtesy of Alexandra C. Ayres, Sally Azer, and Kelly Robinson.

BELOW: 3.10
Residential and commercial projects have different scopes, clients, users, and end products. Design work courtesy of Elaine Hu.

and restoration. The commercial and residential areas of design each have their own unique aspects.

Leaning Toward Residential or Commercial Design

One difference between the areas of commercial and residential design is the client or end user. Commercial projects have clients who may or may not be the end user. For example, a large public office building will have many users, including employees, customers, and visitors to the space. The client who makes most of the decisions (and pays the designers' fees) may not even work in the building. The designer must consequently service the needs of the client who is designating the project requirements, and the needs of the users who will be occupying the space. On the other hand, residential projects are normally smaller in scale and require the designer to work closely with the client. This client is the end user of the space; therefore, the space must be customized to the needs, requests, and preferences of the individual. Another difference between the two clients involves how the designer is paid: by an individual or by a business or corporation. Furthermore, the occupancy of the interior or exterior determines its category. Single-occupancy dwellings are considered private residential spaces, whereas multiple-occupancy dwellings are considered public spaces (see Figure 3.10).

What type of work do you lean toward? Although you may be skilled in a variety of areas, you probably favor working on a certain type of project. The results of these projects are more rewarding to you and better formulated. These are the projects of which you are most proud. If you really enjoy residential design, why would you target your portfolio toward large commercial firms? It is common knowledge that you will spend more time at work with your clients and

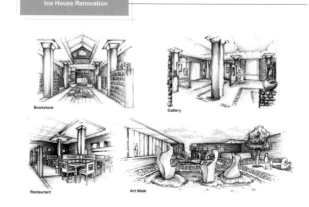

colleagues than you will at home with your family and friends. Why would you want to be in an environment that does not motivate and energize you? Determine what you enjoy doing and target those types of firms when seeking an internship or job. Have passion for what you do and, ultimately, you will get paid for doing what you love.

You should be able to identify at least three types of job areas or specializations in which you would feel qualified and inspired to work. Don't overlook a single avenue. The more options you have identified, the better your chances are of finding a suitable position. Start with the ideal specialization, but build in alternatives. See Box 3.5 for a list of additional design-related career opportunities.

There are other considerations besides the type of work you'll do. Finding a place where you belong can transform an ordinary career into a successful adventure. The number of people you work with will influence your decision to pursue a certain specialty. A small firm ranges in size from a single person (known as a sole proprietor) to 10 or 15 people. A large firm can have over 200 employees. These firms typically design and build millions of square feet of commercial space every year and are ranked in lists of giant firms published annually in design magazines. Obviously, in the middle lie the equally adept medium-sized firms.

Residential firms tend to be small firms, while the majority of commercial firms are the larger ones employing more people. There are advantages and disadvantages to working for either a small or a large firm. In a small firm, you have the chance to do a bit of everything, from preclient meetings, to designing, to installation on the job site, and so on. In a larger firm, you have the opportunity to work on a range of complex projects or in a specialized area. You also gain exposure to top clients and prestigious projects that you wouldn't get in a smaller firm. In a medium-sized firm, you encounter some of the advantages and disadvantages of both small and large firms.

DESIGN CAREER OPPORTUNITIES

Residential Designer	Home Theater/Media	Color Consultant
Contract Designer	Specialist	Production Designer
Facility Manager	Furniture Designer	Colorist
Historic	Textile Designer	Transportation
Preservationist	CAD Draftsperson	Specialist
Historic Restorationist	Furnishings Buyer	Window Treatment
Environmental	Manufacturer's	Specialist
Designer	Representative	Art Director
Lighting Consultant	Manufacturer's	Theatrical Set Designer
Accessibility Specialist	Distributor	Design Journalist
Wallcovering Designer	Showroom Manager	Design Educator
Kitchen and Bath	Sales Associate	
Specialist	Product Specifier	

Box 3.5

Tailoring Your Portfolio

Focus your portfolio to highlight your specialty. Each time you interview, you will tailor your portfolio to a firm, market segment, or targeted area of practice. Look at work done in that area and see how it communicates visually. Each area of practice has a unique approach to presentation. For example, a rendering of a personal residence is presented quite differently than that of a commercial sports facility (see Figure 3.11).

Put together your portfolio in a way that impresses these firms. Select work samples that focus the employer's attention on your expertise. Include a range of projects, from small to large, simple to complex, graphic to technical. Some pieces will be removed, some added, some moved closer to the front or back, and so on. Try to relate your examples to the firm's work. Try to match "what I can do" to "what the firm needs." Know your target audience. If you are applying for an internship in a commercial firm, a kitchen and bath design does not belong in your portfolio. In the end, you'll need to decide what area of design is right for you and make sure this desire is reflected in your portfolio.

WHAT'S RIGHT FOR YOU?

Knowing your audience goes right along with knowing who you are and knowing what your strengths and weaknesses are as a designer. The goal is to make the perfect match: you are happy with the academic program or job, and the school or employer is happy they accepted you. A thorough self-analysis will prepare you to speak intelligently about yourself and your design work in an interview. The better you understand who you are and what you're looking to achieve with this portfolio (i.e., entry into school, an internship, a full-time position), the better

3.11a and 3.11b Each area of design has its own presentation and communication methods. Design work courtesy of Kim H. Nguyen and Charudatta Joshi, respectively.

able you will be to include those key components in it and to talk about them in an interview. During the portfolio process, you'll learn more about yourself and your profession. You will put your own knowledge to the test by combining professional knowledge with your technical skills to produce a tangible product.

Before you can address the requirements of a portfolio, you must deal honestly and effectively with yourself. You should begin with yourself because if what you do is in harmony with who you are, self-fulfillment is very likely to occur. Too many students neglect this prerequisite to career planning and end up frustrated. A key to your future is what has happened in the past. Take the time to complete a detailed self-analysis.

Self-Analysis Questions

The purpose of a self-analysis is to identify all the components that have interacted to produce the kind of individual you have become. What you discover will also be invaluable later when you construct your resume and go for interviews. You will find the answers to many of the questions you'll be asked by prospective mentors and employers. The questions listed below should act to jog your memory, ensuring you don't omit important details later. The self-analysis process helps to organize your thinking in order to identify your strengths and weaknesses.

The following questions are included for your personal use. The questions are meant to help you and should not represent a good or bad value judgment. This set of questions relates to you and your personal characteristics as a designer. The answers to these questions will only help you if you answer them directly and honestly.

1. Do I like to work with people, data, things, or ideas?
2. Do I have the ability to make decisions quickly?
3. Am I theoretically or technically minded?
4. Am I patient?
5. Do I mind close supervision or criticism?
6. Am I a self-starter?
7. Do I like to assume responsibility, or do I prefer to work under someone else's direction?
8. How heavily do I weigh time invested and quality of work, versus satisfaction?
9. What are my design strengths? Design weaknesses?
10. What aspect of design gives me the most satisfaction? The least?
11. What do I want to achieve in my profession?
12. Can I complete a designated task with professional conduct?
13. Is it clear to me what I want to do for a living?
14. Do I need additional education to get my dream job?
15. What deficiencies will I need to overcome?
16. Do I express myself well?
17. Do I prefer to communicate orally? In writing? Graphically?
18. Do I see myself as a leader of a group or as an active participant?
19. Do I work well under pressure or does pressure cause me anxiety?

20. Do I seek responsibility?
21. Do I enjoy idea development and conceptualization?
22. In my chosen profession, what are the things I do best? Are they related to people, organizational skills, or technical skills?

The next set of questions relates more to the type of work and work environment you'd prefer. Again, ask yourself these questions and give an honest answer.

1. In what kind of physical setting do I like to work?
2. Do I prefer an urban or a rural environment?
3. Would I be happier in a small, medium, or large organization?
4. Do I want to work for a firm with few employees or a mega-firm?
5. What is the likelihood of job growth in my area of design?
6. What are the interesting trends in my field?
7. Does my knowledge of technology give me an edge over the competition?
8. Am I free to move to other geographic locations?
9. Would a change in geographic location enhance my job opportunities and prospects?
10. Do I want the security of a salaried position or would bonuses and commissions inspire me more? What about a combination of both?
11. How can I modify my design work to fit the market need?
12. Do I want to work a regularly scheduled workday or work week?
13. Would I like to travel for my job? Am I willing to travel more than 50 percent of my working time?
14. Are there other important persons to be considered in my career decisions?

If you are in college, know that only a few college students are absolutely certain of what is required to help them be successful in their chosen career. Therefore, you are not alone. Many students encounter difficulty in the internship or job search because they place too many limitations on themselves, such as location or salary, and are unaware of the numerous career possibilities. You may think you can pursue only one option in your career. You may end up putting all your eggs in one basket, only to discover too late that you have to modify your plans (when time is working against you). In the end, only after you identify who you are, what you are happy with, and what your objectives are will you be able to design a portfolio that accurately reflects who you are and what you want in a career.

CONCLUSION

Once you have a handle on the type of work and work environment that will satisfy you, you can target your portfolio for that area of design. The professors and practitioners who will review your portfolio can then look at it from a particular perspective, such as residential or commercial design. In the next chapter, you will be exposed to the typical contents of a design portfolio and will begin gathering the materials appropriate for your own unique portfolio.

GETTING IT TOGETHER

Gathering Material

The first three chapters introduced you to the design professions and who will be reviewing your work. You may be asking, "When do I start working on my portfolio?" *Now*. Congratulations! You are reading this book and therefore starting the portfolio process right now. In this chapter, we will talk about selecting your material. How you organize your portfolio says a lot about who you are and how you think. The typical contents of a portfolio based on educational standards and skill sets will be discussed. The inclusion of artifacts in your portfolio involves careful collection, selection, connection, and reflection. Before you dive into developing your portfolio, it is a good idea to understand the scope of the entire development process. It is recommended you read this chapter in its entirety before you begin designing your portfolio. This will offer you a holistic view of the procedure.

If you think about it, a portfolio is a collection of unrelated, fragmented tasks. It may include a complete project and pieces of many other diverse projects. There is little rhyme or reason to the inclusion of these tasks, other than to illustrate important skills in your specific design discipline. With so many varied artifacts available, carefully consider what is to be included. As illustrated in Figure 4.1, it's your job to form the parts into a cohesive whole. Do not arbitrarily throw a bunch of projects into a zippered portfolio case and declare your portfolio done.

The process of gathering your materials provides a great opportunity to learn more about yourself and your profession. Do not think of this as a waste of your time or an arduous task that takes too much effort. The act of creating a portfolio is a learning experience in itself. You will gain additional design and organization skills that will make you that much more marketable and desirable to firms. You'll need to do some self-directed learning to understand how to organize your portfolio. Let's start by looking at what is typically included in a portfolio.

4.1
The overall view of the model provides context, while the close-up images provide more detail. Both are necessary to create the "whole" package.
Design work courtesy of Daniel Childers.

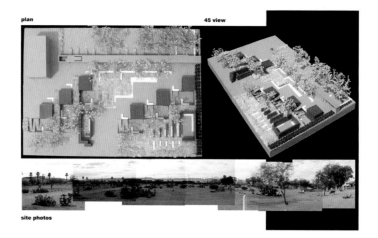

WHAT IS INSIDE A PORTFOLIO?

The typical contents of your portfolio will be similar to those of other designers but also unique to your profession and of course, unique to you and your special skills. Every design discipline has different portfolio requirements and alternative ways to determine what is good design. A designer's portfolio should exhibit a wide array of experiences and illustrate the designer's capabilities to meet any design challenge (see Box 4.1). You can organize your work in a few ways: by project, by theme, or by skill set.

Go for diversity! Show aspects of the full range of your skills, knowledge, interests, and abilities. Show projects at different stages of completion, from rough concept sketches, to polished renderings, to details.

Beverly Brandt, Ph.D.
Professor
Department of Interior Design, College of Design
Arizona State University
Tempe, AZ

Box 4.1

Organizing by Project

Your creative pieces should be selected to demonstrate competency in several areas. If you are using only a few completed design projects to illustrate your aptitude as a designer, select works that are far reaching, ones that really show your versatility as a designer. The portfolio is a window into your achievements and offers valuable insights to an interviewer who is evaluating your potential as an employee or a professor who is assessing the likelihood of your success in a program. Maximize the potential of these insights by including projects that appeal on various levels (see Figure 4.2).

Including three commercial design projects of office environments will not show your versatility as a designer. Although most architecture and design offices have a particular area of expertise, many also dabble in other specialties of design. For example, a commercial firm that specializes in retail and hospitality design may also design corporate offices or educational facilities. Cover your bases by including several different yet related projects, like an office environment, a restaurant, and a shopping center (all commercial projects).

The right balance of design content will determine the success of your portfolio. But what is the right balance? That is difficult to say. It's like trying to describe a dash of salt. What is a dash? Is it a pinch, a smidge, a couple shakes of the saltshaker? If you have too much variety in your portfolio, the reviewer may think you do not know your design strengths. If every project exemplifies the same set of skills, this lack of variety will convey that you can only do one or two things really well, when in fact you are probably quite accomplished in many aspects of the profession. How do you strike the right balance? No one can answer this but you. It is suggested you show a little variety, but not too much.

4.2
The list of projects in this table of contents illustrates the diversity of projects available inside the portfolio.
Design work courtesy of Jeffrey Lothner.

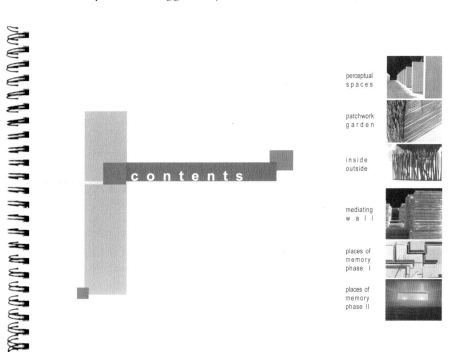

contents

perceptual
s p a c e s

patchwork
g a r d e n

inside
outside

mediating
w a l l

places of
memory
phase I

places of
memory
phase II

4.3
The school's admissions committee defined the skill sets identified in this table of contents. Design work courtesy of Ellen Barten.

For academic portfolios, the school may predefine criteria. Show the most complex work you have. Elemental work is acceptable for a first-year portfolio but a higher level of learning should be reflected in a high-level portfolio. Also, it would be unwise to ignore a skill when requested to show it. For example, schools often have a list of required skills they wish to see in your admissions portfolio (see Figure 4.3). You must show the skills listed, even if your work is not good. If it stinks, rework it. To completely omit a skill set (such as manual drafting and drawing) when requested to show evidence of it will hurt your chances of getting into the program.

The professional portfolio is more flexible in its contents. If you dislike working in a particular medium (like hand rendering or computer modeling), do not include that kind of work in your portfolio. It's important to show a variety of work but also only work that brings you joy. Why would you include examples of work you cannot stand producing? For example, if a firm is very impressed with your examples of product specification tables, they may want you to do that for a majority of your time with their firm. If you detest writing specifications, do you think you would enjoy waking up each day to go to work? Probably not. If a particular segment of the profession frustrates and depresses you, avoid promoting it in your portfolio.

Organizing by Theme

You can also organize your portfolio around a theme. A theme is a unifying idea that is a frequent element in your portfolio. It is the message or meaning behind

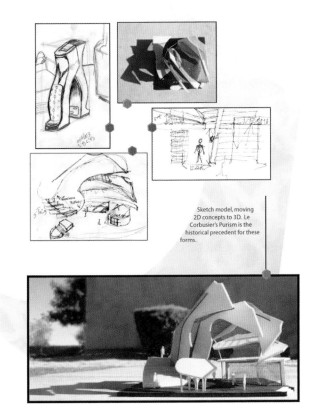

Sketch model, moving 2D concepts to 3D. Le Corbusier's Purism is the historical precedent for these forms.

4.4
A simple hexagon theme is seen in the gray background image and the smaller graphic elements. This theme was carried throughout the student's work examples. Design work courtesy of Aaron J. Kulik.

your work, an underlying concept that is consistently demonstrated in the way you arrange your work or add additional graphic elements. This can be a good way to illustrate your talent and creativity. Design the portfolio so the theme is reflected in every part of your portfolio, like the repeating hexagon theme in Figure 4.4.

Designing your portfolio around a theme can be a challenge. A theme may be stated and apparent, such as nature (with flowers) or a patriotic theme (with flags). It can also be abstract and implied, such as formal and elegant, or casual and crisp. A very successful use of theme was seen in a portfolio I reviewed recently. The student treated the images of her work as photos hanging on a wall in an art gallery. She put scanned images of actual picture frames around each image and added a shadow underneath. The images popped off the page. She also scanned hooks and cables and put these at the top of each image. On the outside edges of the two-page spread, she drew and hand rendered a few tall candles on metal stands. As the sections of the portfolio changed to show different skill sets, the color of the candles changed as well. It was a pleasure to review this portfolio. Her images themselves were well done and the presentation made it that much better.

Organizing by Skill Set

Let's discuss organizing your portfolio by skill set. It is suggested the portfolio be organized by skill set or category so reviewers can focus on the areas of most interest to them (McKenna 2000). If you are an architect, interior designer, or landscape architect, your profession's appropriate educational accrediting body has identified a set of skills. Remember that the National Architectural Accrediting Board (NAAB) is the authorizing agency for accrediting architecture programs in the United States. Likewise, the Council for Interior Design Accreditation (CIDA) accredits interior design programs in North America, and the Landscape Architectural Accreditation Board (LAAB) accredits landscape architecture programs in the United States.

There are common skill sets in the CIDA, LAAB, and NAAB standards that can be reflected in your portfolio. Skills commonly needed in our design disciplines may include, but are not limited to, work that represents Design Fundamentals, History, Design Development Skills, Communication, Building Systems/Site Construction, Codes and Regulations, Contract Documents, Programming, Project Management, and Business and Professional Practice. Review these standards. Which ones are most appropriate to your situation? Write these skills down. Put them in a chart and leave some space below each item. Select projects that demonstrate competence in these standards. Write the title of each project (or part of a project) under the appropriate skill. Now look at your list. Do you have too many items under one or two skill sets? Do you have absolutely nothing under a few others?

These skill sets represent the overall breadth of knowledge required by the profession to practice in the field (see Box 4.2). You may or may not have pieces that represent each and every skill listed above. Moreover, when you are just starting out on your professional path, you will have more pieces in some areas (like drawings and basic design work) than in others (see Figure 4.5).

That's okay. You would not be expected to have full construction documents, custom models, and animated walkthroughs represented in your portfolio if you are only applying for upper division courses in your program. These skills would more likely be evident when applying for an entry-level job or when seeking a promotion in your current firm (see Box 4.3).

Organizing your portfolio around recognized industry standards is useful for two reasons. First, these national standards signify the collective endeavor of

In reviewing a portfolio, I consider both breadth and depth based on the individual's level of education and professional experience. High school and undergraduate portfolios tend to have more breadth, whereas persons holding graduate degrees or professional positions are expected to have greater depth.

Kathleen Gibson
Associate Professor
Design and Environmental Analysis, Human Ecology
Cornell University
Ithaca, NY

Box 4.2

- hand drawing & rendering
- modeling
- principles of composition & order
- instrument assisted drawing
- influences
- miscellaneous

4.5
The first four categories represent skill sets. Additional categories were added to showcase special skills and knowledge. Design work courtesy of Ashley Delph.

numerous knowledgeable practitioners and educators who have identified indicators of good design. These are benchmarks for gauging competence. Second, these standards are nationally recognized. Therefore, a portfolio organized around these skill sets will have added meaning to practitioners. The standards recognized in California are the same ones recognized in New York, Florida, and elsewhere.

Putting together your portfolio will help you identify gaps in your design work. You can determine where you need to grow and expand. An area that is not adequately addressed may be an area in which you would want to invest some time.

The optimal design portfolio should include enough work samples to talk through your designs for approximately ½ hour. There should be a variety of work samples that show your "well-rounded" skill sets. You should include examples of 3-D images; construction detailing; standard floor plans, elevations, and sections; images of physical models; hand rendering and sketching; and any other extracurricular activities that are field-related (photography, sculpture, painting). Portfolios must include "Process." Many portfolios only focus on the final, finished images of projects (physical models, CAD images, and the like) and neglect to show process sketches, bubble diagrams, and more.

Greta Gillisse
Recruiting and Employee Relations Manager
Callison
Seattle, WA

Box 4.3

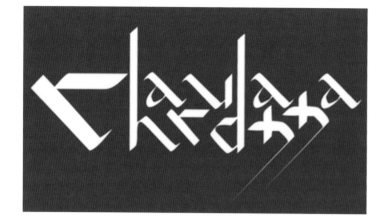

4.6
Calligraphy like this is ornate and highly stylized. It can be used to complement your design work. Calligraphy courtesy of Charudatta Joshi.

You also may not have good work in all of these areas. Don't try to cover all the bases by including inferior work. A poorly rendered perspective is not better than having no perspective at all. (We will talk more about this later.)

How can you differentiate yourself from the hordes of other job applicants? An awareness of other cultures developed through reading and possibly travel abroad can add appeal to your design solutions. Have an understanding of legal issues that affect your industry. If you draft a construction detail specifying a material that no one uses anymore (such as asbestos), that's a clear indication that you are not using the most up-to-date information. Knowledge of your industry should be apparent in the design samples you select. If you call out a material sample as green or sustainable and it isn't, practitioners will notice. Similarly, if you state specific criteria for a certain project, make sure that project meets those criteria.

Students often ask me if they can include additional material in their portfolio, to help them stand out in the crowd. Maybe they are artists or have developed an expertise in photography. Many designers have additional skills in fine arts. These are examples of personal expression, a glimpse into your inner vision and passion. The portfolio should appear to have focus and unity. Creative work such as a few stand-alone photographs, illustrations, and fine art prints should be removed. You may be a talented photographer, but if your photos are not of designed buildings, interiors, or exteriors, they will compete for the viewer's attention and could diminish the entire force of your portfolio. There is a difference between fine art and hobbies. Let's use calligraphy as an example. Calligraphy like that shown in Figure 4.6 is a stunning form of penmanship. It is definitely a learned skill as it can take years to become an accomplished calligrapher. This type of additional skill would be valuable in our design disciplines, where artistic visual communication with clients and colleagues is a necessary component of the professions. You could use your calligraphy skills to embellish your portfolio with artistic titles and captions. This would add, not subtract, from your work samples.

TYPICAL CONTENTS

Regardless of how you choose to organize the work inside your portfolio, the work will typically include examples of process work, drafted drawings, computer-aided drawings, presentation boards, three-dimensional (3-D) work, material samples, and written material (see Figure 4.7). If you are really good at sketching and have six pages devoted to that, but have almost nothing on any other skill, you're not showing breadth of skill. Professional portfolios typically are heavier on images than writing; academic portfolios are the reverse (see Figure 4.8).

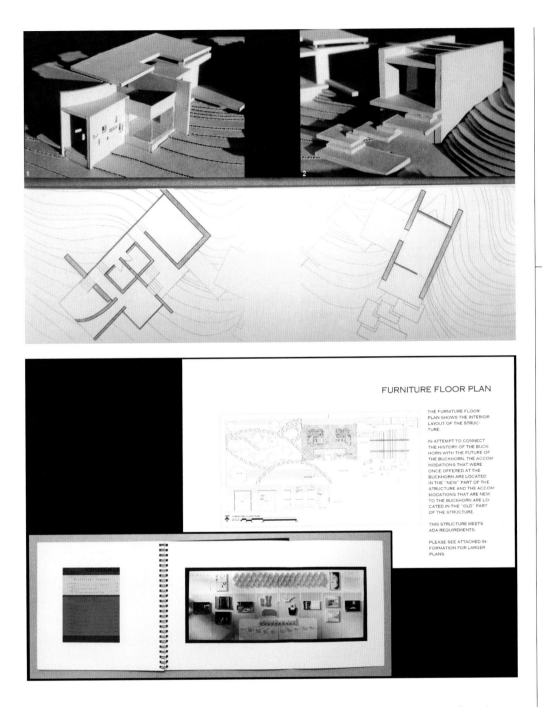

LEFT: 4.7
This page layout shows both the 3-D physical model and the drawings that accompany it. Design work courtesy of Jeremy Gates.

BELOW: 4.8
Some of your pages may work best with only images, while other pages would benefit from text to describe your design. Design work courtesy of Lauren Maitha and Ellen Barten.

FURNITURE FLOOR PLAN

THE FURNITURE FLOOR PLAN SHOWS THE INTERIOR LAYOUT OF THE STRUCTURE.

IN ATTEMPT TO CONNECT THE HISTORY OF THE BUCKHORN WITH THE FUTURE OF THE BUCKHORN, THE ACCOMMODATIONS THAT WERE ONCE OFFERED AT THE BUCKHORN ARE LOCATED IN THE "NEW" PART OF THE STRUCTURE AND THE ACCOMMODATIONS THAT ARE NEW TO THE BUCKHORN ARE LOCATED IN THE "OLD" PART OF THE STRUCTURE.

THIS STRUCTURE MEETS ADA REQUIREMENTS.

PLEASE SEE ATTACHED INFORMATION FOR LARGER PLANS.

There are many things to include in your portfolio. There are also a few things you should *not* include. Never put a picture of yourself in your portfolio. Never include any personal information such as race, age, social security number, and so on. This is a clear indication that you are unaware of professional etiquette and hiring procedures. Leave out any reference to your own political affiliation, sexual preference, or religion. If any project could be considered offensive or the intent could give the wrong impression to the reviewer, remove it from your portfolio. When in doubt, leave it out! Let's focus next on some of the artifacts you might include in your portfolio.

Process Work in a Design Sketchbook

Architects, interior designers, and landscape architects can be very artistic individuals. But there is more to design than the aesthetic. One aspect of design in the built environment that separates it from other more aesthetic design professions is its inherent problem-solving responsibility. A client has a problem. The client seeks a design professional to solve that problem. The designer gathers important information regarding the parameters of the problem and its potential solution. This is sometimes referred to as design programming, conceptual design, or the design process. This information is critical in the formulation of your design solution and should be included in your portfolio (see Box 4.4).

Drawing is the predominant form of communication used in the design process (Pressman 1997). Freehand drawing and quick sketches help in concept visualization and are an important part of your process work (see Figure 4.9). Many practitioners prefer to see examples in a portfolio of work representing the entire design process, from rough sketches to final construction documents. Preliminary process work includes sketches, doodles, notes, drawings, flowcharts, bubble diagrams, block diagrams, interaction networks, quick sketches, wayfinding exercises, concept exploration, space plan studies, construction and material research, decision trees, quick perspectives, graphic models, inspiration images, and other visual references. Concept models like the one in Figure 4.10 are also good examples of your thought process.

Quick sketching techniques are invaluable in our design fields. Sketches such as the one in Figure 4.11 can quickly communicate your ideas to others. But one sketch does not qualify as a representation of your design process. One sketch is just that, one sketch. A process is a series or progression of elements. Make sure your sketches are graphically developed. Incomplete sketches are fine as long as they can express your intended concept.

You have two ways to showcase your process work: in your portfolio or as a separate book. A few select pieces of your process work can be integrated into your portfolio. Or you can showcase all process work in a design journal or

An important portfolio component is the documentation of the designer's research and process for various problems and solutions. Students can show parts of their conceptual development, programming evidence, and schematic sketches in ways that take the viewer through the student's creation and decision making. Additionally, annotated drawings can identify evidence-based design criteria, three-dimensional expression, or code compliance research.

Denise A. Guerin, Ph.D., FIDEC, ASID, IIDA
Morse-Alumni Distinguished Professor
College of Design
University of Minnesota
St. Paul, MN

Box 4.4

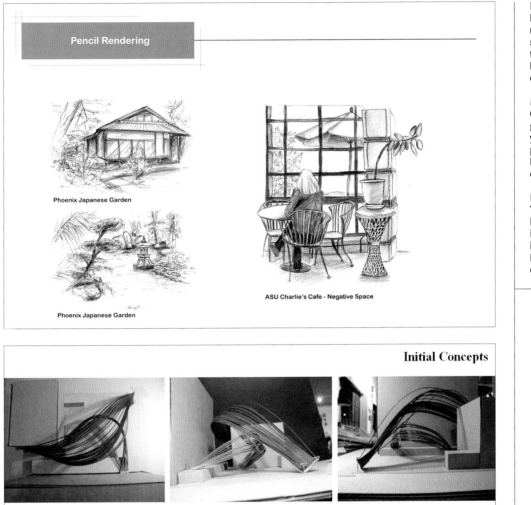

Pencil Rendering

Phoenix Japanese Garden

Phoenix Japanese Garden

ASU Charlie's Cafe - Negative Space

Initial Concepts

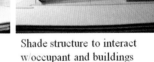

Opposed arcs

Visual interest to link 1st Ave
w/Adams St & Second Ave

Shade structure to interact
w/occupant and buildings

sketchbook, as a supplement to your portfolio (see Figure 4.12). This sketchbook can be tucked into the back of your book or case. If the interviewer wishes to see it, it's available. Also known as a concept journal, this compilation of raw documents and drawings shows your brainstorming process in action.

A sketchbook provides a glimpse into your personality and your work process—of your mind at work (see Box 4.5). It is a journal you carry with you at all times, allowing you to jot down notes or do a quick sketch of something that inspires you. A great idea usually evolves slowly and is actually a compilation of several thoughts rolled into one solution, like the pen sketches in Figure 4.13. A sketchbook often includes ideas that are rejected

and ideas that are merged, altered, and recycled into other projects. It is a good way to show a potential employer how your mind functions when seeking answers to design challenges. Many designers like to see this so they can ascertain if you will fit into the culture of the firm.

A journal, notebook, or sketchbook can showcase how your ideas evolve, how you think, and how you solve design problems. Not showing any of your design process work may raise the reviewer's suspicions. Remember that our design disciplines involve more than flashy images. They are disciplines that solve problems for clients and require careful decision-making ability. Demonstrate this skill in a sketchbook as a supplement to your other portfolio work (see Box 4.6).

You say you don't have one? Start one now. Buy a bound journal or sketchbook from any bookstore or art supply store (see Figure 4.14). Start documenting the development of your ideas. If you want more drawing freedom, you can photocopy individual sheets of your process work and have all of them bound into one booklet. Another option is to reformat these documents to match the format and layout of your other portfolio pieces. If you have your sketches and concept drawings spiral bound into a book, design a front and a back cover. You may even want to have these covers laminated so they stay neat and clean. Make the sketchbook beautiful and tempting. If it looks good, the reviewer will want to open it and handle it. If you like to do everything digitally, convert your sketches and other hand-drawn work into digital format. A good time to do this is throughout each project, rather than waiting until the very end of the project to search around for your preliminary sketches.

4.12
A sketchbook should show more than sketches. It should include any imagery that helped you solve the design problem. Design work courtesy of Rachel K. Dankert.

The inclusion of a project's evolution in the form of developmental sketches is something I have come to understand from employers as a critical component and almost the thing they are more interested in seeing than the "finished product." A separate sketchbook of freehand ideation is critical and should be included to show an employer a designer's range of skills. It's nice if it can be separate so it can be passed around if there happens to be more than one person present at an interview.

Ann L. Black
Associate Director
School of Architecture and Interior Design,
College of Design,
Architecture, Art & Planning
University of Cincinnati
Cincinnati, OH

Box 4.5

Drafted Drawings

The act of creating architectural drawings is known as technical drawing or drafting. The mechanics of drafting require the use of drawing tools such as paper, pencils, pens, T squares, triangles, and other drawing apparatus to create precise line drawings. These line drawings can be of structures, interiors, exteriors, or objects. They are often drawn in multiple views, such as plan, elevation, section, and various orthographic projections (see Figure 4.15). They are also drawn at a known scale much different than the actual size of the object or space, such as ¼" =1'0" or 1" = 500'0".

Although the computer has advanced technical line drawings at an accelerated pace, your portfolio will need to display your ability at both hand and computer drawings. Complex software packages are helpful in the design process, but they

ABOVE LEFT: 4.13
A final design is often the result of many initial concepts and attempts. This concept work can be shown as evidence of your thought process. Design work courtesy of Stephanie Fanger.

ABOVE RIGHT: 4.14
Sketchbooks come in various shapes, sizes, styles, and prices.

> **The presentation clearly** provides the ability to understand how the "design thinking" progressed and matured into a refined design solution. In some cases this may best be done within a project, while in other cases it may best be done in a supplemental sketchbook or journal. It may even be the case that in some instances both avenues of presentation may be appropriate within a single portfolio. Whatever mechanism best describes the designer's strengths is the way to go.
>
> Jo Ann Asher Thompson, Ph.D., FIIDA, FIDEC
> Vice Chancellor, Spokane
> Professor of Interior Design, Interdisciplinary Design Institute
> Washington State University
> Spokane, WA

Box 4.6

RIGHT: 4.15
An example of hand drafting shows your design skill and your technical ability with pencil and drafting instruments.
Design work courtesy of Ashley Delph.

BELOW: 4.16
Computers are precise but hand drawing is still an expected skill to have in the design disciplines.
Design work courtesy of Jeffrey Prince.

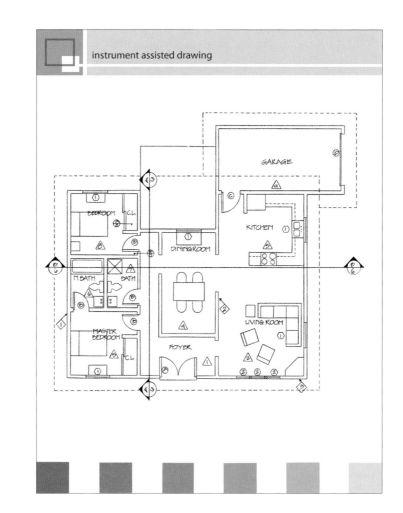

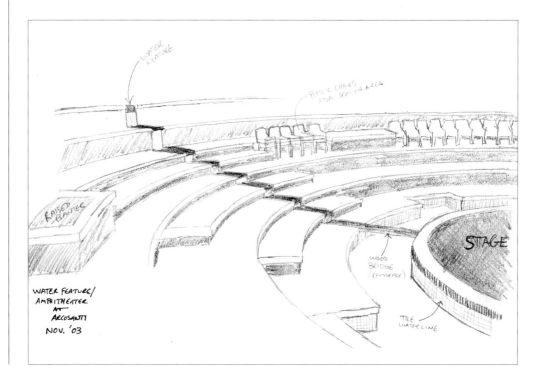

cannot replace the conceptual energy in freehand drawing. Practice your drawing skills to continually improve your presentation proficiency (see Figure 4.16).

Some authors and practitioners would advise you to bring your large, original drafted or CAD construction drawings to a job interview. These drawings can be rolled up and carried in a tube. Others say you can adequately reproduce these drawings or close-up views in a smaller size that is consistent with the rest of your portfolio. It is best to find out from the contact person at the firm if you should bring these types of large drawings to your interview. Regardless of how you present examples of your drafting and drawing, know that you need to include either some hand drafting or computer-aided drawings.

Computer-Aided Drawings

Computer-aided design (CAD) involves the use of a wide range of computer-based tools that assist architects and other designers in their daily design activities. Initially developed for the aerospace and automotive industries, CAD has now progressed to desktop applications used in all areas of construction. Many different software packages are available, ranging from 2-D vector-based systems to 3-D parametric surface and solid modeling systems. CAD is used to fabricate drawings and specifications that can subsequently be used to estimate the correct amount of needed materials, determine the cost of development, and, in the end, provide the meticulous drawings necessary to build the finished product (see Figure 4.17). Construction drawings in interior design, architecture, and land-

4.17
CAD drawings are precise and accurate. They can be fairly simple or fairly complex.

1042 N. Opal - Brian Twet Front Yard Landscape Plan

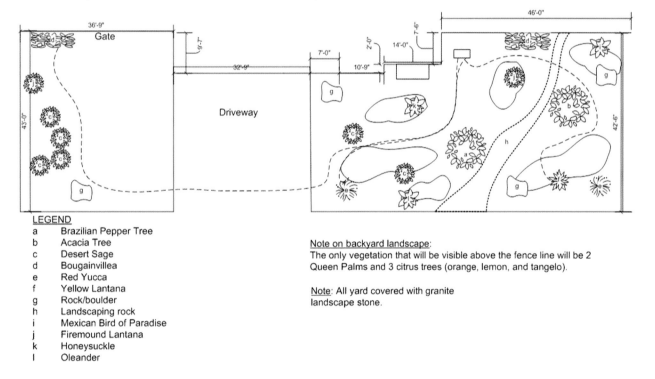

LEGEND
a   Brazilian Pepper Tree
b   Acacia Tree
c   Desert Sage
d   Bougainvillea
e   Red Yucca
f   Yellow Lantana
g   Rock/boulder
h   Landscaping rock
i   Mexican Bird of Paradise
j   Firemound Lantana
k   Honeysuckle
l   Oleander

Note on backyard landscape:
The only vegetation that will be visible above the fence line will be 2 Queen Palms and 3 citrus trees (orange, lemon, and tangelo).

Note: All yard covered with granite landscape stone.

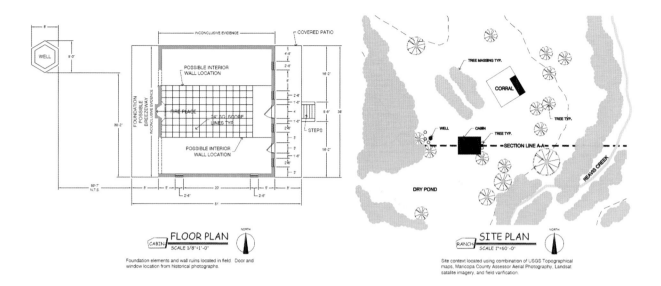

FLOOR PLAN
CABIN SCALE 1/8"=1'-0"

Foundation elements and wall ruins located in field Door and window location from historical photographs.

SITE PLAN
RANCH SCALE 1"=60'-0"

Site context located using combination of USGS Topographical maps, Maricopa County Assessor Aerial Photography, Landsat satalite imagery, and field varification.

ABOVE: 4.18
A benefit of CAD drawings is the ability to display multiple drawings from the same project at different scales. Design work courtesy of Jeffrey Prince.

RIGHT: 4.19
Several modeling software packages are available to help you in designing. Use the tool that works best for you.
Design work courtesy of Sally Azer and Joanie Liebelt.

scape architecture can be drafted manually but are more often created with CAD tools (see Figure 4.18).

Using CAD as a design tool is becoming more prevalent in today's design firms (Mitton 2004) due to its reliability, flexibility, clarity, accuracy, and efficiency. As one author states, "The computer is designed to store, process, duplicate, transmit, and retrieve vast quantities of information" (Pressman 1997, 265). CAD is a benefit to design through its increase in worker productivity, ease of revising drawings, retrieval of imagery, and the accuracy of the finished product (Clemons and McCullough 1989).

Computers are useful when doing repetitive tasks. They cut costs and speed up the design process. Skill in CAD and other computer imagery software is an expectation of today's architecture and design students. Designers generally use a multitude of 2-D and 3-D software programs, such as AutoCAD, FormZ, ArchiCAD, Microstation, Revit, Sketchup, and 3D Studio Viz and Max (see Figure 4.19). However, you will want to use the right tool for the job. If a computer cannot accomplish what you need in order to solve the design problem, don't be afraid to divert your

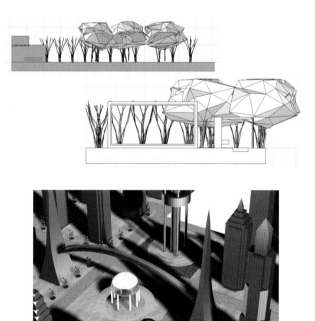

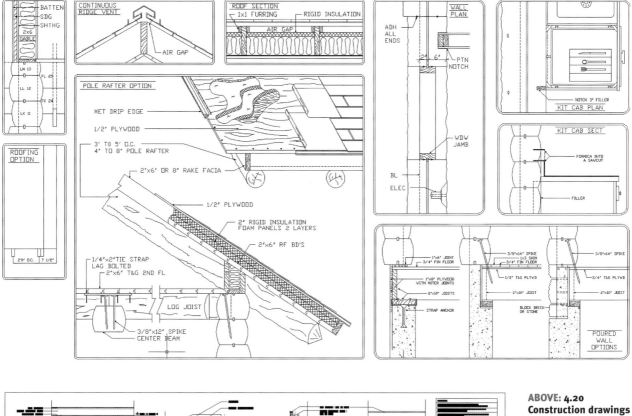

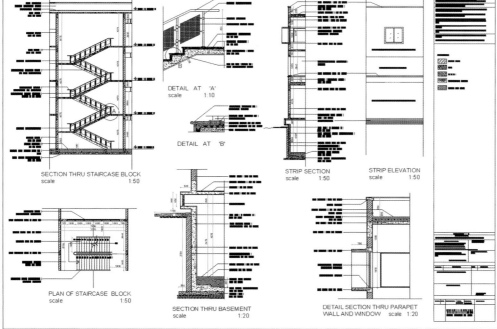

attention to traditional communication tools (i.e., use a pencil). Designers should have a working knowledge of many software applications, from office software like Microsoft Excel to image-editing software like Adobe Photoshop.

CAD is used to its fullest potential when making construction drawings. The inclusion of construction drawings in a portfolio is essential. This is one type of project that makes our disciplines of the built environment unique. Artists don't have these types of drawings. Neither do fashion or graphic designers. A full set or sampling of construction drawings illustrates your comprehension of materials, structure, details (as in Figure 4.20), and your ability to communicate with 2-D plans, elevations, sections, and details. It also represents your ability to organize a project, because these drawings include title blocks, keys, legends, construction notes, and all the symbols necessary to communicate your design (see Figure 4.21).

If possible, print your construction drawings directly from the software in which they were created. This will give you the cleanest, clearest production of the drawings. Line drawings created in vector-based software will pixellate when reproduced in raster-based software. (You'll learn more about this in Chapter 9.)

Presentation Boards

Presentation boards are used in the design disciplines to communicate and sell an idea to the client. No matter how great you think your idea is, no matter how well you can verbally explain it, a picture is worth a thousand words. Clients prefer visual presentations, often with multimedia and large-format presentation boards. They need to see what you are talking about.

Most presentation boards are flat and 2-D, with pictures, images, and drawings adhered to the board surface. Boards with a 3-D quality may add interest to a presentation. These boards may include line drawings, rendered elevations and perspectives, written information, and even material samples (see Figure 4.22). Admirable drawing and rendering skills, along with proficiency in visual layouts,

4.22
Presentation boards visually communicate to others with 3-D qualities.
Design work courtesy of Han Yoon Lee, Shelby Bogaard, and Tracy Franson.

are very important skills to have in order to execute a successful presentation board. A project may require only one board. More likely, the project will require several boards to adequately convey your design ideas.

Boards can be created manually by cutting and pasting your drawings, color copies, and samples onto the board. They can also be produced electronically by laying out your entire presentation in available software applications, and then producing a large poster-size print. This print can then be adhered to a stiffer backing board that can stand on an easel or be pinned to a wall. You can also combine the two methods by doing some work on the computer, printing to a large-scale printer, and then adding other elements by hand. This approach is actually the most successful because these boards tend to be more 3-D, with some work extending out toward the viewer. This invites the viewer to touch the board and engage another human sense. Whether you choose to include the actual boards as part of your portfolio, or smaller, digitally altered versions, presentation boards exhibit your ability to visually communicate with others.

3-D Models and Full-Size Work

Let's face it. Not every project you create as a designer is flat. Unlike graphic designers, we work in 3-D space. When you create a building, interior, or exterior design, you are considering the design from all three directions—X, Y, and Z. Sometimes you need to create a 3-D form to relay your design intent to a client, or in school to your peers, professor, and jury of critics. You may produce foam core, balsa wood, or mat board scale models (see Figure 4.23). There may be courses where you are exploring form and mass and you create 3-D sculptures as well.

Computer renderings can be utilized to highlight the complexity of 3-D forms, like the one in Figure 4.24. Unfortunately, a 2-D representation of 3-D is never as powerful as the original. You lose the presence of the piece when it is forced into a less effective format. That's one benefit of taking the original work with you to an interview. But how do you get these models to fit nicely inside your portfolio case? You don't. Unless it's very small, you cannot easily cram a 3-D model into your relatively flat portfolio. The trick is to go from a 3-D object to a 2-D representation. You have a couple of options to do this. You can photograph the object from all sides. This would generate a nice series of prints, showing the

4.23
Working models are a good way to experiment with your design. Design work courtesy of Paul Marquez.

4.24
More and more architecture and design work is being accomplished with computer media. Among other things, this illustration shows the impact of light on an atrium area. Design work courtesy of Brian WinThant Tong.

work from all angles. You can also videotape the piece, convert it to a digital movie, and put that movie into your digital portfolio.

Full-size work lends itself to its own unique challenges. You may have designed full-scale furniture, construction details, or process models. When building the piece, take pictures of the process along the way. When done, you can take more pictures of the finished piece or even create a video by moving slowly around the object.

If you were fortunate enough in a previous employment position to see your design work produced or brought to fruition, photograph the work. Large-scale work like an exterior patio, an interior lobby, or the building itself is another story. First, get permission from the firm to use these photographs of the space in your portfolio. Give credit to the firm and head designer whenever these photographs are used. Make copies of concept sketches, construction documents, material selections, presentation boards, specifications, and other materials from the project *before* you leave the firm. (Again, ask for permission first.) Once you are gone, you will have limited or no access to these materials again. It is frustrating for your supervisor (no matter how nice he or she is) to have to gather copies of these materials for you six months or a year later because now you need a copy in order to apply for a job or for graduate school. Material is often discarded once a project is built, especially odd-sized presentation boards and 3-D models. If the object is difficult to store, it is more likely to be destroyed. Therefore, any record of your work on these boards or models has vanished. Take the photos while you can.

Material Samples

Most design projects are constructed of more than one building or finishing material. We use concrete, glass, steel, upholstery, paint, and many other materials. To demonstrate these various materials and finishes to clients, we rely on presentation boards with tangible examples mounted to them, such as the one in Figure 4.25.

Upholstery samples should be pressed, trimmed, and securely fastened to the board. One way to present your fabric samples is to wrap the fabric around a piece of foam core board or mat board and secure the fabric on the backside. Another way is to have the fabric edges visible. If this is the case, use pinking shears to pink the edges of the fabric so they won't fray. Hard samples such as laminate, thin slices of metals, slender glass pieces, and other relatively lightweight objects can be mounted with various household glues and cements. How do you secure heavier material samples, like tile, wood, or stone, to your board? You can use professional cement glue, such as Mastik or Liquid Nails. Secure them very well to the board. You don't want them to fall off the board right when someone is reviewing it. Keep in mind that once you glue these samples to your boards, they are not coming off!

Unfortunately, there is no easy way to represent material sample boards in a digital format. The closest you can get is to take a high-resolution photo of all your materials individually or of the material boards (see Figure 4.26). Digital

BELOW LEFT: 4.25 The samples of materials shown on this presentation board would allow the client or juror to experience the sensation of touch. Design work courtesy of Lisa Perrone, Cindy Louie, and Kristy Harline.

BELOW RIGHT: 4.26 A high-resolution composite of your intended material samples can substitute for the actual sample itself. It loses the tactile quality but can still convey the visual essence of your design.

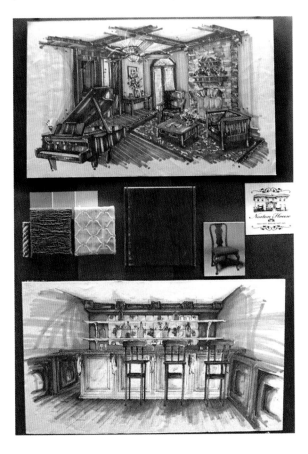

photographs do not always convey accurate levels of execution. Some practitioners believe there is no substitute for original work because the tactile properties of the materials are completely lost. It is appealing to hold and scrutinize a physical sample. A small materials sample board can be used in your portfolio to complement one of your complete projects. While the interviewer is looking through your portfolio booklet, you can pull the sample board out of the case and present that, too.

Design in the 21st century fuses function and sustenance into a cohesive whole. The successful integration of these two concepts, in my opinion, is critical to the future of our ever-changing culture and environment.

Functionality means creating spaces that not only accommodate the broadest range of people but also meet the client's needs and specifications. It is also exceptionally important to not only meet the demands of the clients but to take into account the future needs and management of the space. This in turn denotes that functionality is the universality of design and prepares society for the future.

Sustainability creates designs of spaces that not only take into account the needs of immediate users but also consider its future use in regards to costs, efficient proper use of materials, and their ultimate effect on the environment. One approach to sustainability is to use regional materials as well as useful designs from history. Adobe shelters originally designed and built by Native Americans living in the Southwest region of the United States are an example of sustenance in design. Ecologically conscious materials such as compacted mud are made into shelters that retain heat in the winter and stay cool in the summer, which is highly important in the deserts of the Southwest. The significant characteristic of sustainability is to enhance rather than blemish the landscape by designing non-obtrusive structures of simple design that respect local climatic, environmental, and cultural traditions within surrounding environments.

Before entering into the program here at ASU I had a rudimentary awareness of the various issues that designers face as we enter into the 21st century. By partaking in the College's well-regarded curriculum along with its knowledgeable and experienced professors, I have been able to expand basic understanding of design and its implications for society and culture. As I continue my education here at ASU, I expect that as I progress through the program, my education will prepare me for my professional career. Technical knowledge, coupled with my own instinct and intuition, will ultimately ensure that I will be able enter the Interior Design field with pride and confidence.

4.27
A statement of personal design philosophy is often required for an admission portfolio and can be a positive option for a professional portfolio too.
Design work courtesy of Shelby Bogaard.

Design Philosophy

An optional component of your portfolio is the design philosophy. Also known as an artist's statement, this short essay describes your beliefs and philosophy as a designer. This statement is a description of your attitude about design and the world around you. It should be a reflection of your viewpoint and perspective, and be interesting enough to keep the reader's attention (see Figure 4.27).

Before jumping into writing this statement, think about what you want to achieve with your designs and what you are trying to say with them. This can be one of the most difficult essays to write. There is no magic formula for constructing your philosophy. Some designers spend time in contemplation, jotting down notes over the course of weeks and months. Other designers sit right down at the computer, pull up their favorite word processing software, and begin writing.

Start by filling in the information in Box 4.7. This is intended to help you think about the strategy for developing your own unique philosophy. Describe your qualifications for being a good match for the academic program or employment position. This does not mean changing your philosophy to meet the expectations of the school or firm. If you researched the philosophy of the school or firm, you

THINKING ABOUT YOUR DESIGN PHILOSOPHY

Three reasons I enjoy design are:
1. _____
2. _____
3. _____

Three words that describe me as a designer are:
1. _____
2. _____
3. _____

Three beliefs I have about designing are:
1. _____
2. _____
3. _____

Three possible themes for my philosophy are:
1. _____
2. _____
3. _____

Three ways I can integrate my philosophy into my portfolio are:
1. _____
2. _____
3. _____

Box 4.7

can acknowledge its philosophy and point out where yours meets it. Recognizing where you stand with regard to current design trends, theories, and issues can be helpful in writing your philosophy as well.

Graduate school applications often ask for this type of statement (see Figure 4.28). Parts of your statement can be recycled but not the whole thing. You wouldn't send the same letter to 10 different graduate schools with the name of one school right smack in the middle of the first paragraph. Always proofread text you intend others to read. Use the spell-checking feature of your software program, too.

The design philosophy statement is a sample of your writing. Terminology you have learned in design classes or garnered from being in your firm or on the job site should be reflected in this statement. If you need to, get out your thesaurus and dazzle the reader with a plethora of eloquent vocabulary (i.e., a lot of nice words).

There are several sections to this philosophy statement. The first paragraph should be informative but brief. This is the reader's introduction to you. It invites the reader to learn more about your aspirations and ambitions. Some designers start and end their philosophy statement with a quote from an artist or designer who has influenced their design thinking. This part of the statement should be only three to four sentences long.

The body of the design philosophy statement is longer and will allow you to elaborate on several of your more challenging and rewarding projects. How did you approach the design solutions? What is unique about these projects? What strong statement does your design make, and why is it important to notice it? The reader will probably want to see the projects you are discussing so please make sure they are included in your portfolio. Furthermore, this is the time to talk

4.28
A short philosophy or intent statement tells the review committee what you intend to pursue in your graduate studies. Design work courtesy of Melissa Zlatow.

As designers, we have a unique opportunity (and oftentimes an obligation) to help shape and define the attitudes and beliefs of generations to come. Minimizing the destructive consumption of our resources should be a constant objective. However, bombarding society with pictures of tree huggers and an infinite supply of biodegradable "save the whale" bumper stickers is hardly the answer. In fact, it can have the opposite intended effect. In order to understand how to best attain the desired behavior, we must first identify the barriers that prevent its execution. This type of research will increase public awareness regarding the design community and the holistic role designers play in today's business world. Illustrating the impact of "good design" in the lives of the masses can lead to an increase in the notion that designers do not simply make things "stylish"; they strive to improve everyday life. With careful research, we may discover pertinent information regarding why so many people still choose to recycle infrequently or maybe even not at all, and design our products accordingly.

about your mastery of certain techniques or your interest in a current design topic or trend, such as sustainability, designing for the aged, or historic preservation.

As you close your statement in the last few sentences, express your final thoughts clearly and directly. Explain how your design philosophy has a positive impact on your designs and why this makes your design solutions so successful. Take time to carefully craft this statement. Remember, this is yet another promotional tool. It just happens to be a written promotion, rather than a visual one.

What does this look like? Overall, your philosophy statement should be no more than two pages. Strive for 400 to 500 words when using a 10- to 12-point font. Keep it short. The design philosophy should be well written, articulate, and confident. Try to maintain a serious tone that is sincere, not pompous or overbearing. Your desire to use design research and inquiry to expand your understanding should be included in the content of this statement. You will probably need to rewrite it several times before it truly communicates your ideas and achieves a smooth grammatical flow.

Some designers prefer to send their design philosophy statement to schools or firms along with their resume. It is also perfectly acceptable to include it as part of your traditional portfolio. However, practitioners disagree about including your design philosophy in your digital portfolio. It involves a great deal of text, which is difficult to read on a computer monitor. In a web-based portfolio, it can simply be a link to another web page. (A web page is a single document found on the web and is usually part of a larger web site that has graphics, media, and content all linked together.) In a more linear portfolio, you would have to devote time and space to this writing. The choice is up to you.

Written Materials

Decisions will be made based on what is seen in your portfolio, including photos and images of your work, as well as the written commentary that goes along with them. With that in mind, there is no need to write pages and pages of descriptive text to accompany your visual images. No one will take the time to read them. But even a portfolio with minimal text needs some captions and titles, as shown in Figure 4.29.

4.29
A portfolio contains more images than text. Use labels to guide the viewer to the aspects you want to emphasize. Design work courtesy of Shrikar Bhave.

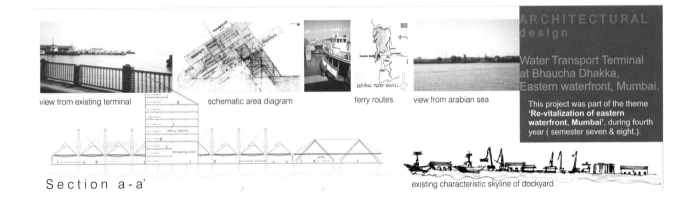

view from existing terminal   schematic area diagram   ferry routes   view from arabian sea

ARCHITECTURAL
design

Water Transport Terminal at Bhaucha Dhakka, Eastern waterfront, Mumbai.

This project was part of the theme 'Re-vitalization of eastern waterfront, Mumbai', during fourth year (semester seven & eight.).

Section a-a'

existing characteristic skyline of dockyard

FINISH SPECIFICATIONS

CODE	ITEM	QTY	MANUFACTURER	DESCRIPTION	REMARKS
CNC-1	Ready Mix	6610 sq. ft.	Davis Colors	Concrete, light fast, lime proof, weather resistant color, use W-1000™ concrete cure and sealer.	Light Gray-8084
CPT-1	Chamber #7216	115 sq. ft.	Masland Contract	Carpet, DuPont Antron Legacy Nylon, 28 oz./sq. yrd., textured loop pile, 18w" x 28.5L", beck dyed, 1/12 gauge, .250"/.188".125" pile height, 74oz.sq.yrd., woven polypropylene primary and secondary backing.	#12606
MIR-1	N/A	5	Reflection Products	Mirrors, columns, 2'6" x 8'. Flush mount polished steel.	
MTL-1	Radians	95 sq. ft.	Ceilings Plus	OB-19, 3/17" x 5/8" Obround @ 7/16" x 15/32" Staggered Centers, 27% open.	Kryolite
MTL-2	Waterslide	2	Moz Designs Inc.	Aluminum Paneling, 3' x 5', .040 thick. Applied to dressing room doors.	Sapphire
PAD-1	RSP-600 Kwick-Stik	700 sq. ft.	Resilite	Padding on columns, 2" thick tough PVC Rubatex foam core. The front surface of the mat is coated with Resilite #457 coating. 5.5–7.5 lbs/cu.ft., 5.5–7.5 25% compression resistance, 75 tensile strength per min., 125 elongation %per min., 0"/min max flammability, 3yr guarantee.	Black
PNL-1	N/A	339 sq. ft.	Fabri Trak	Fabric wall panels for columns. Custom brand logos printed on fabric.	COM-4
PT-1	1017	310 sq. ft.	ICI	Flat, apply 2 coats. Apply to cash wrap wall.	1017 Touring Green
PT-2	815	3075 sq. ft.	ICI	Flat, apply 2 coats. Apply to walls as marked.	815 Natural White
PT-3	1016	490 sq. ft.	ICI	Flat, apply 2 coats. Apply to super graphic wall.	1016 White on White
RB-1	N/A	610 lf.	Roppe	Pinnacle Rubber Base, 4"h.	100 Black

4.30
Written work can also be included in your portfolio.

A short title will include the name of the project and the client (if any). A slightly longer title will include a brief description of the design problem. This provides some context for reviewing the project. A project description can include the title, client, project goals, design problem, date or duration of project, and your solution. This is sometimes referred to in industry as a "design brief."

Samples of other written material may be included in your portfolio. Specifications (commonly referred to as specs) are written requirements for the production of your spaces and buildings. These written descriptions are for finishes and materials, workmanship, equipment, construction standards, and so on. They are technical reports used to relay project requirements to the general contractor. The four common types of specifications are descriptive, performance, proprietary, and reference (Reznikoff 1989). You may have one of these types of specifications in your portfolio as evidence of your ability to write technical reports (see Figure 4.30).

You may perhaps include business memoranda, detailed budgets, cost analyses, spatial studies and other written materials in your portfolio (see Box 4.8). These forms of written communication are not as commonly found in a designer's portfolio as images of professional work. But if you are pursuing a graduate degree in business or are looking for a position in design management, you will want to show your expertise in these areas.

Proofread your written material over and over again. In whatever software you are using to type the text, use the spell-checking feature. Have others read the written material, too. You may omit something or consistently misuse a word. Others reviewing your work can catch your mistakes. If English is not your first language, have a native speaker review your work. (Your ability to work or attend school in a different country will depend in part on your mastery of the language in that country.) Although writing is not the focal point of your portfolio, it can detract from your designs if done incorrectly.

COLLECTION, SELECTION, CONNECTION, AND REFLECTION

Now that you have an idea of what artifacts *can* be included in your portfolio, it's time to consider what *will* be included. The next section talks about a simple process that involves the collection, selection, connection, and reflection on your work (Kilbane and Milman 2003). These four stages will help you identify what must be in your portfolio.

Collection

Many designers start gathering and sharing their material with friends and family long before they receive any formal training in portfolio design. Think about it. You have probably been putting together a portfolio for quite a while. You just never knew your compilation had a name. The collection of your work is the first step in creating a design portfolio.

Start by collecting the objects and projects you think are good enough to be included in your portfolio. Go for quantity first. Ultimately, you will narrow down your choice of projects to the highest quality items. But for starters, gather as many good examples as possible. This gives you a large pool of potential projects.

Your first attempt at collecting and arranging your work will consist of school projects. These are basic visual exercises and case studies. As you progress in school and your projects become more complex, your portfolio will morph into a larger body of work.

Save all of your work (see Box 4.9). After all, how can you document your skills if you don't have any evidence? Even if you absolutely despised the project and you never want to see it again, save it anyway. A portion of it may be exceptional. That's the portion you should put in your portfolio. Maybe it was the lighting or demolition plan, or the presentation board, or the foam-core model that was really outstanding (see Figure 4.31).

You must begin collecting materials *now*. The last week of the semester is not the time to start pulling materials together. Besides work done in school projects, don't forget about work done through jobs, internships, or volunteer opportunities. These experiences also provide a wealth of items as possible samples.

Students often ask me, "What items from my courses and field experiences should be saved for my portfolio?" My answer is always to keep everything you do. Take care of this work. Put a date on it, especially your design process work. After a time, you won't be able to rely on your memory to accurately recall when you did this and when you did that. Collect as much of your work as you can. At this stage, it is okay to be a pack rat.

> **A portfolio should** document not just the end of the design journey, but also the path of that journey.
>
> Jane Britt Greenwood, AIA
> Associate Dean
> College of Architecture, Art, and Design
> Mississippi State University
> Starkville, MS

Box 4.9

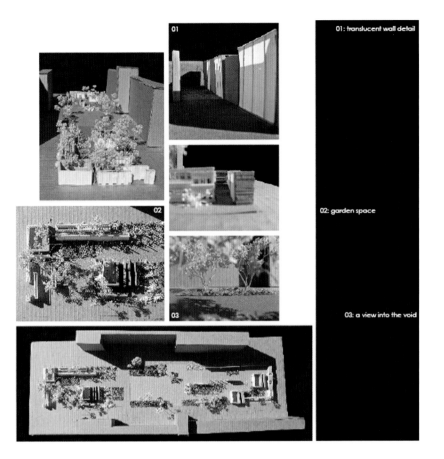

01: translucent wall detail

02: garden space

03: a view into the void

Selection

As a second step, narrow down the collection of projects and select the ones that best fit your needs. If you were successful in the collection stage, you should have a vast quantity of projects from which to choose. Selecting your work is a challenging yet rewarding step. It involves decisions about what kind of projects to include, which examples are your best, and how many projects should be in your portfolio. Now is when you shift your energy from gathering *quantity* to selecting *quality*. Of course, keep in mind that in your first few years of school, you won't have a large number of projects to select among. On the other hand, if you are a graduating senior, you will have too much work. You could include every single project you ever did. But why would you? It's not feasible, not desirable, and makes you look unfocused.

In this stage of selecting your items, consider the self-analysis you completed in the previous chapter. Recall your strengths and weaknesses. Your projects should focus on your strengths. Which projects exemplify your design power and would present your design work in the best possible light? It is suggested that you examine your work and divide it into the four categories listed below (Berryman 1994). Focus your energy on the projects in category #1.

1. The work is ready to be presented to others.
2. The work needs minor adjustments or modification.
3. The work needs major adjustments or modification.
4. The work has no potential and should be discarded.

To help you select your projects, take a look at each project and ask yourself a few questions:

- What is this design about?
- How does it solve the design problem given?
- How does it represent the client (if there was one)?
- Why would I include this in my portfolio?
- What is it about this project that I am most proud of?
- Does this represent my best abilities and skills?
- Is there anything I would apologize for in this project? (If so, do not include it.)

Box 4.10

Keep in mind the reviewer will be looking at a large amount of information. Whether he is a professor or an employer, he will be looking at numerous portfolios. You do not want to ask your audience to look at too many projects when looking at a few could accomplish the same goal. If it takes too long to review, the practitioner may mentally tune out before experiencing your best work. You will have a better chance of success if you choose your work wisely. A few exceptional examples of your potential as a designer are all that are needed to secure a position in a firm or a place in an educational program. See Box 4.10 for some additional help in selecting your projects.

The need to be selective is particularly important when you work on your digital portfolio. The technology to create, present, store, and even distribute your digital portfolio allows you to include tons of projects. But this mass quantity does not make it a better portfolio. It's a bigger portfolio, but not necessarily a better portfolio. Too much information is perceived as disordered, muddled, and disorganized. Be as selective for your digital portfolio as you are for your traditional portfolio.

After deciding the content of your portfolio, you may realize you have a few gaps in your skills. Do you need to create a piece just for your portfolio? If your education or work experience has not provided you an opportunity to do a certain kind of work or show a certain set of skills, you might consider creating a new piece on your own (as discussed shortly). You might be tempted to include design work from high school. If you are pursuing a college degree, never include these earlier samples. This suggests you were not productive enough in college to generate anything worth putting into your portfolio. It certainly sends the wrong signal.

Connection

As a third step, you need to connect your work to who you are as a designer. Connection is the relationship between things, of bringing two diverse entities together. Ask yourself how the projects you have selected connect to who you are as a creative individual. Seriously ask yourself, "Does my work correlate with my design philosophy? Are these projects a reflection of who I am as a designer? Of my strengths and abilities? Do they correlate to form a unified whole? Or are they simply a jumble of little bits that don't stick together? How can I tie my portfolio pieces to the direction I have chosen for my career? Does this portfolio say 'commercial designer' if that is my focus? Or does it say I don't know what my focus is because I don't know what I'm doing?" Be honest. If there is a project that you really love but it does not connect to the other projects, pull it out. Don't delete or destroy it. Simply pull it out for use in a later portfolio. For example, I remember doing a residential design project for my undergraduate degree that earned top marks. But my focus was commercial design. I really hated to put the project aside. There was one particularly good rendering in the project. I pulled that one rendering into my portfolio as an example of my rendering ability. You may need to do something similar when connecting your projects to your design focus.

Remember that your portfolio should illustrate what you *can* do and not what you *cannot* do! It documents your strengths and accomplishments. It is a mirror image of yourself, connecting your work to who you are as a designer. Consequently, no one else will have a portfolio quite like yours.

Reflection

Lastly, purposefully reflect on how these projects collectively form *one* portfolio. If you put the necessary thought into completing the connection stage, your projects should all correlate. A critical element of the portfolio process is reflection, the careful consideration of the contents. This is the time for examination and introspection. Now is the moment to seriously *think* about your portfolio as one project, not a series of separate pages or web links.

It is said that a portfolio completed without reflection is no more than a fancy resume or scrapbook collection. Deliberate on each project. Purposefully consider *why* you would include this project and why it reflects well on you. You may gather all the projects together, put them aside for a few days or weeks, and then come back and reflect on them again. This is also a good time to have friends, professors, and fellow designers look over the work you have collected. They should be able to ask intelligent questions about your work, what it represents, and why you would include it. These are the same type of questions an interviewer may ask you when reviewing your portfolio. Reflect on what you have learned over the past few years, through education and experience. Ask yourself, "What did I learn from my education? My experiences? How can I document my growth as a designer?" There may be a particular project that indicates an area of new knowledge. More importantly, think about what you would tell interviewers when they ask about your work. What is the goal of your portfolio? Why are you creating (or recreating) it? As there will be other applicants for the position you want, what sets your work apart from everyone else? What in your portfolio makes you stand out and gets you noticed?

REWORKING PROJECTS AND CREATING NEW ONES

As you have read, many different types of projects could be included in your portfolio. Now that you've gone through the process of collection, selection, connection, and reflection, you will have identified many superb projects. You also may have some that are not as exceptional but still represent an important skill or viewpoint. A project that is good but not great does not belong in your portfolio, but don't throw it away. Some projects may just need to be reworked slightly. They may have great potential but for whatever reason (time or financial constraints, limitations of the project description, and so on), you never expounded on it.

Never include a project in your portfolio just because it is neat, fits the size of your portfolio, and received a passing grade. A particular project may have taken you a lot of time or may have been a very complex project. That does not necessarily mean it is a great project and deserves to be in your portfolio (see Box 4.11). In addition, work that seemed exceptional a year ago may now look primitive. Be open to removing older, simpler work and replacing it with newer, more exceptional work. Continually refine, remodel, and revise your work.

As a student in the first years of education, you may need to bulk up your portfolio by including a copy of your resume, award certificates, and additional graphics such as carefully designed pages to divide the sections of your portfolio (see Figure 4.32). One way to add more project examples to your portfolio is to create new work. For another example of your technical skills, try reworking an existing project in a new medium. For example, if you need more computer-aided drawings, redo some of your drafted work in CAD. Two versions of the same drawing can illustrate your mastery in multiple mediums. The same principle applies for illustrations (see Figure 4.33). If you have a rendering done with marker and pencil, why not try the same rendering in watercolor or done with rendering software?

You may not have many examples now. As you progress in school, you'll have the opposite problem—you'll have too many projects and not enough room in your portfolio. If you have a required booklet to fill for a school admissions port-

A design portfolio is a showcase of the presenter's work and the last page should be just as outstanding as the first. If certain parts of a project within the portfolio are not up to par with the rest of the work, either redo that section or eliminate it totally. I like to see a well-balanced portfolio that includes decision-making processes, sketches, hand drawings, and computer-generated drawings. Portfolios tell me a lot about the presenter without the person saying anything. The organization, the selection of work, and the quality of work tell me a lot about their abilities and even their work ethic.

Sue Markham, FASID
Sr. Facilities Administrator
Gulf Power Company, A Southern Company
Pensacola, FL

Box 4.11

folio, never leave blank pages. A portfolio with blank pages says you do not have enough experience or you produce low-quality work not worthy of inclusion. If the design of your portfolio allows you to remove the blank sleeves, do so. Your portfolio may appear thinner to you but it will look quite full to the reviewer. (We will debate quality versus quantity in Chapter 5.)

YOUR PORTFOLIO'S PERSONALITY

Your portfolio is more than a random collection of work, more than a scrapbook of educational and experiential memories. It is a personal expression not only of your skills but of your personality as well. Once you have collected, selected, connected, and reflected on your work, you should be extremely intimate with your portfolio. One way to help you understand the reasoning behind your portfolio as a single entity is to attempt to succinctly explain it to others. In one sentence, explain the thinking behind your portfolio. Think of this as a mini-design philosophy statement. Maybe this story will help you in narrowing down your work. When I was working on the dissertation for my doctorate, one of my professors asked me the title of my dissertation. As I was in the early stages of its development, I launched into a short epitaph epistle. She cut me short and told me that I didn't have it together yet. I went away deflated and continued refining my dissertation topic, and along with it, the title. For the next four weeks or so, every time I saw this professor, she would ask me for the title. I would again launch into a lengthy explanation (though a bit shorter than the last time). She would again cut me short and send me away. Finally, I saw her on campus one day and blurted out my 10-word title.

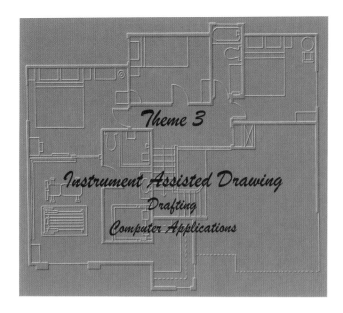

COFFEE DR.

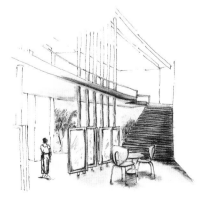

She smiled and said, "You got it!" Until I could succinctly explain the essence of my work, I didn't fully understand it any better than anyone else. That is how you need to be with your portfolio—up close and personal. From going through this chapter, you should have an idea now of how to organize the content of your portfolio. In the next chapter, we will discuss in detail the process of organizing your material into a coherent whole.

CONCLUSION

Carefully consider what elements to put in your portfolio. It's more than a random collection of work. Every image in your portfolio is a reflection of who you are as a designer. You should have a good idea of what artifacts to save from your classes and which of these items are in a state worthy of inclusion in the portfolio. Once you have decided which artifacts to include, you can begin planning the format and flow by using helpful planning tools such as a storyboard and a table of contents. These tools, plus the ordering of projects and the optimum number of projects to include, are all discussed in the next chapter.

5

Organizing Your Design Work

Are you ready to get things together? This chapter discusses the organization of your portfolio materials. Now that you have an idea of the different types of portfolios, who will be reviewing it, and how to gather and select your portfolio pieces, it's important to tackle the problem of getting all this information into a coherent structure. A storyboard and a table of contents will be discussed as planning tools. The order of your projects and the argument of quantity versus quality will also be covered.

MULTIPLE FORMS OF YOUR PORTFOLIO

In today's design fields, we use both traditional hand methods and technology to communicate with each other and with our clients. The portfolio is no exception. It is likely you will have multiple forms of your portfolio (see Box 5.1). The days are gone of walking around town, interviewing with your original projects or one paper copy. Nowadays, you need to show your expertise with technology

I have observed about a 50/50 proportion of digital versus traditional printed portfolios. I personally hold no preference for one over the other. Like any tool, hand techniques versus digital processes can be well or poorly managed. However, digital processes may have ease of dissemination advantages over traditional strategies.

Jill Pable, Ph.D.
Assistant Professor
Department of Interior Design
Florida State University
Tallahassee, FL

Box 5.1

RIGHT: 5.1
This digital model
represents the
building's assembly
process and the
student's skill with
technology.
Design work courtesy
of Zubin Shroff.

BELOW: 5.2
Draw where items on
your page will be
placed. Use a computer
or sketch by hand.
Remember to include
blocks of text.

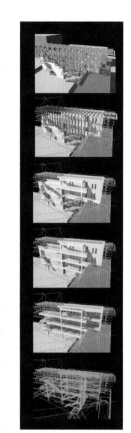

by showing something in digital form, like the computer model depicted in Figure 5.1.

You can achieve consistency between your traditional and digital portfolio with thought and planning. The easiest way to have multiple presentation formats is to duplicate the information. You can have a digital portfolio on a web site and include some of the printed web pages in your traditional printed portfolio. You can create a layout for your traditional printed portfolio and duplicate it in your digital portfolio, or vice versa. With this in mind, select a background color and fonts that are the same or very similar between the two formats. A benefit of this is obviously the smaller amount of time you'll need to invest.

Ultimately, your choice of presentation format must never overshadow the work itself! You may have a fabulous design solution, but if you choose to present it on bright neon mat board or show it in PowerPoint in only grayscale, you may be diluting the power of your project. Likewise, if you spend all your time creating a beautiful web site for your projects, but each digital image is small, pixellated, and of poor quality, your portfolio's value will decrease.

CREATING A STORYBOARD

Putting your portfolio together can be a formidable task. Plan well now. It will pay off later. It is important to know why you are organizing your materials in one way over another way. A storyboard can be helpful in this organization process. A storyboard is a visual plan that guides the reviewer through your portfolio. It reveals the layout of your portfolio and how a reviewer will read through it. A storyboard is not a list of elements or a table of contents. Besides listing what each page contains, it is helpful to sketch out what is included on your pages and where graphic elements, images, and text will go (see Figure 5.2).

Linear Format

There are two popular storyboard formats: linear and nonlinear (Kilbane and Milman 2003). In a linear storyboard, projects are presented one after another in a predetermined

Title of Project
Date & Location

Project Description

Maybe two sentences, talking about the design challenges and how you solved them.

IMAGE

IMAGE

IMAGE

IMAGE

IMAGE

LEFT: 5.3
A linear sequence is good for projects that are interrelated and must be viewed one after another. Illustration courtesy of Aaron J. Kulik.

BELOW: 5.4
A nonlinear format allows the viewer to decide which part of your portfolio to view after the opening page. Illustration courtesy of Aaron J. Kulik.

sequence (see Figure 5.3). You control the order of your projects and the way they will most likely be viewed. A good example of this format is a book, with a definite beginning and a definite end. However, you cannot guarantee that the reviewer will read through your portfolio like a book from start to finish. I know people who read the last page or two of a novel before they begin reading it so they know the end before they begin. To me, this seems strange. But the same thing could occur during an interview. The interviewer looks at your first project, skips through to the fifth page, and then flips it over to the last page. Some practitioners may even start at the end and work backward, expecting the front project to be the best. A linear format is actually an attempt but not a guarantee at controlling the review process.

Nonlinear Format

A nonlinear format has many variations and allows the reviewer far more freedom (see Figure 5.4). He can navigate or flip to any portion of your portfolio that he desires. He is in control of the review process. A logical example for a nonlinear format is a web site (see Box 5.2). You know that once you are on a web site's home page, there are links to other pages housed in the site. Nonlinear navigation can be in the form of branching or star structures.

As shown in Figure 5.5, a branching structure is a nonlinear format that starts with a core element and then splits or branches out to other elements. Think of this as

In regards to a digital portfolio either on CD or the web, I would prefer a nonlinear digital portfolio that may have images grouped according to type. With that format, I could easily review various types of work based on my interests or priorities.

Edward A. Cook, Ph.D.
Associate Professor
School of Architecture and Landscape Architecture
Arizona State University
Tempe, AZ

Box 5.2

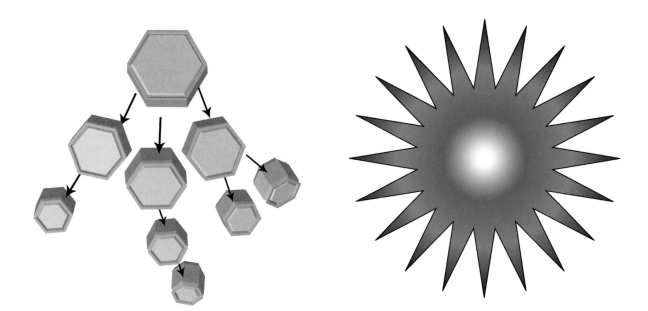

ABOVE LEFT: 5.5
Like this series of hexagons, a branching navigation pattern does not require a symmetrical number of pages or projects. Some projects may be given more attention than others. Illustration courtesy of Aaron J. Kulik.

ABOVE RIGHT: 5.6
A star represents a simple branching system, in which parts of your project break out from the main project in the center. Illustration courtesy of Aaron J. Kulik.

a tree. The trunk is your core portfolio element, such as technical drawing skills. The main branches on the trunk become the next level of elements, such as drafting, computer-aided design (CAD), and rendering. Each of these branches then has other elements (like leaves), which could be a few samples of work done in each area. The number of samples does not need to be consistent among the branches. And some branches can be longer. For example, you may want to show another level of CAD drawing, such as plans, details, and three-dimensional (3-D) work. This makes another level of work that the other areas do not have.

A star structure is another nonlinear format and begins with a core element (see Figure 5.6). The next level of elements and the one after that are all consistent. Think of a star that has equal segments around its central point. Using the same technical drawing example, you would consistently show two examples of drafting, two examples of CAD work, and two examples of rendering. In a web-based portfolio, this format allows the user to easily work forward along a path and then work backward along the same path with only a couple clicks of the mouse.

To create your portfolio storyboard, you can use a high-tech method (i.e., concept-mapping software) or a low-tech method (post-it notes, note cards, or drawing on a whiteboard) as shown in Figure 5.7. Concept-mapping software is a visual tool based on concept map theory. It shows the elements in boxes and the links between the elements with different types of lines. There are many different packages available; just search online for concept mapping software. Either method (high-tech or low-tech) will result in a list of categories that make a great table of contents.

BEGINNING PAGES

The first page of your portfolio (whether traditional or digital) is an introductory page. An introductory page is a good place to put a title, personal logo, and con-

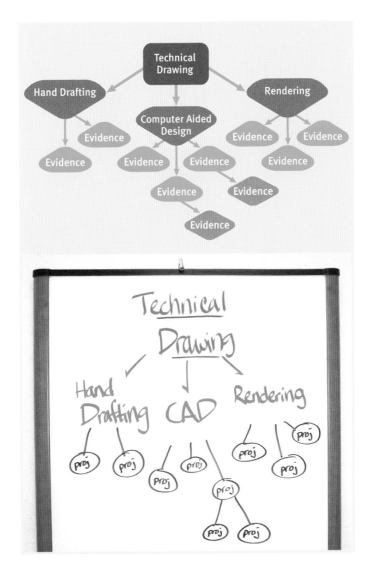

5.7
Drawing out your storyboard helps to show how the project pieces relate together and how the projects can be grouped.

tact information (see Figure 5.8). This is the same logo and information that you can repeat on your resume, business card, and other promotional material.

The next page can be a table of contents, like the one in Figure 5.9, which communicates how your portfolio is organized and what can be found inside. It states the categories that will organize your work and is often used as a navigational tool to see the various parts all in one glance. The standard skills listed in Chapter 4 are a good way to categorize your work. If you are organizing your portfolio around a theme, you'll need to come up with creative names for each category.

If you can, put page numbers in your table of contents and on your printed pages, like the one in Figure 5.10. This limits your ability to switch pages around or quickly alter the content of your portfolio. But if the portfolio will be submitted for admission into a design program, the page numbers will help the reviewing faculty quickly find a particular section of your work. You won't be rearranging these portfolio pages anyway. Once it is submitted, it's out of your hands.

RIGHT: 5.8
The first page of your portfolio should contain your name, contact information, and possibly some illustrations of your work.

BELOW LEFT: 5.9
A table of contents like this one is easy to read and simple to navigate.
Design work courtesy of Aaron J. Kulik.

BELOW RIGHT: 5.10
Here is an example of a table of contents that includes page numbers. These are helpful for reviewers who wish to flip to their favorite part of a designer's portfolio.
Design work courtesy of Shelby Bogaard.

Your Name
Your email address

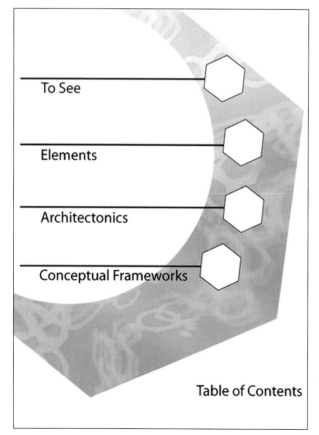

To See

Elements

Architectonics

Conceptual Frameworks

Table of Contents

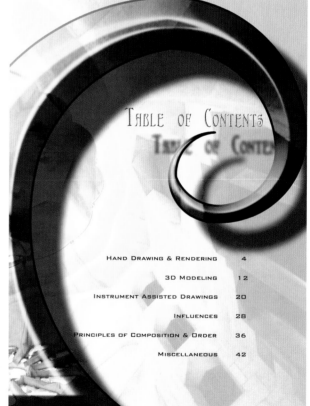

TABLE OF CONTENTS

Box 5.3

ORDER OF PROJECTS

There is much discussion about the order of your portfolio pieces. Remember, any portfolio should present only your best work, illustrating key skills and capabilities. Undeniably, there is little argument your *best* work should be shown *first* (see Box 5.3).

Should you show your simplest work first and end with your most complex work? This is known as a chronological portfolio, which represents the designer's progress from beginning work to most current work. Avoid this type of organization. You only have 10 to 15 seconds to make a good impression with your graphic work. If you don't catch the attention of the reviewer in your first work, she won't want to look at the rest of your portfolio. It must be engaging and provoking.

Overall, most practitioners and educators would agree that the *first* and *last* pieces should be your absolute best work. The first piece sets the tone for the remainder of your portfolio. When you open your portfolio, the first piece needs to be your strongest, like the one in Figure 5.11. If your finest piece is viewed first, you have already created a positive impression for the viewer. Interviewers are actually expecting to see great work right at the beginning. If you have some other strange strategy and they don't see dazzling work at the beginning, their view of you has just been deflated. Your first piece deserves special consideration. This may or may not be your most recent work, although more recent work is in all probability your best.

So what comes after the first brilliant page of work? Should you show your best work first and last, with other great work in the middle? Should you show your three best works right at the beginning (i.e., the knockout strategy)? What if you don't really have enough good work to

5.11
When practitioners open your portfolio, they should see a piece of your finest work.
Design work courtesy of Jeffrey Lothner.

I prefer to see examples of two to four of a student's best projects—period. A portfolio should not be representative of every project you have ever done, but the crème de la crème. I prefer to see a two- to three-page spread of one project which takes the viewer from process through finished images over the two to three pages. Other work (design build, studios, paintings, etc.) goes toward the back.

Greta Gillisse
Recruiting and Employee Relations Manager
Callison
Seattle, WA

Box 5.4

completely fill your portfolio? The decision is up to you. The order of the projects in your portfolio will determine the pace at which a practitioner reviews it. The order will influence the reviewer's mood, too (see Box 5.4).

DIVIDER PAGES

Once you decide how you are going to organize your portfolio, you need to decide if you will have section dividers that repeat the categories listed in your table of contents. Portfolios arranged by themes are best organized with dividers. Create something unusual with your choice of materials and decorative elements. This need not take a large amount of time, as a change in theme should be apparent. If you are organizing your portfolio by project, these divider pages separate one project from another (see Figure 5.12).

The divider pages can contain an explanation of what the reviewer will be seeing in the next few pages, and maybe a summary of the design challenge and how you masterfully solved the problem. This is a wonderful way to "sell" your work and heighten the anticipation of the viewer. Include both graphics and text for maximum visual stimulation. After reading a short two- or three-sentence description, who wouldn't want to turn the page to see the result?

QUANTITY VERSUS QUALITY

When you start your design career, you may have few projects you would be proud to put in your portfolio. Once you've gone a bit further on your career path, you will have *too* many projects. Although it is incredibly tempting, you cannot feasibly include them all in your portfolio. Besides, you don't want really old material in your portfolio—the more recent the work, the better. Face it, your portfolio will be judged by its weakest piece. So don't include anything that you are embarrassed to show or for which you would feel compelled to offer excuses. It is important to understand there is a difference between design and art. Art is a personal visual expression of the artist's idea and beliefs. Design is the designer's solution to someone else's problem. We are hired by a firm or client to create designs that function, look good, and solve a problem.

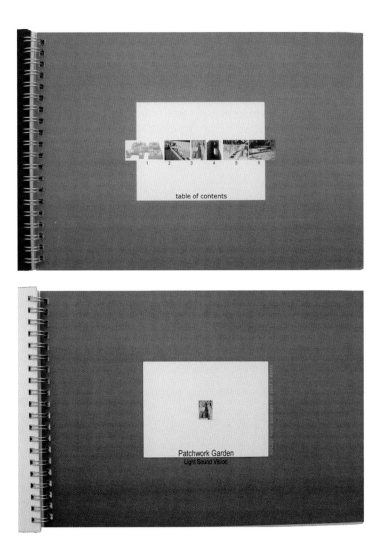

We are not hired to make pretty pictures. Keep this in mind when weeding out the weakest projects in your portfolio.

Although there is no set number for the projects or pages in your portfolio, 10 to 15 original works is plenty. Some of your projects, like the one in Figure 5.13, may include only one or two pages, while other projects may have more than five pages each (see Box 5.5).

Include no more than two pages per project and no more than 7 to 10 *quality* projects for a typical interview. The quantity could increase for significant, key hires, or someone with highly varied experience. Those with less experience should expand one or two projects into three sheets (four if the project is super-significant) but "fill in" the remainder with skills areas such as hand sketching, hand rendering, computer rendering, and more.

Tom Horwitz
Principal
FRCH Design Worldwide
Cincinnati, OH

Box 5.5

For an internship or lower-division admission portfolio, it may be difficult to compile more than 10 good projects because you don't have a large number from which to choose. It's better to have fewer good projects than many mediocre projects. Your portfolio layout may be the most beautiful piece of artwork in the world. But if the projects represented within are only of mediocre caliber, the portfolio will not help you be competitive in the field.

So how do you increase the number of projects if you feel you don't have enough? Look for one- or two-day training workshops and seminars given by companies in design-related areas. Software companies in particular can provide local and Internet-based training, which can result in a nice piece of work. Take a short art course on drawing through your school or community center. Did you have a good idea for a past school project but (due to other influences or project restrictions) never pursued it? This may be the time to redesign and refine an alternative solution to a previous design problem. Don't throw out any good ideas. You'll find that a good idea is still a good idea. It may be worth developing an alternative solution from a fresh perspective and getting another portfolio piece out of it.

When all is said and done, practitioners reviewing your portfolio will not take the time to go through all of your projects. They may end up flipping casually through your portfolio and may miss your *best* project. Most practitioners have experience reviewing work and will be able to tell if you are qualified for the position after viewing only a few pieces. Don't waste their time. Include less than 10 of your best projects. There's nothing worse than being asked to stop presenting during an interview. If this does happen, it would be great if you had a web site to direct them to for viewing more of your work at a later date or at their leisure.

COPYRIGHT ISSUES

What is a copyright? A copyright is the claimed right to any original work held by an individual or organization. Copyrighted material can include documents, images, artwork, drawings, multimedia, and more. Using these items without obtaining permission from the author or artist is punishable by law and can include fines and even jail time.

You may have heard someone mention the term *intellectual property*. What is the difference between intellectual property and owning a copyright? Intellectual property is a creation of your mind. It's new knowledge. Because knowledge is an intangible asset, it is harder to pin down than a copyright. You are welcome to say your work is your intellectual property. This does not prevent someone else from copying it. According to the United States Copyright Office (2006), a copyright is intellectual property with exclusive rights defined by the granting government, often denoted with the copyright symbol shown in Figure 5.14.

5.14
The copyright symbol represents work that is protected by law.

Copyright law extends beyond traditional media to include digital media. The Digital Millennium Copyright Act of 1998 extends copyright protection to computer-related work, including text and graphics. This has implications for the distribution of your digital portfolio over the Internet and in distributed multimedia formats.

What all this means is simple: Never use a drawing or image that is not yours! It is an infringement on someone's copyright. I know this sounds logical. Yet, I recall a recent admission portfolio that showed a computer-aided design model on one of the applicant's pages. It was the same model that was included on the course CD. It wasn't the student's work at all but was presented on the page *as if it was*. This made me wonder whether the other materials were original or someone else's work. Please do not put your future career in jeopardy by taking the work of others and passing it off as your own (see Box 5.6).

Manipulating Existing Work

Design concept creation often requires the use of existing graphics and images that inspire your design. You see a magazine ad or hear a music clip and it inspires you to design a building or landscape. Or you design a new object based on the inspiration of another object. Let's say you have designed a new playground

Am I worried about students doing touchups of hand-drawn work, that what I see isn't necessarily "what I get"? Not at all. I see the future direction of graphic communication as an integration of hand and digital skills to allow for a better dialogue, a better exchange of information, a better understanding of design ideas. Competition work designed by our students at the University of Florida integrates hand-drawn work and digital interface to great success. It's all about a new generation of graphic thinking and communication.

Margaret Portillo, Ph.D.
Department Chair
Department of Interior Design, College of Design,
Construction and Planning
University of Florida
Gainesville, FL

Box 5.6

seating system based on an existing system. How do you know if you are violating a copyright? If the owner of the original work is losing money or the ability to promote and sell his piece based on your design, then yes, your design is in violation of the original copyright. There is a difference between using an idea that someone else has in a new, creative way and actually using the artifact that someone else created.

This brings us to a discussion on fair use. The United States Copyright Office (2006) defines fair use as the use of copyrighted material without permission from the copyright holder for purposes such as scholarship or education. Section 107 of U.S. copyright law lists different purposes for which a particular work can be reproduced without violating copyright. These include comment, criticism, news reporting, research, scholarship, and teaching. Any use of copyrighted material other than for these purposes is an infringement of the copyright. For example, if in one of your projects you display a copyrighted image that you took from a magazine or web site, you must cite the source of that image. And you cannot claim it is yours or make any type of profit from using that image.

Contractual Obligation

After working for a firm part-time or in an internship, you may want to show some of that work in your portfolio. You may not be aware of which aspects of the work are copyrighted or protected. Ask your supervisor. The client on the

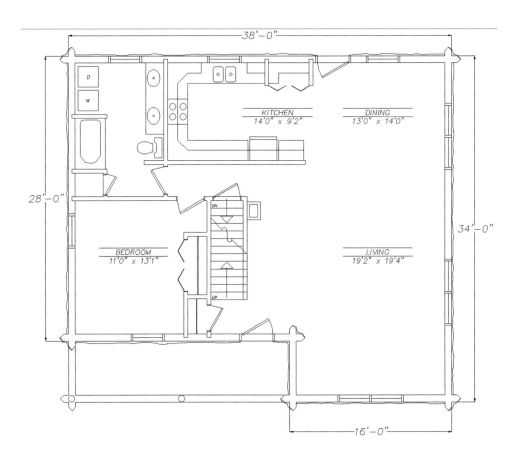

5.15
Ask about using work done under contract or while employed before putting it into your portfolio.

project may have paid for all concept and sketch work, plus final ideas and designs. By putting some of this work in your portfolio, you would be violating the rights of the client.

If you created a design on your own time, with your own resources, you own it. It is your intellectual property. You can duplicate it, change it, manipulate it, and alter it to your heart's content. But if you create a design while under contract to work for another person or firm, that person, firm, or even client owns the design (see Figure 5.15). In order to have a copy of that design in your portfolio, you will need to ask permission and get that permission *in writing*. After receiving permission, make a photocopy of the work or a copy of the electronic file. Never take the original piece from your employer!

Collaborative Projects

There are times when you'll include the work of others in your portfolio. The underlying principle is to give credit where credit is due. Did you take part in a large project? With an honest attitude, what role did you play? Everyone knows that large projects like the one in Figure 5.16 require large groups of people.

Our professions in the built environment are all about teamwork. Seldom do we design and construct a building, interior, or exterior completely on our own. Some of your work will have been completed with the assistance of peers, instructors, friends, and family. This is the direct result of engaged learning and good classroom instruction. How much of your project did you really do? Be honest

5.16
A group project like this one is hard to divide into individual parts. Who worked on the concept? The sketches? The renderings? The images? The layout? Be able to articulate your role and contribution. Design work courtesy of Alexandra C. Ayres, Sally Azer, and Kelly Robinson.

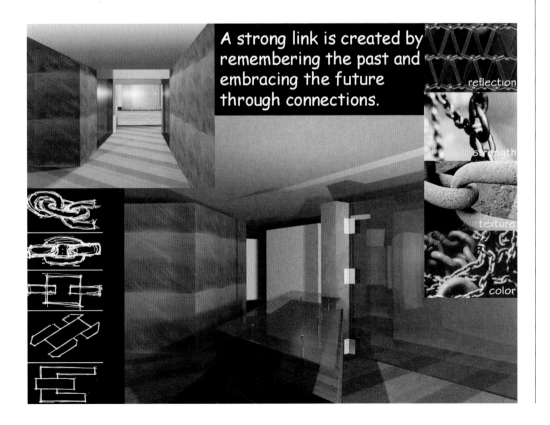

A strong link is created by remembering the past and embracing the future through connections.

reflection
strength
texture
color

SAMPLE PERMISSION REQUEST STATEMENT

I do hereby grant permission to _____ to reproduce images of my work from a team or group project in his or her printed and/or digital portfolio. When applicable, I request a credit be given near the image.

Signature _____   Date _____

Box 5.7

about your role. If you feel uncomfortable putting something into your portfolio because you know it's not really yours, omit it. You should have plenty of other projects to use instead.

Saying that you were a part of a team (rather than hogging all the credit yourself) is honest and believable. It's a good thing to illustrate in your portfolio not only that you've had the experience of working on a team, but also that you are willing and able to share the glory with your colleagues. Give credit to your employer and colleagues and clearly state what you contributed to the project.

Even if you are not sure you are going to include a sample of the team's work, ask the team members for permission to use it in case you decide to do so later. A sample permission request statement is provided in Box 5.7.

Asking for permission now will save you time later. You won't end up having to track down this person or that person. You can include a permission statement on that page of your portfolio, usually as a small footnote at the bottom of the page. A permission statement clarifies that you have received permission to present the work of others in your portfolio. A sample statement could read, "I have received written permission from colleagues, supervisors, and anyone else whose images are shown in my portfolio. When applicable, credits are indicated near the image."

Theft of Your Work

What will prevent others from stealing your designs? Not much. This is particularly true for digital portfolios. Once you mail off your CD or place work on your web site, it is now available to the world. Unfortunately, it's possible that your work will show up in someone else's portfolio (see Box 5.8).

Your images are unlikely to be reproduced because they are at a low resolution. But others will take your ideas. In today's society, the reality is that unauthorized copying and false claims of authorship exist. The ultimate protection of your work and your creative ideas is to never share your portfolio with anyone. But is this the right approach? If you fear someone will steal your ideas, you will never show your work to others. If you become so paranoid about someone else lifting your ideas, you will never show anything in a digital format. You limit your expo-

Box 5.8

sure to potential employers, plus you restrict your ability to demonstrate your technology skills. By exposing your designs to others, you are only increasing your visibility. Don't let the shadow of theft stop you from showing your work on the web.

You may want to include an authorship statement in your portfolio. An authorship statement communicates who is responsible for the materials contained in your portfolio and articulates the authenticity of these materials. It could read something like, "This digital portfolio contains my original works, unless otherwise noted." This statement can be on your web site home page, or the first or last page of your traditional printed portfolio. Put it at the bottom, where it is not immediately noticeable but definitely present.

TIME MANAGEMENT

Thinking about your portfolio and putting it together takes time. Getting it done means getting it done well. You will need time to go through a couple of storyboard drafts, time to fine tune, time to re-photograph projects if necessary, and time to manage unexpected problems. I know you've heard it before. Give yourself plenty of time. Start early. Your portfolio will not get done unless you commit some time to getting it done. Make it a priority. Create a timeline and stick with it. After all, a goal is only a dream with a deadline!

Realistically, creating your portfolio will take some time out of your busy schedule. Allot enough time to get it done because it will take you twice as long as you think (see Figure 5.17). Avoid the 11th-hour rush of putting your portfolio together the night before it is needed. It is most common to make a blunder when you are tired and weary. You never know when you'll have a major problem or a series of minor setbacks. I remember a former student of mine telling me about putting his portfolio together the night before a big interview and working into the wee hours. He got little sleep but did finish it. Unfortunately, he was not as sharp during his interview as he should have been and consequently was not asked to join the firm.

Another student was working on her portfolio one evening and her roommate was in the room talking with her. Without knowing it, her roommate set her

5.17
A layout like this one that has a vellum overlay with printed text takes time to create and execute. Give yourself plenty of time to design unique layouts.
Design work courtesy of Liisa Taylor.

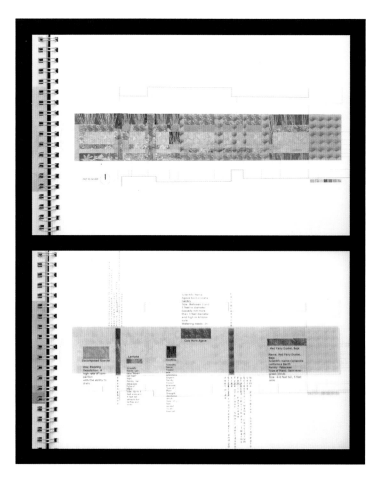

coffee cup down on one of the projects. When the roommate picked up her cup, she left a brown ring right in the middle of this student's presentation board. The student had to recreate her entire presentation, which took time away from working on her portfolio layout. Prepare for the unexpected.

Every year before admission portfolios are due at my school, students are printing their portfolio the night before. Invariably, the printer dies or runs out of supplies in the middle of the night. So they head out to the local copy center and stand in line there with classmates who are also printing at the last minute. If you're ever going to have computer or printer problems, it will happen the night before your portfolio is due. I was once working on a project and was on a very tight schedule. Wouldn't you know it; a virus hit my computer and completely knocked it out. I had to rent a laptop from a local computer store and rush to get the job done on time. This meant a few late nights. Don't let this happen to you. Plan for extra time because mistakes will occur and accidents will happen. As these anecdotes prove, it's common to experience problems, which result in reproducing portions of your portfolio. If you need to rework something, think positively. You can raise the project to a higher standard so all is not a complete waste of time. Remember, the time and expense you invest in your portfolio is an investment in your future.

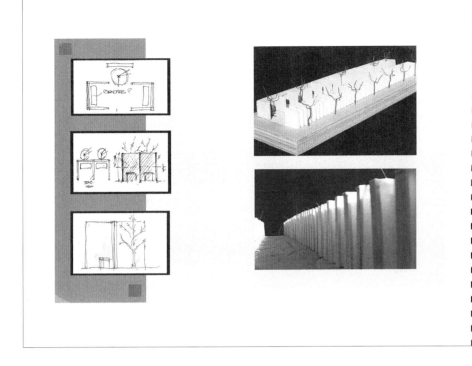

5.18
The three sketches and two color images give the reviewer enough to see without cluttering the page. Design work courtesy of Jeffrey Lothner.

KISS Strategy

One way to complete your portfolio on time is to keep it simple. Avoid overly complex graphics because it's easy for the viewer to get lost in an overly complex design that's not developed completely. This means too many images on a page or too many little extras. As the page in Figure 5.18 demonstrates, having four or five small images per page is a good rule of thumb. Some pages will have fewer, some a few more, depending on your layout. Besides being difficult to review, an overly complicated portfolio will result in more time and money for you.

You may have heard the KISS acronym used before. It stands for "Keep It Simple, Stupid." Now, this is not intended to insult you. It means to keep everything simple and easy. Simple is sometimes far more preferable than complex. Have you ever started a design project with high aspirations? You wanted to do this exciting thing and that fabulous thing. But when time became precious, the simple solutions proved the most useful and practical.

CONCLUSION

This chapter covered a great deal of information on the structure and flow of your portfolio. You may have wonderful work and tantalizing images. But if the content of your portfolio jumps all over the place, no reviewer will be able to understand it. Determine if you will use a linear or nonlinear format. Decide which project is your absolute best and put it at the beginning. This chapter has, I hope, raised your awareness of copyright issues and the amount of time it will take to create your portfolio. In Chapter 6, we'll talk about the appearance of your work, how different colors affect the reviewer, and how to use various design elements and graphic principles as guidelines for laying out your work.

Portfolio Layout

Regardless of the format of your portfolio (traditional or digital), it should have a consistent appearance. People will review your portfolio in various ways. Some will flip through it from start to finish, some will jump around your pages, and some will start at the back and work forward. Because you have little control over how someone will view your work, all of your pages should have some elements of consistency to them.

This chapter covers basic elements and principles of design, along with specific principles related to the graphic layout of your pages. An understanding of color and how individuals perceive it is helpful in choosing colors for your portfolio. What's more, what you write and how your text looks will sway how your portfolio is reviewed. Lastly, the visual layout of each individual page, how you arrange and rearrange the images, text, and graphics on the page, will be discussed.

DESIGN ELEMENTS AND PRINCIPLES

The images representing your work are the essence of your portfolio. How you present those images is a significant part of how they can be displayed to your best advantage. In this section, we'll talk about the elements and principles of design. These are the basic components of any creative work. By using the elements together with the principles, you can create a visual language for communicating your design to others. Use them to make your layout even more stunning and appealing than a haphazard, random distribution of items.

The goal of using the design elements and principles is ultimately to help reviewers read your portfolio (see Figure 6.1). Lead them around your page. Imagine you are standing at the end of a hotel lobby. Someone places a blindfold on you and tells you to quickly walk to the other end. You could do it, bumping into a wall or a piece of furniture; you'd get to the other end eventually. Now

6.1
A layout that is clear and easy to understand will help the reviewer focus on your professional skills.
Design work courtesy of Zubin Shroff.

The attempt after the mid term review was to find a device by which the differences between the two communities on the site could be architecturally articulated. Since housing typologies and family structures are similar for both communities, orientation was adopted to express this. The band was now composed of two masses, one oriented towards Mecca and the other conforming to site geometry.

imagine that you still have the blindfold on but someone leads you by the hand. This person walks you around furniture and keeps you away from any obstacles. You'd get to the other end just like before, but more quickly and safely. You might even enjoy the experience. The same is true for using the design elements and principles to guide the reviewers around your portfolio pages. Help them see what you want them to see.

Design Elements

Let's talk first about design elements. There is some debate over the names and number of design elements. Some sources say there are five elements, others seven, and different sources include different topics. The most common design elements are considered to be line, shape, form, space, texture, pattern, and color. Design elements are concrete and quantifiable. They can be isolated and defined in any art or design object. They are the objects used *in* the design, the building blocks of your portfolio layout.

Line

Line is one of the most basic elements of all designs. A line represents an edge and sets boundaries for our designs. Lines can be loose and free or defined and sharp.

They can be straight, curved, vertical, horizontal, angled, thin, broken, wide, and so on, depending on how they are drawn and how the user perceives them (see Figure 6.2).

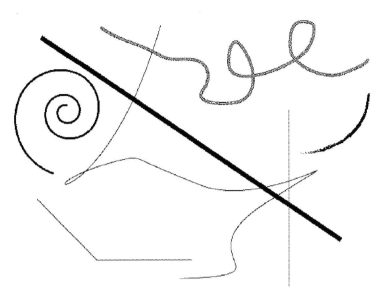

All lines have direction. They lead the reviewers around your pages, telling them what to see and interpret. They can have implied meaning. Horizontal lines imply stability, serenity, and tranquility, while vertical lines imply formality, vigilance, and a sense of balance. Oblique or angled lines imply progress, movement, and action. Think of these types of lines as apparatus for communication. Use them on your portfolio pages to guide the viewer through your work. A scattering of random lines around the page is confusing to the eye. Thoughtfully use lines to direct attention to the most important item on your page. Help the reviewer read your portfolio.

The edges of your work on the page will themselves create an implied line. Implied line is a succession of visual elements that suggest a nonstop linear relationship. It is actually an invisible line created when objects are positioned in order, drawing your focus to them while your brain mentally connects them together. The best example of implied line is a dotted line, like the elements in Figure 6.3. Your brain will want to close the gaps between the dashes. If you are putting all your portfolio work together electronically and then printing out each page, you know that you cannot print to the very edge of the page. Therefore, you will have limits to where your work stops. Elements in your work that come right up to the margins on your pages form implied lines, as shown on the page in Figure 6.4.

ABOVE: 6.2
Line is a popular design element. Use lines in your layout to direct the reviewer to sections of your work, or to frame the page and images.

BELOW: 6.3
A broken or dotted line implies that a line is there when it is not. Illustration courtesy of Aaron J. Kulik.

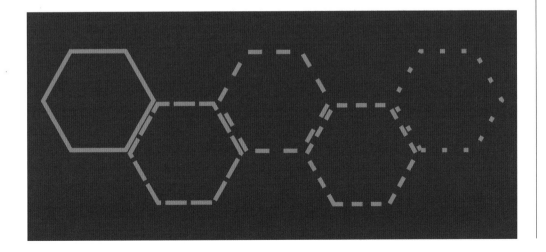

RIGHT: 6.4
Elements aligned on your page can create implied lines. The eye "sees" these lines without their existence on the page. Design work courtesy of Alexandra C. Ayres, Sally Azer, and Kelly Robinson.

BELOW: 6.5
A shape can be as clear as these three geometric shapes with black outlines. Or a shape can be loosely defined by color, pattern, or another design element.

Shape

The next design element is shape. Shape is defined by the outline or identifiable contour of an image or object. Lines or colors define the edges of basic and complex shapes. Like lines, shapes can convey different feelings. Rectilinear shapes convey a feeling of clarity, stability, and formality. Triangular shapes seem to imply direction and action as they reach toward a terminal peak. And curvilinear shapes imply movement by creating a feeling of continuity and protection (see Figure 6.5).

Where are shapes found in your portfolio? Every image on every page has a definable shape. Most people keep these images in rectangular shapes because it's easy and economical to put them in this format. After all, most of the work we do as landscape architects, interior designers, and architects is structured and rectangular. (Face it. We live in a square world.) But you can use any shape that you want. Keep in mind that the portfolio page itself is a shape and it dominants your entire presentation. This again is most likely a rectangle.

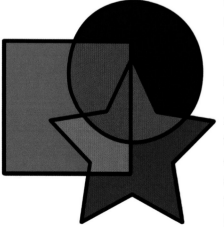

A word of caution is warranted about mixing too many different shapes because this can look sloppy. The viewer may question whether you know what you're doing. You'll also want to limit the number of shapes and their sizes. Try grouping smaller shapes together to form visually larger shapes. If you have several images of your design process work for one project, keep them all the same size and shape and group them together. This avoids the mistake of using a few smaller shapes when one large shape does a better job (see Figure 6.6).

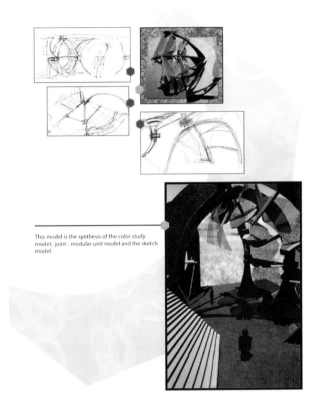

This model is the synthesis of the color study model, joint - modular unit model and the sketch model.

LEFT: 6.6
The smaller process work images are grouped together. They are then offset by the larger rendering on the page.
Design work courtesy of Aaron J. Kulik.

BELOW: 6.7
Form takes into account all three dimensions—X, Y, and Z. It is likely you will show forms and models in your portfolio.
Design work courtesy of Christy Phifer.

Form

Form is the next design element. It is the visual appearance or spatial arrangement of objects. It can mean more than physical or substantive mass. It can include substance (such as solid or liquid form) and weight. Form is often used synonymously with shape, although they are different. Shape is a two-dimensional (2-D) outline, where form is a three-dimensional (3-D) configuration. For example, a circle is a shape while a ball is a form. A drawing is a shape, while a sculpture is a form (see Figure 6.7).

pattern sculptures

RIGHT: **6.8**
To make flat, 2-D objects (i.e., shapes) in your layout possess more depth, use shading techniques. The green shapes here almost look 3-D because of the light and shadow.

BELOW: **6.9**
Light is used to create shadow. The combination of the two can make any 2-D shape look 3-D. Illustration courtesy of Aaron J. Kulik.

You are going to have some semblance of form in your portfolio, as the portfolio itself is a 2-D representation of your 3-D work. Shading makes 2-D objects in your portfolio appear more 3-D (see Figure 6.8). This involves understanding the direction of light. Shading uses a series of values based on the way light would hit a 3-D object. When shading objects in art, you use various kinds of light (see Figure 6.9):

1. The highlight, which is the brightest area on the object's surface.
2. The transitional light, which is the middle tones of color.
3. The core of the shadow, which is the darkest area on the object's surface.
4. The reflected light, which is where the light is reflected from a nearby object or surface.
5. The cast shadow, which is the shadow cast by the object onto another object or surface.

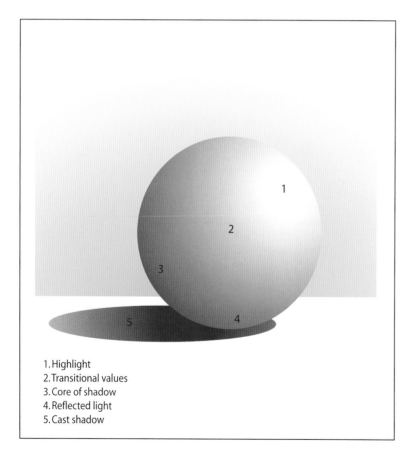

1. Highlight
2. Transitional values
3. Core of shadow
4. Reflected light
5. Cast shadow

Anything you can do to imply the appearance of depth in your layout will turn a boring 2-D presentation into a quasi–3-D experience. Using something as simple as a gray shadow box under one of your project images lifts that image off the page, giving it the illusion of being closer to the viewer. Or you might consider using the bevel and emboss options in Adobe Photoshop's layer blending options, as in the images in Figure 6.10.

Framing the image with a contrasting color or even black separates it from the background. Overlapping or placing one of your images in front of another implies depth. You can overlap some text onto one of your project images to not only link the two elements together, but also bring the text forward. Without implied

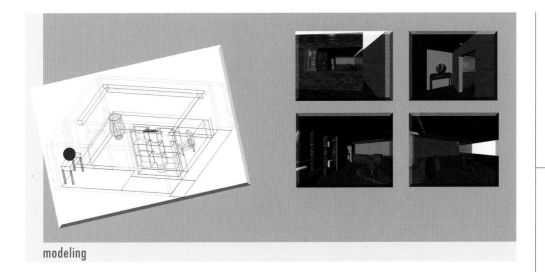

modeling

6.10
Raster editing software like Adobe Photoshop has several features that can be used to embellish your images. This layout shows Photoshop's Layer Emboss and Bevel options. Design work courtesy of Christy Phifer.

depth, the page remains comparatively flat. See Box 6.1 for tips on creating drop shadows, like the ones in Figure 6.11, using Photoshop.

Space

If you think about it, space is invisible until it is defined. Space is an empty or blank area, which needs to be defined by a boundary. Spaces in the built environment are defined by boundaries such as walls, floors, and ceilings.

Space on a page layout can be considered positive or negative (see Figure 6.12). Positive spaces are the elements on the page, whereas negative spaces are the areas of emptiness that surround them. The images, graphic elements, and areas of text represent positive space. The background of each portfolio page is negative space; it's where your work is *not* located. Both are equally important. A balance of both positive and negative spaces will allow your eye to focus on what is important and then rest when it sees *nothing*. Too much negative space around your images can make them look isolated and unimportant. Too little space is claustrophobic. You are seeking a balance between the two.

PHOTOSHOP DROP SHADOW

One way to make your flat images appear more 3-D is by adding a Drop Shadow in Photoshop. To do this, open your image. Select the Effects button in the bottom of the layer window. It's the fancy F on the left. If it is not available, duplicate the layer (make a copy of it) and then push the Effects button. From the pop-up menu, select Drop Shadow. In the Layer Style box, change the opacity and light angle of the shadow if desired. Increase your canvas size to something slightly larger than your image. The shadow should now be visible. Crop the image to include the shadow.

Box 6.1

RIGHT: 6.11
We all know the page is flat. Anything you can do to make the items on the page "jump" toward the reviewer will add interest and variety to your presentation. Design work courtesy of Allison Saunders and Pamela Stradling.

BELOW: 6.12
Either the white or the purple areas can be considered positive space, depending on which is considered the foreground color and which is considered the background color.

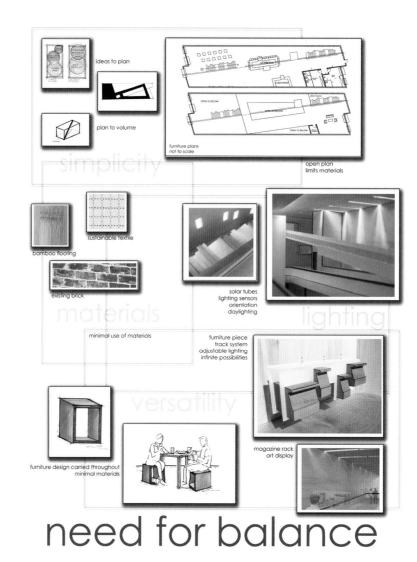

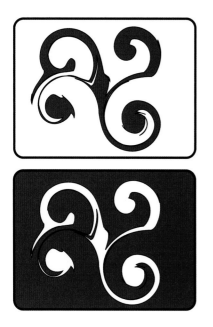

Texture

As revealed in Figure 6.13, the next element of design is texture. Texture refers to the visual or tactile characteristics of natural and man-made objects. Most people only think of rough surfaces as having texture, though *every* object has texture, even smooth surfaces. Of all the design elements, texture is the subtlest. It can add interest to your portfolio images and pages, but it won't impact your presentation as much as other elements like color and shape.

Real textures can actually be seen and felt. Implied textures are those that can be seen but not felt, like the ones in Figure 6.14. For implied textures, your mind will recall the physical sense of touch when viewing a texture. For example, seeing a picture of a sandy beach may recall memories of walking along the seashore, feeling the sand squishing between your toes. Therefore, textures can imply psychological feelings. Smooth textures are passive and pleasing to the

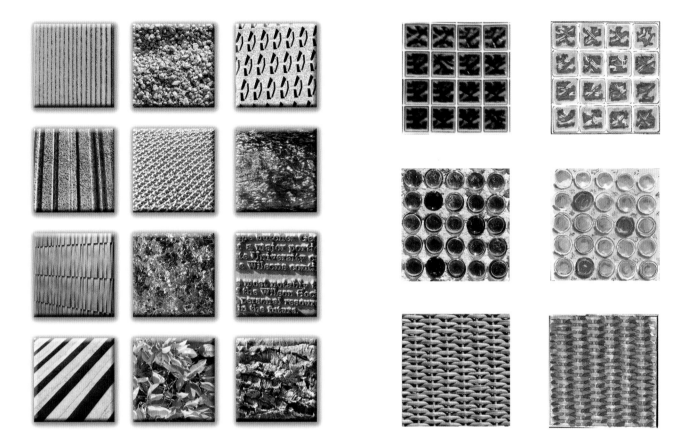

eye. They are associated with reserved, graceful, and subdued moods. Rough textures can seem unpleasant. They tend to create an informal mood and will visually dominate your design. The use of texture creates sensual and visual excitement. Combine both smooth and rough textures for drama and interest. Too much of either one is boring.

Keep the impact of light in mind when selecting papers for your portfolio. Because smoothness is also a texture, don't ignore the effect of shiny finishes on your pages as backgrounds or added elements in your design. A glossy finish on a background might reflect light into the reviewer's eyes. Someone viewing your portfolio might be distracted by the glare.

Lastly, the use of texture can make your design distinctive. It can add fascination to a dull surface. The texture of the paper you choose for your printed portfolio (pages, cover, or case) will have an impact on your portfolio. This will be the most obvious use of texture. Do you want a rough-textured background such as watercolor paper? Or a smooth, clean surface like cold press illustration board? Read more about paper choices for constructing your printed portfolio in the next chapter.

Pattern

Pattern is the repeating structure of any art or design work, the arrangement of forms to create an orderly whole (see Figure 6.15). In general, patterns are more

ABOVE LEFT: 6.13
All objects, either in nature or the human-made environment, have texture (even smooth objects have a texture).
Illustration courtesy of Aaron J. Kulik.

ABOVE RIGHT: 6.14
Texture in a printed or digital portfolio will be visual texture, as the tactile features of the original material will be lost.
Illustration courtesy of Han Yoon Lee.

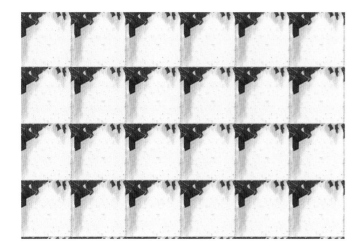

ABOVE: 6.15
The organized repetition of one element forms a pattern.

RIGHT: 6.16
The repeated elements on these and subsequent pages create a pattern for the entire portfolio. Design work courtesy of Katie L. Fulton and Jennifer Gozzi.

perceptible than textures, which make them a stronger visual element for capturing the reviewer's attention. Repeating similar elements over and over again in your portfolio will produce a pattern. Four things can be evaluated in any pattern: placement of emphasis, pattern character, color scheme, and pattern scale. These aspects of pattern are actually design principles.

Patterns can be seen in nature but are far more apparent in the built environment. You may be reading this text while wearing a geometrically patterned shirt and sitting in a chair with a floral pattern, on a floor with a Persian carpet, in a room with striped wallpaper. Pattern is evident in your portfolio in the background paper of your traditional portfolio or the wallpaper on the web page for your digital portfolio. Pattern can also be seen in the arrangement of elements on each page. Pattern (combined with texture and repetition) can enhance your portfolio images (see Figure 6.16).

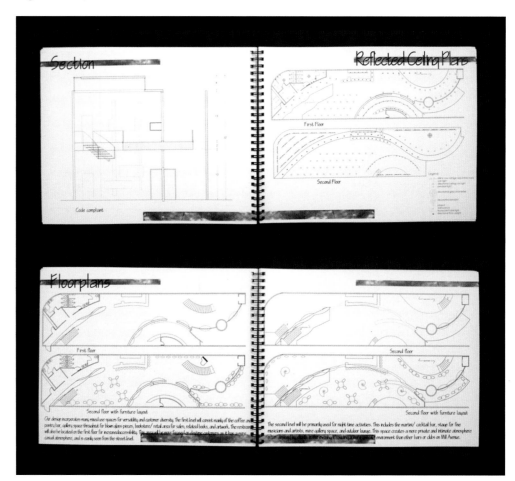

Color

Color is an extremely important design element. Why? Because we don't function in a black-and-white world (see Figure 6.17). Of all the design elements, color in your portfolio will have the *most* impact on reviewers. Their appraisal of your use of color is quite subjective and up for interpretation. Color has symbolic, emotional, and psychological meanings unique to every individual who reviews your work.

Color is defined by three components: hue, saturation, and value. A color's hue is its name, such as red or green. This name represents the wavelength where the color is found on the visible spectrum, such as in the color wheel in Figure 6.18. The saturation of a color is its purity, intensity, or chroma. It is the amount of gray added to the color's hue. A saturation level of 0 percent would be a very gray color, whereas a saturation level of 100 percent is a fully saturated or pure color. The value of a color is the level of brightness. A value of 0 percent is black and a value of 100 percent is white. These three components determine the *color* that you see.

Choose your portfolio colors wisely, especially for the background, borders, and text. For example, a deep blue and a pale yellow would provide a pleasant, yet forceful, contrast. A bright green and a bright magenta would be too overpowering for the viewer's eyes. Whatever colors you choose, keep in mind that the love–hate relationship with any color or color combination is subjective. You may love it but someone else may hate it.

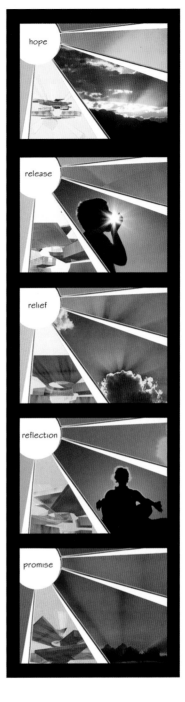

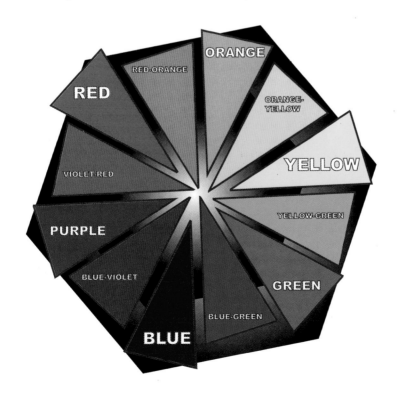

ABOVE: 6.17
Color is such an important design element. It can affect a reviewer more than any other element.

LEFT: 6.18
Primary colors on this color wheel can be divided into secondary colors that are formed by combining the adjacent primary colors.
Illustration courtesy of Aaron J. Kulik.

Design Principles

Having design elements in your work is a good start, but it is not enough. You must arrange them properly using the principles of design. These principles are the abstract and conceptual laws of designing. Design principles use the design elements to create objects, buildings, interiors, exteriors, and just about anything (including your portfolio). They guide the organization or arrangement of the elements. The design principles are universally accepted as *rules* or *philosophies*. Frequently recognized design principles include scale, proportion, balance, repetition, emphasis, and harmony.

Scale

The first design principle is scale. Scale is primarily viewed as the size and dimension of figures and forms relative to some universal standard for measurement, such as a ruler or the human body (see Figure 6.19).

In architecture and design, we compare the size of an object or our environment to ourselves, our size, our shape, our body. For example, a car parked next to a person is normal because the car appears at the correct scale. Yet, a scale model of the car can fit in the palm of your hand (see Figure 6.20).

Keep in mind the size of one object on your page can influence how the others appear, as shown in Figure 6.21. For your portfolio pages, the difference in sizes of elements on your pages will tell the viewer where to look first. The largest image on your page will obviously command the most attention (see Figure 6.22). Make good use of this design principle by guiding the viewer to that largest, most important element on your page.

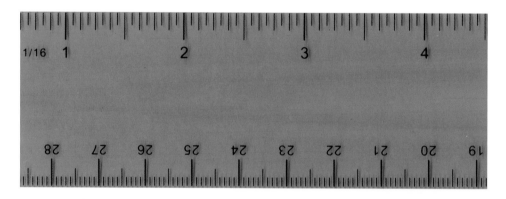

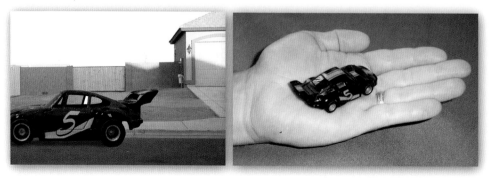

RIGHT TOP: 6.19
A scale is a common element of everyday life. We in the design professions constantly relate our buildings, interiors, and exteriors to a ruler like this . . .

RIGHT BOTTOM: 6.20
. . . or a recognizable structure like a home, or even our body.

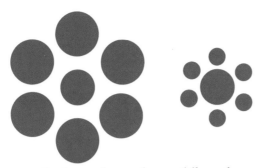

Which circle in the middle is bigger?
(Answer: They are both the same size!)

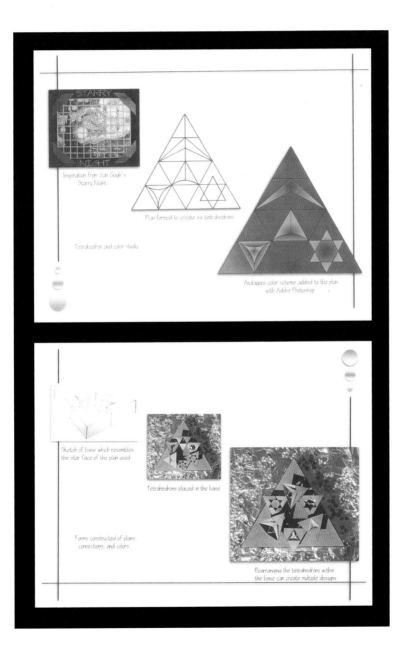

ABOVE: 6.21
All the objects on your page layout or web page will influence the perception of the other objects.
Illustration courtesy of Aaron J. Kulik.

LEFT: 6.22
The large triangle in the top page and the large square in the bottom page dominate the layout. This can represent a wise use of scale if you want the reviewer to focus the most attention on those elements.
Design work courtesy of Katie L. Fulton.

Proportion

Proportion is closely associated with scale. It is the comparison between size and quantity of parts as they relate to a total form (see Figure 6.23). Proportion guides the relationships between objects in your design. Where scale focuses more on the object itself, proportion focuses on the relationships between those objects. Therefore, the context in which you discuss an object becomes very important.

Like scale, we judge the appropriateness of an object's or a space's size in relationship to our body. In Figure 6.24, you can see the stylized human figure in each layout is proportional to the plant on the left. Architectural spaces that are meant to impress us (such as a big church or athletic stadium) are scaled so large that we (the humans) are dwarfed in comparison. In contrast, think of the living room in your home. Its proportions are more in scale with the size of our bodies, resulting in a friendly, comfortable setting. Use the principle of proportion to lay several images on your page. You may have one important image that is scaled larger and possibly several more that are ½ or ¼ its size. Do not haphazardly scale the images to several different sizes, but keep them logically proportional to one another.

Balance

Balance is a principle of design that can be physical or visual. Physical balance relies on gravity and equilibrium. The weight of one object must be counter-balanced by the weight of another object on the opposite side of a fulcrum. Human-made structures must maintain balance in relation to a perpendicular surface. In other words, for a building to remain standing, it must be balanced on the ground. However, there is no scientific method for determining the weights of shapes in art and design. We as designers deal with visual balance, how objects *look* balanced on paper.

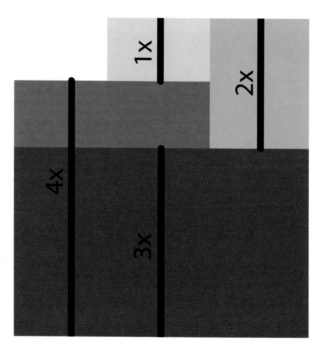

6.23
Proportion forms a relationship between objects. Think of this design element as a building block for the layout of your printed or web pages.

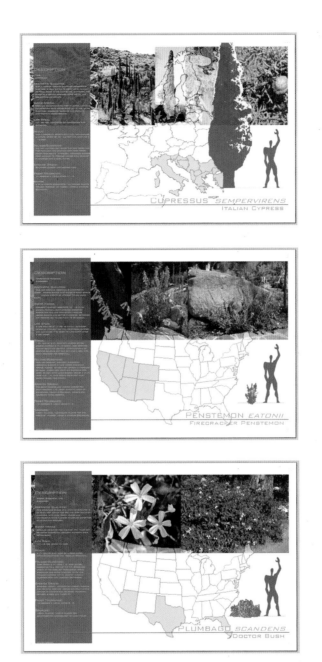

6.24
Notice the use of the gray figure to show the sizes of the plants selected in this landscape architecture project.
Design work courtesy of William Iadevaia.

A key concept in both physical and visual balance is equilibrium. The point where the axes meet is the strongest focal point, the center point. When elements are in visual balance, there are equal elements (or the appearance of them) on either side of the center point.

There are two types of visual balance: symmetrical and asymmetrical. Symmetrical balance is the equal weighting of elements on either side of the center point or central axis (see Figure 6.25). It is formal in character and gives the impression of permanence and stability. Also known as bilateral balance, this type of balance produces designs that are restful, restrained, and peaceful. But symmetrical balance can be bland and boring. Too much symmetrical balance is not

PORTFOLIO LAYOUT 117

interesting. A form of symmetrical balance is radial balance, where objects are equally distributed around a central point. This core point is the place from which all the elements extend or radiate. Some everyday examples include the spokes on a bicycle wheel and the iris of the human eye. Radial balance can be seen in the fanciful snowflake in Figure 6.26.

In asymmetrical balance, visual arrangements are neither identical nor mirror images. However, they still tend to stabilize one another (see Figure 6.27). Asymmetrical balance is achieved by positioning a large object against a few smaller objects, a little area of bright color against a bigger area of a muted color, one object in the center of your layout against a few objects along the edge, and so on. Changing the size or shape of objects can increase the intensity of the asymmetrical balance. This results in contrast in shape, wherein the visual elements are intentionally arranged to be in variance with one another. Be patient when trying to achieve winning asymmetrical balance. Successful asymmetrical balance takes experience and careful planning.

Attempt to use both symmetrical and asymetrical balance in your portfolio. Where symmetrical balance is formal and structured, the informality of asymmtetrical balance creates visual interest. Asymmetrical balance allows for the white space in your layout to be used more dynamically. Symmetrical balance can be used well in two-page spreads, where the same project is spread over two facing pages in your traditional portfolio. Digital portfolios can have thumbnail images equally balanced on the web page.

ABOVE: 6.25
Symmetrical balance is the most formal and traditional type of balance. You can't go wrong by balancing elements equally on a page.

RIGHT: 6.26
Radial symmetry can be seen in this stylized snowflake. All elements and spaces repeat themselves around a central point. Illustration courtesy of Aaron J. Kulik.

Repetition

Repetition can be thought of as organized movement at regular intervals, or the consistent recurrence of an element in your design. Generally defined as duplication, repetition uses the design element of pattern to its optimal effect. There are several forms of repetition. Rhythm is a type of repetition in which elements are repeated in a structured or organized manner. Progression is another type of repetition that suggests movement and draws the eyes into a directional sequence. It is the gradation of smaller elements to larger ones, subtle colors to brighter ones, lines to shapes to forms, smooth textures to rough textures, and so on (see Figure 6.28).

Repeating one or more design elements introduces a sense of order to your page layout. It helps the viewer's eye to move around your page. It is the timed movement or the pace at which someone reviews your page, like the assembly drawing in Figure 6.29.

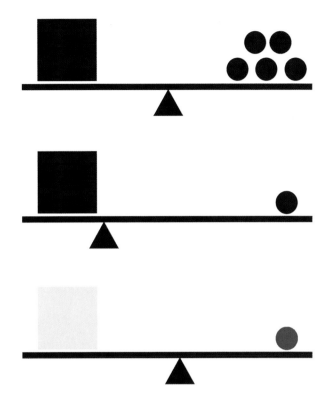

ABOVE: **6.27**
Asymmetrical balance still involves an equal weighting of objects, but the objects no longer need to be the same.

LEFT: **6.28**
Repetition can be created by the progression of shapes or even colors. Illustration courtesy of Aaron J. Kulik.

RIGHT: 6.29
A typical example of repetition in a designer's portfolio might be an assembly drawing of a building or a piece of furniture, like this metal frame sofa.
Design work courtesy of Jon Vredevoogd.

BELOW: 6.30
The emphasis in this image is in the lower right corner.
Design work courtesy of Jeffrey Prince.

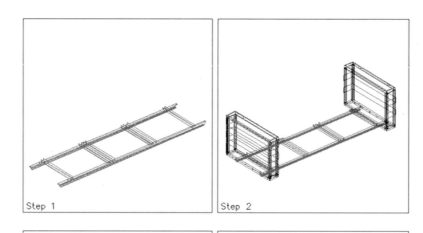
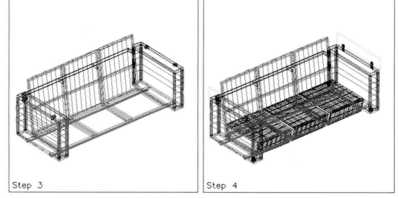

Step 1

Step 2

Step 3

Step 4

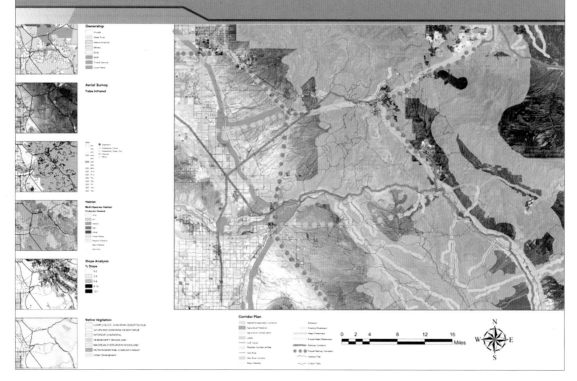

Corridor Network Design

Emphasis

Emphasis happens when certain elements are accented more than others, creating a relationship of dominance and subordination. It is the tendency for one object to dominate all other objects. If everything is equal in emphasis, you will have a very boring page layout. The dominant element in a composition will immediately seize the reviewer's attention, like the large image in the bottom right of Figure 6.30.

Remember to use the design principle of emphasis in conjunction with the design elements. Make one object brighter, larger, more textured, or different in color; surround it by a shape, or point to it with a line. What is important in your design? Most likely, it will be your main project image, rather than titles, lines of text, and smaller supporting images.

Harmony

The last design principle is harmony. Harmony is defined as oneness, a singleness of style, or the state of being one. It is the opposite of emphasis. Also known as unity, it refers to the totality of related parts. Harmony helps the individual elements on your portfolio page be seen as a whole page, rather than a collection of random parts.

Repeating elements and being consistent can achieve harmony. It is the visual linking of elements on your page. A simple example in your portfolio is placing the titles of your work in a similar location. The viewer will not have to search for the title each time he turns the page. Bang! It's in the same spot on every page, as seen in the sample in Figure 6.31.

Not only that, but a consistent use of font, size, and color for your titles will make every page a harmonious part of the whole portfolio. Keeping your page backgrounds the same color, texture, and possibly pattern (three of the design elements) will also create a visually pleasing cohesiveness. As mentioned earlier, the opposite of harmony is emphasis. Having differences in your design can give it liveliness and verve. This helps develop a pleasing tension that holds the viewer's eye. Strive for a balance between harmony and emphasis.

FORMAT GUIDELINES

How you lay out and present your designs says a lot about you as a designer. Designs that display too much variety are visually disorganized. On the other hand, dull designs fail to evoke any sort of reaction and this is just as bad. This section covers basic principles of graphic design that will help you both in laying out your pages and in understanding the psychological impact of the colors you choose to use in your portfolio.

6.31
Consistent placement of titles beneath images helps the series of images relate together as one element.
Design work courtesy of Adel Bagli, Karl Mascarenhas, Zubin Shroff, and Karl Wadia; Academy of Architecture, Mumbai.

Roadside Internet booths.

Light transit system within the settlement.

Local vendors integrated into the streets.

Community spaces with pedestrians.

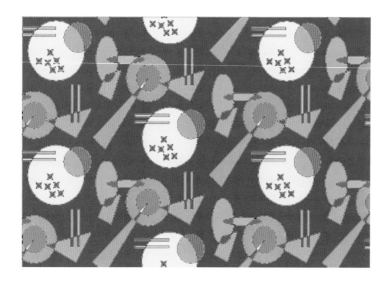

6.32
Additional graphic elements for your layout can be a shape, a band of color, a personal logo, or a personal touch on every page.

Layout Principles

The graphic design of your portfolio is important. As a designer, you have a talent for designing. Yet you may not be aware of how graphic elements can influence page layout. Graphic elements are any item on your portfolio page (whether printed on paper or displayed on a computer screen). These elements include images, text, one shape or a row of shapes, a personal logo, some color, single or double lines, and so on (see Figure 6.32). These elements are as much a part of your portfolio as the projects themselves.

Your design work is the most important aspect of your portfolio. But you know as well as I do that the visual appeal of the entire portfolio should sway the opinion of your reviewer. It will entice or repel. Certain colors and shapes have the power to turn someone on or off. It's difficult to gauge the reaction of a reviewer because visual design is often a subject of individual preference, affected by personal experiences, cultural persuasions, and environmental influences. There is no way to know that someone viewing your portfolio dislikes yellow because it is a reminder of something negative from his or her childhood. (I grew up in a bedroom with yellow-checkered wallpaper. To this day, I dislike yellow in any interior environment.) On the other hand, you may perceive yellow as a bright, cheerful color. Remember, your pages will be reviewed subjectively.

There are four basic principles of graphic design that can help you in your page layout. They are contrast, repetition, alignment, and proximity. Your use of these principles can enhance your portfolio and differentiate it from other portfolios. Let's briefly discuss each one.

Contrast

Contrast is produced when two or more elements are dissimilar to one another. Contrast of color can be between the background color and the color of your text. In order to easily read the text, the background needs to be significantly different, with at least 75 percent contrast (Kilbane and Milman 2003). After putting text on your portfolio page, look at it with your eyes squinted or half-closed. If you struggle to read it or if the text blurs into the background, you do not have enough contrast. For example, light gray text on a medium gray background doesn't work. Contrast can also be achieved with your selection of text. You can use large text for titles and smaller text for project descriptions, or you can use two different fonts. Too much of the same thing gets boring. Very large pictures combined with smaller pictures (as in Figure 6.33) will invoke contrast.

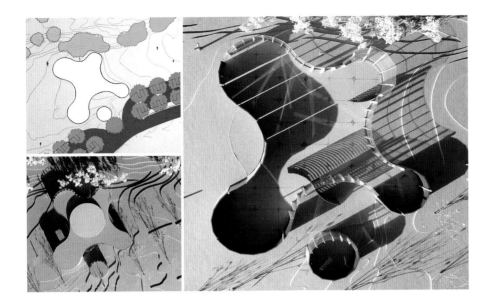

LEFT: 6.33
The dominant image on the right provides contrast with the two smaller images on the left.
Design work courtesy of Daniel Childers.

BELOW: 6.34
The repeated visual element of the plans themselves creates repetition on the page.
Design work courtesy of Paul Marquez.

Repetition

Repetition is not only a design principle, but also a layout principle. It is formed by continually using the same visual element, such as a font, shape, color, or text.

Repetition creates a sense of unity and consistency, but is not monotonous or boring (see Figure 6.34). It is often used to organize a design so the reviewer can understand your layout. A word of warning: before you repeat the same element over and over, make sure the element is worth repeating. If you have a poorly designed logo, redesign it or omit it.

Alignment

Alignment is the arrangement or positioning of page elements. It is a consideration in your decisions about where to place these elements (see Figure 6.35). The placement of these elements should be deliberate, so that the page is enticing rather than a collection of things stuck here and there just to fill up space. Elements are typically aligned to the left, right, center, top, or bottom. Ask yourself, "Does the page flow? Is there a visual connection between the graphic elements?" If not, realign everything so your page flows and is connected together.

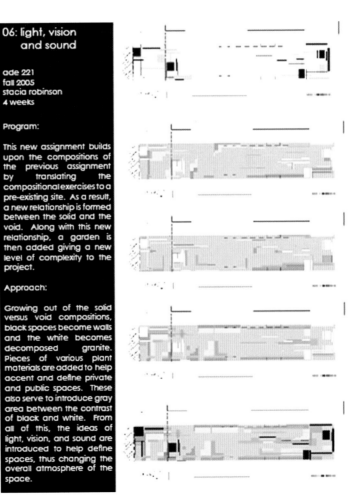

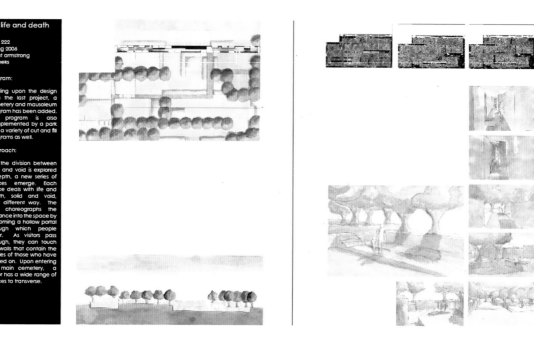

ABOVE: 6.35
The black bands on the page edges assist in lining up the images, especially the series of smaller images on the right page.
Design work courtesy of Paul Marquez.

RIGHT: 6.36
The four renderings in close proximity tell the reviewer that they are part of a whole and should be evaluated as such.
Design work courtesy of Alexandra C. Ayres, Sally Azer, and Kelly Robinson.

Proximity

Proximity relates to the unity of similar elements. Elements that are meant to be together are grouped together, like the four images from the same project in Figure 6.36. Likewise, elements that are unlike are kept apart from one another. You can help the viewer's eye travel over the page by grouping similar elements close to one another. What elements should go together? The answer to that question depends on the information you want on a page. Proximity ties your pages together.

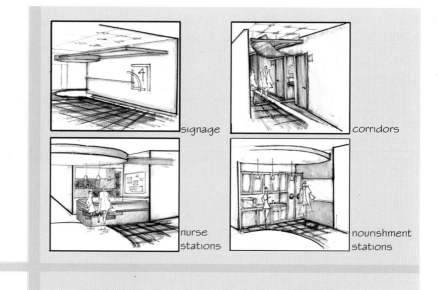

wayfinding

"It is important to provide a variety of cues to assist people in finding their way. Some people pay attention to one kind of cue, some pay attention to others."
Janet R. Carpman, Ph.D., healing by design

With these four principles in mind, be consistent in your use of project images and graphic elements. Even if you decide to be inconsistent, make sure it's obvious that you intentionally want to be inconsistent so the reviewers don't think you have overlooked this part of your design. If your intent is not apparent, they will think you have made a huge mistake. In addition, when using supplementary layout graphics, don't let them appear stronger than your own work. Your work is the priority, then the text, and then the extra elements you may add to pull the entire page together.

PSYCHOLOGY OF COLOR

Color can add to or subtract from the emotional impact of your printed or digital portfolio. Color communicates information as much as words. The colors you choose for your page backgrounds, text, and other graphic elements can divide or unify the entire page or entire portfolio. As seen in the color spectrum in Figure 6.37, you have numerous colors and color combinations available for use in your portfolio.

The emotional and psychological effects of color are undeniable. People have differing color preferences. They also have differing psychological and physical reactions to color. After you read through these next few pages, you will be able to make an astute selection of colors.

Color symbolism is the representation of something abstract. It's something a person feels that a color represents, such as an experience, feeling, or personal meaning. The meaning of a color may be learned from experience or through the customs of society. Colors mean different things in different cultures (e.g., brides in the United States wear white; brides in China wear red). Colors can also change in meaning over time. If you're old enough, you may remember Crayola brand crayons once had a crayon called *flesh*. The same color now has a more politically correct name, *peach*. Colors can also have various meanings. What you may think is white can be described with hundreds of different names by the Inuit Eskimos. White is not white.

Colors can invoke physiological responses as well, making you feel physically cold or warm. Colors considered to be cold or cool are blue, violet, and green. These colors affect the mind and body by slowing the metabolism. These colors can be powerful and frigid, or clean and refreshing. On the opposite end of the spectrum are hot or warm colors, such as red, orange, and yellow. They stimulate the body and increase the level of activity, as well as body temperature. They tend to be viewed as aggressive and attention grabbing. Use these sparingly in your portfolio.

6.37
A spectrum of color can be used to your advantage. Choose all your portfolio colors wisely, not just background and font colors.

RIGHT: 6.38
Seek a balance between light and dark colors. Too many light colors are hard to see and too many dark colors may overpower your presentation. Illustration courtesy of Shrikar Bhave.

BELOW: 6.39
Don't forget that black and white are colors too! With black and white also comes gray. From viewing this illustration, what do you think? Illustration courtesy of Aaron J. Kulik.

A color can be considered light or dark. Light colors are those that have only the faintest hint of color. They are subtle and open up a layout. Dark colors are strong, sober, and seem to diminish rather than expand space. In Figure 6.38, you can see that light colors recede into the background, while dark colors advance toward you.

Pale colors, or tints, are colors with a large amount of white. These soft pastels evoke a feeling of youth, romance, and femininity. Bright colors, on the other hand, are clear and distinctive. These are pure colors with no addition of black or white. Too much of a bright color will make the page visually vibrate.

The Interaction of Colors

What's more, colors can interact. Our perception of an object's color is a constantly changing, highly dynamic process (see Figure 6.39). It depends on what colors surround the object, how long we have been exposed to the scene, what we were looking at before, what we expect to see, and perhaps what we would like to see (General Electric 2005). Colors can appear different when next to other colors, or in varying proportions with other colors. Common color schemes are listed in Figure 6.40.

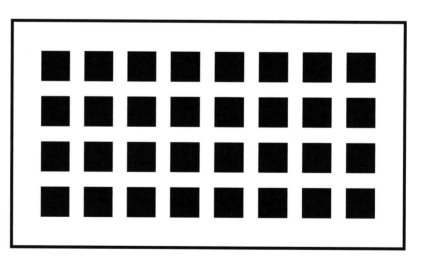

*Do you see gray areas in-between the squares?
(Are your eyes playing tricks on you?)*

Analogous	Colors next to each other on the color wheel
Neutral	Lacks color and is good for backdrops
Monochromatic	Shades, tints and tones of one color
Complementary	Opposite colors on the color wheel
Primary	Red, yellow and blue
Secondary	Orange, green and violet
Tertiary	Any color between the primary and secondary colors (i.e., blue-green)
Warm	Reds, oranges and yellows appear to advance toward the viewer
Cool	Greens, blues and violets appear to recede away from the viewer

Simultaneous contrast is a term that describes the optical effect that adjacent colors have on one another. When placed together, contrasting colors like the ones in Figure 6.41 will emphasize their differences even more. A color will tend to shift toward the adjacent color's complementary hue. For example, a gray circle on a green background will take on a reddish tint. Or directly placing something red next to something green will make the red look more intensely red.

A light color against a dark background will appear even lighter than it is, and vice versa (see Figure 6.42). Light backgrounds tend to darken objects and dark backgrounds tend to lighten objects. Which will you choose for the background of your pages?

LEFT: 6.40
Color schemes are often used in our design professions to create style and appeal. They typically involve one, two, or three colors to produce aesthetic context.

BELOW LEFT: 6.41
Stare long enough at any of these color combinations and your eyes will start to jump and water. Be careful when using strong contrasting colors or you may hurt the eyes of your reviewers! Illustration courtesy of Amol Surve.

BELOW RIGHT: 6.42
The background color influences how the other colors appear against it, even in grayscale. Illustration courtesy of Aaron J. Kulik.

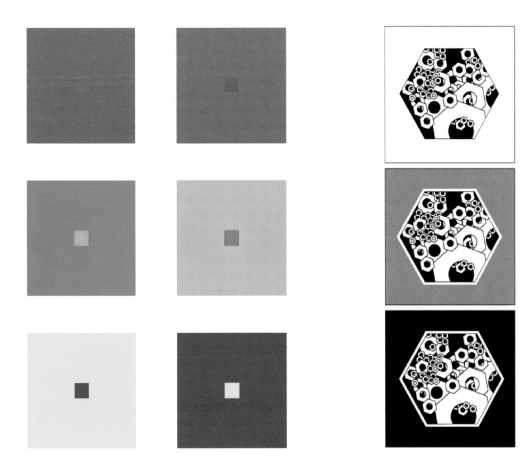

Light and color are intricately connected. Light is the radiant energy that your eye perceives. Your eye perceives wavelengths of radiant energy (or light) as different colors. The perceived colors are transmitted to your brain, where they are recognized as distinct colors. This occurs when your eye perceives a rainbow similar to the one in Figure 6.43 and your brain acknowledges it. Likewise, the amount of light, the quality or comfort of the lighting, and the function of your brain as it interprets what your eye sees are major factors influencing how others will see the colors used in your portfolio.

The aging eye requires more light, interprets color differently, and is more sensitive to glare. By age 60, an average lens receives one-third less light than at the age of 20. As individuals grow older, they become more sensitive to glare. Indirect or reflected glare is caused by light bouncing off a polished surface. The viewing zone for reading your portfolio on a horizontal surface (such as a desk or table) is between 25 and 40 degrees. A shiny finish on the paper of your portfolio will bounce light back into the reviewer's eyes.

In addition, the eye perceives color differently as we age. As the human eye ages, the lens thickens and turns more yellow. This doesn't mean that older individuals see everything as yellow. There is simply a reduction in the eye's ability to discriminate differences in the blue wavelength of the color spectrum. Light blue and pale blue elements used in your portfolio may look different to you but not to older individuals. To them, the two elements appear as one. Overall, the visibility of your portfolio pages depends on:

1. The size of the page and its elements;
2. The brightness of the page and its elements;
3. How much time the eye has to adjust to what is seen; and
4. The contrast between the elements on the page and the page itself, or even the page and its background; the higher the contrast, the easier it is to see.

The Meaning of Colors

Let's look at each color individually to help you wisely select colors appropriate to use in your portfolio. More details can be found in available books on color symbolism.

White

White is the ultimate in lightness. In the color system of visual light, it represents the totality of all the colors combined. White is rarely represented in its pure state. It always has some warmth or coolness to it. Its positive connotations are purity, birth, cleanliness, innocence, and peacefulness. Its negative connotations are weakness, surrender, and cover-up (i.e., whitewash or whiteout). You must be careful not to use too much white in your portfolio design because

6.44

it is highly reflective. Darker objects against a white background will appear even darker and will provide a high contrast. Without texture, white areas may appear blank, empty, and boring.

Black

Black is as dark a color as you can get because it absorbs all light. Actually, it is the absence of color. From one perspective, it symbolizes sophistication, power, and sexuality. At the other extreme, it symbolizes death, emptiness, and depression. It is often combined with white for an authoritative presence. Keep in mind that black is harsh and tiring when overused. As with white, too much black is not good.

6.45

Gray

Gray is considered a neutral color because it is neither positive nor negative. It is serious, anonymous, and silent. It represents technology, work, industrialism, intelligence, and modernism. Because of its implicit neutrality, gray is an excellent background for presenting work with more vibrant colors (like your design projects). Gray can be tinted as either warm gray or cool gray. These subtly tinted grays are restful and pleasant. Keep in mind that too much use of gray

6.46

implies confusion, loss of distinction, and old age. Have you ever been to London? The color gray comes to mind, as the color indicates a wet, stormy, or foggy environment.

6.47

Red

Red has the greatest emotional impact of all colors. It is attention grabbing, powerful, and stimulating. It represents love, passion, festiveness, and importance. It is a color full of drama. A word of warning: use red in moderation! A reviewer's eye will gravitate toward it because it is an aggressive and strong color. It represents revolution, prostitution, and fire. It signifies danger and is the color for stop signs and fire trucks. If used in large areas, it can become irritating. A better use of red is as a small accent color.

6.48

Orange

Orange is often the central hue in a friendly color scheme. Uncomplicated, direct, and warm, it implies the pleasures of family life and a sense of community. Orange is symbolically considered light-hearted, bright, humorous, cheerful, and fresh. Orange is vivid and stands out well, even more so when balanced with green or blue.

6.49

Brown

Brown is the color of many organic materials found in nature. It is associated with comfort and security and is predominantly considered a masculine color. It signifies richness, affluence, dignity, and harmony. Accents of brown can bring harmony to your designs. If used in excess, it can make a design gloomy and melancholy. It is also quite dull and depressing in tints, such as tan, beige, and buff.

6.50

Yellow

Yellow is symbolically cheerful, spirited, uplifting, happy, hopeful, and optimistic. Yellow is best used in pale tints. In maximum saturation, yellow can in fact be more aggressive than red. This intense yellow is associated with caution, sickness, betrayal, and cowardice. Use yellow in moderation, as overuse can make a design dull and boring. The human eye easily perceives yellow and it visually advances toward the viewer. Combined with small accents of blue or violet, yellow is stimulating and suggests a sense of movement and energy.

Green

Green is the largest color family visible to the eye. It promotes a sense of renewal and relaxation, harmony and tranquility because it combines the extroversion of yellow with the peaceful effects of blue. Green is generally considered to represent growth, spring, freshness, youth, and refreshment. However, green is dull and depressive if used in institutional shades. These are shades commonly used in health care uniforms to contrast with the afterimage effects of red (i.e., blood). Strangely, green tends to recede and is often combined with red to create a sense of energy and excitement.

6.51

Blue

Blue is the coolest of the cool colors. In many cultures, it implies protection and is often the color of military uniforms. Stability, faithfulness, trustworthiness, and responsibility are symbolic meanings. It is the color of truth, tranquility, conservatism, and security. When used with its complementary color orange, blue is vibrant and effervescent. If overused in your designs, it can create a sense of sadness and despair.

6.52

Violet

Also known as purple, violet is the hardest color for the eye to distinguish. It's not quite warm and not quite cold, making it magical, whimsical, regal, unpredictable, and fascinating. A major problem with using too much violet is its association with mourning and death in some societies. Use of violet in strong saturation can evoke feelings of hopelessness or irritation. Add a bit of yellow with violet for freshness and balance.

6.53

CONCLUSION

Now that you have been exposed to both design elements and principles, you should have a better understanding of the foundational components that form any good portfolio layout. Combine these with the graphic design principles of contrast, repetition, alignment, and proximity. Finally, add meaningful color to your page, text, and other graphic elements to further stylize your portfolio. In the next chapter, we'll build on these fundamentals to create a printed portfolio. We'll talk about the page format, text, size of work, and even the paper and optional presentation case.

7

Constructing a Printed Portfolio

This chapter will continue with the presentation of your printed portfolio. Specific attention will be paid to the format of your printed pages, including the text you add with your images and the type of paper you select. The size and format of your presentation are important considerations. Your decisions in these areas will ultimately have an impact on the packaging of your work.

PHYSICAL SIZE AND LAYOUT

Projects in each discipline have different parameters and requirements. Apparel designers have flat boards of dress sketches; urban planners may have 3-D topographic models of entire cities. Some disciplines rely more on 8.5" × 11" work while others need much larger presentation boards, such as 24" × 36", or even 36" × 42". These will fit into different-sized presentations and portfolio cases.

You probably have work in a multitude of sizes, as represented in Figure 7.1. What do you do now? It's best to select one single portfolio size. This makes the portfolio easier to handle and present during interviews. You want the reviewer focusing on your work, not your format. If you include random shapes and sizes, you convey to the reviewer that you are unorganized and cannot comprehend visual association.

Stick with a manageable format size. Larger formats waste material, require big, expensive cases, and are awkward to transport. This doesn't mean that you exclude excellent work done in a larger format. You include these larger items at a reduced size. Will the size you have selected accommodate both horizontal and vertical pieces? Just because you may not have both layout formats now does not mean you won't in the years to come. Plan ahead. Make sure the format you choose is flexible enough to accommodate future formats.

RIGHT: 7.1
You may have projects of many different sizes. A traditional portfolio is formed in one consistent size.

BELOW: 7.2
An extremely large board is great for a public exhibit, but would be nearly impossible to bring to an interview.
Design work courtesy of Megan Williams and Zsavay Andrews.

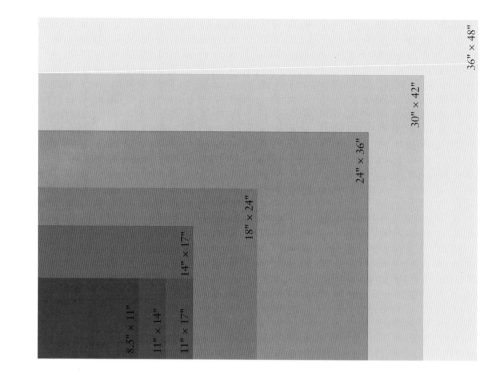

Although architects and designers typically create large presentation boards like the one in Figure 7.2, most interviewers would have difficulty balancing this size board on their desk during an interview. (You'd be surprised at the number of job interviews conducted at the local coffee shop.) Reproduce your larger drawing sheets and presentation boards to a smaller format, such as 8.5" × 11" or 11" × 17". If the projects are in electronic form, you can simply print them out at a smaller scale. If not, you will need to reduce them and get them into electronic format. You can do this by either scanning or photographing them (more on this in Chapter 10).

What kind of work are you showing? Does it need plenty of presentation space around it? If your images are small, a large background might bring out the best in your work. Or is your work lost in a large background? In addition, the size of your portfolio is in part dictated by printing constraints. If each page is created electronically, you can only design on a certain amount of the page before you exceed the printing margins.

Visual Layout

In this section, we'll discuss the visual layout of your portfolio and its pages. This is the process of arranging

Box 7.1

and rearranging your images, text, and graphics on the page (see Box 7.1). Each page of your portfolio is considered one individual layout. In addition, two facing pages and the portfolio as a whole are also layouts that must be thoughtfully designed. Important considerations in your portfolio's visual layout include the concept, the type of layout, and the arrangement of your elements.

Layout Concept and Format

Let's start with the underlying concept of your portfolio. What is it? A concept is more than the style of your portfolio. A concept is the idea and the reasoning behind your portfolio design, layout, and presentation. Elements of your portfolio layout should visually relate. The grouping of these elements creates the look and feel of your portfolio and determines why a good layout outshines a bad one, as shown in Figure 7.3.

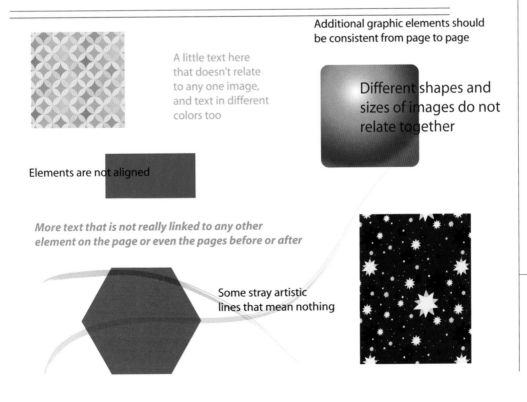

Additional graphic elements should be consistent from page to page

A little text here that doesn't relate to any one image, and text in different colors too

Different shapes and sizes of images do not relate together

Elements are not aligned

More text that is not really linked to any other element on the page or even the pages before or after

Some stray artistic lines that mean nothing

7.3
A consistent and organized layout has few of the errors shown in this illustration of a poor layout.

Your layout should never overpower your work. Someone reviewing your portfolio should notice your impressive layout, creative use of color and graphics, and obvious organizational finesse. They should notice it, not focus on it. How you lay out your work *does* make a difference—just ask any graphic designer.

Figure 7.4 shows the three types of layouts: portrait, landscape, and the two-page spread. A vertically oriented presentation, in which the format of the presentation has greater height than width, is known as a portrait layout. This type of upright presentation works best in books with left and right pages that can be turned. The opposite layout is known as landscape. This is a horizontally oriented presentation, in which the format has greater width than height. This type of presentation works best in an easel portfolio, where the reviewer is flipping pages one over the other. You can also create a book portfolio in landscape, as long as *all* pages are landscape, including the front cover. By doing this, you are immediately telling reviewers to turn the book sideways before they even open it.

Either portrait or landscape is acceptable, as long as you use the layout consistently throughout your portfolio. You are either going to present everything horizontally, everything vertically, or some of each. If you have pieces in different formats, put all the horizontal pieces together and all the vertical pieces together. This way, the reviewer is not constantly rotating your portfolio from portrait to landscape and back again, which gets tiring. Will this require you to reformat some of your work to remain consistent with the viewing direction? Probably. It's worth it though, as your portfolio will appear more organized and cohesive.

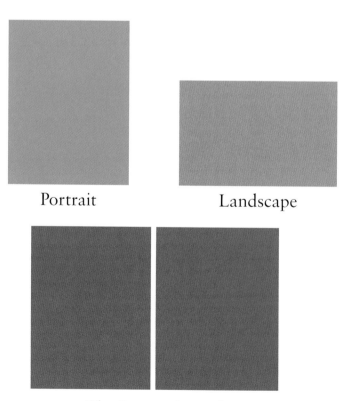

Portrait   Landscape

The 2-page Spread

7.4
Three typical page layouts are the vertical portrait, the horizontal landscape, and the two-page spread (which can be used vertically or horizontally).

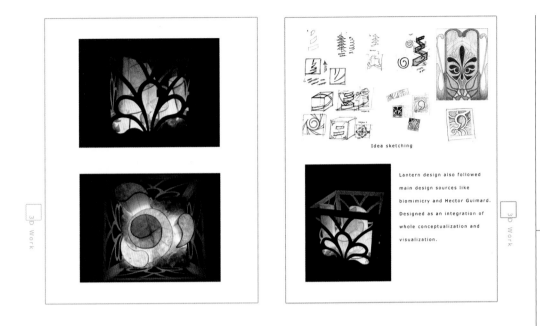

Idea sketching

Lantern design also followed
main design sources like
biomimicry and Hector Guimard.
Designed as an integration of
whole conceptualization and
visualization.

LEFT: 7.5
This two-page spread allows enough room to show the finished product, a short description, and some of the concept drawings for this 3-D lantern.
Design work courtesy of Han Yoon Lee.

BELOW: 7.6
A butterfly fold allows you to include a larger 11" × 17" page in your 8.5" × 11" format book.

If you are using a book format for your portfolio, use both sides of the page. This provides a sense of continuity for reviewers and is a resourceful use of their time (Seguin 1991). Placement of these two pages facing each other is the third type of layout—the two-page spread. (This is sometimes referred to as the double-page spread. It's the same thing.) Someone viewing this layout spread will inherently view it as one item, rather than two separate pages. Use a two-page spread to show a set of projects or projects related to the same concept or skill set. Use it to show your most important work or larger, complex projects, like the one in Figure 7.5.

A foldout page is one that is larger than 8.5" × 11" and is folded to fit inside. For example, you may have a construction sheet that is 11" × 17". You can either fold it in half and let the viewer flip it open, or fold it in half and then fold the edge back over like a butterfly (see Figure 7.6). This enables you to show slightly larger pictures while maintaining the consistency of your book layout. You can also use both sides of the page to create an unusual butterfly fold like the one in Figure 7.7.

Sketching Your Layout

How do you begin? Start laying out your pages by sketching them first. If you are working with digital files, make a copy of each file and manipulate the copies to form your layouts. If you make a mistake, you can trash the file and open the original again.

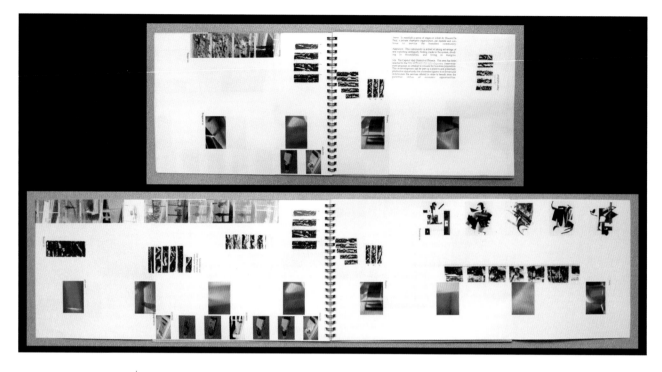

For original printed materials, never grab the adhesive and start gluing things to the pages of your portfolio without first intelligently laying them out. This would be a huge mistake. Instead, take pen and paper and begin roughly sketching where the various elements would go, like a storyboard for each page (see Figure 7.8).

A key factor in reviewing your portfolio is how it is read and interpreted. In our society, we tend to review everything from left to right. Therefore, take advantage of this natural tendency and place your most important item in the upper left corner.

Regardless of the format you choose, use as much of the page as possible. Strike a balance between postive and negative space, as discussed earlier. Again, your audience comes into play. Although I do not consider myself over the hill (or even that close to it), my eyesight is not as

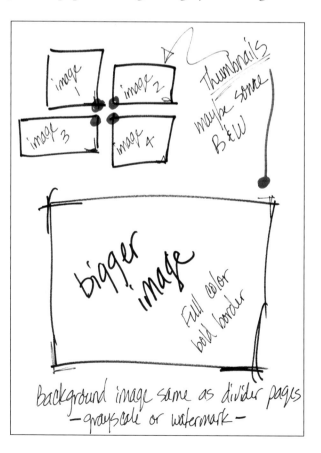

ABOVE: 7.7
Do not limit yourself to only one layout size if an ingenious fold or two could make your portfolio so much better.
Design work courtesy of John Milander.

RIGHT: 7.8
A quick sketch showing where you can place your images and how they relate together will save you a lot of time when you sit down to put it all together later.

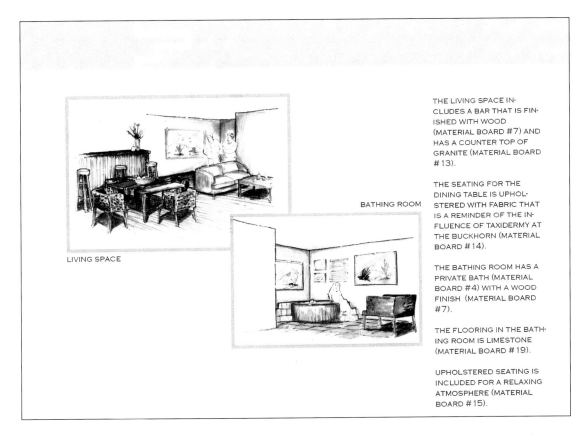

LIVING SPACE

BATHING ROOM

THE LIVING SPACE INCLUDES A BAR THAT IS FINISHED WITH WOOD (MATERIAL BOARD #7) AND HAS A COUNTER TOP OF GRANITE (MATERIAL BOARD #13).

THE SEATING FOR THE DINING TABLE IS UPHOLSTERED WITH FABRIC THAT IS A REMINDER OF THE INFLUENCE OF TAXIDERMY AT THE BUCKHORN (MATERIAL BOARD #14).

THE BATHING ROOM HAS A PRIVATE BATH (MATERIAL BOARD #4) WITH A WOOD FINISH (MATERIAL BOARD #7).

THE FLOORING IN THE BATHING ROOM IS LIMESTONE (MATERIAL BOARD #19).

UPHOLSTERED SEATING IS INCLUDED FOR A RELAXING ATMOSPHERE (MATERIAL BOARD #15).

7.9
It is assumed by the reviewer that the two images outlined in blue are related because of their close proximity and overlap. Design work courtesy of Lauren Maitha and Lindsay Miller.

good as it was 15 years ago. I need large enough images in a portfolio to see the details you want me to see. If you have room on the page, use it. Small images with too much negative space on the page make the page look empty. If an example isn't large, include more than one per page.

Establish a balance between your photos, drawings, text, and other elements. Two or more items placed in close proximity (like the two renderings in Figure 7.9) create an immediate visual relationship. Likewise, elements placed far apart represent distant proximity. This could be two images, some images and blocks of text, or some images, text, and other graphic elements like logos, lines, and shapes. Elements on the page that relate together should be grouped together. If something doesn't quite fit, remove it. Images of varying size can add personality to the layout (see Figure 7.10). A two-page spread like Figure 7.11 can be consistent but have images of more than one size on each page, too.

Extra design elements can be added to your pages, such as logos, borders, titles, shapes, lines, backgrounds, and so on (see Figure 7.12). Avoid cute design elements added to your page, like solid circles in rainbow colors. You are not scrap-booking. Could you pick a few elements only please? Too many elements or even too much variety can detract from your work. Keep it simple but not so barren that your layout looks as if it is lacking in substance. Strike a balance between just enough and too much. Unnecessary elements on your pages will do nothing but create visual noise. A simple layout is a successful layout (Figure 7.13).

RIGHT: 7.10
If all the images on this page were the same size, it would be boring. Note that the smaller images, although slightly different sizes, are not widely disparate. Design work courtesy of Aaron J. Kulik.

BELOW: 7.11
When the traditional portfolio is laid flat, the two pages are viewed as one. The sweeping graphic element at the bottom assists in tying the two pages together. Design work courtesy of Shelby Bogaard.

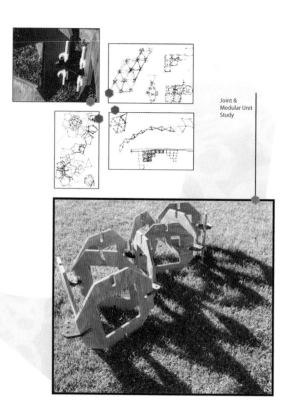

Joint & Modular Unit Study

PATTERNS based on designer Frank Lloyd Wright

PATTERNS based on flower biomimicry resource

COMPOSITION AND ORDER

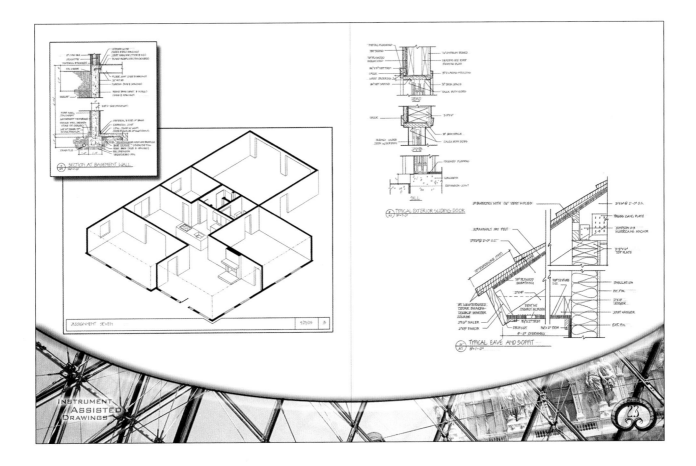

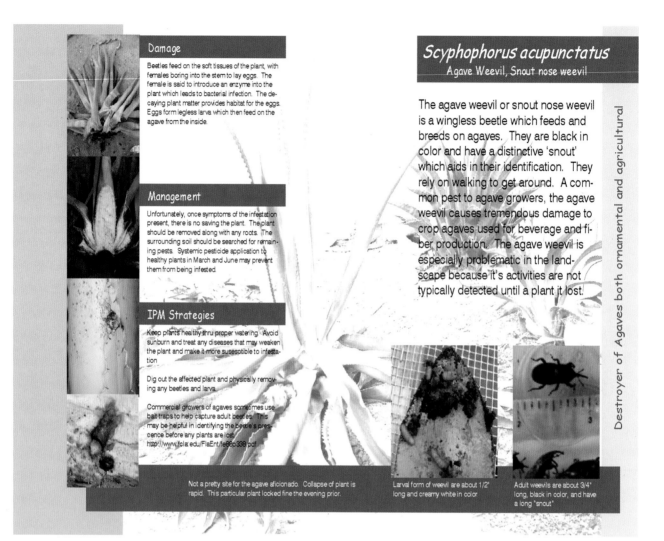

Within the graphic:

Damage

Beetles feed on the soft tissues of the plant, with females boring into the stem to lay eggs. The female is said to introduce an enzyme into the plant which leads to bacterial infection. The decaying plant matter provides habitat for the eggs. Eggs form legless larva which then feed on the agave from the inside.

Management

Unfortunately, once symptoms of the infestation present, there is no saving the plant. The plant should be removed along with any roots. The surrounding soil should be searched for remaining pests. Systemic pesticide application to healthy plants in March and June may prevent them from being infested.

IPM Strategies

Keep plants healthy thru proper watering. Avoid sunburn and treat any diseases that may weaken the plant and make it more susesptible to infestation

Dig out the affected plant and physically removing any beetles and larva.

Commercial growers of agaves sometimes use bait traps to help capture adult beetles. This may be helpful in identifying the beetle's prescence before any plants are lost.
http://www.fcla.edu/FlaEnt/fe86p338.pdf

Scyphophorus acupunctatus
Agave Weevil, Snout nose weevil

The agave weevil or snout nose weevil is a wingless beetle which feeds and breeds on agaves. They are black in color and have a distinctive 'snout' which aids in their identification. They rely on walking to get around. A common pest to agave growers, the agave weevil causes tremendous damage to crop agaves used for beverage and fiber production. The agave weevil is especially problematic in the landscape because it's activities are not typically detected until a plant it lost.

Destroyer of Agaves both ornamental and agricultural

Not a pretty site for the agave aficionado. Collapse of plant is rapid. This particular plant looked fine the evening prior.

Larval form of weevil are about 1/2" long and creamy white in color

Adult weevils are about 3/4" long, black in color, and have a long "snout"

7.14
The vegetation in the background image gives context to the presentation without overpowering the graphic.
Design work courtesy of Jeffrey Prince.

One or more background images on your pages can add depth and personality to your work. These images should be subtle and not dominate the viewer's attention. (That's why they are known as background images, rather than foreground images.) Stick with one or two images only, possibly in grayscale (see Figure 7.14).

Too many images that change from page to page confuse the viewer and do not help to coordinate and tie your pages together. Try to use images that relate to your discipline or to your project. For example, a background image of a planting plan that is like a watermark would tie in well with a landscape architect's portfolio. I reviewed an admission portfolio one year and the background image tied in to the theme: sight. That's a solid theme. Scattered throughout the portfolio were several quotes from famous architects, designers, artists, and philosophers that related to sight and seeing design in various ways. But the background image on all the pages was a hand-sketched eyeball. I can tell you, it was very strange trying to evaluate each page when the page seemed to be staring back at me.

Lastly, do not forget to design your layout to accommodate later additions. Make it simple to update. Leave room for future work. You will definitely update your portfolio. How easy is it to remove a few images from a page? A few pages from your portfolio? Will adding something significantly alter your concept? If you've carefully thought out your concept and layout design, adding or deleting material later should not upset the flow of your portfolio presentation. (Unless you are using a book portfolio in which pages can be moved around, you would want to bind the pages together right before you go out to interview.)

TEXT

Because the most powerful sensory mode is visual, using images to convey meaning is important (Barrett 1998). Remember the saying, "A picture is worth a thousand words"? Images can convey a message much faster than text. Nonetheless, as in Figure 7.15, some explanation of your work is necessary.

You cannot have a portfolio with 100 percent images and no text. It's just not practical. Titles and short passages of text combined or overlaid with your images will accompany your work. Text is used in both traditional and digital portfolios. (More specific information on using text in digital presentations is presented in Chapter 12.) Therefore, the text can be as short as a title or as long as a project description. It is important to consider not only *what* you write but also *how* you write it and *where* you place it on your page. Let's begin with what is written.

What to Write

The text you include in your portfolio says as much as your images. Text is helpful because the portfolio must speak for itself (see Box 7.2). Only in an interview can

7.15
In a design portfolio, images are the focus, yet some text is necessary to explain complex design problems.
Design work courtesy of Charudatta Joshi.

ARCHITECTURAL VOCABULARY

The architectural vocabulary should be a scripture of the site's intrinsic character; echo to its idiom. It should garner the potentials of the site & course them for appropriate effect.

Hence, the architecture that emerges from the site & grows on its resources can approve of its essentiality & reason to exist. The usage of locally available materials & vernacular construction strategies imparts an everlasting simplicity to its creation. The almost ascetic quality of space that evolves from such humility conveys a profound message.

The design typology to be adopted should pragmatically respond to the local climate simultaneously, balancing other aspects such as economy, scope & nature of development & long-term impacts.

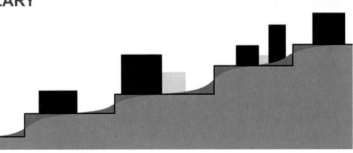

Minimum cutting & filling

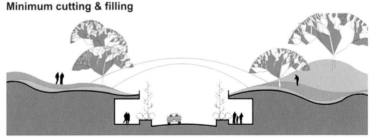

Follow site levels

Text is most effective when it serves to inform the audience why the portfolio images represent valid examples of the student's work and character. Distinguishing between an objective description and a persuasive description of the portfolio images may inform the audience about the body of work in the portfolio as well as what type of team member the potential employee may become within the workplace. Ultimately, the choice of language and the textural features reflect purpose and personality that help to determine where the student will fit successfully within a workplace environment.

Julie Hutchison
Interior Designer/Project Manager
Gensler
Phoenix, AZ

Box 7.2

7.16
An admissions portfolio submitted for review must speak for itself. Include enough text to adequately explain the design problem and your solution.
Design work courtesy of Paul Marquez.

you provide a verbal explanation for the process, idea, or product. If you are asked to leave a *copy* of your portfolio at an office for review later, your work stands on its own. This is especially apparent when submitting a portfolio like the one in Figure 7.16 for admission into a degree program, as few schools allow you to verbally explain your portfolio.

Text is placed in several key locations in your portfolio, such as the introductory page, titles under your images, table of contents, divider pages, and project descriptions. On the introductory page, use text to provide some general informa-

Approach:

The concept for this project emerged from studying the concepts of light, vision, and sound. Upon researching the terms, one word seemed to encompass all three - illumination. Illumination is defined in this project as the degree of visibility of the environment and an interpretation that removes obstacles to understanding. This concept helped to organize the building program to illuminate light, vision, and sound throughout the project.

tion about yourself, such as your name, design area, and contact information. After all, what if someone really likes your portfolio and you are not present at the review session? You'd like them to get a hold of you, right? A phone number and email address on that page are essential! Some students like to include quotes from their favorite designers or artists, sprinkled throughout their portfolio. (As famous people are well known, please spell their names correctly.) If the quotes are short and sweet, go right ahead. Too long a quote, or one written in Old English or Latin, won't be very helpful.

You must label your work. Use some text to clarify the intentions of your design, particularly those that are not apparent just by looking at your design. Without some indication of your intent, the reviewer will not understand the emphasis of the project (see Figure 7.17). Let's say you have a drawing of an exterior seating area drawn in plan view and also presented in a rendered perspective. Should the reviewer be looking at your technical drafting skills or your rendering skills? Is the seating an original design or are you trying to show how you used an existing seat in an innovative manner? Help the reviewer identify the strength you are trying to illustrate.

Remember your audience is either educators or practitioners, not your mother or roommate who doesn't understand a plan view or perspective. These professionals understand the language of design communication. Rather than a one-paragraph description of the drawings or images, a description of the project context would be more helpful. For an example see Figure 7.18. What were the most challenging obstacles to overcome? How did you overcome them? What is the strength of this project? Why is *this* image or project so important that it belongs in your portfolio?

7.17
For reviewers unfamiliar with this project, the images alone would not adequately explain the designer's intent. Design work courtesy of Shrikar Bhave.

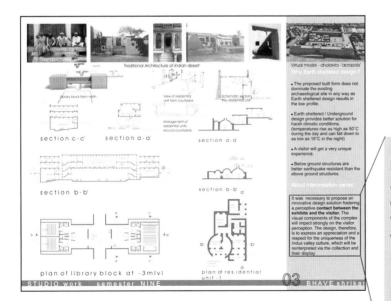

It was necessary to propose an innovative design solution fostering a perceptive **contact between the exhibits and the visitor.** The visual components of the complex will impact strongly on the visitor perception. The design, therefore, is to express an appreciation and a respect for the uniqueness of the Indus valley culture, which will be reinterpreted via the collection and their display.

7.18
A description of the project parameters and challenges you faced in your design is beneficial.
Design work courtesy of Yang Peng.

Of great importance are spelling and grammar. Nothing turns off a practitioner (and especially an educator) more than misspelled words. As this text is often *not* created in word processing software with a spell-checking feature, typos in headings and titles might accidentally be overlooked. A common typographical error involves homonyms, which are words that sound the same but have different spellings. Think of words such as there, their, and they're. Your computer's spell checker may not catch these errors. Capitalization must also be checked, especially if your text includes proper nouns that should be capitalized. Proofread your work at least three times and do so when your mind is fresh, such as first thing in the morning and not two hours before the interview.

Lastly, you will need to balance the amount of text against the number of images (see Figure 7.19). Too much text is like too many images. It waters down the focus of your work. No one wants to spend five minutes reading a page of text. As you can see, you need to give careful thought to what is written in your

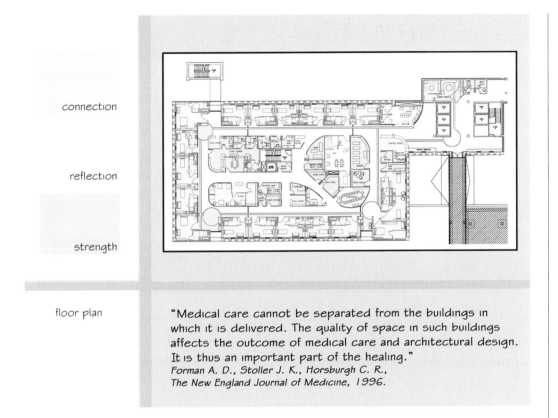

connection

reflection

strength

floor plan

"Medical care cannot be separated from the buildings in which it is delivered. The quality of space in such buildings affects the outcome of medical care and architectural design. It is thus an important part of the healing."
Forman A. D., Stoller J. K., Horsburgh C. R., The New England Journal of Medicine, 1996.

portfolio. There is no guarantee that the reviewer will read every single word in your portfolio. But if every line of text has been carefully crafted, you can be assured that it will make a good impression if read (see Box 7.3).

How to Read It

The context of your text is as important as the content. What does it look like? How is it placed on your page? Text is viewed as a part of your graphic presentation. Short statements will form visual blocks on your layout. Plan these into your layout as you would your images, on the page or as a separate component, as in

7.19
Seek a balance between the text and images. Design work courtesy of Alexandra C. Ayres, Sally Azer, and Kelly Robinson.

I think the composition on the page is equally as important as the number of images. For instance, four images with an intended message or a descriptive caption can be successful if all of the images work together and clearly communicate the message. I look for message first, whether it takes one image and a description or it combines several images together. Graphics are not just eyewash meant to dazzle the reader. They tell a story about the interviewee and his or her abilities.

Lorraine Cutler
Associate Professor and Chairperson
Department of Interior Design, College of Design
Arizona State University
Tempe, AZ

Box 7.3

ABOVE: 7.20
This ingenious divider page uses text on a vellum overlay to describe the project shown on subsequent pages.
Design work courtesy of Liisa Taylor.

BELOW: 7.21
Notice the stylized elements in the serif fonts that are not present in the sans serif varieties.

Figure 7.20. Often, architecture and design students believe the image is everything and the text is an afterthought. Not so. There are several considerations when using text. These include the amount of text, and its location, size, appearance, and color.

The amount of text makes a difference on your portfolio pages. Occasionally, you may want to include a few paragraphs of project description. It is helpful to break a large amount of text into columns. It's preferable to format this copy as short lines of text with ample space between columns for ease of reading. Be consistent about where you put your text. If you put the title of a project under one image, above another image, and up the right side of a third image, reviewers will be confused.

Serif and Sans Serif

The kind of font you select is critical. The font is the letters and numbers of a particular design. (The terms *font* and *typeface* are often used interchangeably.) There are two types: serif and sans serif (see Figure 7.21).

SANS SERIF FONTS	SERIF FONTS
Arial	Garamond
Gill Sans	Palatino
Helvetica	Times New Roman

The small adornments on the ends or edges of the letters are called serifs. These fine lines extend from the tops (known as ascenders) and bottoms (known as descenders or feet) of the letters. It makes the letters easier to read. Serif fonts are used for large amounts of text, like the text of a book. They are more frequently used because the serifs form a linkage between letters that leads the eye across each line of text. Examples of popular serif fonts include Garamond, Palatino, and Times New Roman.

Sans serif fonts lack the stroke at the ends of letters found on serif fonts. Simply put, they are *not* serif fonts. Sans serif fonts tend to strain the eye so use them sparingly. Appropriate choices for sans serif fonts include titles, headings, and other short passages that stand alone. Examples of popular sans serif fonts include Arial, Gill Sans, and Helvetica.

The font you choose and its placement will affect the structure of the page. A great font selection can contribute to the look and feel of your portfolio, whereas a poor selection can ruin your design intent. Use only one or two fonts! Too many fonts are confusing. Although text is not an afterthought in your portfolio, your text should never overpower your images. Too many fonts or variations of different fonts (i.e., bold, italic, underline, or shadow) can draw too much attention to the text or destroy its legibility. Use these variables sparingly.

Fonts like those in Figure 7.22 can support or oppose the message you're sending in your portfolio. Think carefully about the font for different parts of

THINKING ABOUT YOUR DESIGN PHILOSOPHY

Adobe Caslon	Design	Janson Text	Design
Arial Narrow	Design	**Kabel Black**	**Design**
Avant Garde Bk	Design	Lucida Sans	Design
Barmeno Regular	Design	Minion	Design
Chalkboard	Design	*Mistral*	*Design*
Clarendon	**Design**	Modern No. 20	Design
Colonna MT	Design	Optima	Design
Eras Demi	**Design**	Papyrus	Design
Frankie	**Design**	PLASTIQUE	DESIGN
Geneva	Design	Sabon	Design
Harrington	Design	**Swiss921 BT**	**Design**
Improv	Design	Verdana	Design

7.22
Compare the aesthetic of each font shown in the word "Design." Which font would reflect the look and feel of your own design portfolio?

The contents should be clear to anyone looking at the portfolio. Each project should be clearly explained, in a type size that people can actually read. And, make sure everything is spelled correctly.

Fritz Steiner
Dean
School of Architecture,
University of Texas at Austin
Austin, TX

Box 7.4

your portfolio. Fit the font to the audience. If you are applying for a graduate program that specializes in historic preservation, use a legible font that has historical connotations (like Gothic, French Script, or Papyrus). The fonts you select must be legible and easy to read. If your overly stylized font looks spiffy but is very difficult to read, your message will not be read. Exotic fonts such as gothic scripts, handwriting, and fantasy fonts will overwhelm your work.

Text Size and Color
Next, consider the size of the text (see Box 7.4). Set a hierarchy for your text. Titles and dates should be one size; project descriptions another size. Titles work best at a slightly larger size, such as 14 or 16 point; other text a bit smaller (Mitton 2004). Do not go smaller than 10 point. It's a fact of life: older eyes need larger text. But bigger is not necessarily better. If you have a font that is still difficult to read even after you enlarge it, it's not any better. It's just bigger. Ultimately, know your audience and plan accordingly.

Often overlooked is the color of your text. Pay heed to this when selecting your portfolio's color palette. Most likely, you will use black text. Therefore, the more text you have on your pages, the more dominant black will be in your final layout design. As shown in most of the text in Figure 7.23, text that is similar in value to the background color of your pages will disappear. You must have enough color contrast for the text to be legible. In a recent batch of admission portfolios, I reviewed several that had illegible text. These included blue text on a black background, red text on a blue background, and black text on a dark background image.

PAPER

A printed portfolio obviously requires paper. There are a variety of papers you can use in constructing your portfolio pages and possibly the cover and case as well. Some papers come in pad forms, some in individual sheets. Some are letter size. Some are oversized. Some can be purchased at office supply stores, some at specialty art stores, some online. Experiment with these different types of paper to determine what you like and what works best for the intent of your design.

People seldom see the halting and painful steps by which the most insignificant success is achieved.
Anne Sullivan

The dictionary is the only place where success comes before work.
Mark Twain

There is only one success - to be able to spend your life in your own way.
Christopher Morley

It takes 20 years to make an overnight success.
Eddie Cantor

One's best success comes after their greatest disappointments.
Henry Ward Beecher

Success seems to be largely a matter of hanging on after others have let go.
William Feather

Success usually comes to those who are too busy to be looking for it.
Henry David Thoreau

People rarely succeed unless they have fun in what they are doing.
Dale Carnegie

7.23
The text within the two purple boxes is the most visible. All other text is too close in value to its background color to be clearly read. Illustration courtesy of Amol Surve.

For mounting your work, use durable paper with a heavier weight than typical office paper. If your portfolio is impressive, it may be passed around the office. Select a sturdy paper that can handle this abuse, paper that won't get messy and torn from wear. Ninety- or 110-pound cardstock is not much more expensive than regular paper and comes in a variety of neutral colors. It takes color from a laser printer well and can be sent through a copier. Remember that ink-jet printer ink smears. Wait until it dries completely before putting the page into the book sleeve. (Yes, I've seen images smeared because someone was running late and was too impatient to wait.)

Some paper will start to yellow in as little as a few weeks. Purchase acid-free paper, which is paper made from pulp with almost no acid added to it. It will resist deterioration. Also called alkaline paper or neutral pH paper, it is an option available in a variety of papers and boards.

When purchasing your supplies, remember to buy extra. You will add more information to your portfolio later and you'll need to repair it if it becomes damaged. Having extra paper supplies on hand will save you time and effort trying to add or mend pages later. Moreover, paper products show slight variations in color by batch. Buy more than enough of the same batch to ensure you will have an ample supply of the same color paper later. An everyday 20-pound paper at a brightness of 92 is acceptable for regular copies. For the needs of your portfolio, it is suggested you use at least a 32-pound paper at a brightness of 98 (Marquand 1994). The colors of your work will really jump out on high-quality paper.

Types of Paper and Boards

Different types of commonly used paper in our design disciplines include Bristol board, watercolor paper, chipboard, illustration board, poster board, foam core, mat board, linen paper, vellum, and bond paper. There are many other types of papers, as well—too many to include in this writing. I'll review some characteristics of these popular materials to give you an idea of what they are used for (and when they should *not* be used).

Most design work is executed on white paper such as vellum or bond paper. Vellum is a translucent paper used for presentation drawings. Pencil, pen, and colored markers flow across either side of this paper. Vellum is usually mounted against another sheet of paper because it appears hazy. You could even place this against other decorative paper with color or texture. If you plan on printing your work directly onto vellum, purchase photographic quality vellum, as shown in Figure 7.24. It is a heavier weight and will survive the trip through a laser printer.

Bond paper is a type of business paper commonly used for writing, printing, and photocopying. It's what you probably call copy or printer paper. It is strong and durable, consisting of wood, cotton, or both. This may be a good choice for book portfolios where you slip the pages into plastic sleeves. If not using sleeves, use cardstock. It will survive the wear and tear of use much better. This is the best choice for presentation book portfolios, such as the one in Figure 7.25.

Bristol board is similar to vellum in its smoothness but heavier in its weight. This thin paperboard is made of cotton fiber and is suitable for writing, drawing, and printing. Another heavy paper is watercolor paper. It can have a smooth or slightly rough surface. Watercolor paper is a good choice if you prefer textured cream or white paper. It is durable, standing up to frequent handling, and comes in a multitude of styles, weights, and textures. However, it is not suited for direct printing or copying.

Linen paper is a high-quality paper made of linen fibers. It is a good choice for resumes and other written materials. Because of its fine texture, it can serve as a

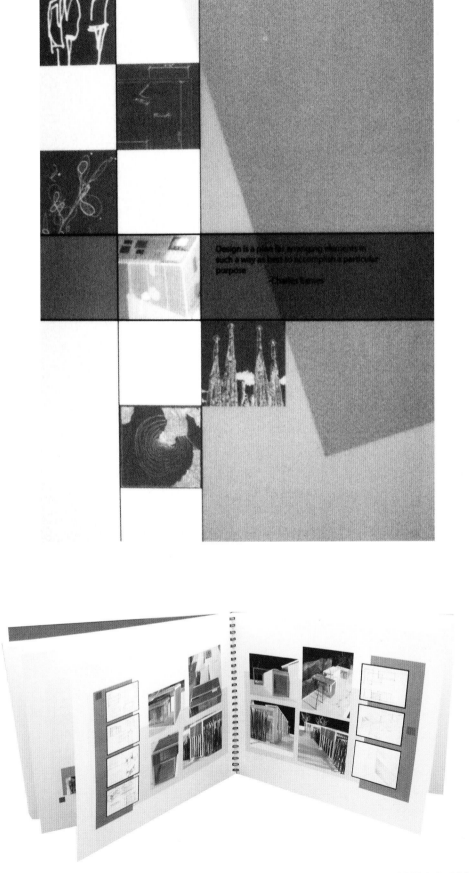

LEFT: 7.24
Photographic vellum is heavier than regular vellum and can be run through a laser printer. This type of paper gives you a translucent surface with which to experiment, as shown in this example with darker paper beneath. Design work courtesy of Cindy Louie.

BELOW: 7.25
Cardstock is stiff paper that works exceptionally well in bound portfolios. Design work courtesy of Jeffrey Lothner.

7.26
**Small amounts of
textured paper can
enhance your printed
pages, introducing
tactile qualities into
an otherwise smooth-
surface portfolio.
Design work courtesy
of Hayley Johnson.**

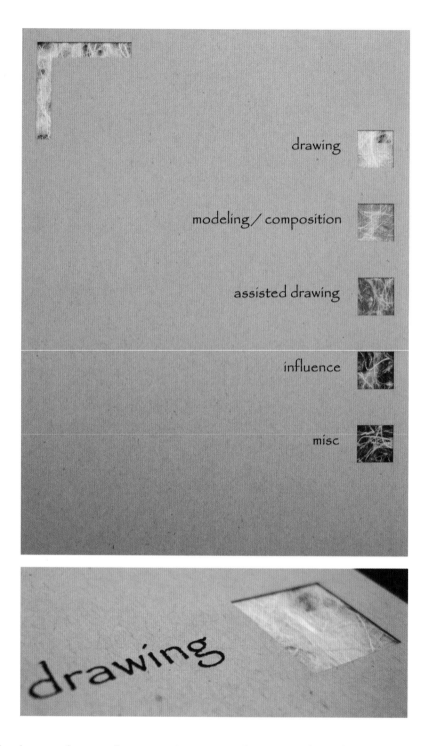

nice background paper for mounting your other printed work. Background and accent papers include decorative papers, which come in a wide variety of textures and colors. Design projects are seldom executed on decorative paper, because it has too much of a novelty impact (e.g., shiny, corrugated, floral, and so on). Be careful about over-emphasizing the background paper. You do not want to take away from your design work by overpowering it with the background paper (see Figure 7.26).

Boards are also available that are heavier in weight and more durable than other paper stocks. These are good choices for the front and back covers of your portfolio. Although you can create all your pages with boards, the sheer weight of your portfolio would discourage anyone from picking it up. Illustration board is a sheet of cardboard with a sheet of drawing paper mounted on one side. Illustration boards are mostly used by commercial artists and come in both cold and hot press varieties. Cold press has a slightly textured surface, while hot press can have a super-smooth, acid-free surface.

Thicker boards include foam core and mat board. Foam core board has a layer of plastic foam sandwiched between two layers of paper. It is available in a variety of sizes and thicknesses (typically 3/16"). It is limited in color to black or white. It is commonly used to mount photographs and display materials because it is so lightweight. This is a good choice for a plate portfolio, along with mat board. Mat board is a 1/8" thick fiberboard used to mount artwork or frame pictures. It comes in a variety of colors and is commonly sold in large sheets. You can use it to enhance and showcase your work by framing it inside cut windows.

Keep in mind that the core of mat board is often white or cream. Use mounting board if you want the same color throughout the board. As shown in Figure 7.27, it has the same look and consistency as mat board, but with a solid color on one side through the core to the other side. The only limitation is that it is available only in black and white. As mat board weighs more than foam core, it may be the best choice for a sturdy cover of unique design but not for the inside pages.

Don't forget the back of your pages. Many new designers focus all their attention on the front of their portfolio pages and completely neglect the back. When

7.27
Mounting board works well for framing work in a plate portfolio because the beveled edge is the same color as the rest of the board.

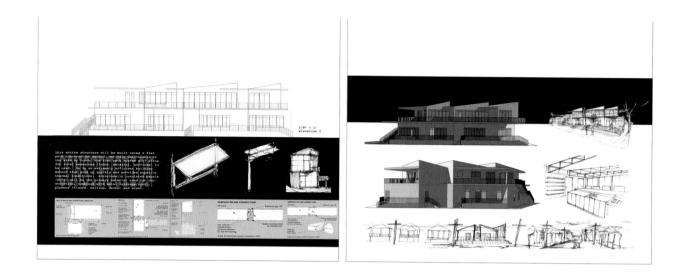

7.28
Reviewers expect to turn a page in your book portfolio and see work on the back. Avoid blank pages unless absolutely necessary.
Design work courtesy of Daniel Childers.

your portfolio is being reviewed, particularly if it is in a book format, the reviewer will flip through your pages and will certainly see the backs of the pages. Frugally use both sides of the page with different projects or images of the same project, as in Figure 7.28.

And do not forget the *very* last page. This last page needs something, even if it is a blank sheet of your background paper. Reviewers do not want to see the back of your photo paper with the manufacturer's name all over it.

Paper Color

From the previous chapter, it is clear that there is much to know about color. You may be wondering, "What color would be best for the background of my projects?" You want to choose a background color that is visually appealing, yet won't overwhelm your work. Black, white, and gray provide wonderful background environments on which to present your work. These are considered neutral viewing surfaces. Each has its own benefits. Black hides marks and smudges (especially fingerprints), adds a sense of drama, and is the most forceful and dramatic (see Figure 7.29).

White can be dramatic, too, providing wonderful contrast if the majority of your work is dark. Gray is not as shocking as either black or white. A warm gray is inviting and pleasant while a cool gray is cleaner and more sterile. The value of a gray may influence the colors in your work. Other neutral alternatives include cream, ivory, and beige. These alternatives are natural and convey a sense of value and worth in your portfolio.

Printing directly on colored paper will alter the colors of your images. A black-and-white line drawing should appear black and white. For example, the line drawing in Figure 7.30 is displayed as black lines on a white background, with a color surrounding it. It is best to apply any color in your layout software around the images with their white backgrounds.

LEFT: 7.29
Black is a popular background color as it adds a sense of drama to your work. If most of your work is dark in color, stick with a lighter background to provide contrast. Design work courtesy of Aaron J. Kulik.

BELOW: 7.30
Stick with a white background for your work and use color around your images.

Look at your printed portfolio under different lighting conditions. What looked great in your bedroom under an incandescent light source may look terrible in an office environment under fluorescent lights. In addition, papers with a glossy finish can be reflective like a mirror. Without light, you would never notice the gloss. With light, a page with this type of finish can look completely different. It can also make reviewing difficult, as light is bouncing off the page (see Figure 7.31).

When my colleagues and I were last reviewing admission portfolios, we kept noticing the same dull, olive green background paper used in many of the portfolios. We were wondering why we kept seeing this same colored paper over and over again. Then someone mentioned that the purchased portfolio books *came* with that paper. Many of our students just kept that very unattractive background paper in their portfolio because it was there. The color of your background *does* have an impact on how your work is perceived. A small stack of paper in a better color (not dull, olive green) is worth the price in order to offset your work. You want the reviewer to look at your work—not your background paper.

As you can tell, how you display a project in your portfolio can be influenced by the color of the background, the colors of the other projects surrounding it, and what is visible on the back of your pages. Experiment with various backgrounds and color combinations before deciding what works best for your design intent. One student applying to our program used a bright red background paper. I couldn't figure out why the student would use this obnoxious color. Did it have something to do with her theme? No. Her design philosophy? No. All of the admission portfolios are reviewed anonymously, but when a colleague of mine

MATTE   SEMI-GLOSS

GLOSSY

7.31
Matte finish paper is a better choice than gloss paper to avoid glare.

later found out whose portfolio is was, she asked the student, "Why red?" The reply was, "I like red." Liking a color is not enough. In this case, the portfolio was not as strong as it could have been and weakened the student's chances of getting into the program. Please think of the reviewers and what their eyes will see. Remember that color can be used to energize, inspire, subdue, or agitate. Select your colors wisely.

PORTFOLIO CASES

There are several considerations when choosing your portfolio case, such as its presentation format, size, style, and how you plan to use it. This section will discuss these considerations and provide some visual examples. We all know that fashion is fleeting. What is popular today may not be popular tomorrow. Therefore, I am presenting only a few commercially available portfolio books and cases. Search online or check your local art supply store for more options.

Presentation Formats

A traditional printed portfolio can be presented in several formats. These include plate, book, and easel portfolio formats. Each has its unique advantages and disadvantages. One is no better than the others. You will need to determine which format best suits your individual needs. You may even decide to use multiple formats or a combination of several designed into one presentation. You can then decide if you'd like to showcase your work inside a purchased or handcrafted case.

Plate Portfolio

A plate portfolio consists of your work mounted on individual boards. You can rearrange your plates any way you deem necessary, allowing you to customize the presentation. A plate portfolio provides the flexibility to choose the pieces you want to include, in the order you want. An unusual benefit of a plate portfolio is that matted board invites the reviewer not only to see your work but to touch and feel it as well. This engages yet another human sense. Unfortunately, unbound portfolios can be difficult to manage and keep organized. It is essential to number and put an identification tag on the back of each plate.

You have several options for presenting your work: illustration, mat, mounting, or foam core board. You can either mount your work on the front, or cut a bevel-edge window into the front and place your work behind it. To keep the edges intact, trim them with vinyl adhesive tape (preferably in the same color as your board). You may think foam core board provides the best advantage because it is so lightweight. But its biggest disadvantage is the $\frac{3}{16}$" thickness, which makes a 20-piece portfolio about 4 inches thick. You may need to get a larger portfolio case or show fewer pieces.

A plate portfolio can include full-size 24" × 36" presentation boards. It is more likely to be smaller, like the 8.5" × 11" plates in Figure 7.32. Here are some tips for cutting your boards: Always work on the backside. Carefully mark the measurement

RIGHT: 7.32
A plate portfolio contains your work mounted on mat, mounting, or foam core boards. Artists and graphic designers use this type of portfolio more often than landscape architects, interior designers, and architects.

BELOW: 7.33
A book portfolio can have a unique cover made of various materials, such as paper, boards, leather, or even cork.

in three locations, then line up your cutting edge with at least two of the marks. Use a sharp blade in your cutting instrument. Cut on a rubberized mat, a spare piece of cardboard, or even another board. (Cutting on your dorm room carpet or on your roommate's coffee table is not suggested.) Keep your blade straight and perpendicular to the board. Press evenly and firmly to cut through the board in one stroke. If the board is thick, score the cut line by making several passes along the same line. Ensure the cut has gone through the entire board *before* trying to pull apart your pieces. Lastly, smooth down the edges and corners using some fine sandpaper. If you are cutting windows into your board and the inner corners are rough, try using a four-sided nail-filing block.

Occasionally, you may wish to show your original work in its original format. (This depends on the purpose of the portfolio and the audience.) A laminated portfolio is a type of plate portfolio that includes your original pieces mounted on board or cardstock and then laminated with transparent film at a commercial establishment.

Book Portfolio

A book portfolio is the most popular format that uses a binding system to secure your pages in place. Because it reads like a book, little explanation is required to guide the reviewer. As shown in Figure 7.33, most book portfolios are small in format, as a larger one would have pages that were too big and awkward to turn.

Book portfolios obviously do not show your original work, such as large presentation boards and 3-D models. These portfolios are created digitally and then printed on paper, which means the images are one step away from the original. The experience is different for the viewer, as he cannot touch your paper, material samples, or 3-D work (see Figure 7.34).

Bound presentation books are available. These have a plastic cover and are filled with many polypropylene sleeves. The binding style is book bound, as pages are stitched right into the binding. You cannot add pages. You can subtract (permanently) by cutting extra pages out of the binding. These are typically used for academic portfolios.

The focus should be on your work and not on your binding system. It is best if a book portfolio can lay flat with a wire or plastic coil binding. Avoid plastic comb bindings like the one in Figure 7.35, because the pages catch on the teeth.

BELOW TOP: 7.34 A book portfolio created electronically demands all hand-drawn work to be scanned, all 3-D models to be photographed, and all electronic imagery to be merged into one software application. Design work courtesy of Jeremy Gates.

BELOW BOTTOM: 7.35 A comb binding like this is not recommended, as paper will catch on the individual teeth.

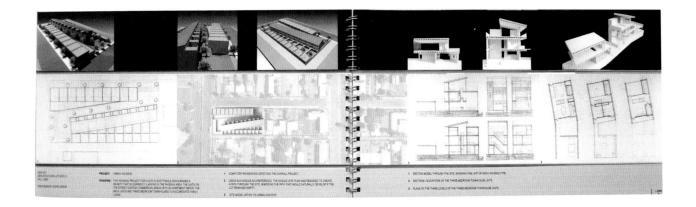

RIGHT: 7.36
Binders and folders such as these are great for class papers and organizing your notes. But they do not convey the professional tone you are seeking to present in a portfolio.

BELOW: 7.37
A screw-post binder is often metal. The page sleeves are drawn together with a small metal post that you literally screw into the case backing. Design work courtesy of Elaine Hu.

Especially, steer clear of cheap plastic covers and office binders like those shown in Figure 7.36. These scream "student." This type of simple binder is good for submitting a term paper but is not good enough for a professional portfolio. Among the several types of binders deemed durable enough to hold your portfolio pages are ring, toothed, and screw-post binder systems.

Ring binders use rings as pivot points. Three-ring binders should be avoided at all costs. The polypropylene sleeves used in three-ring binders noticeably only have three holes. Every time you turn a page, you are putting stress on one of

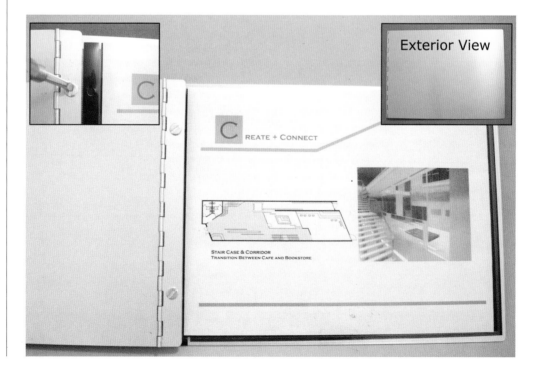

those holes. In time, the holes will tear and rip. In addition, the metal clasp of the binder rarely closes properly. Tooth systems have a ring every ½" to hold the pages more securely in place. Occasionally, a page may get hung up on the rings, yet it is more stable than a three-ring binder.

Screw-post binders like the one in Figure 7.37 requires pages to be added or removed with a screwdriver. It is relatively easy to switch out pages, and the pages are certainly secure in the book. You can purchase extenders, which are ½" metal tubes that allow you to put more pages inside.

Another trendy binding method is a wire binding. Also known as a coil or spiral binding, this type of binding permanently fastens your pages together. The wires fit inside holes created in your cover and pages as shown in Figure 7.38. The loops are pinched to securely hold the wire. The biggest advantage of wire binding is it allows the portfolio to lay flat when open.

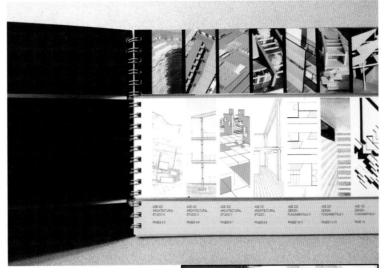

Easel Portfolio

An easel portfolio is another type of book portfolio that turns the case into the stand for presentation. This puts the work in a comfortable, upright position for viewing, keeping your hands free during an interview. The book itself attaches to the easel case with a ring or screw-post fastening system (see Figure 7.39).

ABOVE: 7.38
A wire binding permanently gathers your pages together. This cover is different in that it is a sheet of Mylar sandwiched between two pieces of black cardstock, with openings created to showcase the Mylar. Design work courtesy of Jeremy Gates.

LEFT: 7.39
An easel portfolio is like a book portfolio, but it has a stand that flips out so you can present your work during an interview to more than one person. Design work courtesy of Lauren Maitha and Lindsay Miller.

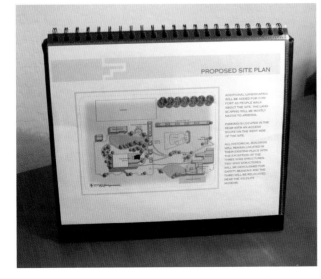

Most easel portfolios allow you to display your work only in portrait format or landscape format, but not both. Others are square and can present work in both directions. Expensive easels have an integrated stand and are exceptionally stable when sitting on a desk. Less-expensive easel binders are used for business presentations. They are cheap and look like it. It is difficult to maneuver the little easel tab to pop out behind your book, and they are not as stable as the portfolios with an integrated easel stand.

Page Inserts and Sleeves

The popular book format allows you the option of permanently binding the pages together. This is known as a one-off or single-edition book, and it allows you create and bind specifically for one interview or one academic program (see Figure 7.40).

There is one major drawback to a permanently bound portfolio—it lacks flexibility. Once the projects are bound together, there is no way to take them apart without sacrificing the entire portfolio. For example, I am aware of a student who sought an internship in Barcelona. She knew the firm's specialty area and created the one-off book shown in Figure 7.41, a collection of her work presented expressly for them. This was feasible considering the availability of personal computers and high-end printers. The expense is going down as the available technology continues to rise.

7.40
This single-edition concept booklet has only six pages of individually cut cardstock.
Design work courtesy of Julia Kancius and Allison Saunders.

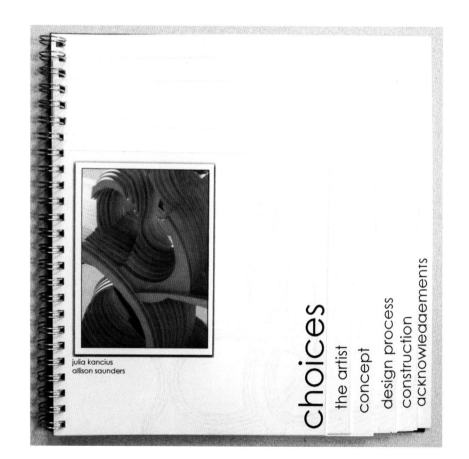

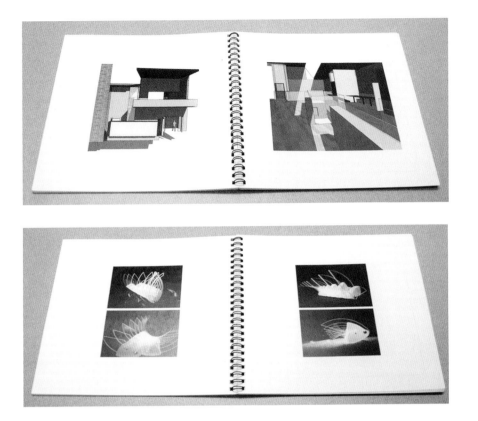

LEFT: 7.41
A single-edition book allows you to tailor your presentation to one firm or one school. Design work courtesy of Ellen Barten.

BELOW: 7.42
Page inserts or sleeves allow you to reuse a professional portfolio book by swapping the drawings.

Instead of a permanent binding, many designers use page inserts for maximum flexibility. Page inserts are transparent jackets or sleeves that hold your work in place (see Figure 7.42). These sleeves are usually secure on the sides, and your work is loaded from the top. They must be slightly larger than the work you will put inside. Secure your work to the sleeves with small pieces of double-sided tape so the pages will not slide around, or worse, fall out.

You can purchase sleeves in acetate, Mylar, vinyl, or polypropylene. Depending on the work you will present, one type of insert will work best for you. Acetate functions best with thin inserts but will become scratched and worn with heavy use. It will yellow and become dull over time. There may also be some warping due to heat and humidity. Mylar is the trade name for a type of polyester (polyethylene terephthalate) known for its high tensile strength and stability. It is commonly used in museums and libraries for protecting stored artifacts. Unfortunately, Mylar is stiff and rips with rough handling. Acetate and Mylar sleeves can be shiny. Add this to the white background you may have selected for your paper and the result will be extreme glare. Either change the sleeve or change your choice of paper to reduce this glare.

Vinyl sleeves are softer and more flexible than other sleeves. Vinyl is better at dealing with heat and humidity and is the clearest of all sleeves. But it is heavy. The sleeve may cling to your work samples, even possibly lifting portions of your design right off the page. Here's a helpful hint: To keep the sleeves from sticking together, try rubbing them with a fabric softener dryer sheet. This dryer sheet will also pick up lint and dust from the page.

Polypropylene sleeves are lightweight and the most flexible of all sleeves, being durable, stable, and tear resistant. There may be several other types of sleeves and inserts available, as new advances in synthetic resin technology bring more products to market. Keep your options open. The portfolio format you use today may not be the one you will use three years from now.

Selecting the Case

An important portfolio decision is the selection of the case. There are several aspects to consider when selecting a case, such as its size, appearance, and transportability. Each option must be weighed against the others. If you plan to carry your portfolio around a metropolitan area, a lightweight case may be more important than durability. If you are shipping your portfolio around the world, its ability to easily fit in a standard shipping container will save you money. Look online for product and vendors, such as RT Innovations and Portfolios-and-Art-Cases.

A good portfolio case should last throughout your design career. You should tire of it before it wears out. This case must be tough; able to resist water, punctures, and scratches; and sturdy enough to withstand frequent handling. Carefully examine the case before you purchase it. Consider the durability of the hinges, interior pockets, corners, zipper or other closure, finish, and other features. For example, an aluminum case is durable and well built (see Figure 7.43). It makes a strong impression. It also must be lightweight enough for you to carry around and small enough for the interviewer to easily handle during an interview. Sounds like a tall order to fill, doesn't it?

You may think that you do not need a case, that you can throw your work into a backpack and show up for an interview. This might not be a good idea. Your case provides a container to protect your plates or book and is another part of your professional presentation. Think of the opening of your case as a dramatic event. It's like opening a birthday present. We all like gifts, but gifts that are beautifully wrapped are more fun to open. Have you ever opened a large wrapped box, to find another smaller box inside, and another box inside that? Think of the drama this added to the experience and how your anticipation increased as you closed in on the prize. Your portfolio in its case can be the same way. Your work is the prize and the case is the elegant wrapping.

Case Size and Style

We discussed the sizes of your projects earlier in this chapter. The size of the case should be big enough to hold your largest project with a little extra room inside. You do not want the case to fit so tightly around your projects that you ruin your boards because the zipper gets stuck at the corners. Likewise, if your design book is thick, be sure the case properly closes. Your case must be larger than your work, yet snug enough so everything inside doesn't slide around and get banged up. Consider using a piece of foam to tuck smaller pieces into a larger case.

Measure the dimensions of the case before you buy it. The *interior* dimensions are most important, because you want your portfolio plates or book to fit *inside*. If you are purchasing the case online, seek out the interior dimensions before purchasing, even if you have to call the manufacturer's customer service number to get this information.

There is no *one* case size that is optimal—no perfect size. Some people prefer a larger case, while others like a smaller one. There are advantages and disadvantages to both. A large case will give you space around each piece. The key is to put your work inside the case without folding it. The work should not be stuffed tightly together or appear crowded. You want to convey the impression that it is very important work. A large case will also give you more flexibility in terms of the content you present to others, such as a materials board, sketchbook, and 11" × 17" book format portfolio.

On the other hand, cases that are too big may be difficult to handle in an interview. It is common to be asked to open your case and present your portfolio right on someone's desk. You may end up tipping over the coffee sitting on the interviewer's desk! Moreover, a case that is much larger than your work will jostle your work around, damaging corners and edges of boards and books.

Therefore, the current trend is moving from large portfolio cases to smaller ones (Hungerland and Hungerland 2002). Presenting smaller work makes the

8.5" × 11"

7.44
If your design work tends to be larger than traditional letter size, opt for a larger portfolio, like the 11" × 17" books shown here.

viewing experience more intimate and personal. Larger 11" × 17" portfolios like the ones in Figure 7.44 are an optimum size. They can be transported easily, mailed in a standard size box, and presented right on the practitioner's desk during an interview. A letter-size case is easy to carry but will only showcase smaller work.

What if you want to buy the case while in school but don't know the sizes of future projects? Do you purchase the case before you have a pile of work to put in it? Or do you accumulate your work and then see which case fits best? There are no right or wrong answers to these questions. Most students begin assembling their work into a portfolio book and case after two years of education. It may be worth waiting to purchase a case until you have compiled several pieces of work. You can then purchase one that fits the majority of that work.

Typical case sizes are 11" × 14", 18" × 24", and 24" × 36". You may have to seek out the size case you truly desire and have it made specifically for you, as a special order. If you really are set on a particular yet unusual size, do not settle for something standard. Purchase a special-order case. Made-to-order cases available from bookbinders and other companies are worth considering. Give yourself enough time in your planning to have the case delivered.

The look or style of your case speaks volumes. Cases come in a variety of colors, although black is traditionally favored (see Figure 7.45). Cases can be aluminum, vinyl, leather, cloth, wood, canvas, or whatever resource you desire. Think about the durability of your case. For example, vinyl cases are the least expensive but also the least durable. Leather is more expensive but will last you for years. Other materials such as cloth and wood can be used to create an interesting, one-of-a-kind appearance. But will they last? Are they easy to transport and carry? The color, material, finish, and details of your case will all be scrutinized in an interview situation just like your clothing and shoes.

Pockets created on any of your presentation boards for odd-sized work (such as brochures or booklets) will bend and break in time (Scher 1992). This gives your portfolio an unkempt appearance. Many portfolio cases and binders come with pockets on the inside covers to hold these types of items (plus some extra resumes). Some cases even include a few special pages to store your digital portfolio CDs. Keep in mind that this information can slip out as the pockets stretch with wear and use.

Put an identification tag on both the outside and the inside of your portfolio. Laminate your business card or other form of identification to the inside of your

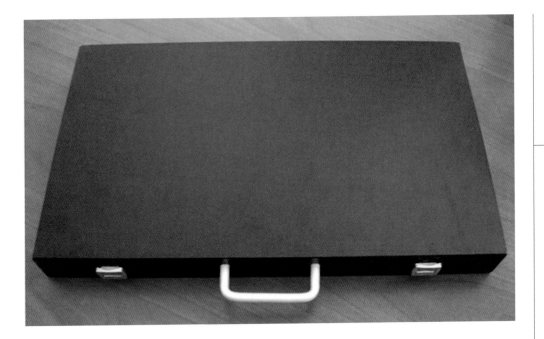

7.45
A black artist's case can hold your portfolio book, sketchbook, additional resumes, a pen, questions for an interviewer, and just about anything else you'd need at an interview.

case and make sure you include your name, phone number, and email address. Identification that cannot easily be removed is best. You can also create a stylish luggage tag that can be attached to the outside of your case with a leather strap, purchased in a local luggage store. If your portfolio case is valuable, you may even offer a reward for its return if you ever lose it.

Transportability

Your portfolio is a traveling document. It must be tough and durable, beautiful and creative, organized and easy to use . . . all at the same time! Another consideration when selecting your portfolio case is how you will transport it. Will it have a handle? Will you tuck it under your arm? A very large case or a portfolio with heavy plates inside may need to be transported on wheels. I would strongly suggest the case have comfortable handles because you never know how long you will need to carry it. A former student told me he went to interview for an internship in New York City. This was shortly after the tragedy of September 11, 2001. He took the subway into lower Manhattan and exited at what he thought was the correct station. Because of construction near the former Twin Towers, he could not walk directly to the office where he was expected for his interview. He ended up walking over a mile around the perimeter of the construction site, all the while carrying his portfolio case. Thankfully it had handles. Save yourself some blisters and buy a case with comfortable handles or even a shoulder strap that can free one of your hands. You never know if you will need one hand to hold an umbrella or open doors. I would also advise staying away from book-style portfolio cases without handles. These are very nice-looking vinyl or leather cases that store your book of sleeves (see Figure 7.46). The only problem is that they have no handles. People carry them around by holding them close to their body. One good bump from someone when you are in downtown pedestrian traffic and you could drop your portfolio, scattering your work all over the sidewalk or plaza.

If you need to send your printed portfolio for a review, determine what type of mailer it will require. You will need some space between your portfolio and the mailing case for cushioning. Or, select a mailing case that snugly fits around your portfolio so it cannot move during shipping. If the case is an unusual shape or excessively heavy, your shipping options will be limited. Keep this in mind when selecting your case. Another option is actually creating the mailing case for your portfolio. Again, this takes time and money. If you are sending your portfolio on CD, pack it carefully as a CD can break in the mail. Use a padded mailing pouch or a box with padding wrapped around the CD inside.

Additionally, do not assume a mailed portfolio will be returned. Specify if you want it back. If you do, figure out how much it will cost to have it sent back and include a self-addressed stamped envelope. A flat-rate mailing package measures 12" × 3.5" × 14". Check the full range of mailing package dimensions and rates at the United Postal Service website (http://www.usps.com), or any other delivery service web site. Keep in mind the weight of your case when shipping it. The cost of shipping a heavy portfolio can be quite staggering.

If you plan to travel by airplane, it would be best to bring it on the airplane as a carry-on item. Typical carry-on size is 16" × 10" × 24". Anything larger than this must be checked in as baggage. Do you trust the airlines to deliver your portfolio to your destination? What happens if you are flying to Denver but your portfolio ends up in Detroit? If the portfolio is very large or heavy, it may be subject to excess baggage fares. If traveling abroad, determine if it will clear customs and security screening. With increased security measures being taken internationally, your portfolio case may not even be allowed to be put on an airplane or transported through an airport. Check with the airlines for international restrictions on both size and security.

Purchased or Handcrafted

You have two options for acquiring a case. You can purchase one or you can make your own. Purchased cases may not be very original, but they convey a sense of professionalism and are readily available. Cases can be plain or fancy. Keep in mind that it is what's *inside* that really counts. The work you place inside must live up to the packaging (see Box 7.5).

The best way to know what sizes and formats are currently available is to visit your local art supply store or check various vendors over the Internet. Using the

7.46
A leather portfolio can be reused many times with page inserts inside. It will last longer than a vinyl or plastic book and looks more professional. Design work courtesy of Stuart Braiman.

Box 7.5

Internet will increase the options available to you, especially if you reside in a smaller town with fewer retail stores. (A case may be found when searching online under the word *portfolio*, but try *presentation cases, artisan albums, display easels*, and *art cases* as well.)

Price does play a factor. What can you afford? How often will you use it? If you can afford it, buy a nice case in leather or a sturdy aluminum one. If you remain in the design fields, you will use it throughout your professional years. Invest in a quality case. Torn and ripped cases, mangled pages, and split sleeves tell others that you do not care much about your work. The practitioners who interview you may then wonder if you will have the same disregard for client work. Invest in the best portfolio case you can afford.

Estimate how many portfolios you will need before purchasing. If you are applying for graduate school, you will not present your portfolio in person but will mail it to the school for review by an admissions committee. You will probably not get this portfolio back. If you select a case that is impressive yet extremely expensive, you will be investing a great deal into this process. Multiply this by the number of schools to which you are applying. How much are you willing to invest? Do you need a case at all or can you bind your work in a book format like that shown in Figure 7.47?

Instead of a purchased case, you have the opportunity to make your own hand-crafted case (see Figure 7.48). This will take more time yet will give your portfolio an air of distinction. Just like you would in a design project, do a mock-up or rough model before investing time and expense in the final construction. A hand-crafted portfolio can be a plus in your favor. It can also be a negative if it is poorly crafted, dirty, and falling apart. This is professional suicide. Use a sharp cutting instrument and the finest adhesive. This is not the time to skimp on supplies.

Quality products are wasted if they are used improperly. Bad craftsmanship reflects poorly on you as a designer. Spray adhesive, glue stick, and rubber cement are not recommended. In time, drawings will peel off your boards, and it also causes vellum and paper to yellow. Use dry mounting instead, in which heat is

RIGHT: 7.47
If you plan to mail your admission portfolio to several schools, you may want to create a single-edition book instead of investing money in a case that may never be returned to you. Design work courtesy of Charudatta Joshi.

BELOW: 7.48
You also have the option of creating an innovative presentation system like this portfolio of square pages inside a handmade acrylic case. Design work courtesy of Julian Sin.

used to bond one surface to another. This can be expensive yet is resistant to abuse. (The difficulty may be finding a dry mounting machine.) Another popular option is StudioTac, which is a smooth, dry adhesive sold in sheets. You position the little white dots on your work and on the mounting surface and then adhere them together. They are acid-free and won't bleed through your sheets. StudioTac even comes in a super-strength version that you can use to attach heavier materials or 3-D objects to your boards.

A handcrafted portfolio case that is difficult to open is worthless. The practitioner may be very impressed with your inventive case design until he realizes he cannot get it open or figure out in which direction to begin viewing your portfolio. It is best to avoid frustrating the reviewer before he has even seen a single piece of your work. Make the case simple to open and browse.

The same can be said for the organization of the contents. How can someone reassemble your work *back* in your case if you are not there to do it? Complex inserts and pieces will confuse and frustrate the reviewer. Your work must be trouble-free and instinctive to reassemble. I recall looking at a unique portfolio case submitted by a prospective graduate student. The pieces inside were interesting (CD, resume, letters of recommendation, work samples) but it took me some time to figure out how to get it all back in the right order. As another professor had previously reviewed it, it's likely I didn't even see it as the student originally intended. Someone else must have struggled with the repackaging before me.

CONCLUSION

It is clear there are many considerations when constructing your printed portfolio. Decisions must be made that range from the minuscule details of layout and text to larger issues of paper selection and case. All of these choices will influence how others perceive your work. There are no right or wrong choices. But the decisions you make reflect your pride and investment in your work and ultimately in your future. Think carefully before jumping into portfolio construction. In the following chapter, we will begin our discussion of the digital computer by reviewing the technology you may need to produce a digital portfolio.

THE DIGITAL PORTFOLIO

8

Digital Portfolio Production Tools

As design professionals, media are pushed in our faces every minute of every day. We are experiencing information overload. With this plethora of information, we are becoming far more critical of the information that is placed in front of our eyes than ever before. This contributes to the need for your digital portfolio to be top-notch. If it's not, it will be viewed as more unnecessary noise in the usual barrage of information. As designers we need to make a good impression with our visual presentation, and we have to do it quickly by grabbing the attention of the viewer.

Making that good impression means using the right tool for the right job. If a traditional medium achieves the best results, use it. If a computer can produce a better effect, use that. Remember that print portfolios have fewer obstacles. The reviewer can get right to the evaluation without dealing with technology. Several elements have an impact on how you construct your printed portfolio and how your images and pages are perceived. These include the type and size of paper, the type of printer, the resolution of the images and the printer, the type of image, and the levels of integration between the software applications you use and the printer. The quality of your digitally created portfolio will depend on what technology tools you use and how you use them. There are no standard hardware and software in our professions. We use whatever tool we need to get the job done. Therefore, you may be exposed to many applications and processes during the creation of your digital portfolio. This chapter will present various types of hardware that may be useful in creating your digital portfolio. Specific attention will be paid to the tools you'll need, such as multimedia computers, scanners, printers, digital cameras, and digital storage devices.

DESIGNERS AND COMPUTERS

As computer-aided design (CAD) is replacing drawing as a mode of communication, the essential work of architecture and design is being radically transformed. The designer's job description has been comprehensively transformed because of the digital revolution. We no longer work only in print. We work with a combination of media.

As designers, we use technology every day in our attempts to design places and spaces, and in our communication of those designs to others. The use of the Internet has revolutionized the design process. We are now able to read about new products, download material specifications, access code information, transfer CAD drawings from manufacturer's web sites into our own design projects, and even collaborate in real-time with colleagues in other time zones. (To download or upload means to send or receive an electronic file from a computer server.) Researchers surveyed 275 designers and found they use the Internet for communication, research, sharing resources, and providing information on products and services (Black and Waxman 2000). It is important for you to understand computers and digital media because you will continue to use technology in your fields to acquire online continuing education units (CEUs) throughout your career (Bender 2003; Pablo 1999). As a designer, you will use many computer graphics and presentation applications that will demand much from your computer. These applications require higher processing speed, more memory, accelerated video display cards, and higher resolution monitor displays.

Platforms: Windows and Macintosh

An operating system is the software that controls the fundamental functions of your computer. Operating systems in widespread use today include Windows 98/NT/XP, Macintosh OS X, and an assortment of UNIX systems, such as Linux, Solaris, and A/UX. The platform is the underlying system on which your applications run. Two major platforms are used today in industry: Windows and Macintosh. (Personal computers on the Windows platform are sometimes referred to as Wintel because they use a microprocessor manufactured by the Intel Corporation and run the Microsoft Windows operating system.) Most designers use a Windows or Macintosh platform. Some designers even use both platforms on a daily basis.

Although you may use one platform more than another, it's very important to understand *both* platforms and how your digital work will appear on each. For example, the system settings for image values are different. Macintosh machines tend to be darker than Windows machines. Macintosh and Windows systems also have different color palettes, making your portfolio's color combinations look different on either platform. A fabulous combination of colors on your Windows system may look dull and lifeless on a Macintosh. Or a subtle background color on a Macintosh may be glaring on a PC. Platform differences will be discussed in several later chapters. For now, it's enough to know there are two commonly used system platforms.

COMPONENTS OF A MULTIMEDIA COMPUTER

The computer you use is a significant factor in the creation of your digital portfolio. The decisions you make if purchasing a new computer or using an existing one will determine what kind of software applications you can use, how many you can use at the same time, how long it will take to do certain tasks, and what types of other components you can use, like scanners and speakers. Know what kind of processor, speed, amount of memory, and hard drive space are available on your computer. When you purchase software, check the side panel on the box to determine the hardware requirements necessary to successfully run the software.

Processor

Like blood pumping through your veins, the processor is the heart of your computer. It is also known as the central processing unit (CPU). It includes all the circuitry and the processing chip to handle high-speed computations. Without the CPU, the computer will not work. (This is the same as if your heart stopped beating.) Your processor determines how fast information is understood and exchanged with the rest of your computer and its peripheral devices. Processor speed is measured in megahertz or gigahertz. Every year, processor speeds increase. They range from 3.2 gigahertz on up. You are probably most familiar with the processor being called by its brand name, such as Pentium, manufactured by the Intel Corporation. The higher the Pentium number, the better the quality. Just keep in mind that every year, the speeds increase.

Memory

In order for your computer to run, it must have space to work. This is called memory. Like your brain's memory, a computer's memory is its holding place for data and information. There are two forms of memory: RAM and ROM. Random-access memory (RAM) is your computer's short-term memory, its holding space for instructions and data. It's where the computer's CPU stores its operating system and the software that is currently in use. Information kept in this memory is more rapidly accessible to the computer than that stored on a hard drive, which makes your open software applications run faster. Every time you turn off your computer, the RAM is erased. On the other extreme, the built-in section of memory that contains basic instructions for allowing the computer to start or "boot" is known as read-only memory (ROM). This kind of memory is not erased when you turn off your computer. The hard drive is your computer's storage space for software programs, and files. Unlike RAM, the hard drive stores the long-term memory for your computer. It is usually measured in gigabytes (GB) or terabytes (TB). The more space that's available to you, the more programs and files you can store on your computer.

Memory is measured in data units. The smallest unit of digital data is called a bit, has a value of either zero or one, and is abbreviated as a lowercase b. A byte is a portion of digital data that is eight bits long and is abbreviated with a capital

B. Similar to the prefixes used in decimal measurements, a kilobyte (KB) is approximately one thousand bytes (1,024 to be exact), a megabyte (MB or a meg) is just over a million bytes, a gigabyte (GB or a gig) is 1,073,741,824 bytes, and a terabyte (TB) is approximately a thousand billion bytes (or a thousand gigabytes) (Cohen 2000). With the use of multimedia in your design projects, you will use up your computer's memory so fast, it will make your head spin.

Monitor and Video Card

A monitor shows all images generated by a computer and processed by a video graphics card. Different sizes are available, which are measured from corner to corner. Standard sizes are 15", 17", 19", 21", and so on. Monitor resolution is the basic measurement of the amount of information on the screen. This is defined by the product of two numbers, such as 480 × 640. The first number indicates the number of pixels down the screen vertically, the second, the number of pixels across the screen horizontally. The higher the resolution, the better, as higher-resolution screens allow you to display more details.

A video card is a circuit board mounted inside your computer that generates signals necessary to drive, or manage, a particular type of monitor. If you plan to do extensive 3-D graphics and image editing, you'll need a video card with a graphics accelerator, which has a dedicated video processor and RAM of its own. Several types of video memory are available so check your computer's specifications before purchasing video software.

Sound Card, Speakers, and Headset

Your computer may have some sort of sound system, composed of a sound card, speakers, and a microphone. A sound card is the device needed to accept audio input and produce audio output. It is a card installed in your computer that has

8.1
A headset keeps the microphone a consistent distance from your mouth when adding a monologue to your digital portfolio.

the ability to record and play back samples of digital audio. Speakers allow you to hear voice, music, and other sounds from your computer, generated by the sound card. Of course, if sound is not a necessary component of your portfolio, you can always do without speakers.

If you are planning to make audio recordings, you might consider purchasing a headset (see Figure 8.1). A headset includes an earpiece or headphones with a built-in microphone. It allows you to both listen and respond while leaving your hands free to work on the computer at the same time.

CD-ROM and DVD-ROM Drives

CD-ROM and DVD-ROM drives are the parts of the computer that allow you to record data onto various types of optical discs. CD-ROMs, or CDs, are optical storage discs and can hold more than 500 MB of data. These optical discs are recorded with laser technology and are used to store data, text, images, and music. They are becoming more inexpensive every day and can be purchased in bulk quantities at most office supply and electronic stores.

There are two types of discs: CD-R and CD-RW. A recordable compact disc (CD-R) is an inexpensive blank disc on which data can be stored. However, data on this type of disc cannot be erased and re-recorded. You can store data on it one time only (i.e., a read-only CD). The storage capacity of CD-R media is measured in minutes as well as in data capacity. Currently, there are two main CD capacities: 74 minutes (650 MB) and 80 minutes (700 MB).

A rewritable compact disc (CD-RW) is a type of CD to which you can write data multiple times. These discs support Universal Disc Format (UDF), which allows for read–write capabilities on Windows and Macintosh systems (i.e., a hybrid disc). However, the data on CD-RW discs may only be readable by CD-RW drives, and may even need the same software that was used to produce a disc in order to read it. They are also more expensive then CD-R discs.

Two types of CD drive are available, as well: one that reads data only (CD) and one that reads and writes data (CD-RW). Today, most software applications and data are distributed on CDs, so a CD drive is almost mandatory to have on your computer. In order to store data on a disc, the drive uses a laser to burn or etch data onto the CD. Among the many software applications obtainable to do this are Roxio's Easy CD Creator (see Figure 8.2), BurnatOnce, and NCH Express Burn. (New products are always coming on the market, so do your homework before selecting one. Some cost money; others can be downloaded for free.)

Another option for your digital media is to use a DVD-ROM, or DVD, which stands for digital versatile disc. A DVD recorder drive can record and read data from both a CD and a DVD. A DVD disc is the same size as a regular CD yet can hold far more data. DVDs can also be double-sided or dual layer. A DVD can handle more intensive graphic downloads and will run interactive multimedia presentations as well. A DVD can be viewed on either a Windows or Macintosh platform, and it can even be viewed through a DVD player connected to a television.

8.2
A special software application is necessary in order to "burn" data onto a CD.

**8.2
A special software application is necessary in order to "burn" data onto a CD.**

A DVD-R is similar to a CD-R, in that it is a write-once medium. It can store from 4.7 GB (single layer, single-sided) to 17 GB (double layer, double-sided). Like a CD-RW, a DVD-RW can be erased and rerecorded over and over again without being damaged. These are more expensive than one-time recordable DVDs. It is not suggested you burn your digital portfolio for distribution on DVDs. Although they will hold more information than a regular CD, not everyone's computer can read this type of disc.

Networks

Because digital portfolios can be reviewed over the Internet, it is important to understand connection speeds, or the quantity of data that can be relayed from one computer to another through a particular connection in a designated amount of time. Although more and more people are using a dedicated Internet connection that is always on, there are still those who continue to use a dial-up connection over an ordinary telephone line. A modem is a device that converts digital signals to analog and back again. Dial-up modems have a low bandwidth and are quickly being replaced by higher bandwidth connections, such as cable modems and integrated services digital network (ISDN) cards.

PERIPHERAL DEVICES

In addition to the components inside or attached directly to your computer, there are several peripheral devices you might use to create your portfolio. These include scanners, printers, digital cameras, and digital storage devices. You can purchase these items, rent them, or use ones available in your school's computer lab. These will probably be connected into Universal Serial Bus (USB) ports with USB cables. The nice feature of a USB port is the ability to plug and unplug a device while the computer is running because it will recognize that a device has been added or deleted (without having to reboot your system).

Scanners

The term *digitizing* refers to the process of scanning an image on a scanner or taking a digital photo and converting analog information into digital information. A scanner is a peripheral device necessary to capture an image off paper and convert it into digital media (see Figure 8.3).

A high-quality scanner is better than a low-quality one. It will render colors better, provides an image preview faster, and comes with software that has features that will save you time when editing photos in other software later. Different types of scanners include flatbed, sheet-fed, slide, transparency, and portable. Each has its own advantages and disadvantages.

I find that a flatbed scanner is the most useful because material sitting on it can be three-dimensional (3-D), like a design model. Flatbed scanners are not as fragile as portable scanners and have more versatility than photo and sheet-fed scanners. They come in several sizes, such as 8.5" × 11", 11" × 17", and so on. Large flatbed scanners are great for digitizing large drafting sheets or oversized presentation boards. You can have this kind of work scanned at copy centers or commercial printing companies because it is *not* economical to buy one of these yourself.

8.3
Scanners are used to transform something on paper into electronic data. Scanners come in a variety of types, sizes, styles, and brands.

Resolution is as important for scanners as it is for monitors and printers. The quality of a scan is determined by its resolution, represented in dots per inch (dpi). Dpi is the number of dots on a printed page in a linear inch. A high dpi will give you a high resolution, which results in a crisp, clear image. (We'll learn more about image resolution shortly.) For example, there are 600 dots horizontally and 600 dots vertically for 600 dpi resolution. This gives you 360,000 dots per square inch, resulting in a sharp image. Keep in mind that scanner, monitor, and printer resolutions are all interrelated. If you scan a photo at a low resolution (e.g., 150 dpi), make adjustments to it on a monitor with 72 dpi, and then try to print it at 1,200 points per inch (ppi), your image will look terrible. Ppi is the number of pixels on a screen in a linear inch. We'll discuss scanning and printing tips for your design work a bit later, too. For now, know that images should be a high-resolution *dpi*, which needs to be printed at a high-resolution *ppi*. (The terms *dpi* and *ppi* are often used interchangeably, even though they do have distinct meanings.)

Every scanner has a color capacity. A scanner is programmed to distinguish between various colors and shades in the original scanned document. Scanners always produce raster images, in which a bit depth number represents each pixel. This tells how many colors an image can hold. The higher the bit depth, the more colors can be represented. For example, a 24-bit color scanner gives you 16.7 million possible color definitions (Kilbane and Milman 2003). We cannot even distinguish that many variations, much less find a printer that can print them.

Lastly, scanners need software. When you purchase a scanner, you will get compatible software to connect it to your computer. Most scanner software has basic capabilities for modifying an image, such as brightness and contrast, resolution, color adjusting, cropping, and rotating. Advanced image editing will require software such as Adobe Photoshop. Tips for editing your images are provided in Chapter 10.

Printers

In order to have others see your digital work on paper, you'll need to print it. Printing directly from a digital copy (rather than a photograph or slide) is known as digital printing. Primarily two types of printing are widely used today: ink-jet printing and electrophotographic printing (otherwise known as laser printing).

Ink-jet printing is a type of inexpensive printing in which the ink is literally sprayed onto the sheet through a series of little nozzles in the printer. Most ink-jet printers have four cartridges to spray the ink: cyan, magenta, yellow, and black. This is the printing mode of CMYK.

Resolution is significant in determining the quality of the printed page. Resolution for a printer refers to the number of ppi produced by the ink-jet or laser printer. Most printers have a minimum of 600 ppi, with some capable of producing photo-quality prints (provided that the image has adequate resolution to begin with). An ink-jet printer's resolution relies on a number of factors, such as the number of nozzles, the regularity of ink droplets, the position of the droplets, and the quality of the paper used for printing.

The other type of printer is an electrophotographic printer, or laser printer. (Because Hewlett-Packard is the pioneer in printer technology and LaserJet is one of its brand names, most people refer to electrophotographic printers as laser printers). The technology in these printers is similar that of copy machines, which produce high-quality text and graphics. Laser printers come with black ink only, or full CMYK color.

Use a laser printer for your printed portfolio! Although the resolution on many of today's ink-jet printers is very high, remember that the ink is simply laid on the paper whereas a laser printer burns the ink into the paper. Therefore, a print from a laser printer will not smear or smudge. Furthermore, prints from a laser printer will not fade in time, as ink-jet prints will. Colors from an ink-jet printer are generally not accurate for representing the original digital work. To maintain the quality of your prints, store them in a dark place (like a drawer or closet) and keep them out of direct sunlight. (This is also good advice for any unused paper supply as well.)

Digital Cameras

A digital image taken with a digital camera is a good way to preserve precious, often irreplaceable material. Advantages include the ability to control the resolution of the image right on the camera. Pictures can be seen immediately, so you can decide if you want to keep them on the camera's storage space or delete them. Digital pictures can be shared via email or printed like a traditional photo. Finally, because they are digital, pictures can be enhanced and improved digitally. Let's talk first about your camera's resolution.

Resolution

Resolution of images taken on digital cameras is measured in megapixels. A megapixel (MP) is a unit of measurement equal to one million pixels and indicates the number of pixels that can be captured by the camera's image sensor. The more pixels packed into an image, the sharper and more vivid it will be. A high-resolution camera will have a high megapixel number and will produce high-quality images. You should use a digital camera with at least three megapixel capability (or three million pixels), although more expensive cameras used by professional photographers are eight MP or higher. As a rule of thumb, a three MP file can make a photorealistic 11" × 14" print.

With the settings on your digital camera set to a high resolution, the pictures will download from your camera to your computer at a large size. You can reduce it later in your camera's software or in other image editing software. If you immediately reduce the image size on all of your photos (because then they will be smaller size files), you will have to increase them later if you want larger prints. This defeats the purpose of photographing with a high resolution in the first place.

Images can be saved in a variety of formats. A good suggestion is to save the file in an uncompressed format, known as RAW images. RAW is short for "raw data." The RAW file format contains untouched raw pixel information right from the camera, without any in-camera processing. A great advantage of RAW is that it postpones applying any image adjustment (such as color saturation or contrast) until you can get your hands on the image. These can be manipulated *before* the image is converted into 8-bits per channel and compressed into an image (McHugh 2005a).

Although RAW files sound appealing, there are several disadvantages, such as the extremely large file size. With these large file sizes, you cannot save as many images on your camera's memory card as you could with images of a lesser quality. And you need to find space on your computer to store them. You will be required to manually manipulate the photo. This takes time and patience. I would encourage you to seek more information regarding the RAW file format if you are serious about photography and wish to maximize your digital camera's image quality potential.

Storage Capacity

Digital cameras function very much like conventional cameras. Instead of capturing images on exposed film, information is stored on a portable storage device called a memory card. Sometimes referred to as flash cards or memory sticks, memory cards come in a variety of formats, shapes, and sizes. There are several formats of digital camera memory cards, such as a CompactFlash (CF), MultiMedia (MM), and Secure Digital (SD) card. The significant difference between them is physical size. A CompactFlash card is about the size of a matchbook, while both a MultiMedia and a Secure Digital card are much smaller, like a postage stamp. Check the type of card required for your camera and make sure you purchase that format of card. A 256MB memory card correlates to 256 megabytes of computer memory, 4G to four gigabytes of memory, and so on. This can be a drawback, as the number of pictures you can take is limited by the amount of memory on your camera's memory card. The highest-capacity memory card available today will shy in comparison to the cards of tomorrow. Upgrade to more memory when economically feasible.

Speed and Accessibility

One of the benefits of using a digital camera over a conventional camera is that there is no need to wait for your film to be processed and developed. (It's less expensive too as you're not paying for terrible photos.) A digital camera allows you to see in an instant whether the picture you just took is acceptable by viewing it in the camera's viewfinder. This is a small window on the back of the camera that shows your picture. Known as a liquid crystal display (LCD), it is a full-color display screen used on digital cameras to review pictures and menu information. Granted, the display screens are small and will not show every detail. But they are large enough for you to preview the pictures and delete the ones that are unsatisfactory. You can then reshoot until you are satisfied with the results.

One drawback can be the battery. Many digital camera batteries are special to your camera and are rechargeable. It would be worth the investment to purchase an additional battery pack for your camera. A number of times when I was out photographing one thing or another, my battery began losing its charge. With an additional battery, I could continue on. Some of the newer cameras will take regular batteries, although you will use these faster than a rechargeable one. Needless to say, buying, renting, or borrowing a digital camera to take photos for your portfolio is essential in today's technology-driven world.

DIGITAL STORAGE DEVICES

When you begin working on your digital portfolio, you will have some images and a few files of your work. The more you work on it, the more files you will have and the larger these files will become. If you get into any type of sound, video, or animation, you will have *very* large files and a *very* large problem— where do you store all this stuff? It is a good idea to occasionally store old or seldom-used files on an external storage device, freeing your computer's RAM. Storage devices are a means to back up and archive your data as well. It's not a question of *if* your system goes down, it's a question of *when*. Back up all your portfolio files frequently.

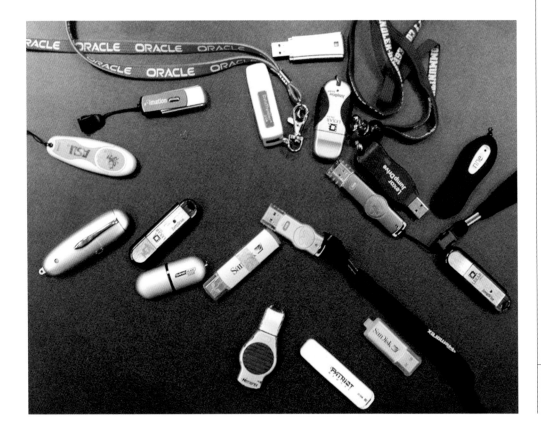

8.4
A wide variety of USB drives are available.

A good option is a USB drive. It is a small, lightweight, portable, and rewritable mass storage device. It comes in a variety of memory sizes and styles (see Figure 8.4). It contains flash memory, which is a form a memory that can be electrically erased and reprogrammed. The entire memory device does not need to be erased, only the block of data you want to erase. Also known as a jump or flash drive, this little device provides an effortless way to transfer data from computer to computer. Just plug it in and you have access to another drive on your computer.

Storage devices do not guarantee that you won't lose data on them. I can think of two examples from years past. One involved a student who stored her files on a few floppy disks (remember these?) and then put those disks in a tightly sealed car on an extremely hot day. The disks literally melted together into a freeform blob of plastic (quite an artistic blob, too). The second example was a former colleague's data, which was stored on a Jaz disk that somehow became corrupted. That was 1 GB of memory down the drain. So even expensive memory and storage devices are not guaranteed or exempt from data loss.

CONCLUSION

It is obvious that the computers and other technologies you use for developing your digital portfolio will have an impact on the quality of your work, plus how fast you can get it done. Use whatever technology resources are available to you to get the job done right. If you decide to purchase computer components and various peripheral devices, know that what is the latest and greatest today will be quickly outdated tomorrow. In the next chapter, we'll start making decisions about what work should be included in your digital portfolio and how the technology itself will influence that selection.

Digital Imagery

Now that you have selected work you would like displayed in your printed portfolio (and know what technology you will need), you may choose to show the same (or similar) work in your digital portfolio. Knowing how your work will appear displayed on a computer monitor or projected onto a large display screen may cause you to rethink what you include in your digital portfolio. This chapter explores computer display basics, such as color systems, pixellation, resolution, image interpolation or distortion, and raster versus vector graphics. We'll end by identifying various types of digital files you will use, how to use them, and how to save them for optimal performance in your digital portfolio.

COLOR SYSTEMS

Keep in mind your work, which you originally created on paper, will now be displayed on a computer monitor with transmitted light. You do not want wildly unpredictable color shifts when you go from one color system to another.

Recall our discussion of light and color from Chapter 6. They go hand in hand. But light and pigments mix differently to form colors. The light displayed on a computer monitor will affect the colors of your digital portfolio projects. In addition, no two computer monitors are the same so even though your design looks fabulous on your own monitor, that doesn't mean it will look as great on someone else's monitor. Knowing this in advance, focus your time and attention on the presentation and content of your portfolio rather than on whether the blue in your design is the exact blue displayed on the screen.

Subtractive Color System

The subtractive color system is based on the color wheel developed by Isaac Newton. In this system, colors are seen by reflected light, as white light reflects off

RIGHT: 9.1
The subtractive color system is used for print media and has primary colors of red, yellow, and blue. Illustration courtesy of Aaron J. Kulik.

BELOW: 9.2
The additive color system is used for digital media and has primary colors of red, green, and blue. Illustration courtesy of Aaron J. Kulik.

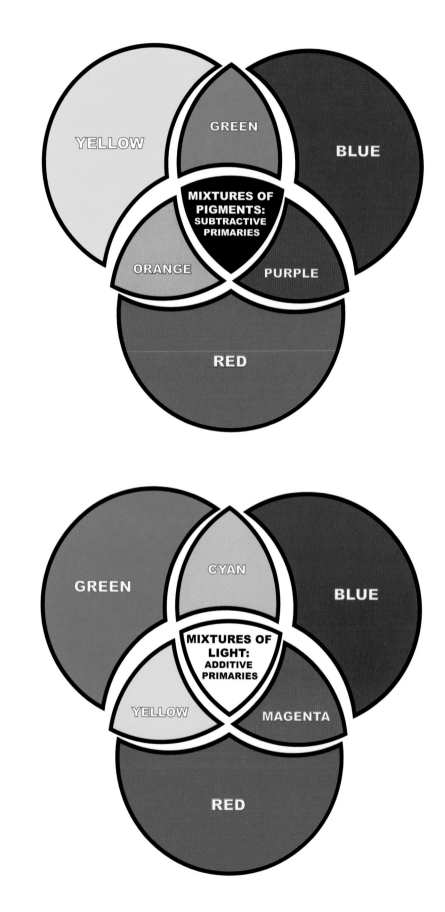

a colored surface to your eye. An object absorbs (or subtracts) all other colors except the color of the object, which is the one your eye sees. For example, a red apple absorbs all colors except red. Red is then bounced back to the eye and a red apple is what you see. The primary colors of the subtractive color system are red, yellow, and blue. Secondary colors are orange, green, and purple (see Figure 9.1).

Additive Color System

Television screens, computer monitors, and theater lighting all use the additive color system. This is the color of light. Its primary colors are red, green, and blue (RGB). These can be added together to produce the secondary colors of cyan, magenta, and yellow (see Figure 9.2).

A secondary color of light mixed together in the correct proportions with its opposite primary color will produce white light. For example, yellow and blue are complementary colors, as are magenta and green, and cyan and red. If you combine the three secondary colors, the result is not black but an unappealing dark brown. Printers in the printing industry therefore must add black ink to do CMYK printing (which stands for cyan, magenta, yellow, and black).

PIXELS, PIXELLATION, AND RESOLUTION

Let's begin by discussing the smallest indivisible piece of a digital image or display—the pixel (see Figure 9.3). Each point of light and color on your monitor is a pixel. The word *pixel* comes from the combination of *picture* and *element*. Together, these dots create a matrix of squares that form the image. The quality of your portfolio depends on the quality of your images. The quality of your images depends on the resolution of the image, the number of pixels it contains, and whether it is created in raster or vector software.

An image's pixels help define its resolution. Pixels directly affect picture quality. A basic definition of resolution in an image is the number of pixels in it. The more pixels you have in an image, the higher its resolution. The higher the resolution, the better the picture will be. An image with low resolution will show only large features. Low-resolution images appear blurry and rough, with jagged edges. High-resolution images are clear with sharp, crisp edges. They can show numerous tiny details that go unseen in a lower resolution image. Therefore, an image's resolution will control how smooth or jagged the picture appears.

The number of pixels in an image will also describe its overall dimensions. This is measured in dots per inch (dpi) or its number of pixels per square inch. A low number of pixels

9.3
Each point of colored light on a computer display is a single pixel.

SUGGESTED RESOLUTIONS FOR GRAPHICS

TYPE OF GRAPHIC	SUGGESTED RESOLUTION
Web graphic	72 ppi
Newspaper printed image	100–150 dpi
Newspaper line art	300–600 dpi
Magazine and art book	225–300 dpi
Commercial print line art	600–1200 dpi
Photo-quality prints	240–600 dpi

Table 9.1

(say, 72 dpi) will result in a small image, about an inch or two in size. This is called a thumbnail image because it is as small as your thumbnail. A higher dpi results in a larger image, which obviously is easier to see.

In addition to providing information on the quality of the image, each individual pixel has exactly one integer value that provides specific color information. These values range from 0 to 255, giving an array of 256 integers. A pixel's resolution, or depth, determines the number of colors available to that pixel. For example, one-bit images are black and white. Eight-bit images have 256 levels of colors, and 24-bit images have over 16 million colors from which to choose. The higher the bit depth, the more color possibilities you'll have. Better resolution with more pixels results in more intense color. Of course, a tradeoff we'll discuss later is that the digital file will increase in size. Resolution guidelines are offered in Table 9.1 by authors Smick and colleagues (2006) to aid in selecting the correct resolution for your images.

IMAGE INTERPOLATION

Image interpolation occurs in all digital photos. It happens whenever you resize the image or distort it in some way by stretching or skewing it. When you take a small digital image like the one in Figure 9.4 and enlarge it, it will pixellate. The computer software determines mathematically where new pixels will go and what color these pixels will be. When doing this, the individual pixels become quite visible, often causing a stepped or jagged effect.

Interpolation is the method of using a mathematical formula to compute all the values between two known pieces of information. It is a way to create missing data. For example, if you weighed 150 pounds on May 15 and 156 pounds on June 15, you could estimate your weight on June 1 by interpolating the data. (A good estimate would be 153 pounds.) The more data you have, the more exact the interpolation would be. If you weighed yourself every 5 days, you would have more data points to consider. Image interpolation works the

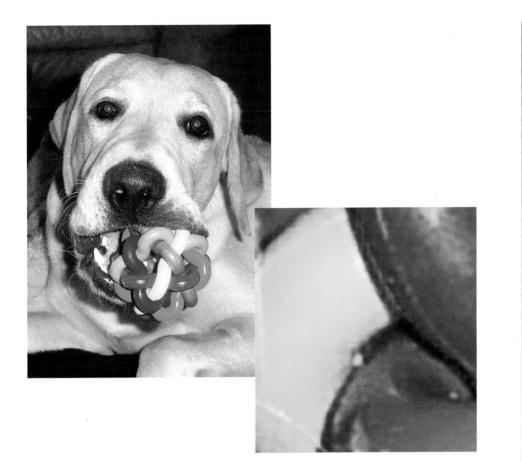

9.4
The close-up view of the colored ball breaks down, or pixellates, into individual pixels when scaled larger.

same way. If you wish to increase the size of a digital image from 100 pixels to 200 pixels, image-editing software (such as Adobe Photoshop) would create a new pixel by using the average color and intensity of the two pixels on either side of the one to be produced.

Whenever you scale an image, the number of pixels in the image is not changed, only the resolution. Downsampling is what you do when you scale it down without changing the resolution. When you do this, the software must throw away many pixels. When you enlarge it, you are upsampling, making the software add more pixels by interpolating amid the extra pixels in the image. Each method results in some image distortion.

Interpolation occurs every time you rotate or distort your image, as illustrated in Figure 9.5. Each time you do this, you will lose image quality. Interpolation changes an image's file size. The first time you rotate your image, it distorts a little bit. Every consecutive rotation causes the image to degrade more and more. A good rule is to avoid rotating your images more than once if possible.

There are many different types of interpolation algorithms available in various software applications. An algorithm is a process in the program designed to solve a particular problem, such as fixing distorted images (Visek 2006). If you really desire to know more about these processes, it is worth reading about.

9.5
Each time you rotate a graphic object, the image gets slightly worse. See how the rotated S in the lower right corner is a little blurry compared with the original above? Illustration courtesy of Aaron J. Kulik.

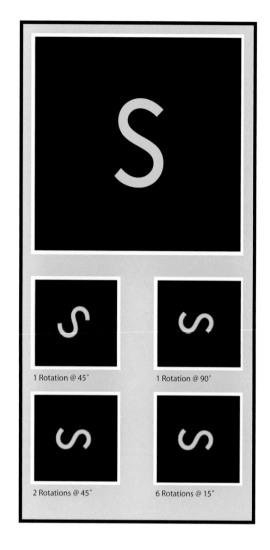

1 Rotation @ 45°   1 Rotation @ 90°

2 Rotations @ 45°   6 Rotations @ 15°

For the purposes of this book, know that Adobe Photoshop CS and CS2 both use a bicubic interpolation. In short, when you increase the size of an image, the software considers the colors and intensities of the neighboring pixels (four on each side, 4 × 4 = 16 total pixels referenced). Those neighboring colors are averaged to create new pixels of color around the interpolated pixel (McHugh 2005b). This bicubic process produces sharper images than other methods and is an ideal pairing of output quality and processing time.

This next section addresses what to do when *things go wrong*. If you enlarge or decrease an image's size and you see no residual problems from the resizing process, you can ignore this discussion of artifacts. Many photos don't have the level of detail or resolution to cause these problems. But even the best interpolation algorithm may produce image residue or artifacts.

Image artifacts are repetitive flaws in your image that negatively affect it. Poor interpolation algorithms, used when you edit or compress your image, often cause these undesirable effects. When interpolating an image, you will have a trade-off between three artifacts: aliasing, blurring, and halos.

1. Aliasing is the visual effect of pixellation. When a line or curve is visible in a shape or text, its edges are neither perfectly vertical nor perfectly horizontal. Some pixels are completely covered, while others are not. The result is a jagged edge, which is said to be aliased (Visek 2006). If the image has a high resolution, it will have more pixels to display and the aliasing won't be very noticeable. Increase the size of your image and you risk seeing these jagged edges (like the ones in Figure 9.5).

2. Blurring an image means to soften the details on part of the image or on the entire thing. This is good for shadows and background effects, or to smooth the jagged edges previously formed by aliasing.

3. Halos (sometimes called edge halos) are the light lines around the edges of objects in your image. Sharpening the image too much produces these shadowy halos.

Even good interpolators will have some of these effects. As the interpolator tries to reduce blurring and aliasing, you may notice your image has a slight halo. You can minimize pixellation by using an anti-alias feature, found in both fractal and art software programs such as Adobe Photoshop. Anti-aliasing removes an image's jagged edges by giving it the look of higher resolution and softer edges (McHugh 2005b). It blends pixel colors on the perimeter of hard edges in the image, such as shapes, text, and lines.

Images with fine geometric patterns, high-quality textures, and thin lines (like the CAD drawing in Figure 9.6) have the greatest chance of being affected by interpolation. After resizing an image, it can become hazy with dull edges. For example, you may have an image that shows the use of brick. If the brick pattern on the existing image has a resolution of a single pixel, when you decrease the size, you'll lose the fine pattern. Imagine the teeth of a hair comb. Each tooth represents one line of pixels; so do the spaces between the teeth. Now make the comb smaller. The teeth would just squeeze together because you cannot have half pixels.

9.6
Interpolation artifacts are likely to appear in digitally manipulated line drawings.

RASTER VERSUS VECTOR

There are two classifications of images: raster and vector. Each has its own advantages and disadvantages. You will need to be comfortable working with each format, as not every piece of software is capable of importing and exporting all file types. Some graphic software applications now allow you to merge both raster and vector images together in the same page layout. Files are then printed in one shot from this one piece of software, rather than from numerous software applications and then adhered by hand onto a presentation board.

Raster Images

Raster images are formed one pixel at a time. You edit individual pixels rather than entire shapes. Raster images are created with a set resolution, such as 72 dpi, 300 dpi, and so on. Images for your printed portfolio should be scanned or created at 300 dpi. For use on a web site, compress all files down to 72 dpi because the Internet defaults to this resolution. Why waste time with a higher resolution when 72 dpi is all you get?

9·7
The larger you scale a raster image, the more jagged it will appear. Illustration courtesy of Aaron J. Kulik, Dick & Fritsche Design Group.

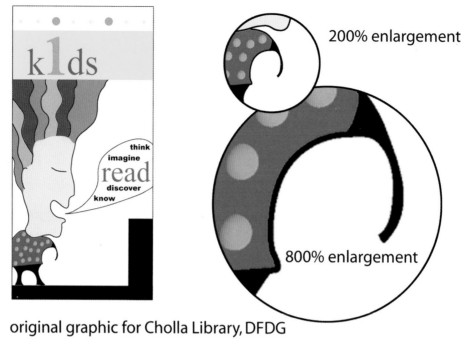

original graphic for Cholla Library, DFDG
raster image

Raster images are sometimes referred to as bitmapped images. (The term *bitmap* can actually refer to a raster image that consists of pixels, or it can refer to black-and-white images when discussing color. I've heard it used both ways.) The thing to remember is these images have a *fixed resolution*. They contain a set number of pixels and are resolution dependent. When scaled larger, the pixels will stretch. They will appear jagged and will lose detail, as shown in Figure 9.7.

What's more, if you lower the resolution, the image will pixellate. Raster images are best used for continuous tone images like photographs, which represent subtle changes in shade and color. Complex graphics are not advisable in a raster format (McKenna 2000).

Raster Image Editors

Select your images carefully. The images of your work are the means through which you will be known in the profession. It is more effective to have a few very good images than a large amount of mediocre images. With this in mind, never alter an original file! Save the original in high resolution and a large size, and manipulate a copy. If you make a mistake, you can go back to the original.

Avoid severely distorting your images for the sake of art. There is so much you can do with image-editing software to alter your original work. Occasionally, I'll see a graduate admission portfolio in which the applicant has severely altered an image of his or her work by stretching, coloring, and otherwise distorting it. The intent is presumably to make it more graphically exciting. However, it makes the design qualities of the project hazy and more difficult to comprehend. You are a professional in your field. If you are in interior design, someone should look at your portfolio and recognize your work as just that—interior design. Not art. Not graphic design. Not something unrelated to your field. Stay true to your profession when manipulating your images and don't overdo it.

Another word of caution is warranted when distorting or enhancing your work. Do not intentionally mislead the reviewer. What you see is not always what you get. Digital or hand-drawn work scanned into digital format can be altered electronically, such as the image in Figure 9.8. You can change color values, contrast, sharpness, size, scale, and proportions. You can fix many of the mistakes you made in the original design. For example, if the paper on which you drew a sketch has yellowed, you can turn it white again. Or if dirt has found its way onto one of your drafted drawings, you can digitally rub out those specks of dirt. This can be deceptive. Is this your original work? Or did you take another two hours to improve it digitally? Says an art instructor from the United Kingdom (Wood 2004, 190), "With a digital image, you never know what you're looking at. The human touch isn't there at all. There is more interposition or distance between a digital image and myself than there would be with a painted image. Digital art is once-removed." This could pose a problem for those who review the work. Is it representative of your skill if a hand-rendered work has been touched up digitally? Be honest when presenting your work. Honestly tell reviewers (or include in your written project description) if what they are seeing is your honest to goodness original work or something you have enhanced digitally. Some practitioners may appreciate your ability to alter images with technology. All practitioners will appreciate your straightforward and honest attitude.

Seldom is a digital image perfect and ready for your portfolio. You will need to slightly enhance images before putting them into your portfolio. Use a raster graphics editor to modify your images. It would take volumes of text to fully describe all the editing techniques available in various image-editing software programs. Popular programs and their file extensions include Corel Photo-Paint (.cpt) and Adobe Photoshop (.psd).

Corel Photo-Paint

Corel Photo-Paint, sold by the Canadian software company Corel, is a raster-editing software program (see Figure 9.9). It is comparable to Photoshop in many ways, allowing you to create and edit raster images with many of the same tools and features. Its two primary uses are for web graphics and manipulating images.

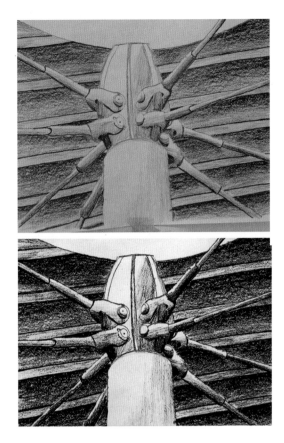

9.8
Adobe Photoshop's Ink Outlines filter can be used to enhance the edges of a hand-drawn sketch.
Sketch courtesy of Rachel K. Dankert.

9·9
Corel Photo-Paint is a raster-editing software program that allows you to manipulate digital images.

Lately, the software's focus has shifted toward the PC photography user. The current version of Corel Photo-Paint is included in the CorelDraw Graphics Suite (no longer sold separately).

Adobe Photoshop

The leading image-editing software program used in industry today is Adobe Photoshop (see Figure 9.10). It allows you to clearly and closely view the image and has many features for precise control. Whether you believe you are an expert photographer or a master with the scanner, images are hardly ever in an ideal state. I have a friend who is a professional photographer. Even she needs to adjust the color, contrast, or brightness of her fine-looking photographs. Tips for enhancing your images with Photoshop's most frequently used features are covered in Chapter 10.

Vector Images

Unlike a raster image that is formed one pixel at a time, a vector image is composed of many individual points based on the underlying mathematical equations of the software. Vector images include illustrations with lines and shapes, typewritten documents, fonts, graphs, flowcharts, and architectural line drawings. Each shape in a vector image has a definite outline and location (see Figure 9.11).

Because resolutions are not predefined as in raster-based programs, graphics from vector software can be output at almost any size *without* sacrificing image

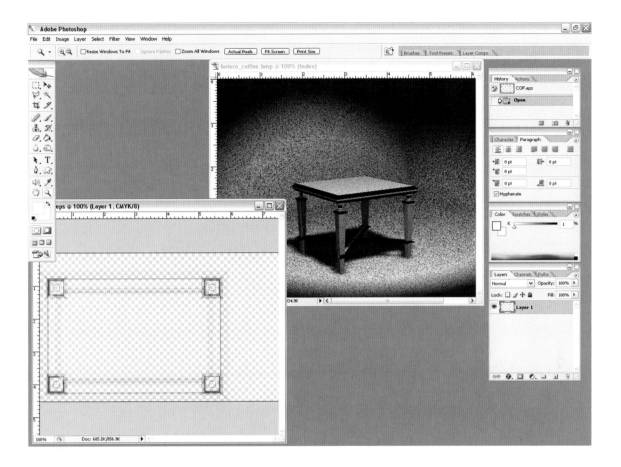

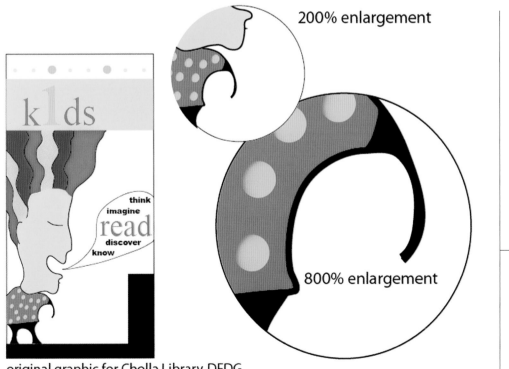

200% enlargement

800% enlargement

original graphic for Cholla Library, DFDG
vector image

ABOVE: 9.10
Adobe Photoshop is the leading industry raster-editing software. It would be worth your time to learn this application.

LEFT: 9.11
Unlike a raster image, a vector image maintains its shape and proportions when scaled larger. Here, the enlarged area remains crisp and clear. Illustration courtesy of Aaron J. Kulik, Dick & Fritsche Design Group.

quality. No matter how close you zoom in to the image, it remains clear. If you are creating a personal logo or introductory page for your portfolio, create it as a vector image so it will always appear crisp and sharp.

Vector images are best used for line drawings and illustrations but are terrible for working with photographs. Think about it. You have a picture of your face. Your complexion has multiple tones. In a photograph, the tones blend from one to another. In a raster program, the pixels adjust when you zoom in and out. In a vector program, this same photo of your face would show each tone in your complexion as a series of pixels. When a tone changes across pixels, one color abruptly changes to another. Not so pretty. Popular vector-based programs and their file extensions include Adobe Illustrator (.ai), CorelDraw (.cdr), Microsoft Excel (.xls), Microsoft Visio (.vsd), and Autodesk's AutoCAD (.dwg).

In summary, vector images are resolution independent, while raster images depend on the resolution to appear sharp and crisp. Vector image files tend to be smaller than raster image files. This can make a big difference when working on your digital portfolio because vector images will download faster in a web-based portfolio than raster images. But raster images are better for displaying lots of photos. The optimum solution when designing your portfolio will be a combination of *both* raster and vector images. This way, you'll get the best of both worlds.

Vector Graphics Editors

Vector graphics editors are software applications that work well for page layouts, typography, artistic and technical illustrations, diagrams, and graphic design. Two popular programs are CorelDraw and Adobe Illustrator. Over the years, these applications have adopted tools and techniques commonly found in raster editors. These editors are closely related to desktop publishing as they can create unique page documents with vector illustrations.

CorelDraw

CorelDraw is good piece of software to use when creating simple drawings and web graphics (see Figure 9.12). It allows you to interactively make and revise vector images. Its ability to produce line drawings, particularly joining multiple paths into a single object, and ease of text control are pluses. CorelDraw was developed for and currently runs only on the Windows platform.

CorelDraw differs in several ways from other vector packages. It is included in a suite of graphics software (all produced by Corel). Time after time, the newest release includes a hefty compilation of fonts and clip art. CorelDraw can do multipage layouts. (Illustrator restricts your design to a single-page layout, although you can print on multiple pages.) And even though each program's native file type can be opened in the other program, the translation is flawed, so moving between programs is not recommended.

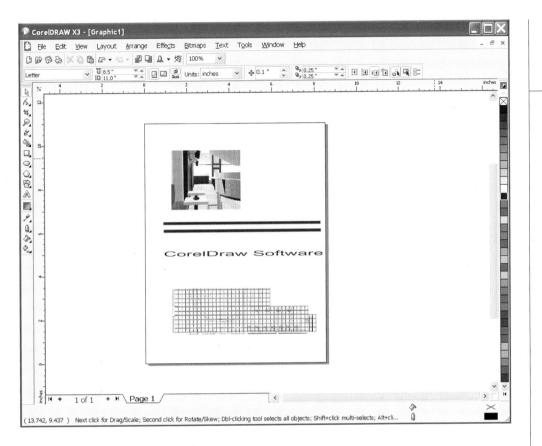

9.12
Drawings, graphics, and multiple page layouts can be created with CorelDraw.

Adobe Illustrator

Adobe Illustrator is a professional vector-based graphics program used widely in the publishing and web design industries for creating clean technical drawings, page layouts, and complex graphics. It works seamlessly with other Adobe products. It is especially good for crisp text, shapes, and line graphics. In Illustrator, you can create complex graphics with drawing tools, color effects, and blended images.

Many of Illustrator's tools (described in Box 9.1) are similar to those found in Photoshop. Although it is beyond the scope of this book to cover all its tools and commands, know that the five color modes in Illustrator are also similar to those in Photoshop (Grayscale, Indexed Color, RGB Color, CMYK Color, and Lab Color). Many of the Photoshop color management tips provided in Chapter 10 are applicable to Illustrator. When saving files in Illustrator, AI is the extension. This file will retain all layer settings. Unfortunately, there are very few options when saving an Illustrator file. To save a copy into a raster image format, you'll need to use the Export command from the File menu. This compresses all layer information and reduces file size.

The Illustrator work area shown in Figure 9.13 looks quite similar to Photoshop, as they share many similar features. The rectangle represents the edge of the image area. Anything outside of this will not print. You can adjust the size of the page from the File>Page Setup menu. The area outside the solid rectangle

ADOBE ILLUSTRATOR TOOLS

Blend Tool	*To incorporate two objects together*
Eyedropper Tool	*To select new colors from existing image colors*
Free Transform Tool	*To skew the appearance of an object*
Gradient Tool	*To create fills that transition between two colors*
Graph Tools	*To create a variety of data charts*
Hand Tool	*To move an image within the window*
Lasso Tools	*To select part of an object, an entire object, or a path*
Line Tools	*To draw separate straight-line segments*
Live Paint Bucket Tool	*To distribute color into a selected area*
Live Paint Selection Tool	*To detect and fill color in-between paths*
Magic Wand Tool	*To select areas based on color similarity*
Measure Tool	*To determine distances*
Mesh Tool	*To design and modify meshes and envelopes*
Paintbrush Tool	*To paint with the foreground color*
Pen Tools	*To draw straight lines and flowing curves*
Pencil Tools	*To draw freeform lines*
Rotate Tools	*To rotate an object or create a series of rotated objects*
Scale Tools	*To resize an object*
Scissor Tools	*To cut a path at designated points*
Selection Tools	*To select an entire object or path*
Shape Tools	*To create various solid shapes*
Slice Tools	*To divide an image into separate areas*
Symbol Tools	*To create and modify symbols*
Type Tools	*To add text to an image*
Warp Tools	*To distort an object*
Zoom Tool	*To view an image at various magnifications*

Box 9.1

is the scratch or play area. This is where you can create and manipulate objects before placing them onto the page. Depending on the printable area of your printer, it's possible that objects close to the rectangle may be cut off.

You can export entire web pages (including the programming coding) from Illustrator using the Save for Web command. It will save the entire page, everything on the page (whether you want it all or not). If you only want one object or area, draw a rectangle around it. (Do not fill it with color.) From the Object menu, select Crop Area>Make. This will export only the area enclosed within the rectangle. Now go to the Save for Web command under the File menu. Use this feature as you would in Photoshop. See what the image will look like on the web by clicking on the button in the bottom right corner of the Save for Web box to preview it in a web browser of your choice.

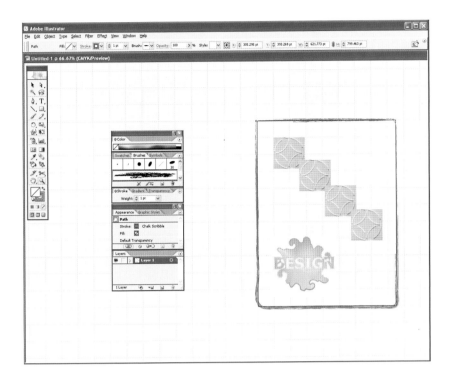

9.13
In contrast to Photoshop, the area outside Adobe Illustrator's on-screen outline is considered the work area and will not print to your printer.

IDENTIFYING DIGITAL FORMATS

There are several formats for digital files that you will be using in either creating or presenting your digital portfolio (see Table 9.2). Although you may not use all formats, be familiar with some of the more fashionable file formats. Know that newer formats emerge in the design industries every year, so this list will grow longer and longer.

The optimal scenario for your digital portfolio would be to have a small file download quickly, with excellent color rendition, a large image size, and clear, crisp image quality. This is absolute ecstasy for image optimizing. This is also a tall order. You will need to make decisions about whether to sacrifice time or quality as you juggle image resolution with file size.

Always begin a new file in your software in what is known as the native format of that software. For example, Photoshop saves as a PSD file, AutoCAD saves as a DWG file, Illustrator as an AI file, and so on. When you are ready to use the file in another application, make a copy to a universal format. Some software applications limit file format options under their Save As command. For example, Illustrator files need to be exported as graphic images. When working with line drawings such as CAD files, you can convert them to image files as Encapsulated Postscript (EPS) files, or export the file from AutoCAD as an Interchange file. These types of files are the best for preserving linear qualities. A word of warning: be aware of your AutoCAD display color. Do you want a black background like the one in Figure 9.14, or a white one?

Always keep your original. Only save an image to a universal or compressed file format when you are completely done manipulating it.

COMMON IMAGE FORMATS

ABBREVIATION	NAME	DEFINITION
DNG	Digital Negative	Publicly available, royalty-free RAW file format; a standard among digital camera manufacturers
EPS	Encapsulated PostScript	Common page layout format; converts CAD files to image files; preserves the linear qualities of the drawing as well as possible
GIF	Graphics Interchange Format	8-bit color depth; good choice for images with only a few colors; excellent for black-and-white line drawings
JPEG	Joint Photographic Experts Group	24-bit color depth; great for photographs; repeated alteration reduces files quality
PDF	Portable Document Format	Maintains consistency of fonts, graphics, and layout; can be viewed on Macintosh and Windows platforms
PNG	Portable Network Graphics	Full depth 24-bit color; offers compression without loss of image quality; not supported by all browsers
RAW	Raw data	Raw data comes directly from a digital camera with no in-camera processing
SVG	Scalable Vector Graphics	Web graphic format similar to a vector-based image that uses mathematical calculations to represent design
TIFF	Tagged Image File Format	Good choice for exchanging raster images between programs; commonly used in desktop publishing

Table 9.2

COMPRESSING FILES

Working with images requires a delicate balancing act between maintaining the quality of the image, while keeping the size of the file manageable. As a rule, JPEG is good, TIFF is better, but RAW is the best. Unfortunately, TIFF and RAW images have great resolution, but also large file sizes. These are fine for print media, but don't work well for digital presentations. Eventually, you will need to compress some of your files. Compression is the process of pushing things together to make them smaller. In digital lingo, it means reducing the number of data bytes that defines a file while maintaining some semblance of its quality. You do this to save storage space and transmission time. The two most common for-

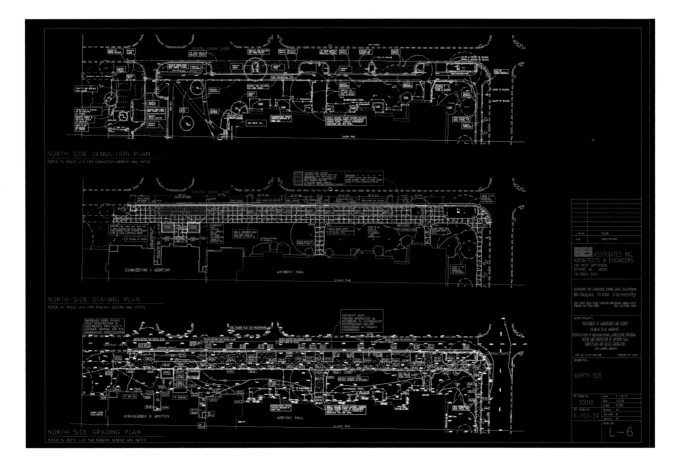

mats for saving and exchanging compressed digital images are Graphics Interchange Format (GIF) and Joint Photographic Experts Group (JPEG). Both of these options will compress the size of the file. As a general rule, photographic images should be saved as JPEG files, while all other graphic images save best as GIF (see Figure 9.15).

Choosing your file format is a balancing act between good looks and fast downloads. When compressing a file, some of its digital data may be thrown away. This is known as lossy compression (not lousy, but lossy). A software program

ABOVE: 9.14
When exporting a drawing from one piece of software (like AutoCAD) to another (like Photoshop), you may get more than just the image. You may also get the background color of the software as well.

LEFT: 9.15
The colored line drawing on the left has few colors and would compress well as a GIF. The rendered perspective on the right has more colors and photographic qualities. It would compress best as a JPEG.
Rendering courtesy of Alexandra C. Ayres, Sally Azer, and Kelly Robinson.

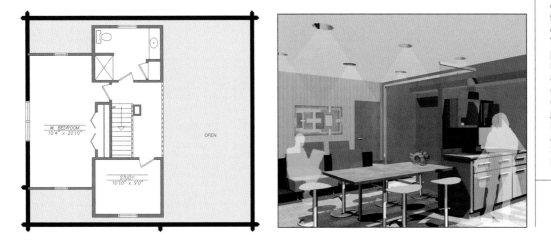

will use this data compression technique to replace a string of code that represents a series of common pixels with a shorter code. This removes redundant or unessential information, thus reducing the size of the file, but damaging the quality of the image in the process. A GIF file compresses, but it does not suffer from lossy compression. When you compress a GIF file, a lot of redundant color information is deleted. GIF compression ratio ranges from 2:1 to 5:1 (Brown 2005c). A JPEG file compresses an image from 10 to 20 times smaller than its original file size (Brown 2005b). JPEG images suffer greatly from lossy compression.

If the downside of compressing an image is reduced quality, why would you want to do this? The main reason is to save disk space. Smaller files take up less room on your computer or external storage device (such as a CD or jump drive). Smaller files also can be transferred to other computers more quickly. You can email a smaller file to someone much faster than a larger file. Smaller files will not clog someone's email inbox. Many service providers limit email attachments to 5 MB. When someone emails me a very large file, my email service provider may not have the capacity on its server to handle such a large file. It will either delete the email entirely (bouncing it back to the sender), or deliver the email with the attached file stripped off. A smaller, compressed file would make it through my email.

Smaller files will also download much quicker from a web site. When others are reviewing your digital portfolio, they will not patiently wait for minutes and

9.16
The JPEG compression box in Photoshop allows you to control the amount of image compression.

minutes to view one of your images. Our culture of instant results has conditioned us to demand everything *now*. Practitioners would prefer to see the image quickly. A smaller file will allow them to do this. Because the maximum resolution that can be displayed in a web browser is 72 dpi, why waste time downloading a higher resolution graphic? A smaller file with a bit less quality and sharpness really won't make much difference in the end.

Compressing a file should be the very *last* thing you do to it. Once it is compressed, you can continue editing it but you don't want to. Every time you open and work on a compressed image (like a JPEG), you lose more information when you save it because it's compressed a bit more (see Figure 9.16). Every time you open that file, alter it, and resave it, you compress it further and lose about 10 percent of the information and quality. The value of your image will degrade each time you do this, ultimately resulting in an inferior image.

Since GIF and JPEG are the most commonly used compression formats, let's discuss the pros and cons of each. GIF images have a limited color range; specifically, 8-bit, which is 256 colors. They are best for images with large color areas and vector illustrations (not raster images). These would be things like line drawings, maps, and vector graphics with little color rendition, as in a personal logo with only two or three colors. They are also good at representing thin text in an image.

GIF images support transparency. This means the background of a GIF image can be left transparent and it will show through to the web page background color. Furthermore, unlike a JPEG, repeated saving will not make the image look worse.

On the other hand, JPEG images are excellent for photographs and other images with varying degrees of light and shadow. After all, the JPEG is named after a group of photographers who created this format. They can contain 24-bit depth of color, giving the image a 16.7 million-color definition (Myers 2005). Be careful when saving and resaving a JPEG file because of lossy compression (discussed earlier). Stick with GIF or JPEG files for web site presentations because they can be opened and read in multiple web browsers on both Macintosh and Windows platforms.

CONCLUSION

Obviously, it is important to know what your work will look like on a computer monitor or projected onto a large screen. You are no longer using the subtractive color system common in printing, but the additive color system of light. This will affect how you manipulate your images, by resizing, interpolating, and keeping them as clear and crisp as possible when saving and compressing them to manageable file sizes. In the next chapter, we'll continue our discussion of digital images. We'll talk about how to scan and photograph your manual work, and then fine-tune it in Photoshop.

10

Creating Your Digital Portfolio

Some designs that can be created with digital media just cannot be produced with traditional media. Because a digital portfolio combines the development of a traditional portfolio with the development of a multimedia project, equal attention should be given to both. The combination of the two is what makes a digital portfolio effective (Barrett 2000). Creating your digital portfolio will require you to manipulate your work by scanning or photographing it and converting to digital files. These files can be further enhanced in Photoshop. All of these topics will be discussed in this chapter.

DIGITAL PORTFOLIO ADVANTAGES

Digital portfolio development is useful to you in several ways. A digital portfolio is easier to maintain, edit, and update than a traditional paper portfolio (Heath and Cockerham 2001). Computers make spontaneity safer. It is now almost effortless to make a mistake and then erase it with one keystroke. Some believe the "undo" button may be technology's greatest contribution to artists and designers (Wood 2004). Art and presentation materials are no longer wasted. With no financial impediment to experimentation, you can try a new artistic approach, knowing it can be discarded at no cost (Wood 2004). In addition, you have created a more permanent record of your design work by having digital copies stored on CD or other storage devices (Leeman-Conley 1999).

By putting your work on CD or the Internet, you can quickly and inexpensively market yourself to prospective employers all around the world (see Box 10.1). This increases your visibility and opens up more opportunities to you than the local job market. The job seeker of today interviews locally for a position. The job seeker of tomorrow interviews by teleconferencing with firms all over the world. Imagine interviewing with a prospective employer overseas. The high cost

There is a benefit to both traditional and digital portfolios. While demand and time seems to be speeding up in our world, having a digital portfolio allows flexibility to show off your work anywhere, anytime. I have friends today who even carry images of their portfolio on their iPod since you never know where you might be. Digital portfolios also show the ability of the designer with technology, which is also becoming more important to our profession.

Paul Hibbard
Project Designer
Mancini Duffy
New York, NY

Box 10.1

10.1
Computer-generated renderings like these showcased in a digital format show a potential employer the candidate's expertise with technology. Design work courtesy of David A. Hobart, Jr.

of sending a traditional color portfolio can be staggering. A digital portfolio can be sent via CD to the interviewer, or the student and the interviewer can simultaneously view the portfolio on a web site while conducting a phone interview. You'd never leave your traditional portfolio with a prospective client or employer; you can with digital media. You can photograph and scan your work into digital format and then make multiple copies to distribute at will. The only expense is the media and the mailing.

A digital portfolio allows you to demonstrate to potential employers that you have the technological skills necessary to create this type of portfolio (see Figure 10.1). You may interview with your traditional portfolio more often because it's just easier to turn pages than to deal with a computer, but a digital portfolio can help raise your apparent value to a design firm (see Box 10.2). Even when designers create the most simplistic digital portfolios, the fact that credentials appear in multimedia format communicates the willingness to innovate and develop new skills.

Invest the time to design a good digital portfolio. A digital portfolio entails a "strong visual foundation of design sensitivities coupled with equally strong technical ability" (Linton 2003, 138). Keep in mind the time you spend on learning a new tool is subtracted from the time you could spend attending to the creative aspects of your digital portfolio. However, this can definitely be considered time well spent if learning a new software application can help you in other classes or projects. It's certainly not a waste of effort to learn new skills. As more of the design process is done in electronic media, use existing electronic files, such as word-processed documents, AutoCAD drawings, PowerPoint presentations, and multimedia files.

Practitioners have their own opinions regarding the creation and dissemination of digital portfolios. Digital

Box 10.2

portfolios sent on CD or via an email link to a web site are great introductions to you and your work. Preliminary findings from a study of employers who reviewed digital portfolios found they requested portfolios to be short and concise, full of multimedia, and easy to use. An additional benefit of a digital portfolio is the opportunity to ascertain a future employee's technology skills by seeing this product (Leeman-Conley 1999).

Digital portfolios may be used more frequently as a screening tool. Firms put much time, energy, and expense into conducting in-person interviews. The number of these interviews can be decreased, because a candidate's digital portfolio provides more comprehensive information than would be obtained from a mailed resume. A firm can look through digital portfolios and narrow down the short list of candidates (see Box 10.3). And while a printed portfolio is an expectation in any job interview, a digital portfolio is an added bonus because your work can be viewed in ways never before available, from graphic presentations with audio narrations, to rendered animated models, to simulated three-dimensional (3-D) environments.

Box 10.3

> **Too many of** the digital portfolios I see appear to be all about presentation using the latest technology and less about application, process, and research skills.
>
> Sue Kirkman, ASID, IIDA, IDEC
> Vice President of Academics
> Harrington College of Design
> Chicago, IL

Box 10.4

10.2
A large isometric line drawing like this will lose much of its detail when presented in a digital format.

DIGITAL PORTFOLIO DISADVANTAGES

Using technology to develop and present your portfolio can have some disadvantages. Keep in mind that technology is helpful to you when developing your ideas. However, it can be a hindrance when its trickery distracts you from the goal of problem solving (see Box 10.4).

Hypermedia (the term is a combination of hypertext and multimedia) may allow you to merge drawings, images, text, animation, sound, and video in an

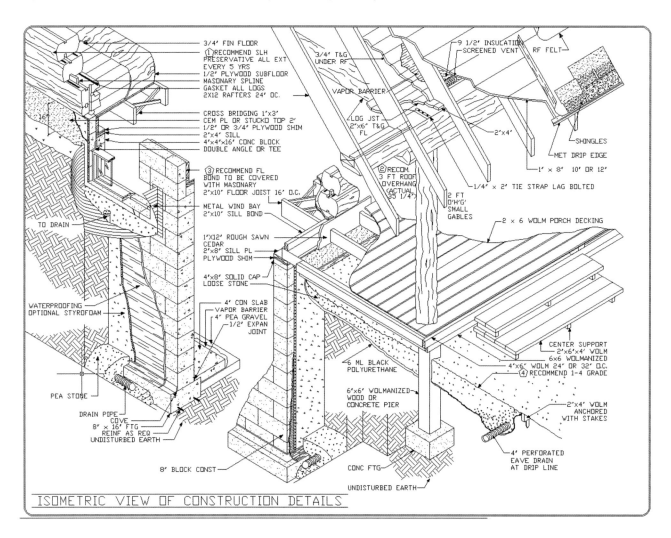

interactive format. But should you? These media have some inherent limitations, as fine lines, weak type, and small, intricate details will not display well electronically (see Figure 10.2).

Designers of digital portfolios must have a strong technical background. As you know, technology is constantly changing. You'll need to keep up with the latest tools to have a cutting-edge portfolio. You may need to devote a considerable amount of time to mastering the software packages you'll use so you can alter your portfolio whenever necessary.

A digital portfolio also removes you from the presentation. A practitioner in another country may review your work. This increases your visibility. But you are unable to respond to his or her comments and questions because you are not present to explain your portfolio. Therefore, your portfolio must answer *all* the reviewer's questions in and of itself.

A digital portfolio may not be for everyone. Just because it's possible to create one, doesn't mean it's the best avenue for you. If technology is not your forte, do not pretend it is. After all, why would you wish to portray a skill you do not have and then be hired to use that skill every day in an internship or job? You would be miserable.

Finally, bear in mind that all the bells and whistles in the world are not an adequate substitute for substance. No matter how wonderful your multimedia presentation may be, your design work is the essence of your portfolio. If that work is poor, a richly executed presentation won't save you. Spend more time on your design work than on its presentation. Don't major in the minors.

SCANNING FLAT WORK INTO DIGITAL FORMAT

Although working with digital media is more and more the norm in today's business world, designers still use good ol' pencil and paper to do some design work, like the concept sketches shown in Figure 10.3. To present this type of media in your digital portfolio, you'll need to scan it. Before scanning, clean up your work. Erase extraneous marks and smudges on your pages. This is especially prevalent in drafted work, which often looks messy because of the pencil lead smeared over the page. Clean your work as much as you can with a traditional eraser before scanning. Remount or reformat the work if it looks sloppy or unprofessional. Get the scanner plate and lid spotless with glass cleaner. Now you're ready to scan.

When creating the initial electronic file, scan it as large as possible. If you scan the image too small and later increase the size, remember that the resolution will decrease and the quality of your photo will substantially decrease, too, because of pixellation. If you are unsure of the resultant image size, it's best to scan it larger than necessary. You can always reduce it later using image-editing software. This will condense the pixels and reduce the file's size, thus maintaining the crispness of your image.

The picture is only as good as the source! Scan at as high a resolution as you can realistically achieve. (Optimally, a digital camera is even better than a scanned

RIGHT: 10.3
This process work represents traditional hand-drawn problem solving, a skill every designer should have. Design work courtesy of Jeffrey Lothner.

BELOW: 10.4
Drafted work must be scanned darker in order for all line weights to appear. Design work courtesy of Elaine Hu.

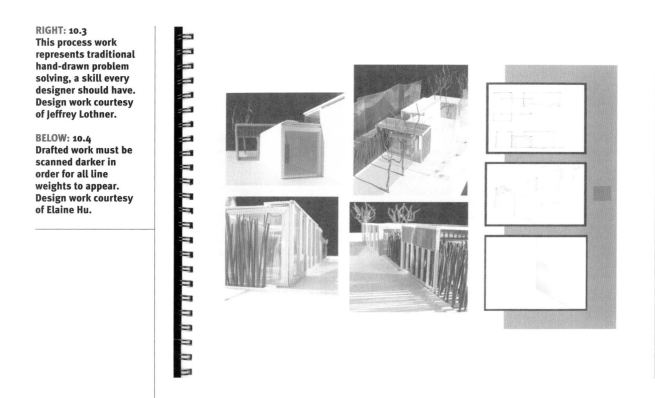

Hand Drafting

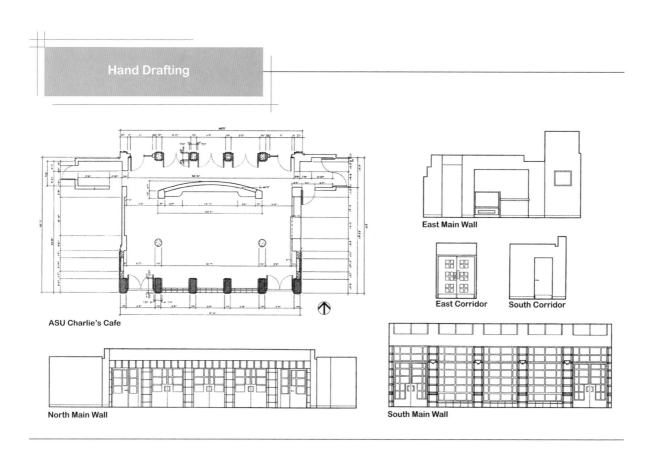

ASU Charlie's Cafe

East Main Wall

East Corridor   South Corridor

North Main Wall

South Main Wall

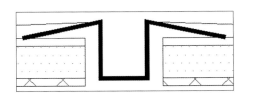

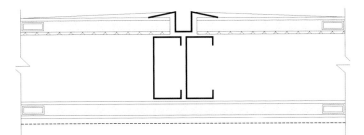

WALLBOARD TRIM

photo because it requires one less step to put the image into an electronic format.) Using a higher resolution will result in a better quality image; a lower resolution will result in an image that is rough and coarse when you print it. For example, scan your work at a resolution of 600 dots per inch (dpi), clean up whatever you need to in Photoshop, and then change the image size and resolution to 300 dpi for printed material or 72 dpi for web-based material. Having a resolution of more than 72 dpi for web-based sharing is pointless, as it will only increase the size of the file without making any substantial improvement in the quality of image. Higher resolution is important only for printing.

Full-color photographs and artwork will scan well because they are raster images. The usual publishing standard is for all images to be at 300 dpi. Never go below 150 dpi or your photos will start to pixellate. Line drawings such as the hand drafting in Figure 10.4 are difficult to scan into digital format. Line drawings with lots of text just do not scan well. Black-and-white images are more likely to pixellate. Think about it. You're taking beautiful vector work and converting it to raster format. When scanning drafted construction drawings and details, typical problems include jagged edges, fine lines that break up (or completely disappear), and thick patterns that clump up and look almost solid (see Figure 10.5).

For line drawings and other images with fine details, consider scanning at a very high resolution such as 800 or 900 points per inch (ppi). Otherwise, they'll look washed out, dull, lifeless. Manipulating a low-resolution image won't help; it will only make those lines disappear into the background. You may need to darken the images in order to see all the details because fine lines and lettering tend to fade into the background (see Figure 10.6). Think about it. A thin line may be only one pixel wide. That's hard to see. Diagonal lines can be the worst, looking like stairs when you zoom close to the image. Crosshatching and other shading mechanisms can look like a sea of pixels. If you can, scan an image larger than the original and at a very high resolution. Use double or triple the normal resolution when scanning or digitally photographing line drawings.

You have color options when scanning your line illustrations. I would suggest you scan in Grayscale mode rather than as line art. In Grayscale mode, you can sharpen, adjust the brightness and contrast, and tweak your image to make it even

10.5
A line drawing will have jagged edges if converted to a raster image and then enlarged. Export your lines drawings directly from the vector software.

10.6
Drawing done by hand needs to be dark enough to be clearly visible when scanned into digital format. Design work courtesy of Ashley Delph.

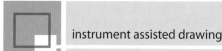

instrument assisted drawing

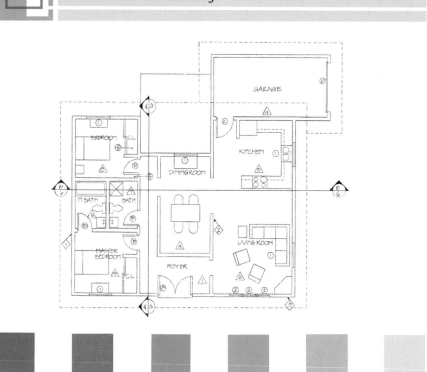

lovelier. Be prepared to clean up the scan further in Photoshop with the Eraser or Clone Stamp tool before scaling it down, keeping the lines and edges crisp (see Figure 10.7).

PHOTOGRAPHING YOUR WORK

For artwork, models, and presentation boards that are too large to fit on a scanner, like the chair in Figure 10.8, you'll need to photograph them with either a digital camera or a traditional 35-mm or 50-mm camera. This is especially useful when designing and building furniture pieces and building models. This progression through the construction process illustrates the work's design process and your ability to logically assemble an object (see Figure 10.9).

In addition to documenting the work in progress, take your final photos when the piece is completely finished and brand new. After you have handled the piece and stored it, it will never look quite as good as it does when it is first completed (see Figure 10.10). With age, wood will crack, paper will peel, paint will lift, and tears and chips will occur from forceful treatment.

Designers should photograph installations of their designs as soon as they are finished. Clients always change a planned interior or exterior slightly to accommodate growth, change, or the need to more thoroughly personalize a space. If

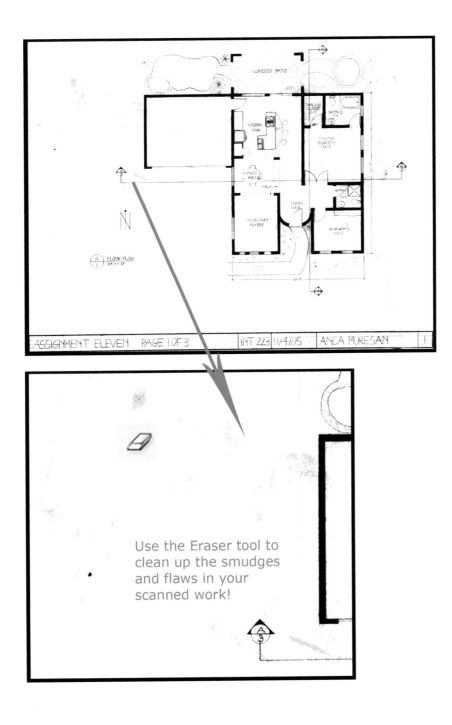

10.7
Small touch-ups are acceptable. Use the Marquee, Eraser, and Clone Stamp tools in Photoshop to remove smudges and minor errors in drawings. Design work courtesy of Anca Muresan.

Use the Eraser tool to clean up the smudges and flaws in your scanned work!

you come back to an installation six months later, it will not look the same as it did on installation day. As an intern, you may be involved in creating design work that is installed *after* you have completed your internship or co-op period. Stay in touch with the firm and your supervisor. Let him or her know that you would like to take photographs of the finished installation for your portfolio. Offer to share the photos with your supervisor. This way, you both win. You get pictures for your portfolio; the supervisor gets pictures for the firm portfolio and for marketing purposes.

RIGHT: 10.8
A full-scale furniture piece obviously cannot be taken to a job interview. Photograph it and place those images in your printed or digital portfolio. Design work courtesy of Elaine Hu and Joanne Huang.

BELOW: 10.9
The construction process for a metal piece of furniture gives the reviewers a glimpse of your work process and your capabilities "beyond the office." Design work courtesy of Paul Hibbard.

LEFT: 10.10
A scale model will never look as good as when you've just finished it. Take pictures immediately to preserve its details and craftsmanship. Design work courtesy of Liisa Taylor.

BELOW: 10.11
A presentation board used to present a project to a jury often contains a multitude of media, such as flat drawings, material samples, concept art, and more.
Design work courtesy of Allison Saunders.

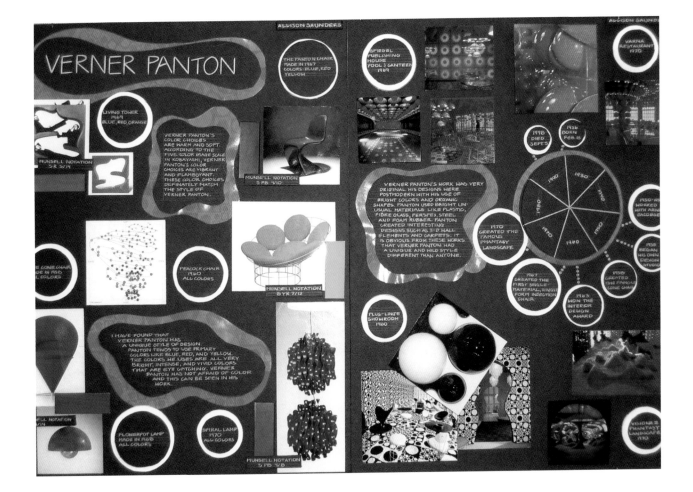

Large flat pieces are sometimes more difficult to photograph than a 3-D form or installation. Presentation boards with a variety of materials and textures on them can be the most difficult. For example, suppose you have a presentation board with a line drawing of a furniture design, a rendered perspective on marker paper, photocopies of furniture hardware, and fabric samples for the upholstery, as in Figure 10.11. All of these objects on the board have diverse textures and will reflect light differently. Taking a photograph of this type of oversized work may be a better solution than trying to scan it in multiple pieces, and then grafting the pieces together.

To assist in photographing large presentation boards and drawings, mount them on an even larger piece of mat board or foam core board. Framing the board with the extra board you have attached in the viewfinder helps to avoid distorting the edges of the actual presentation board. Give the piece a uniform margin around the edges. Pin the board to a wall, set up your camera with a tripod, and start clicking. You could also lay these large boards on a table or floor with a neutral background.

Three-dimensional pieces photograph best when set on a flat surface near a wall, such as a table or counter. Capture the best views, particularly the ones that emphasize the successful construction of the model or furniture piece. Fascinating details like those in Figure 10.12a and 10.12b should be photographed

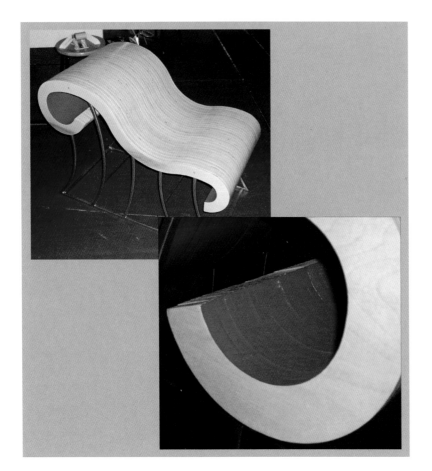

10.12b
Design work courtesy of Lindsay Miller and Lauren Maitha.

closely. Close-up photographs are hard to take, and it's even harder to show the detail you want. Be careful with these shots. Use a camera that has a macro lens, rather than standing extra close to your work to photograph it. If you're too close, everything will end up blurry and none of the detail will show. (To show details from oversized boards, scan those parts and show them as larger digital images.)

Large 3-D work like furniture or a room may be difficult to shoot. Although it's tempting to use a wide-angle lens, it's better to use the panoramic feature found on many digital cameras. The difficulty with panoramic shots is the visual distortion found on the edges, when you try to overlap the tiles or individual images.

What do you put behind the model, sculpture, or piece of furniture as a background? Use a 10- or 12-foot wide backdrop. This can come from a roll of white photo paper, brown wrapping paper, or solid fabric. Even a neutral-colored bed sheet will work. Keep it simple. The focus should be on your work, not on a highly textured or patterned background. Any subdued color in a matte finish will augment your work. Keep in mind the rules of contrast: a light object like the one in Figure 10.13 will appear more prominent against a dark background, and vice versa.

As a designer, you are aware of lighting's impact on the built environment from observation and study. Light is nothing more than radiant energy that can be

sensed or seen by the human eye. Your choice of lighting when photographing your work will determine the range of colors seen in your final image. After all, the appearance of an object undoubtedly relies on the light used to illuminate it.

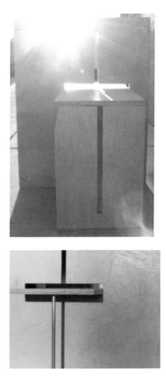

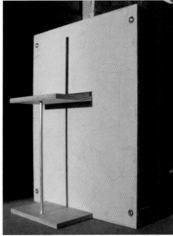

Besides natural day lighting, there are several types of interior light sources you might use to photograph your work, such as fluorescent, incandescent, and halogen. These light sources will alter the colors of your work. Fluorescent lighting will shift all colors toward blues and yellows and away from reds. Incandescent light produces warm color. It will cast a warm glow on your work, similar to that of an open candle flame. A halogen light with a high light rating will give you a close representation to daylight with some emphasis on the color yellow.

For photographing your 3-D work, take some photos with indoor lighting, some on an overcast day, and some in midday sunshine. The best photos will probably be those taken on slightly overcast days around noon. Noontime light provides an almost perfect balance of

LEFT: 10.14b
Design work courtesy
of Elaine Hu and
Joanne Huang.

BELOW: 10.15
Take photographs of
your work and then
manipulate them
digitally.
Design work courtesy
of Elaine Hu.

light. This will most accurately reflect the true colors of your work and you will get diffuse lighting with no harsh shadows. You can see in Figures 10.14a and 10.14b that natural sunlight can be used to highlight your work. In this case, shadows are desirable. This is when using a digital camera is most cost effective. If the photos do not look good, you can just delete them, change the light setting, and reshoot.

Once you have the photos of your work, you can convert them to digital format for manipulation on the computer (see Figure 10.15). The ultimate choice would be to use a high-resolution digital camera and have the photos in digital format from the

start. But you can always use a 35-mm or 50-mm camera and process the photos. Have film developed on a CD so you can easily manipulate the digital images. Request high-resolution images only. Color prints at 8" × 10" size are affordable, small enough to be handled easily, and have just enough visible detail to communicate well.

REDUCING WORK TO A SMALLER SIZE

There are several reasons why you may need to reduce your larger work to smaller, more manageable sizes. Large oversized boards and drawings are difficult to carry. They are also difficult to display in a conference room or on a designer's desk during an interview. Large work will most definitely need to be checked as baggage on airline flights. Are you willing to trust your portfolio to the airlines? Having smaller work means you can include more images of your work without the bulk of large and numerous pages. Finally, you can use smaller images much more effectively on your web site or in a marketing teaser than page after page of larger images.

A large construction document that was originally 32" × 40" will not reproduce well at a smaller scale. The reduction of drawings to a smaller format risks the loss of visible details, as seen in Figure 10.16. Some line drawings just need to be presented at the largest scale possible. Not all line drawings merit this large size. But some will be most effective if presented larger than a tiny image that can't be read. When reproducing your large presentation boards and construction drawings, it may be best to provide an overview of the whole thing in one photo and then use a few close-up photos of parts of the board in a higher resolution and larger size. Detailed views like those in Figure 10.17 illustrate the quality and content of your work.

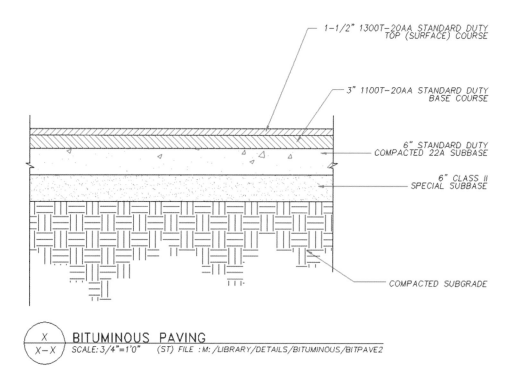

1-1/2" 1300T–20AA STANDARD DUTY
TOP (SURFACE) COURSE

3" 1100T–20AA STANDARD DUTY
BASE COURSE

6" STANDARD DUTY
COMPACTED 22A SUBBASE

6" CLASS II
SPECIAL SUBBASE

COMPACTED SUBGRADE

X | BITUMINOUS PAVING
X–X | SCALE: 3/4"=1'0"   (ST) FILE : M: /LIBRARY/DETAILS/BITUMINOUS/BITPAVE2

10.16
When a line drawing with thin lines is reduced in size, subtle details are lost.

To reduce the size of your work, first make all corrections on the computer while the image is at its largest size and highest resolution. You can then reduce the size and lower the resolution when saving a copy. Work you have done manually cannot obviously be manipulated on the computer unless you scan it into digital format. You can pay to have your oversized flat work scanned professionally on a large-scale scanner at a local copy and print center. This will be more expensive than scanning the work in smaller pieces and then putting it together yourself.

ENHANCING YOUR IMAGES IN PHOTOSHOP

Because the focus of this book is on portfolios, this section will highlight the most frequently used tools and features of image manipulation in Adobe Photoshop. A full list and description of Photoshop's tools is provided in Box 10.5.

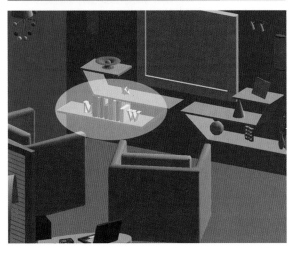

10.17
Detail views of your computer models can enable reviewers to see close-up elements (like the rendered bookends) that might be overlooked in a larger image.
Design work courtesy of Mat Wingate.

ADOBE PHOTOSHOP TOOL DEFINITIONS

Blur Tool	*To blur, sharpen, or smudge an image selection*
Brush Tool	*To paint with the foreground color*
Crop Tool	*To delete selected portions of an image*
Eraser Tool	*To correct mistakes or delete a portion of an image*
Eyedropper Tool	*To select new colors from existing image colors*
Gradient Tool	*To create fills that transition between two colors*
Hand Tool	*To move an image within the window*
Healing Brush Tool	*To correct imperfections*
History Brush Tool	*To revert a portion of the image to a previous state*
Lasso Tools	*To select an area of the image in various shapes*
Magic Wand Tool	*To select areas based on color similarity*
Marquee Tools	*To select a rectangular area of the image*
Move Tool	*To shift the location of a selected image*
Notes Tool	*To add notes to your image*
Paint Bucket	*To distribute color into a selected area*
Path Selection Tools	*To select straight and curved segments*
Pen Tools	*To draw straight lines and flowing curves*
Shape Tools	*To create various solid shapes*
Slice Tools	*To divide an image into separate areas*
Stamp Tools	*To copy selected areas of the image*
Toning Tools	*To lighten, darken, saturate, or unsaturate an image*
Type Tools	*To add text to an image*
Zoom Tool	*To view an image at various magnifications*

Box 10.5

You'll need to know several important concepts and techniques for optimizing an image's appearance. Although the information provided next only scratches the surface of what the software can do, it permits you to fine-tune images for your traditional printed portfolio as well as your digital version. Before we begin, remember that no amount of image adjustment can fix a bad scan or digital photo.

Altering Bit Depth

In the last chapter, we talked about reducing a file's size by compressing it, which often reduces image quality. Another way to reduce file size without sacrificing quality is to reduce the bit depth of the image, or the number of bits used to store information about each individual pixel. Eight bits per pixel yields 256 colors, while 24 bits per pixel will yield 16.7 million colors. By lowering the depth, less color information is stored in an image, which in turn reduces the file size. You can easily change the bit depth of an image in Photoshop, under the Image menu (see Figure 10.18).

Color Management

Color management of your digital images is vital to accurately conveying your design work. Just because the image looks good on your computer monitor doesn't mean it will look good on the Internet or printed on paper. For example, if you're presenting a rendering on the monitor, make it a little lighter. You may

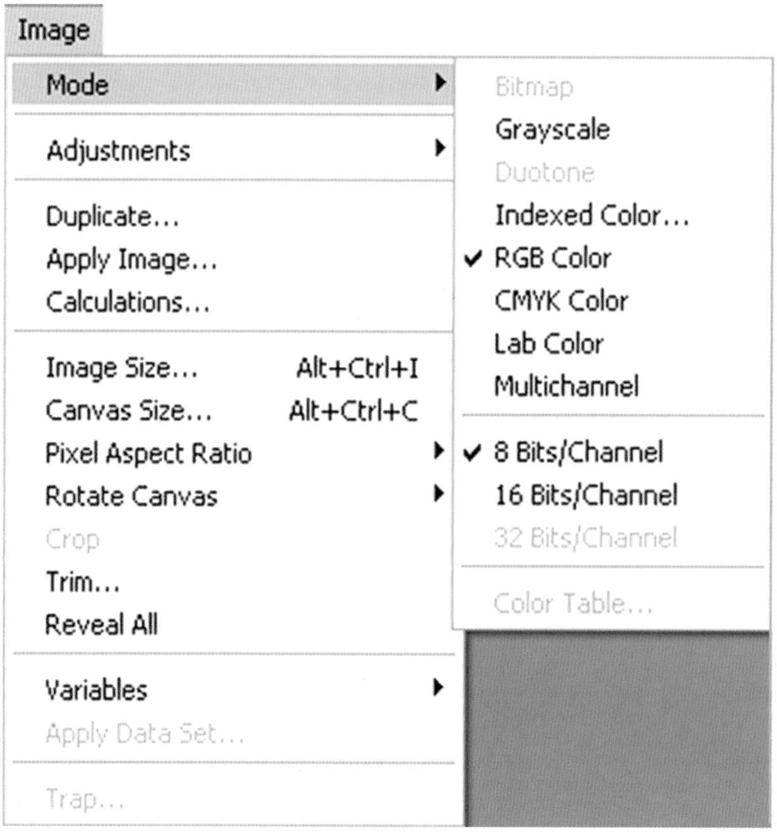

10.18
Change an image's bit-depth, or amount of color information, by selecting from Photoshop's Image menu.

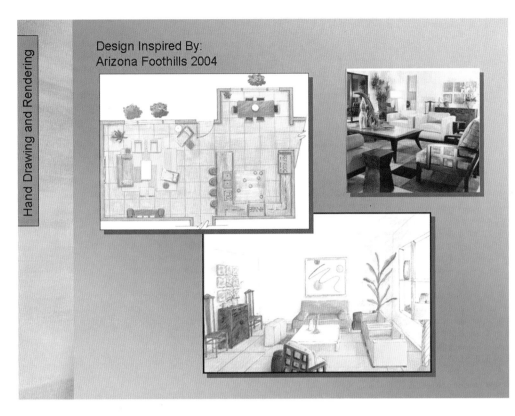

Design Inspired By:
Arizona Foothills 2004

Hand Drawing and Rendering

need to adjust the colors of your images twice: once for a printed portfolio and once for a digital version (see Figure 10.19).

Color Modes

A variety of color modes (including Grayscale) appear on the list under the Image menu. Four modes of full color are commonly used in Photoshop. These are:

1. *Indexed Color,* which has 256 colors. It is useful for GIF files and web design due to its smaller file sizes.
2. *RGB Color,* which uses the additive color system of red, green, and blue. It has 256 colors × three channels, for over 16 million color options. Because of more color options, the file size will be three times larger than that produced with Indexed Color.
3. *CMYK Color,* which uses the subtractive color system of cyan, magenta, yellow, and black. It has 256 colors × four channels, for over four billion available colors. CMYK merges the four colors together so when printed, they represent full color to the naked eye.
4. *Lab Color,* which has consistent color independent of the display device. It consists of Lightness (L) and two color components: A is green to red and B is blue to yellow. LAB images have only three channels.

Grayscale Mode

You may have a quality color image. For artistic reasons, or to add drama to your layout, you can convert a color photo into black and white. The goal is to retain

RIGHT: 10.20
When an original image, like that on the left, is changed into grayscale, color information is lost. Design work courtesy of Stephanie Fanger.

BELOW: 10.21
A better method of converting a color image into grayscale is with Photoshop's Desaturate option.

the brilliancy of your color image without having it appear washed out or lacking in a full range of tones.

Photoshop is all about color. Even if an image is in Grayscale mode, it is not truly black and white as Grayscale mode includes black, white, and 254 shades of gray. Grayscale mode uses an 8-bit color mode whereby Photoshop calculates every pixel's color as a percentage of black. When you switch an image's color mode to Grayscale, you lose the color information for the entire image. The image only keeps each pixel's brightness value. To create strikingly dramatic black-and-white photos from your color images, use the Grayscale option in Photoshop under the Image menu (Mode>Grayscale). This solves the problem of having a limited web-based color palette. Note the difference between the two images in Figure 10.20.

A better method of conversion is to desaturate the image's colors. From the Image menu, select Adjustments> Desaturate (see Figure 10.21). You have the option to desaturate an entire image like the one in Figure 10.22 or only a section you have selected with a

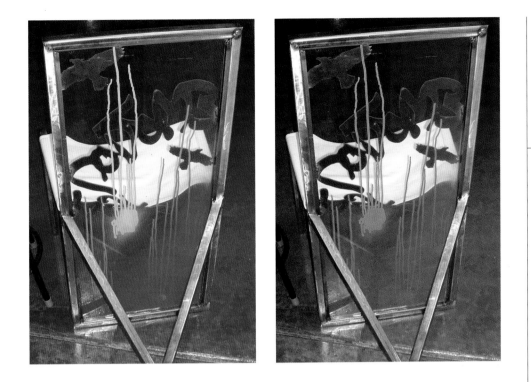

10.22
The Desaturate option in Photoshop retains the image's levels of gradation and converts them to shades of gray.
Design work courtesy of Julian Sin and Amy Oditt.

marquee box. Then only a section of your image will desaturate and become grayscale. Keep in mind that too much desaturation is as bad as too little. If a significant boost in saturation is used to convert an image to black and white, your image can lose detail and inherit additional fuzzy pixels.

Color Levels

The colors of a scanned image or digital photo can shift. All the image may need is an adjustment in tonal levels, which is a range from its lightest to darkest areas. Changing the levels of an image will adjust its values of brightness and contrast so the highlights (or lightest areas) are close to white, and the darkest areas (or shadows) are close to black. The software adjusts all of the other colors in between these two extremes.

There is an automatic adjustment option under the Image menu (Adjustments>Auto Levels) that lets the computer adjust everything for you. This basic automatic correction technique attempts to adjust the image by focusing on a neutral scale for all tones and values (Visek 2006). This option does a satisfactory job for some images but may not give you the precision you need when working on your portfolio images. For precise control, manually adjust the levels by using the Levels option from the same menu.

In the Levels control box, you will see a histogram like the one in Figure 10.23. A histogram is a graph that shows an image's color values and their intensities. (Every image will have a different histogram.) It records the frequency with which pixels of different intensities emerge in an image. A wide range of colors is designated by a histogram with many vertical lines. Few vertical lines means the

RIGHT: 10.23
This is a normal histogram, as the graph has information all the way to the edges of both the left and right sides.

BELOW: 10.24
An image with little or no color has almost no graph information in its histogram.

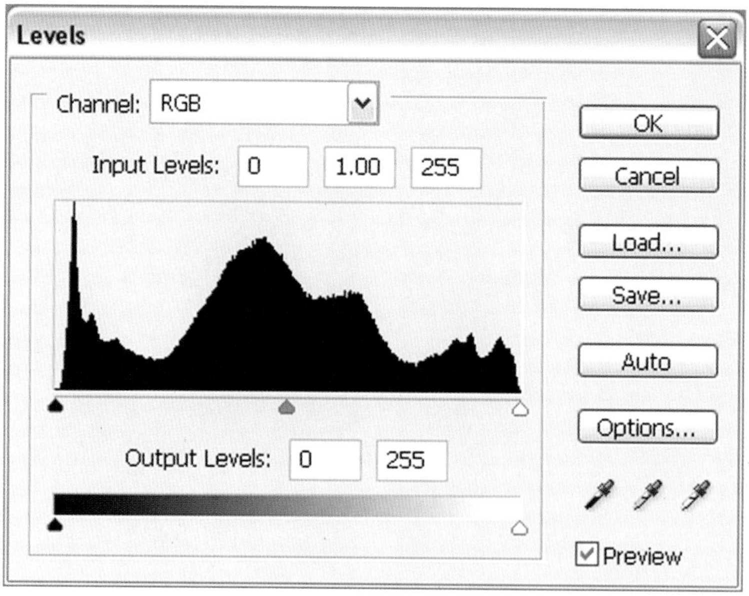

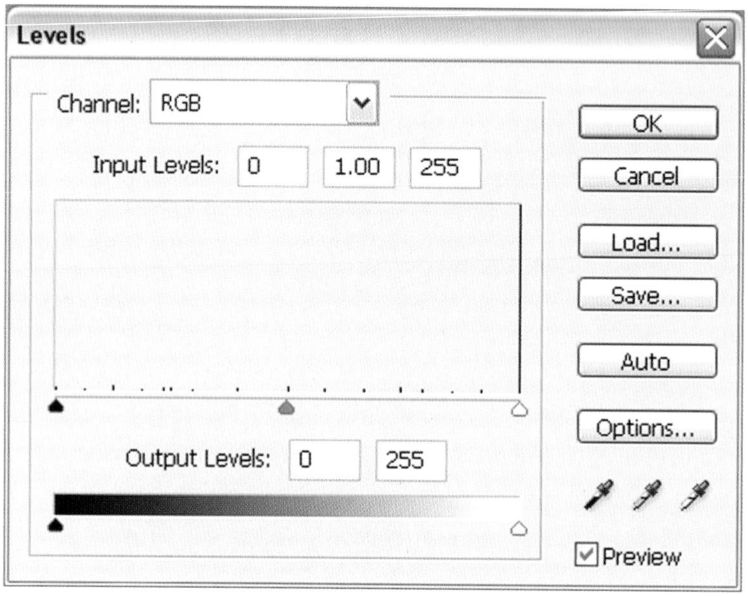

image has little color, as seen in the histogram of the black-and-white illustration in Figure 10.24. A line's height represents the number of pixels of a specific color and brightness. When many of these lines are close together, a shape is formed, like a hill. It shows the distribution of brightness in a range from zero on the left (black) to 255 on the right (white).

There are three triangular sliders that give you three points of adjustment. The black slider on the left is where the darkest pixel of shadow is located. The white slider on the right is where the lightest pixel of highlight is located. When you move either of these two sliders, the grey slider in the middle (representing midrange tones) will adjust itself, always staying in the middle of the two extremes. (You can move this middle slider yourself to increase or decrease the

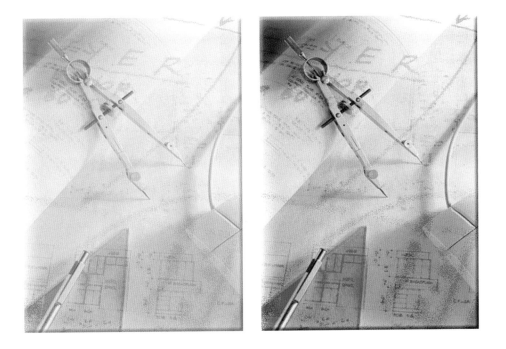

10.25
The compass on the left is the original image. The compass on the right has had its levels adjusted by moving the sliders closer to the edges of spikes in the graph. Notice how the contrast is stronger and the colors are more saturated in the compass on the right.

median color values. I find it best if I let the software manipulate the middle slider while I focus on the two extremes.)

A histogram with no lines on the right or left indicates your image has absolutely no contrast. This image needs some adjustment as it has very few darkness values represented by no line or very short vertical lines. The object is to move the right and left slides to the edges of your histogram. This sets the black point on the left to the darkest pixels and the white point on the right to the brightest pixels.

Figure 10.25 shows the same image before and after a levels adjustment. Notice the contrast enhancement. The compass on the right has a higher contrast and stands apart from the background, whereas the lower contrast on the left blends.

Posterization

Sometimes altering your image can be detrimental to your design intent. When you adjust the histogram levels too much, you can "posterize" your image. Posterization is an effect that occurs when you reduce the number of continuous tones in the image, decreasing the bit depth of an image so much that it has an impact on its quality (Visek 2006). This effect is so named because it can make your photos look like mass-produced posters printed with a limited number of color inks.

How does this occur? By manipulating a histogram too much, changing color modes (i.e., from RGB to CMYK), or overcompressing the image. It is apparent in a histogram when you split the 256 color tones into fewer differentiations. As you alter a histogram that has flat lines, the histogram will adjust itself and spread its levels over a broader range. This forms gaps or breaks between tones where intensity information is now missing (see Figure 10.26a and Figure 10.26b).

ABOVE TOP: 10.26a
Be careful when adjusting the color levels. This original image was photographed at dusk and should be dark.

ABOVE BOTTOM: 10.26b
After adjusting the levels, the tones are spread out. Now the image looks like it was taken in broad daylight!

Color Balance

Color balance is used to adjust the mixture of color in your image. For instance, a black line drawing should have black lines on a white background. That's what everyone expects to see. If the background of your scanned image appears in any other color, such as blue or pale purple, it will look wrong.

Access the Color Balance option from the Image menu under Adjustments>Color Balance. In this box, there are three sliders, each representing two opposite colors (see Figure 10.27). For example, when you move the top slider closer to Cyan, you increase the amount of cyan in the image. As you do this, you obviously are moving it farther from Red and decreasing the amount of red in your image. The other two sliders work the same way. It helps to have the Preview option selected so you can see the changes as you adjust the colors.

Brightness and Contrast

Under the same Image>Adjustment menu is a Brightness/Contrast option that allows you to lighten or darken the entire image (see Figure 10.28). Do this with

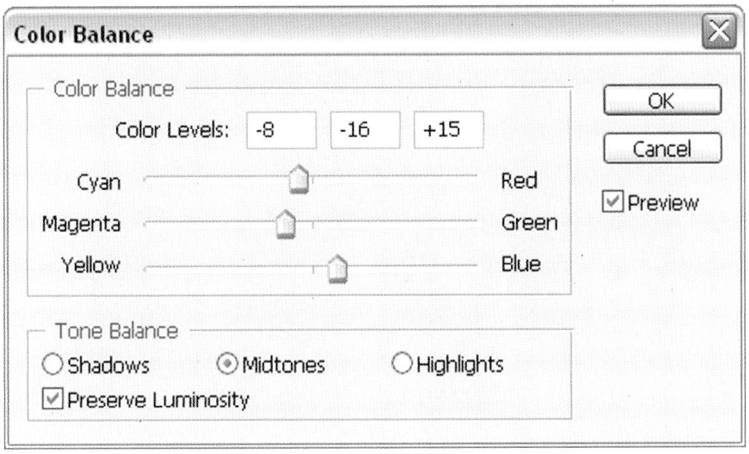

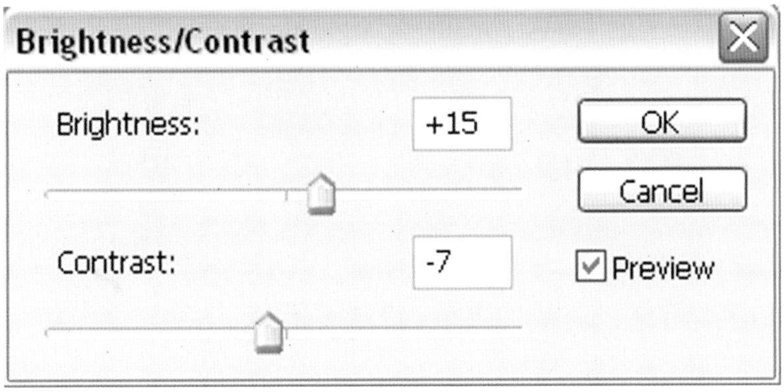

LEFT: 10.27
Color balance can be altered in Photoshop by moving each color slider.

BELOW: 10.28
Brightness and contrast can also be adjusted manually or by using the Auto Contrast option under Photoshop's Image>Adjustments menu.

caution. An image that is too bright will appear washed out. Too much contrast can turn midtone values into very light versus very dark areas, as illustrated in Figure 10.29. Notice the border of the rectangular image is completely lost when the brightness and contrast have been modified too severely.

Using Rulers, Guides, and Grids

In order to consistently place items in your layout from page to page, it might be helpful to accurately place them with the help of rulers, guides, and grids (see Figure 10.30). (Other Adobe products also have these useful features.) Rulers appear along the left and top of the window and are based on architectural inches. To turn the rulers on, select Rulers from the View menu. Selecting it again will turn them off.

A guide is a horizontal or vertical line on the screen that won't print. It is for your reference, only. You create a new guide from the View menu, under New Guide. In the New Guide box, you can select the exact orientation and position of the guide.

You can also click in the ruler area on the screen and drag a new guide onto the page. This is even faster but may not be as accurate. To lock the guides in place so you do not accidentally move them, select Lock Guides from the View menu. To get rid of existing guides, select Clear Guides from the same menu.

10.29
Altering the brightness and contrast too much can negatively alter the original, making it appear washed out or too harsh.
Design work courtesy of Paul Hibbard.

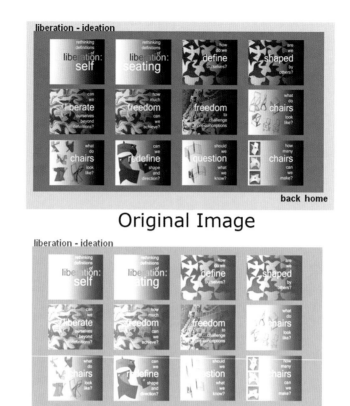

Original Image

Too Bright

Too Much Contrast

Photoshop's Grid can be turned on and off from the View>Show menu. It provides a rectangular reference grid to help you align your images. Like rulers and guides, the grid will not print.

Cropping

The Crop tool is used to delete selected portions of your image and allows you to manipulate the size of the image by defining a rectangular area. When you use the Crop tool, the area being deleted will be illustrated in gray, as in Figure 10.31. Use the crop outline's anchors to shrink or stretch your selection. To go between

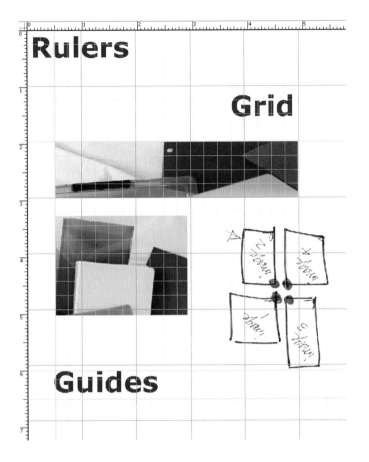

LEFT: 10.30
Several drawing tools, such as rulers, guides, and a grid, are available in Photoshop to assist you in simple layouts.

BELOW: 10.31
The Crop tool will let you select only a portion of an image. Anything outside the cropped area (in gray) will be deleted. Design work courtesy of Shelby Bogaard.

pixels, press and hold the Ctrl key while picking on and dragging the anchors. When you are satisfied with the crop, press Enter. Anything *outside* the highlighted area will be deleted. Never crop an original image, because once the image is cropped and saved, there is no going back.

Resizing

It is sometimes necessary to change the size of part of your image, or the entire image. To change the size of an entire image without cropping it, access the Image Size option from the Image menu. Adjusting the pixel dimensions will automatically adjust the document size and resolution, and vice versa. These settings are interrelated. Unless you wish to alter the shape of your image's outline, check the Constrain Proportions box to keep the new width and height consistent with the original (see Figure 10.32).

To resize a portion of an image, use the Transform, Scale option under the Edit menu. Use one of the Marquee tools in the toolbox to highlight a portion of the image (see Figure 10.33). Marquee options allow you to select an area by picking and dragging a window around it. All options help you stretch or shrink the image with grip points on the selection window (see Figure 10.34). When you are satisfied with the selection, press the Enter key to lock in the new size. Why would you use this option? To create a thumbnail image of a portion of your drawing.

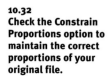

10.32
Check the Constrain Proportions option to maintain the correct proportions of your original file.

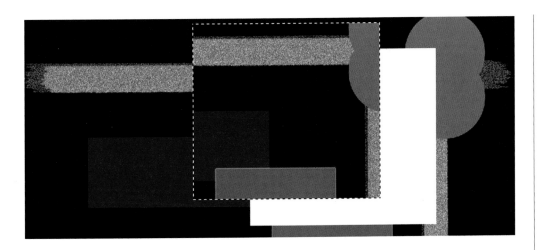

LEFT: 10.33
As this illustration shows, you can use any of Photoshop's Marquee tools to highlight a portion of an image and manipulate it separately.

BELOW: 10.34
The Marquee tools can be used to highlight a section of your image. Under Photoshop's Edit menu, you will find several transformation options, such as Scale.

Rotating

After you scan or digitally photograph your work, you may need to rotate it from landscape to portrait, or vice versa. You can do this under the Image menu (Rotate Canvas). Use either the 90 Clockwise or 90 Counter-Clockwise options. Most likely, your image is oriented in the right direction but is slightly askew. To rotate your image so it is square, use the arbitrary rotation feature (see Figure 10.35).

Exploded axonometric of wall in the kitchen which becomes and outdoor cooking area

Exploded axonometric of wall in the kitchen which becomes and outdoor cooking area

10.35
An unfortunate scanning error seen in the left image is quickly corrected in Photoshop with an arbitrary rotation of 3 degrees. Design work courtesy of Liisa Taylor.

Unfortunately, arbitrary rotation is a hit-or-miss endeavor. First, determine the direction in which the photo needs to rotate. (Clockwise? Counter-clockwise?). Then estimate the amount you need to rotate by entering the angle. This number is usually less than one degree, like 0.5 or 0.25. If this amount of rotation is not enough or too much, you can simply click Undo and try again.

Sharpening

You take a dozen or more pictures and when you begin downloading the files, the picture you really wanted is blurry. Figures! Just how blurry though? An image that is slightly out of focus can be rescued with the Sharpen filter. Incredibly blurry images cannot be revived. Sorry.

To sharpen an image means to make the edges and areas of high color contrast more distinct. An image with low contrast will appear dull and flat, lacking the impact it needs to convey a professional appearance. Sharpening line drawings like the one in Figure 10.36 and other vector-based artwork may help.

The Sharpen options are available under the Filter menu (see Figure 10.37). There are three ways to adjust the sharpness of your image:

1. *Amount:* This controls the amount of sharpening. This is indicated as a percentage.
2. *Radius:* This controls the width of the sharpened edge. A higher number of pixels will produce a wider edge, whereas a lower number of pixels will produce a thinner edge.
3. *Threshold:* This brings back the softer portions of the image.

Never sharpen a photograph. For this, explore the Unsharp Mask filter option instead (see Figure 10.38). You unsharpen a photo to sharpen it. Sounds stupid,

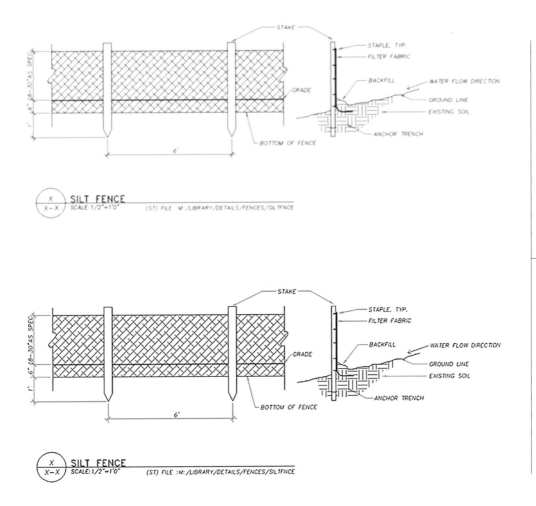

LEFT: 10.36
To give your line drawings more contrast, Photoshop's Sharpen option can be used to make the edges distinct. Notice how the bottom line drawing is crisper and more prominent.

BELOW: 10.37
All Sharpen (and un-Sharpen) options can be found under Photoshop's Filter menu.

right? A long time ago when optical techniques were first being used (prior to the computer age), parts of a film were cut and exposed in order to increase contrast. Other parts of the film were left alone. What happened is the bold edges were pulled into focus while the softer areas were left unaffected. What was inside the masked area was protected; the area outside was sharpened. Hence the term *unsharp mask* was born.

Photoshop's Unsharp Mask increases your image's impact by making the edges more distinct, causing it to "pop" off the page or screen. It affects the areas of highest contrast, while leaving the areas of subtle contrast alone. By escalating the contrast, this tool fools the eye into thinking subtler areas are in focus, too.

Don't oversharpen! Making minimal adjustment gets the best results. Too many adjustments result in visual noise, artifacts, extra shadows,

10.38
Use the Unsharp Mask option to make a photograph's bold areas more prominent while leaving softer areas unaltered.

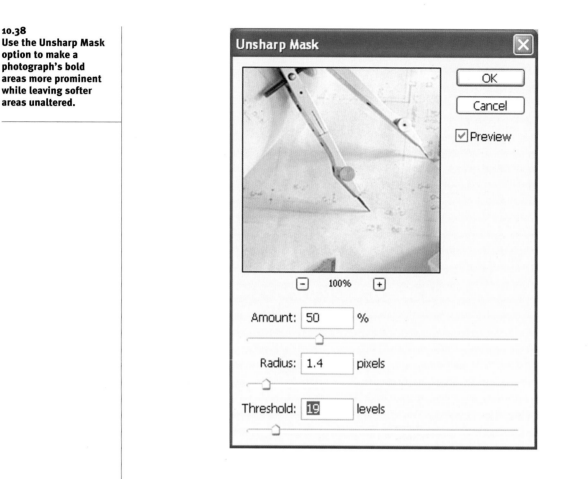

and shifted colors. I've seen some really good images completely ruined by over-sharpening. Occasionally, colors will change or turn out to be oversaturated after filtering. If this happens, use the Fade Sharpen filter available under the Edit menu right after using the Sharpen filter (Penston 2006).

Knowing when to sharpen an image will avoid image artifacts. Avoid sharpening a compressed file. Instead, sharpen the file in its universal format and then save it to a compressed format. Apply sharpening (or unsharpening) *after* you have resized your image to its final size. Resize an image and *then* apply Unsharp Mask with a radius of 0.2 to 0.3 (McHugh 2005c). It makes no sense to sharpen it and then blow up all the pixels. Otherwise, halos you didn't see before will become visible. You won't need to sharpen small thumbnail images for your digital portfolio very much. Larger prints for your printed portfolio might require more sharpening. Use Photoshop's Smart Sharpen option if available.

Using the Smart Sharpen Filter
Photoshop CS2 offers a Smart Sharpen filter, which gives you advanced control over how you sharpen your image. The Advanced mode allows independent control of shadow and highlight settings (see Figure 10.39). Of importance are the three blur removal options: Gaussian blur, Lens blur, and Motion blur. The Gaussian option gives you results very similar to Unsharp Mask. The Lens option

LEFT: 10.39
Photoshop's Smart Sharpen option allows you to have control over the amount of image highlight and shadow.

BELOW: 10.40
Photoshop's Eraser tool will wipe out parts of the image. The white visible here is the color of the image's background.

helps you eliminate halos around the edges of the image if you oversharpened it before. The Motion option helps you counteract a slight blur if you bumped the camera slightly when taking the shot.

Interpolators that preserve sharpness are more inclined to produce a moiré effect (an aliasing artifact). To counter this problem, apply Unsharp Mask right after resizing an image. An image that is downsized by half or more will not show the amount of detail seen in its fuller version. It is also helpful to use the Blur option in Photoshop *before* you downsize the image. This eliminates tiny details that you know will never appear at a lower resolution. Don't blur too much or you will soften the image too much. So, the process would be to (1) blur, (2) downsize, and (3) sharpen your image (McHugh 2005c).

Erasing

To delete a portion of your image, use the Eraser tool (see Figure 10.40). Since the image is really one layer, when you use the eraser, the blank area will return to the background color underneath, which is usually white. The size of the eraser is controlled with the brush sizes. Access these sizes from the Window menu (Show Brushes). It's helpful to keep

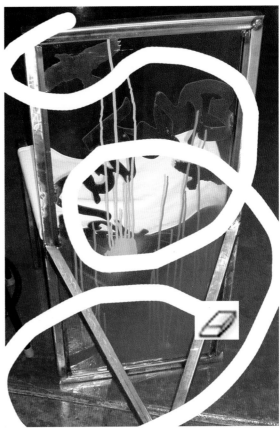

the eraser small and use the Zoom tool to get closer to the image. This gives you a higher level of control and precision. Another helpful suggestion is to make sure you are on the correct layer before erasing a part of the image. I've swiped the eraser across my image only to find out I was on the wrong layer and was erasing the wrong things.

Clone Stamping

The Clone Stamp tool is useful for duplicating selected areas of your image to another location. When you use the eraser (as described above), you wipe elements off a layer and you see the background instead. What if you want to simply get rid of a smudge or some text on your image but you want to keep the same color and texture that the smudge is sitting on? Clone it. Replace what you don't want with a clean background of the same color and texture (see Figure 10.41).

Here's how it works. You first create a color sample by positioning the Stamp tool over the part of the image you want to duplicate. Hold down the Alt key and click on the area of color. Let go of the Alt key. The cursor will pick up the colors and textures of the sample and repeat them wherever you move the cursor. The crosshairs mark the original sampling point. The size of the stamp itself is dictated by the size of your brush, just like when using the eraser. Move your cursor over the objects you want to erase. Click and drag with your cursor. The new color sample will brush over your other objects. Be careful when doing this because you can easily move too quickly and pick up other background colors and objects that you don't want.

10.41
The Clone Stamp tool in Photoshop allows you to pick up one area of color and texture and lay it over another, like duplicating the wood grain across the bottom of this bookcase.

Merging Images

When photographing a large two-dimensional (2-D) presentation isn't feasible, you can scan it in multiple pieces and then bring them back together. There are two ways to merge two or more images into one composite image: with stitching software and by hand.

Large 2-D pieces can be scanned in sections and then merged together in Photoshop. This is known as photomerging, or stitching. Allow a good amount of overlap on each image, such as 25 to 30 percent of the image (Baron 2004). The software has enough information to then determine where to put each image. There are other software options for merging photographs together, known as photo-stitching packages. These are designed for photographers who enjoy creating panoramic images of cityscapes and other large-scale photos, or for web designers looking to create full virtual tours of real spaces. You are looking to use a Flat Stitch option that allows you to merge smaller scans into one large picture. Many of these packages account for focal length, camera tilt, and other distortion effects. When

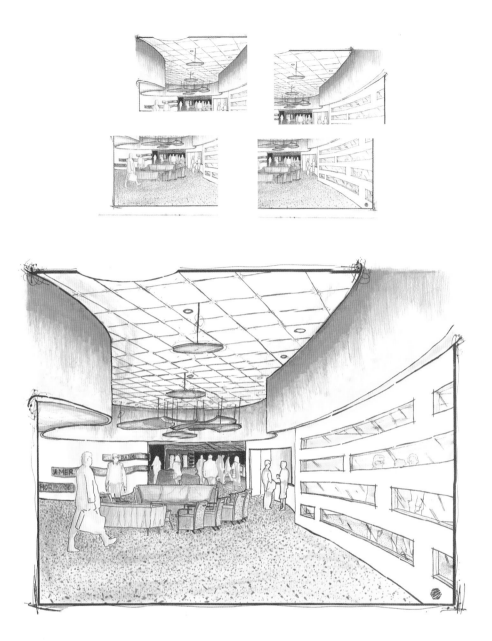

10.42
Four images are combined using Photoshop's Photo Merge automated command.
Design work courtesy of Aaron J. Kulik.

stitched correctly, your composite image should be completely seamless, with no indication of where the images were merged. It is beyond the scope of this book to provided detailed directions for these applications. Search the Internet for stitching software, such as RealViz Stitcher, Panavue, and others.

The second way to merge your images is by hand, as depicted in Figure 10.42. Once you have all of your individual images in digital format, adjust each image for brightness. Rotate the images if necessary to obtain a consistent orientation. Copy and paste two images into a new file onto separate layers and place them side-by-side. Move them next to each other, overlapping them slightly to ensure accurate alignment. It may help to change the transparency of one layer to about 50 percent. After that, you can see when one image overlaps another. Once they are aligned correctly, you can highlight a portion and delete the overlap.

CONCLUSION

Moving from traditional to digital media takes additional thought and consideration. Scanned and photographed images rarely transfer perfectly to a computer. There is always some element to tweak, such as the color, size, sharpness, and more. We will continue in the next chapter to develop a digital portfolio by considering the addition of audio and video elements. Discussion will continue by considering the benefits of Microsoft PowerPoint and Portable Document Format (PDF) files as assembly methods for your portfolio.

Putting Your Digital Portfolio Together

A digital portfolio demonstrates your ability to create multimedia presentations. As mentioned in Chapter 1, multimedia simply means many types of media. Typical media include graphics, text, drawings, audio, video, and animation. But when most people refer to multimedia, they are referring to its two main forms: audio and video. In this chapter, we'll start with tips on optimizing your files for digital media. We'll then explore the formats and software applications typically used for including audio and video in your digital portfolio. In addition, Microsoft PowerPoint and Portable Document Format (PDF) files will be considered, particularly the advantages and disadvantages of assembling your work in these fashions.

GETTING STARTED

A repository of your work will be used in different portfolio formats at different times throughout your education and career. You may need a digital portfolio because one portfolio format does not serve all purposes. Creating a digital portfolio can be a challenge, as different projects require different methods of conversion into digital media. The best way to start is to work from your existing traditional portfolio. After all, you will need a printed portfolio anyway. Why not start from there?

How do you decide in what format to put your portfolio? Weighing heavily on this decision is the audience, because the look and feel of a digital presentation may affect their response to your work. They must have basic computer skills to access and view your digital portfolio. So only those with technical skills and access to computer equipment can participate.

11.1
Once scanned, these renderings can be manipulated digitally for a printed or electronic presentation. Design work courtesy of Paul Marquez.

Another consideration is the software you'll use to create it. The software will restrict or enhance the process. The goal is to take as few steps as possible when converting your conventional materials (like the renderings in Figure 11.1) to a digital format. Determine the best software application for your needs rather than manipulating your images several times in various programs.

Most of the technological aspects of constructing and presenting your digital portfolio can be accomplished with readily available hardware and software. More advanced multimedia production requires high-tech equipment, which comes with an equally high price tag. Colleges and universities usually purchase one or two copies of high-end software and make it available to students. Take advantage of these software packages and other equipment available to you in school while you can.

One dilemma of designing with technology is the constant awareness of the constraints of computers and multimedia. What if you have a fabulous idea but never pursue it because the technology available today just won't suffice? Although using currently available technology is easy, freedom of movement in your portfolio and your own creativity may be limited or restricted if you limit yourself just to the software applications you know. Don't limit yourself or your portfolio's potential. Start with existing tools with which you are familiar. What software can you use now without having to learn new skills? Can your portfolio be made even better by using a piece of software you don't know yet? This is a good excuse to learn that extra application. You can learn new software applications once you begin putting together the basic components of your portfolio. But at least you can get started now.

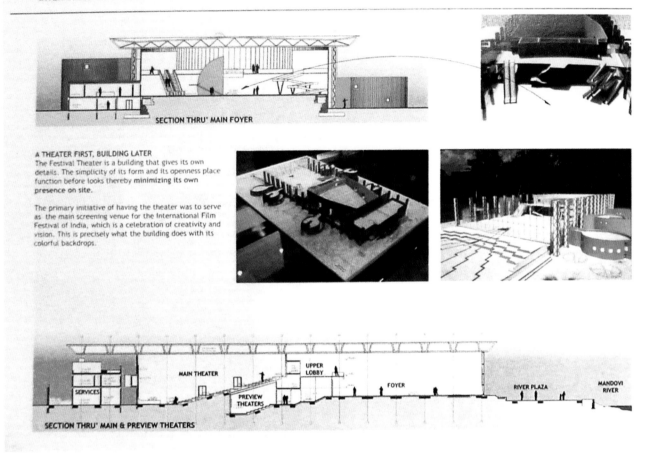

SECTION THRU' MAIN FOYER

A THEATER FIRST, BUILDING LATER
The Festival Theater is a building that gives its own
details. The simplicity of its form and its openness place
function before looks thereby minimizing its own
presence on site.

The primary initiative of having the theater was to serve
as the main screening venue for the International Film
Festival of India, which is a celebration of creativity and
vision. This is precisely what the building does with its
colorful backdrops.

SECTION THRU' MAIN & PREVIEW THEATERS

Selecting the right digital design tools is an important first step in putting your digital portfolio together. How you use the technology tools to produce your digital portfolio says as much about your tech-savvy computer skills as the computer-aided drawings, models, and renderings presented in it (see Figure 11.2).

The vast amount of digital and multimedia technologies available to you is unbelievable, and also overwhelming. How do you know what tools to use? When selecting design tools to create your digital portfolio, ask yourself these questions:

1. What platform will I use (Windows or Macintosh)?
2. What tools are available to me?
3. If a tool I need is not available at my school, where can I access it?
4. If I run into technical problems with either the hardware or software, what support is available to me?
5. What tools can I realistically afford to purchase?
6. What tools do I already know how to use?
7. What tools do I want to use, even if I have to seek training or teach myself to use these tools?

11.2
The integration of several computer applications was required to produce this layout.
Design work courtesy of Charudatta Joshi.

8. How will I display my completed digital portfolio? CD or web site?

9. Will I create one big file for CD distribution? Or many individual files for posting on the Internet?

10. Do I need any special players or viewing software to enable others to see or experience my portfolio?

11. What media formats will I use (i.e., images, sound, movies)? Do the tools I like to use support these formats?

There are many other questions you will ask yourself as you begin your digital portfolio. Bear in mind that "going digital" will not make a bad portfolio better. As in a traditional portfolio, if a project isn't top-notch, don't include it in your digital portfolio. If you have a project that is all ready flawed, trying to convert it to a digital format will only make it worse. And it will take up more of your time too. Be realistic about what you can accomplish in a designated amount of time. Too many bells and whistles will overshadow your design work. Likewise, if you have difficulty managing the digital presentation of your work, your technical abilities will be questioned.

Let's start by talking about some of the core elements of a digital portfolio. You will obviously need images of your design work. You probably have some great images from your printed portfolio. You will need to tweak them for display on computer monitors (see Figure 11.3). And what about audio? Do you want to add sound and narration to your digital portfolio? While we're talking about audio, let's add in video. Video is something you cannot do with a printed portfolio. You can display an actual interior, exterior, or building you designed (or helped design) by walking through the space with a digital video recorder. Animations and motion graphics can be added for an extra special touch. Let's start with optimizing your images and move on from there.

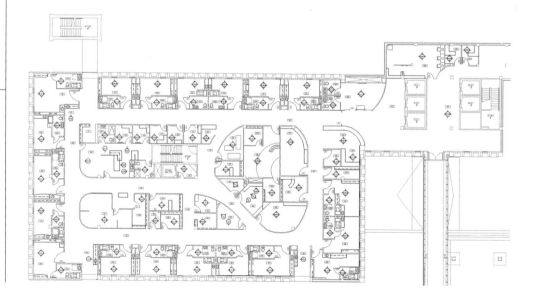

11.3
A line drawing, like this CAD floor plan, may look better in print than on a monitor. Why? Because a single line in the software will fill one pixel only. Angled lines can pixellate if not exported correctly. Design work courtesy of Alexandra C. Ayres, Sally Azer, and Kelly Robinson.

OPTIMIZING IMAGES FOR THE INTERNET

An image that loads and views quickly on your personal computer may drag when accessed on the Internet. Images in your digital portfolio must be of high quality yet quickly accessible by the viewer. You will undoubtedly need to optimize your images. To optimize an image means to adjust it for use on the Internet. You need to consider not only how the image will look and its quality, but also the size of the image file. You'll need to finesse the size, format, and color of an image in order to reduce the file size without sacrificing too much of its quality. You are doing a balancing act with your images. Ask yourself, "Do I want to reduce the size but sacrifice the quality? Or vice versa?"

Are you afraid to do anything with your images now? Do you feel like you can't win? Have no fear. Face it. The people reviewing your work will not pull out a magnifying glass to scrutinize your images. Nor will they spend more than 10 or 15 seconds looking at them (unless they cannot figure out *what* they are looking at). Figure 11.4 is a good example of a portfolio spread with clear focus.

Four ways to optimize your images for the web involve the image's colors, its size or dimensions, the ability to reuse them from one page to the next, and the amount of image compression you select (Brown 2005b). The size of an image is represented by its number of pixels. By defining the size, the browser can block out that area of the web page for your image and start loading the text immediately. The smaller the image's actual dimensions, the faster it will download. You may need to alter the size of an image, like the one in Figure 11.5.

It's important to understand the resolution and color capacity of computer monitors. Years ago, the Internet was created when computer monitors had a palette of only 256 colors. Even if you selected one of these colors, color information on the Internet is limited to only 216 colors. These colors became known as

11.4
**A simple layout with good-quality images to convey the project's look and a short description makes a wonderful presentation.
Design work courtesy of Daniel Childers.**

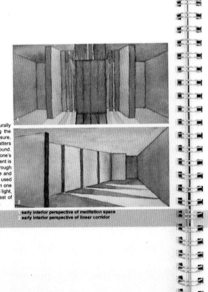

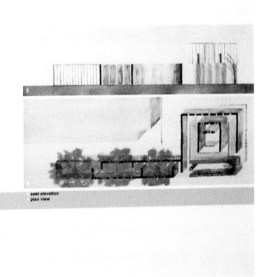

RIGHT: 11.5
An image may need to be resized to display quickly on the Internet.
Design work courtesy of Zubin Shroff.

BELOW: 11.6
When you check the Only Web Colors box in the lower left corner, Photoshop will only let you select among the 216 colors that can be displayed on both Mac and Windows platforms.

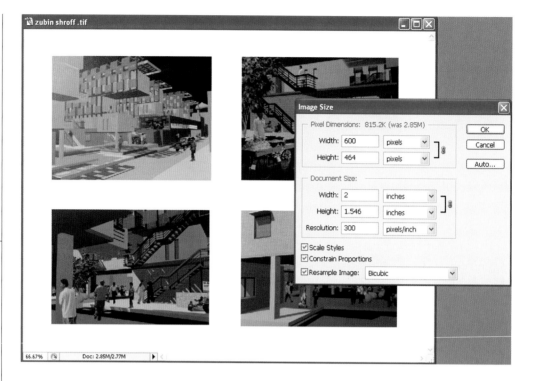

web safe. Not sure which colors are web safe? Simply check the Only Web Colors box in Photoshop's Color Picker box (see Figure 11.6). This restricts you to select only the colors that won't dither on someone's really old 8-bit monitor.

Color can play a role in optimizing your images, too. Use of CMYK for images on your web site is not recommended because this color mode is really intended for print media, only. Stick with RGB format. Know that your online images may

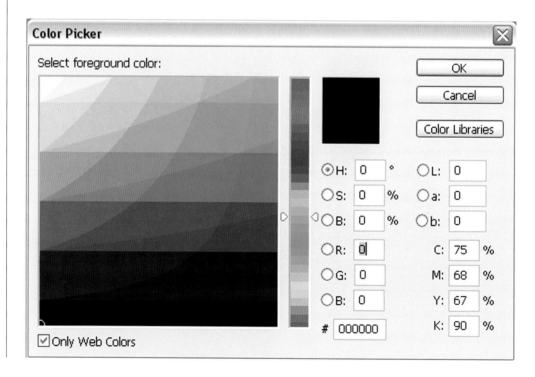

not display all 256 colors in them. If an image's color will not appear on the web page, optimize it. Get rid of color values that will not display anyway. This makes the file smaller. Preview the image first. It may look just as good as the original.

It is impossible to create images that will look wonderful on every monitor and to every person. Once your files are on the Internet, you have no idea at what size your work will be viewed. I could download some of your images and then scrutinize them at 500 percent if I really wanted to. Since the destination monitor is unknown, I would recommend assessing and scrutinizing your web images at 100 percent zoom because that's how most others will see them on the web.

Reusing the same elements from one web page to another can greatly speed up the download time on your web site. These elements can include images, graphic menus, navigation buttons, logos, and so on (see Figure 11.7). When the same elements are reused on successive pages, the user's computer only needs to download them once. Here's how it works. When you access a web site, let's say your school's home page, any images on that web site such as a school logo are downloaded to your computer and stored in cache or temporary memory. When you go to the next page, the school logo is recycled to that page. The computer does not need to retrieve it from the server again because it comes out of cache memory. This saves time.

As connection speeds to the Internet have increased, so have our expectations. We live in an impatient society. Some authors use a 30-Second Rule for seeing the entire page (Brown 2005b). Not just a portion of the page, but the entire page contents in 30 seconds. Text should appear within the first 10 seconds. Smaller images should appear next, within the first 20 seconds of accessing the page (Brown 2005c). After 30 seconds, there is no guarantee that you will keep the attention of the viewer. Few people will wait even 60 seconds for your portfolio page to download and display. Therefore, try to compress files for your web-based digital portfolio to under 50KB apiece (Prociuk 2005b).

Connection speed is intimately connected to file size. For example, an 80-KB file opened on a browser with a 28.8kbps modem connection takes approximately 40 seconds. (This is the speed for downloading over a regular phone line.) You cannot assume everyone has the same connection capabilities that you might have access to at your school or office. You can estimate that 2 KB will transfer every second over a 28.8 kbps modem. What might take you five seconds to download

11.7
Several items are "recycled" on these web pages, such as the gray bar on the left and various graphic elements. This helps the pages load quickly. Design work courtesy of William Iadevaia.

and view at school may take someone at home five minutes on a bandwidth-challenged system (Brown 2005a). Connection speed can become even more of a problem when you consider international connections.

Photoshop Web Features

Let's say you have an image to use for your web-based digital portfolio. How much quality are you willing to sacrifice for a faster download time? There is a quick way to review the same image in multiple formats by using Photoshop's Save for Web feature. (Photoshop and Illustrator both have this feature.) This option allows you to review images at different resolutions and their approximate download times at 28.8 kbps. You can find this under File>Save for Web. You have the option to review one, two, or four versions of the open image with different compression settings and file formats (see Figure 11.8). The exact file sizes listed under each image are estimates. The only way to know exactly how big a file will be is to save the highlighted one in the desired format and check its size outside of Photoshop.

You can mix image formats on your web site. It makes sense. Not everything has to be a JPEG. A very colorful image can be saved as a JPEG file; a black-and-white

11.8
Photoshop's Save for Web feature allows you to review the same image in four different formats.

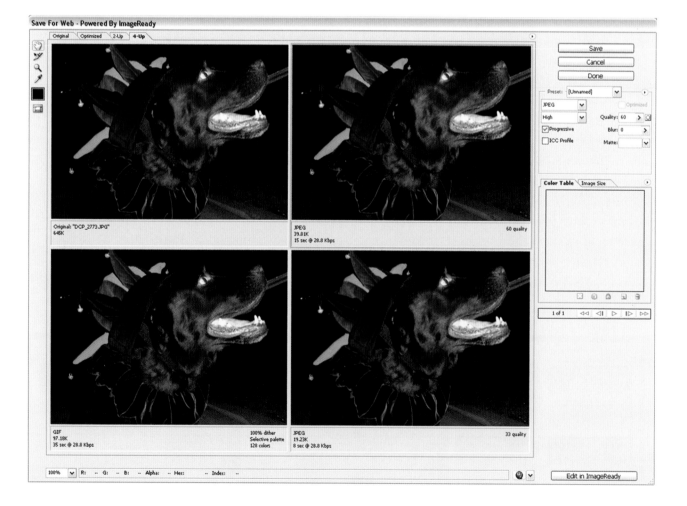

line drawing or one with little color, as a GIF file. Saving as a JPEG once will compress the image to a nice small size. Remember, don't save it as a JPEG more than once, or the result will be lossy compression. As technology improves, I am sure an ideal solution will emerge. For now, remember to go back to your original file if you need to tweak an image all ready saved as a JPEG.

I would suggest you select the Progressive compression option when saving JPEG images. This allows the web browser to quickly display a low-resolution version of the image. Then a high-resolution version replaces it. This is a good thing, as the viewer's patience is not tested. The file size is not increased at all with a progressive JPEG. That's worth it.

Photoshop also has a helpful feature called a Web Photo Gallery that can help you quickly optimize multiple images for the web. This is an automated feature that exports a whole web page of thumbnail images with larger preview images, plus the code to display it. This web gallery feature will automatically convert your images from 16-bit to 8-bit and from CMYK color mode to RGB. Likewise, any layers in your image are routinely flattened, your text is rasterized, and blending modes are applied. How cool is that? However, this feature does not allow for much manipulation or customization, as it has a limited number of layout styles and a confined range of image size and color combinations.

If you are interested, here's how it works. Bear in mind that you can adjust the settings however you want; these are only suggestions to get you started. After accessing the feature from the File menu under Automate, select a source folder (where your images currently are) and a destination folder (where you want the optimized images and coding stored). Select a style of frame from those available in the drop-down menu. As shown in Figure 11.9, the smaller thumbnails can be displayed horizontally or vertically beside the large preview window.

Select the Thumbnail Option and set the size to Medium at 75 pixels. (This will give about a 25-KB image size, although it can fluctuate a little from image to image.) The software will then quickly open and save copies of each image as a JPEG file in your source folder. You'll end up with three folders—one for the thumbnails, one for the larger preview images, and one for the coding of the web pages that will display the images. This is a great way to start getting your images on your web site. If the gallery pages are too bland, you can always spice them up using web-editing software later. After all, a designer's portfolio is so much more!

CREATING AUDIO FILES

Including sound in your digital portfolio is an option you may consider to add dimension and depth to your work. It certainly is something that is not possible with a traditional printed portfolio. Because communication often occurs through speaking and listening (Barrett 1998), the inclusion of sound can be an advantage. But include it sparingly and with much thought. Only use what would enhance your work, not detract from it (see Box 11.1).

11.9
You can create a quick web-based art gallery in either a horizontal or vertical format by using Photoshop's Web Photo Gallery.

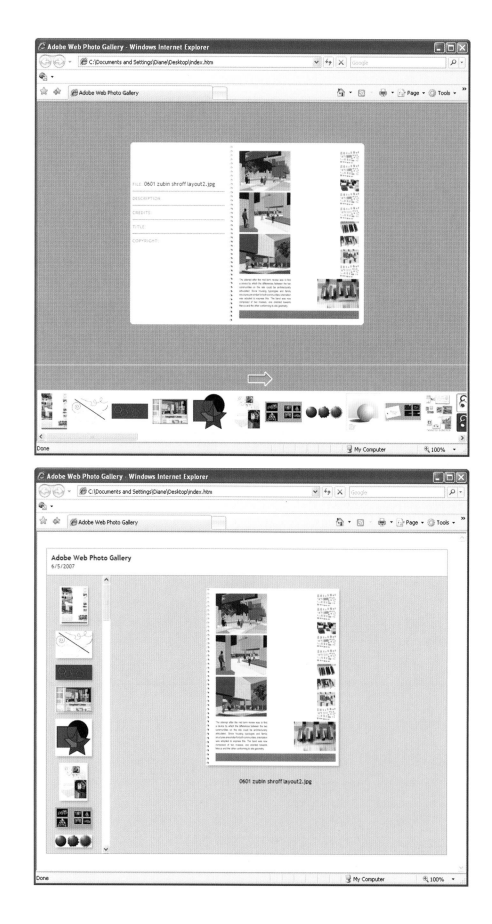

Note that there is a difference of opinion on including sound in your portfolio, either web-based or on CD. Some practitioners find that the use of sound adds another element to the portfolio experience. Others find it annoying when they access your portfolio and music comes blaring out of their desktop speakers. It wouldn't hurt to mention on your CD cover or web site homepage that sound is a part of your portfolio presentation. The viewer can then decide to turn it off or turn it up. Let's begin by discussing the use of sound in your portfolio, the various formats of audio files, and how you can work with them to your best advantage.

Audio Basics

There are two kinds of audio files: streaming and nonstreaming. *Streaming* refers to technology that permits audio and video files to begin playing back before they are completely downloaded from the Internet. These are separate files referenced in your programming. When these files are needed in your portfolio, they download and start to play on the viewer's computer. As the first part is playing, the rest of the file continues to download. It takes little time to start hearing the audio, as these compressed files significantly reduce download time. Viewers can even skip forward to any part of your audio or video without having to wait for the whole thing to download. Disadvantages of streaming files are the programming necessary to use them and the need for the viewer to have a special player to hear them. *Nonstreaming* audio files are fully entrenched in your digital portfolio. They are a part of your production and will play only after they have fully loaded to the viewer's computer. The major disadvantage of this type of file is that large files take longer to download. If viewers have to download a very large audio file before they can even get a peek at your projects, they may get impatient.

There are several typical audio formats. Depending on the software and platform on which you create the audio files, you will probably save in one of these formats: AIFF, MP3, or WAV. AIFF files are common on Macintosh computers. AIFF stands for Audio Interchange File Format. AIFF files are QuickTime compatible, which is a popular Macintosh audio player.

Waveform Audio (WAV) files are the standard recording format for a Windows system. They can play on both Macintosh and Windows platforms. MP3 files are the most popular. MP3 stands for MPEG Layer 3. The format is based on MPEG (Moving Picture Experts Group) technology, which creates exceedingly small files appropriate for streaming or downloading over the Internet. They have high audio quality and the best compression rates.

Some audio files require the user to have a special player or plug-in to hear the audio. Plug-ins are add-on programs that permit browsers to access and display additional file types for documents, audio, and video. Popular plug-ins are free for download from the Internet. The big question is: Will practitioners bother to download a player to simply hear sound in your portfolio? Notify reviewers if they need a certain player or plug-in and provide a link on your web site to that player, or include the actual player on your CD. The most common audio players are Real Player, QuickTime, and Windows Media Player (see Figure 11.10a, 11.10b, and 11.10c).

Real Player is a good quality audio and video software that plays every major media format. QuickTime is audio and video software originally designed for Macintosh systems but available for Windows users, too. It handles many types of file formats for video, sound, animation, graphics, text, and music.

Windows Media Player is for Windows systems and can import various types of file formats. This software comes previously installed on all Windows computers, making it easy to access and, hence, the most popular player for both audio and video files. Most computer users have at least one of these three players already available on their computer.

11.10a, 11.10b, and 11.10c
To hear audio played from your digital portfolio, a reviewer may need to have one of the three popular audio players: QuickTime, Real Player, or Windows Media Player.

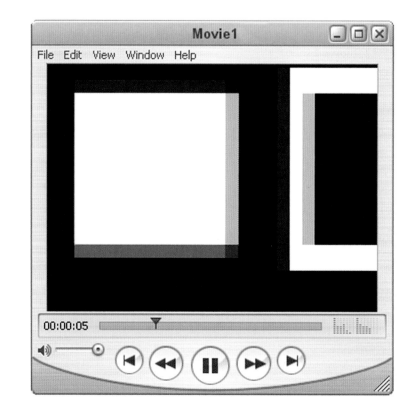

11.10a

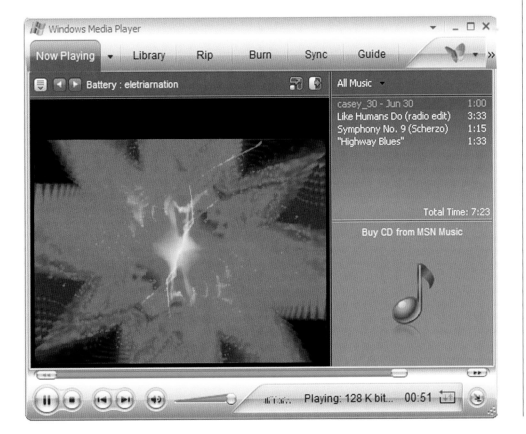

Audio Commentary

Audio explanations of design projects can be helpful to the reviewer. Again, this is something that's not possible with a traditional portfolio and can really enhance the portfolio presentation. Voice-over capabilities allow you to describe the project and provide reflective comments on the design process. This may include you (or a friend with a great speaking voice) talking about your design philosophy while the slides of your projects are fading in and out onscreen. Or it could be a verbal description of a key project, its design challenges, and how you successfully overcame those challenges. You can record this commentary using separate voice software such as Sony's Sound Forge, SoundEdit Pro, or Digital Audio Editor (see Figure 11.11). Or you can record it right in Microsoft's popular multimedia slideshow software, PowerPoint.

Write a script to read. If you don't have a script, you'll be making up your words every time. It will get tiresome and it won't seem as professional in the end. Besides, you cannot assume everyone will be able to listen to the accompanying audio. Think about universal design. Universal design is a concept that describes a design that is so well conceived that it meets all users' needs, regardless of physical disability (Nielson and Taylor 2002). The information you're conveying should be accessible to everyone. Any narrative you read should be identical to written text on the screen, easy to read, and informative. You'll need to read through your script several times to determine the right pace and tone of voice.

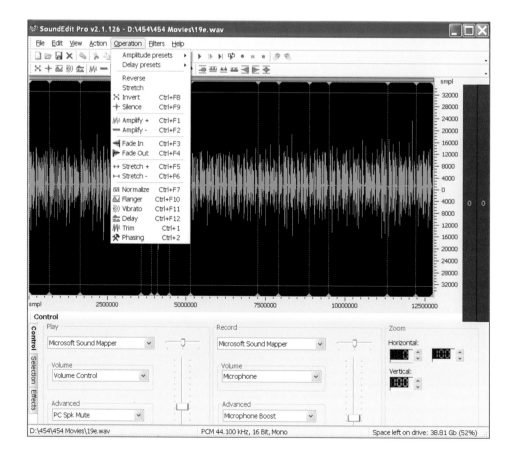

11.11
Several audio-recording software applications are available, such as SoundEdit Pro. Some are free on the Internet; others can be purchased.

Controlling background noise and unexpected disruptions is a challenge when recording audio tracks. You can unplug your phone, close your windows and blinds, and turn off any electronic devices such as fans or microwaves. Yet there are some things that are just beyond your control, like the UPS deliveryman ringing your doorbell and the dog barking at him. (Believe me, these sounds *do* get picked up clearly when you are recording.) Face it, you'll need to read through your script several times and record a number of tracks before you get it just the way you want it.

What if you speak your narrative perfectly but find out later that a low level of background noise can be heard, like a fan or computer whirring? Use the audio software's equalizer to slightly lower the audio track's volume between phrases. This unwanted noise will still be audible but at least you are drawing attention away from it during times of silence.

Other helpful audio-recording tips include using a quality microphone and headphones or speakers. Quality equipment need not cost an arm and a leg. Your local office supply or computer electronic stores have headsets with built in microphones, or a stand-alone microphone that works with your computer's speaker system. Either way, you want to use the best quality microphone to pick up your voice and all its intonations. Try to get a headset with a foam cover on the microphone as this helps diffuse harsh enunciations, such as when you say words starting with the letters "p" or "t." Any little thing you can do to make the audio sound smoother will reduce the number of times you need to record the same commentary.

Background Music

Besides an audio narrative, you can superimpose background music on your digital portfolio. Music played in the background will add another sensory mode to your presentation. It is a backdrop to the main event—the viewing of your work.

What kind of music will you choose? This will reflect on your designs as much as the selection of fonts, colors, and images you have chosen for your portfolio. Soothing jazz or classical pieces can add a touch of elegance to your portfolio. Rough, edgy music with repetitive rhythms can get annoying in time. Know your audience. If you are presenting your portfolio to a practitioner from the baby boom generation, and you are in Generation Y, your tastes and tolerances for music are very different. If others don't like the soundtrack you have chosen, you have just turned them off. You may say, "Well, heavy metal or rap music is a part of who I am and I'll put it in my digital portfolio anyway." That's your choice. Know that it's the practitioner's choice to call you for an interview.

You can record your own music if you are musically gifted. Most of us are not. However, free sound effects and music can be found on thousands of web sites. In light of recent litigation regarding the downloading of music, make sure the music you select is not bound by copyright and is truly free for you to use. You do not want to be in violation of copyright infringement over the audio track you selected.

11.12
Always provide a way to mute the portfolio's music in case the reviewer does not appreciate your auditory selection. Design work courtesy of Manu Juyal.

Lastly, the same advice you read earlier regarding the use of colors and fonts applies to audio. Just because you *can* add sounds does not mean you should. Keep it simple. Let the music or audio commentaries, or both, complement your design work, not compete with it. Be aware that your work may be reviewed in an open office environment. The practitioners who are reviewing your work may be in a situation where they cannot distract those working around them with loud music or other sounds. Do you think everyone in the office wants to hear your commentary or music blaring out of someone's speakers? Provide an "off" button that is clearly visible, like the one in Figure 11.12.

Finishing Your Audio Files

One drawback of audio files is their size. Quality sound will produce a large file. Therefore, after you have recorded and edited your audio file, compress it. Do this at the very end, and save your original audio file in case you need to return to the uncompressed version. Never compress a file more than once because the quality decreases exponentially.

It is important to listen to your audio, not just for the words but also to the level or intensity of the words. The range of sounds we can hear from low bass to high treble is represented in Hertz (Hz). This is a unit of measure for sound representing one cycle per second, or one radiowave passing one point in one second of time. It is named in honor of Heinrich Hertz, the man who discovered the theory of radio waves (Dye 2002). The human voice falls between a low bass of 85 Hz and up to 255 Hz for sopranos (Fegette 2006).

Test your music and audio on both Windows and Macintosh platforms. Test them with tiny computer speakers. Test them with large speakers and a subwoofer (if available). Listen to how your music and commentary sound under all these conditions before burning your CDs or launching your web site. Listen to your audio track several times and let your ear be the judge. Is it of high enough quality to *add* to your digital portfolio? Or does it detract from your presentation?

Lastly, don't forget about copyright or intellectual property infringement. Did you use background music? Did you ask a friend with a melodious voice to narrate an audio commentary? If you have used music or someone else's voice in your digital portfolio, note the title and artist, and provide the narrator's name. Consider having a credits page or section in your portfolio where you can acknowledge the contributions of others.

ADDING ANIMATIONS AND VIDEOS TO YOUR PORTFOLIO

One of the benefits of a digital portfolio is its inclusion of the fourth dimension—*time*. With more and more design practitioners looking for great presentation skills in the people they hire, the ability to develop animations and videos is becoming more common. You can add a dynamic element to your digital portfolio by adding motion graphics, animations, and videos of your work.

Motion Graphics and Animations

Motion graphics is a new term and profession. Although it has is no widely accepted definition, it is in essence animated graphic design. It is a creative discipline that merges graphic design, video, photography, illustration, animation, music, and sound effects. An animation is a type of moving graphic in which a series of images are displayed and then played together to give the illusion of continuous movement. (Ever watch an animated cartoon?) Multimedia presentations use animations to convey a message in a more dynamic way. They introduce compound images, time, and sound to create a short viewing experience. After all, a flash motion graphic on a web page won't run forever—it will play for only a few seconds.

As the speed of computer processors increases and desktop programs such as Apple Motion, Adobe After Effects, and Autodesk Discreet Combustion become more intuitive, motion graphics are becoming ever-prevalent in web-based communication. (An entire book could be written on each of these software applications. Check out your local library or search online for information and tutorials about each package.)

If you do not have the time to design the motion graphics yourself, there are several Internet royalty-free libraries. You can download moving and looping backgrounds and other animated elements. Just remember that these interactive elements are meant to *add* to your portfolio, not pull the attention away from your work samples.

Animated Web Pages

Animation and motion graphics are more prevalent on web sites than in CD-based portfolios. Some animated graphics require HTML programming and some do not. Hypertext Markup Language (HTML) is not software, but a computer programming language that provides the code for both the content and the look of your web site. Ask yourself, "Should my web-based portfolio have any interaction or animated graphics?" Approach this decision realistically. How much time do you have to work on your digital portfolio? Do you have the technology and visual skills to pull this off?

You have three choices for designing your web pages: static pages, simple dynamic pages, or complex dynamic pages. Static pages have no interactive elements. This does not mean they are boring and dreary. They have images, text, and straightforward navigational links. These pages are the easiest to create and maintain. Simple dynamic pages have interface interaction that can be created using the Javascript capabilities of programs such as Macromedia Dreamweaver (discussed in Chapter 12). You start with a static page and add a few animated interactions to achieve a simple dynamic page. One step further results in complex dynamic pages. These pages take advantage of HTML's power by providing the viewer with customized navigation, animated elements, and audio and video capabilities within the web pages themselves (as opposed to having to download these media and then watch them in a separate viewer). Two seminal programs for creating animations are Adobe Macromedia Flash and Microsoft Expression Interactive Designer.

Macromedia Flash

Flash is a well-liked multimedia application useful for creating nonlinear presentations, streaming vector animations and motion graphics, and interactive streaming video (see Figure 11.13). Flash files are built of vector-based objects and

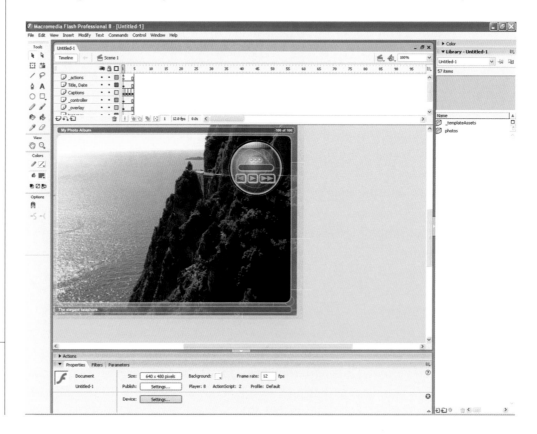

11.13
Flash is a popular application for creating animations and motion graphics.

images. Use of this application requires little programming knowledge. Its graphic interface allows you to create a presentation in a modest amount of time by utilizing a programming code called ActionScript. Many sample scripts (called Behaviors) are provided in the application that allow you to control sections of your presentation without having to write the code yourself. It also comes with design templates to assist you in forming slide shows and video presentations.

Flash provides an array of simple templates to get your web page up and running quickly and has the ability to import files from almost any other program. Because it uses vector-based technology to create its interfaces, file sizes can be kept to a manageable size, while allowing you to resize the video to any size when viewing.

Microsoft Expression Interactive Designer

Although Flash is prevalent in today's animation market, Microsoft Expression Interactive Designer is another application you might consider. Also known as Sparkle, this application allows you to create interfaces with multiple media elements, such as raster and vector images, audio, video, and high-definition text. Its obvious leverage is its seamless integration with the Windows platform.

Video of Your Work

Video is a wonderful way to visually communicate your message and to emphasize your knowledge of design. A good reason why you might wish to include a video in your digital portfolio is to showcase your three-dimensional (3-D) models or full-scale furniture (see Figure 11.14).

You can also shoot video of any completed installations or create a walkthrough of a 3-D digital computer model. Video clips take up a lot of memory so use only one when the project cannot be displayed in *any* other way. Ask yourself, "Can I convey my design just as well with a photo? Do I really need video?" Let's say you have a piece of furniture you have designed and constructed. Several photos of this chair communicate the design nicely, as shown in Figure 11.15. If it were a table, you would want to view it from all sides, particularly if all the sides are dissimilar. In that case, a video would communicate more information than several still images.

Think about why you want to include a video in your portfolio and have a plan before beginning. Why waste your time shooting a large quantity of video that you'll look at later, wondering, "What was I

11.14
The 2-D pictures of this model are nice, but a video that moves the reviewer around it may be better. Design work courtesy of Zubin Shroff.

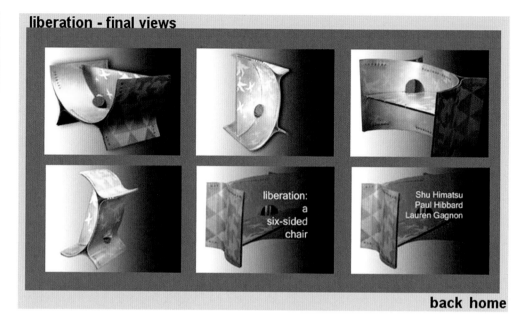

liberation – final views

liberation: a six-sided chair

Shu Himatsu
Paul Hibbard
Lauren Gagnon

back home

thinking?" Know that video takes exponentially longer to process than still images. Do you really *need* video? How much time are you willing to invest? Does it promise a future payoff (e.g., an interview that can only be gained by impressing the socks off the practitioner with a high level of technology)? Case in point, I teach an introductory course in which students complete the semester with a 20-second animated walkthrough created with 3-D modeling software. Ninety percent of the project grade is based on the design of the room and the use of 3-D modeling techniques. Ten percent is the animation. Many of my students develop grand ideas about the video and they spend little time designing their 3-D model. They spend some time rendering it with realistic colors, texture, and lighting. Over half of their time is spent *waiting* for the 20-second video to generate. We're talking 12 or more hours of letting the computer process through 300+ frames of rendered animation (see Figure 11.16). Many of the students never finish the animation because they simply run out of time.

There are several reasons *not* to include video. One is that the software to develop these features is not targeted for the design professional. These applications are intended for animation and video professionals, not the average design student. The various software applications have a learning curve that can be quite steep. How much time is it going to take to learn a software package in order to create, edit, and save a half minute of video? Is this a good use of your time?

Another disadvantage is the need for your personal computer to have a greater storage capacity. Some of these files can be absolutely huge. If you start creating animations and lots of videos of your 3-D work, you may need to purchase more RAM to properly run your files and more external memory to store them.

A further disadvantage has an impact on viewers. The video files will most likely require a player or plug-in to properly run. As for the Adobe plug-ins (Flash and Shockwave), once they are downloaded to your computer, you don't see them.

11.16
A computer-generated rendering of a 3-D model like this lobby may take hours and hours to generate. How much time can you invest in images for your portfolio? Design work courtesy of Eric Cylwik.

But your browser knows they are there and when it encounters a site that utilizes these technologies, the video or animation will automatically play. With all these disadvantages, you might think, "Why do this?" I am not trying to dissuade you from including a video in your digital portfolio. If it is an important part of your job search plan and you believe it will immensely add to your marketability, do it! Otherwise, invest your time in developing the still images and composition of your digital presentation. Still interested? Read on.

Shooting Video

There are several steps to creating a video, such as recording the clip, then editing and saving it. All of these steps require you to make decisions regarding presentation quality and file size. Short video clips can be recorded on most digital cameras or you can rent, borrow, or purchase a higher quality video recorder. Your video can even come from two or three different cameras. Know that the color balance and brightness levels will differ among cameras. Thankfully, video-editing software includes several of the same image control functions available in raster editing software (such as levels, color balance, and balance and contrast). Here are some suggestions for capturing a quality video.

Use a tripod to steady the camera. Even the slightest vibration will distort the video. The background on which you place your 3-D object should be as neutral as possible. The same suggestions provided in Chapter 10 for photographing your work apply to creating video, such as using a neutral background with little contrast and texture, providing extra lighting, considering all angles, and so on. Sometimes having the perfect setting is not possible, as depicted in Figure 11.17.

11.17
When the perfect background and lighting for your 3-D models are not available, be creative with available resources. Here, the chair was photographed against the concrete and glass of a nearby building. Design work courtesy of Katie Crestin and Alexis Raterman.

To see all sides of a model, full-scale furniture, or case goods, experiment with two methods: move the object or move the camera. You can create or purchase an inexpensive rotating device (like a lazy Susan tray) on which to place your work. To move the object, *slowly* rotate it, keeping the camera in a stationary position. Avoid any jarring motions! The other option involves rotating the camera around the object. This may be the only way to capture video of a large case good like a shelving unit or to do a walkthrough of an installation. Keep the camera close to eye level. Keep it steady. You can try recording by holding the camera yourself or setting your tripod on a rolling video tripod dolly. (This is a base with wheels that attaches to the bottom of a standard tripod and can be purchased at any store that sells photography accessories.) Move at a snail's pace. This is not the time to run around your model or literally skip through a building.

Be careful how you handle the camera controls. Zooming in and out, and panning left and right, may produce a dramatic effect. It may also induce nausea in the viewer. The video you'll produce is not Hollywood quality but a low-frame-rate movie. The more movement there is in the video, the harder it is for reviewers to focus their eyes on what is important. You may need to have a pause in the movement. This allows you to add some text or still shots, like the information seen in Figure 11.18, to get your idea across.

The same goes for changing the viewing angle. Keep the camera at the same level as you move around the object or through the space. (Again, a tripod with rolling dolly would help.) It might take some practice for you to get the hang of the camera. Avoid starting and stopping it over and over. Sure, you can edit out

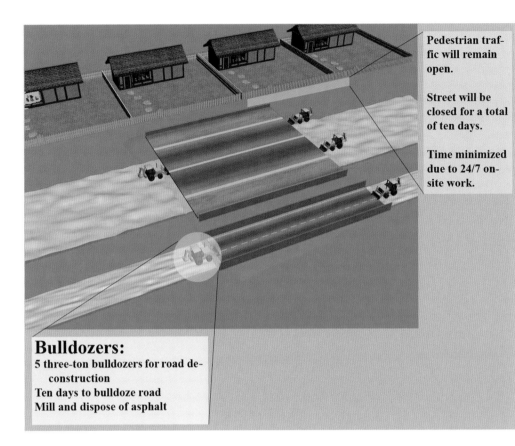

Pedestrian traffic will remain open.

Street will be closed for a total of ten days.

Time minimized due to 24/7 on-site work.

Bulldozers:
5 three-ton bulldozers for road de-
  construction
Ten days to bulldoze road
Mill and dispose of asphalt

11.18
This still image was taken from an animation and enhanced with text to help the reviewer better understand the meaning of the movie. Design work courtesy of Eric Cylwik.

the cuts with video-editing software later, but why not save yourself some time and get it right the first time? If you plan on adding narrative or background music when you edit the video, turn off the microphone while taking the video. This will decrease the file size and save you the time required to delete the audio track later.

Once you've captured the video, you need to put it into digital format. On newer digital video recorders, the output is already in a digital format. Be aware that downloading the video file to your computer will take up large quantities of your hard drive. This video may be compressed or uncompressed, depending on the abilities and settings of your camera.

Video Editor Software

Once you have recorded your video clip, you can edit it with video editor software. Several editing programs are available today and more will no doubt be available tomorrow. Popular products include Adobe Premiere and Premiere Pro, Apple Final Cut Pro, and Macromedia Director. It is beyond the scope of this book to provide detailed instructions for how to use these software applications. Designers in the area of visual communication spend months and even years becoming experts in the area of video editing. You probably don't have that much time. But you should be able to do rudimentary editing after only a few hours of experimentation.

11.19
**Adobe Premiere Pro
may be worth
investigating if you
enjoy creating movies
for your portfolio.**

Adobe Premiere and Premiere Pro Premiere and Premiere Pro are video-editing software produced by Adobe Systems (see Figure 11.19). These applications are intended for professional video editors in the film industry. (An entry-level version called Premiere Elements is oriented more toward the average consumer like you and me.) Premiere runs on both Macintosh and Windows platforms; Premiere Pro, only on Windows. Output can be saved for distribution on CD or on the Internet.

Apple Final Cut Pro If you are a dedicated Macintosh user, you may gravitate toward Apple's popular Final Cut Pro software. It is an all-in-one video editing, compositing, and special effects package. It's a nonlinear editing system, which means you can randomly access and edit any frame in the video clip. (In the past, you would have to select the pieces of the clip, organize them the way you want, and then adjust or modify the sound and images in a linear fashion.) In addition, it allows you to cut video from multiple camera sources, as well as adding filters, dissolves, and 3-D transitions. This is a piece of software worth investigating further if you feel you will be doing extensive video editing.

Macromedia Director Director provides the ability to create multimedia video content and is a solid choice for stand-alone and streaming videos to be disseminated across several mediums. It is a professional-level multimedia package that allows you to build or direct your own movie by integrating audio and video files from many different formats. Director runs on both Windows and Macintosh platforms and integrates well with Flash.

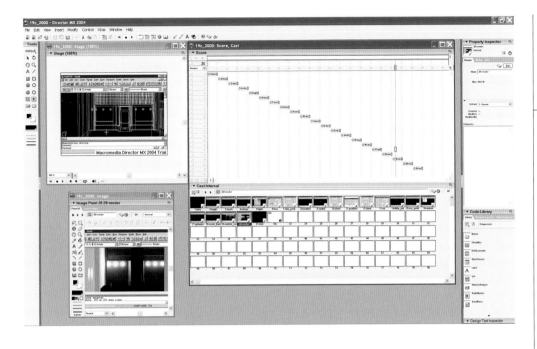

11.20
Director links the
visual and audio with
markers so when the
graphic changes,
the audio is perfectly
in sync.

Director can import a wide variety of graphic formats, video, and even music files by implementing a programming language called Lingo. It places markers at various sections of your presentation that can be linked within the file to other elements. For example, you can take an animated walkthrough you may have created in modeling software and import it into Director. You can also import a narration in which you describe the space. You can then link the two together so when the visuals shift from one area of your space to another, it will be synced with your narration (see Figure 11.20).

Director was originally intended for the creation of stand-alone presentations or CDs. But with its enhanced web-handling capabilities, it can handle online applications efficiently, too. Director exports files with a DCR extension that must be viewed with the Shockwave browser plug-in. Or, stand-alone applications can be exported that execute the movie without a plug-in.

Editing Video

Let's talk about a few tips to help in formatting and editing your clips. The simplest transition between your separate video clips, known as a *cut,* is a quick change from one scene to another. Even a simple cut from one screen to another can support your design intent. It is helpful to the viewer to lead him into your video with black or a neutral color (like gray) and end with the same color. Accommodate the viewer by giving him a title page at the front of your video, to provide context and preparation for what is about to be seen. A closing page is also helpful, telling him the video is over (i.e., Credits).

The size of the viewing window will be small. For online presentations, the screen size works well at 320 × 240 instead of 480 × 360 (see Figure 11.21). This may seem small, but any larger and the video may not fit in the player's window.

11.21
A smaller video screen size allows a reviewer with a smaller monitor to see the same information as one with a large monitor.

Plus, it will take too long to download. Decreasing the window size decreases the file size. Obviously, if you're working off a CD, you can get away with a larger window size and, therefore, a larger file size.

Along the same lines, frame rate will affect video quality and file size. If you lower the frame rate too much, you'll lose video quality and the illusion of movement. If you raise it too high, the file size will grow and the time to download the video will be too long. Finesse the frame rate settings before you commit to capturing a hefty amount of video.

Saving Video
When you are done editing your video (with titles, special effects, and even audio), you have several options for saving your file. See Table 11.1 for typical audio and video file formats. You can save it as an MPEG file. MPEG is not one type of file but a group of compression standards for video and audio, which includes MPEG-1, -2, -3, and -4. (The most common is the MPEG-3, referred to as MP3). These types of files are most often downloaded from the Internet rather than streamed because the files compress frames individually and is valuable for Internet usage. The latest compression standard is MPEG-4. It brings elevated levels of interaction with content and produces a higher quality video with smaller file sizes than any other type of video file format.

These files are usually in Audio Video Interchange (AVI) or Movie File (MOV) format: AVI for users on Windows systems and MOV for users on Macintosh sys-

COMMON AUDIO/VIDEO FILE FORMATS

ABBREVIATION	NAME	DEFINITION
AIFF	Audio Interchange File Format	For storing digital audio; popular on Macintosh platform
ASF	Advanced Streaming Format	A data stream format for multimedia data, including audio, video, and still images, created by Microsoft
AVI	Audio Video Interchange	Moving image files; Windows-based movies
MOV	Movie File	Apple QuickTime movie file format
MPEG MP3	Moving Picture Experts Group	A group of compression standards for video and audio, which includes MPEG-1, -2, -3 (referred to as MP3), and -4; most often downloaded from the web rather than streamed; produces high-quality video with small file sizes
QT	QuickTime	Develops, stores, and plays movies; runs well on Macintosh computers with QuickTime player
RA	Real Audio	Streams the audio to a site for instant sound; runs best with Real Audio Player
SWF	Shockwave Flash File	Supports vector graphics; files are very small and transmit over the Internet quickly
WAV	Waveform Audio	PC audio format but also works on Macintosh platform
WMA WMV	Windows Media Audio Windows Media Video	Small file size that plays through a Web browser; cannot be converted to another format

Table 11.1

tems. You can play both file types on either system, but it's uncommon for Macintosh users to have Windows Media Player installed on their computer. Likewise, a Windows user may have QuickTime installed, but it's unlikely. A flash movie is saved in its own Shockwave Flash File (SWF) format (pronounced "swiff"). It can also be saved as Windows Media Audio (WMA), Windows Media Video (WMV), or QuickTime (QT) file formats.

Any animation, no matter how short in length, will result in a fairly large file size. I remember a student who was completing a rendered animation in the on-campus computer lab. The animation file was so large that he did not have any type of memory storage device on which to store his file. No memory stick existed

11.22
**Provide a simple
button like this one to
indicate that a movie
or video is available.
Design work courtesy
of Manu Juyal and
David A. Hobart, Jr.**

that could house this giant file. He ended up shortening the animation and deleting many of his textures and lights so he could save the file and go home for the night. Large files need to be compressed using video-editing software. If the portfolio is to be put online, the size of the files needs to be drastically reduced.

Try to use streaming video to permit the viewer to begin watching the clip while the remainder of it is still downloading. A streamed file does not have to be downloaded all at once but is downloaded and played in large pieces. While one piece of the video is being played, another piece is being loaded simultaneously, providing continuous streaming of data without a break in viewing. You can activate this setting when saving your video clips for the web.

How can someone viewing your portfolio find and see your video? If your digital portfolio is being distributed via the Internet, you will embed the movie right into your site's HTML files. Make an obvious link, on one of your pages, like the one in Figure 11.22, to encourage reviewers to watch the video. An accompanying still image and a bit of written description may be all it takes to entice them to watch your video. If your digital portfolio is being distributed on CD, put it into another application such as Flash or PowerPoint and provide a button for reviewers to click on to start the video. Speaking of PowerPoint, let's talk about multimedia slideshows next as an option for displaying your work.

POWERPOINT MULTIMEDIA SLIDESHOWS

One of the most popular presentation packages for multimedia slideshows is Microsoft PowerPoint. Many firms use this software for client presentations, and

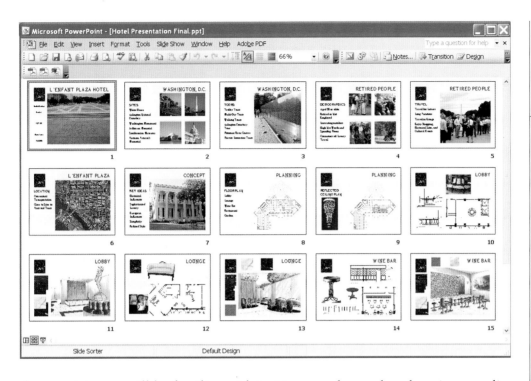

11.23
PowerPoint's linear design makes it easy to follow a presentation. Design work courtesy of Rachel K. Dankert.

the practitioners will be familiar with it. However, know that there is some disagreement in industry regarding the use of PowerPoint for portfolios. PowerPoint is primarily used as a business application; it is not frequently used for creative expression. Several other software applications are useful for portfolio creation and distribution, such as Flip Album Pro, Adobe Photoshop Album, and Extensis Portfolio. Although not as widely used as PowerPoint, they are worth checking out.

PowerPoint is a great choice for a linear presentation in which you show one slide after another to give a guided tour of your work. You can also use a nonlinear style by using the software's hyperlink feature. This allows you to create a table of contents that links to other slides in your presentation.

PowerPoint's linear setup can be a limitation because slides are arranged in a preestablished order, like those in Figure 11.23. You cannot skip from one slide to another without traversing through all the slides in-between. This may frustrate a viewer who just wants to skim your portfolio. Again, here's why it's essential to put your best project first. The viewer may not have the time (or tenacity) to go through your entire portfolio and may only see the first project before exiting the program.

To begin, create a master slide with your preferred background color and texture, text size and appearance, title location, grid lines, and so on. This will help you achieve consistency in portfolio appearance. You can use one of the existing design templates provided in the application (see Figure 11.24). These give you a good base on which to build, but they seldom give you the layout you want. Or, you can be unique and create your own master slide. By this point in the project, you've already sketched out your desired page layouts for single- and double-page

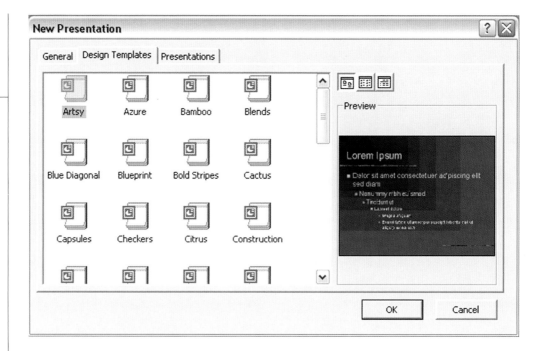

spreads. You can use these as a basis for your master slide. To create this master, I often insert a blank slide and then insert text and images where I want them, adjusting the background color as needed. To make the next slide in the series, I insert a duplicate slide. This maintains consistency in the presentation. You can add and delete text and images as needed.

Once you've placed your text and images on a slide, animations can be added (including sound) to make your presentation extraordinary. Going to the next slide can be more than a boring click. Understated transitions known as *dissolves* can subtly move the viewer from one slide to another. You might consider having a slight pause between each slide to add interest, inducing reflection on what was seen and anticipation of what is to come. A word of warning: Keep it simple. Avoid transitions that move the viewer too dramatically to the next slide. These transitions can be distracting, and in some viewers may almost cause motion sickness. Overly animated presentations with images dissolving and text flying around the screen can be annoying. Remember, your portfolio is about your design work, not the flashy features of the software.

A self-running slide show is another method for displaying your work. You determine the sequence of images and the specific period of time between them (known as the *delay*). You can place an intermediate transition between the images, which is known as a *fade* (Romaniello 2003). The features needed to put this together can all be found under the Slide Show menu.

Audio and video can be embedded in your file. (Look under the Insert menu, Movies and Sounds.) Under the Slide Show menu, the Record Narration option will let you record your narration right in this file and will time it perfectly to your slide transitions (see Figure 11.25). For motion graphics and video, insert a new

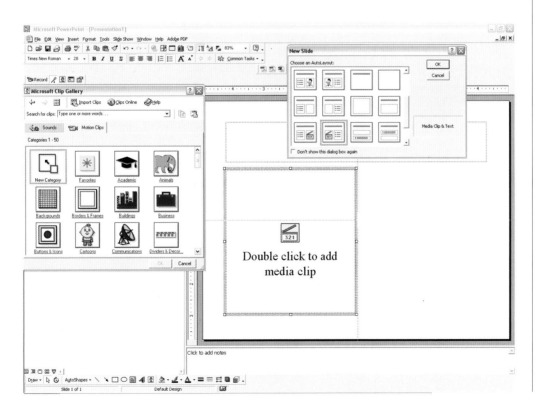

LEFT: 11.25
The opportunity to record narration that is timed with your slides is available in PowerPoint.

BELOW: 11.26
Insert a media clip into PowerPoint with the Media Clip Gallery option.

media slide by double-clicking on the media icon. A Media Clip Gallery box will appear (see Figure 11.26).

When you are done, you need to save your file. If you save it in the default format as a PPT file (PowerPoint Presentation), the recipient of your portfolio must have PowerPoint to view it. Or you can save each slide as a web page. This would be an unproblematic way to copy your CD portfolio right to the Internet. Another option is to use the Pack and Go feature. This function allows you to export your presentation as a stand-alone file. The software embeds the

PowerPoint viewer as part of your file. This way, anyone accessing the file need only click on the "start" icon and your slide show will begin. Creating a Pack and Go file is simple with the software's setup wizard (see Figure 11.27).

LAYOUT SOFTWARE APPLICATIONS

Maybe a PowerPoint slideshow is not your style. Maybe it's not what you want for presenting your portfolio with style and pizzazz. If you are looking for more control over the layout, you might consider using one of the several desktop publishing applications. *Desktop publishing* is a term that describes the use of page layout software to create either small- or large-scale publication documents. These layouts combine text, graphics, and images for print or web publication. Popular layout applications used in desktop publishing include Adobe ImageReady, Adobe InDesign, Microsoft Publisher, Macromedia Fireworks, and QuarkXPress. Let's briefly look at each one of these programs. You'll need to decide which one (if any) is right for you and which one will serve your needs without taking you five years to master.

Adobe ImageReady

Adobe ImageReady is useful for preparing files for display on the Internet (see Figure 11.28). It has many of the same features as Photoshop so the learning curve is less severe if you are already familiar with Photoshop. One nice feature is its ability to slice images. This means it can take a large image, slice it up into smaller rectangular pieces, and reassemble these pieces within a framework that makes it appear that all these pieces are really one big image. This will help speed up your download time, especially if you are relying on large images to make up a good portion of your portfolio.

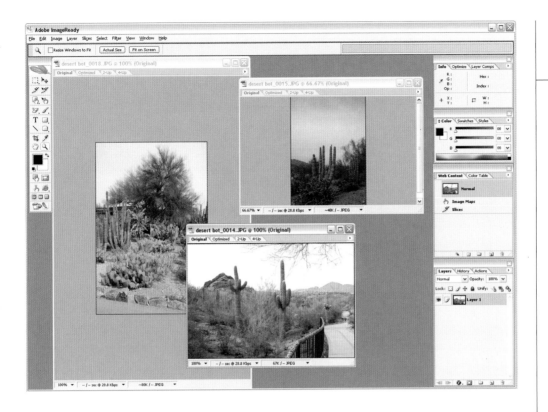

11.28
Adobe ImageReady is
similar to other Adobe
products.

ImageReady has a feature that automatically makes a contact sheet of your thumbnail images, which are all saved in one file folder. You determine the size and location of the images on the contact sheet as you preview the sheet being constructed on your screen. You then need to crop and save each individual image in a web-compatible format. Each file can be compressed independently with varying levels. The software even shows you how long it would take to download an image with varying levels of compression.

Adobe InDesign

Adobe InDesign is a solid page layout program that has all the features you'll need to create smashing page layouts (see Figure 11.29). The user interface is easy to use and even has some of the same features as Photoshop and Illustrator. After you have created images in Illustrator, or manipulated images in Photoshop, you can simply drag-and-drop them into your InDesign page layout. You can then manipulate the images further. Although InDesign is most often used in the printing industry and works with the CMYK color mode, you can export your layout to multiple image formats (i.e., TIFF, GIF, JPEG) for input into web design software.

Macromedia Fireworks

Macromedia Fireworks is an image-editing, web-authoring and publication program maintained by Adobe (see Figure 11.30). It offers a vector-based approach to web design and publication, which is different than its direct competitor,

RIGHT: 11.29
Use InDesign's two-page layout system to create a comprehensive portfolio layout for both print and digital media.
Design work courtesy of Paul Marquez.

BELOW: 11.30
Macromedia Fireworks can create design elements like lines, shapes, and fine text that can be integrated into web pages.

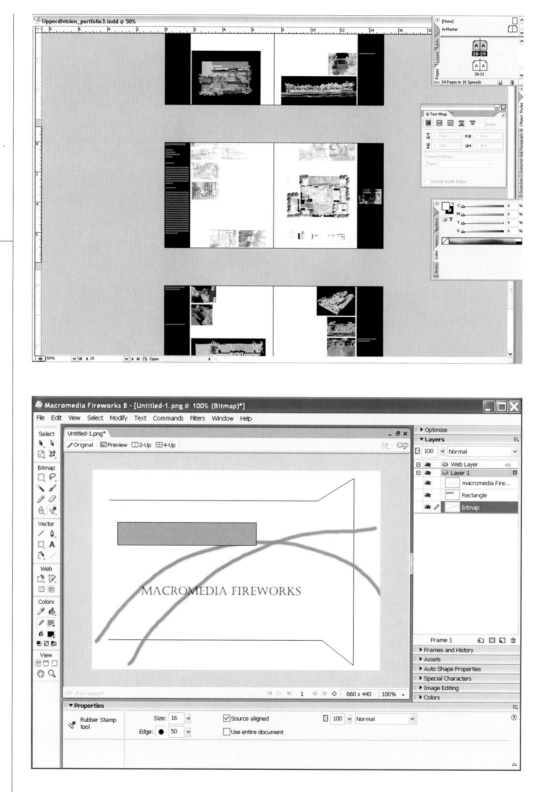

Adobe ImageReady. Its intended audience is web designers as it has limited capabilities for print media. It's sufficient for image editing but much better as a vector program. For example, Fireworks can resize vector objects with no loss of quality but, like other applications, raster images that are resized lose quality.

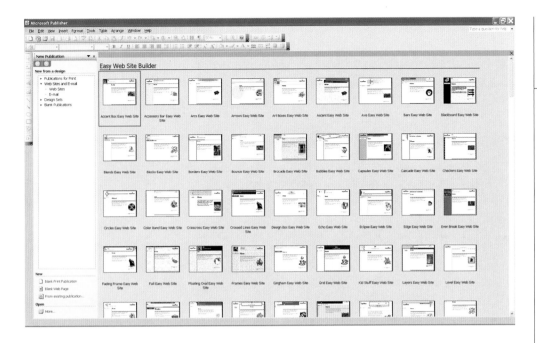

11.31
Microsoft Publisher is
worth investigating
because it has many
web site templates.

Microsoft Publisher

Microsoft Publisher is a desktop publishing package that runs only on the Windows platform (see Figure 11.31). Although it is a good product, complex functions such as text on paths, transparency, and object shadowing are not available in this program. It is bundled into the Office Suite of Microsoft products as an alternative for users in the small business market who may not be able to hire design professionals to create marketing materials.

QuarkXPress

QuarkXPress is a page layout application produced by the company Quark, Inc., that can be used on both the Macintosh and Windows platforms. It is a popular product for desktop publishing and is used to create professional-looking page layouts by professional designers and the typesetting industry (see Figure 11.32). QuarkXPress allows very accurate placement of text and image boxes on the page, plus full color control. Although many of its features are similar to those of InDesign, there are some apparent differences. These include the method of text selection, measurements and transform palettes, and the inclusion of a box or frame around pictures and graphics.

Layout Templates

Try each of these layout applications by downloading a sample of the product from the manufacturer's web site. If one of these layout packages is right for you, use it to create your portfolio layout. Once you have decided on a layout, create a generic template to help you place your objects consistently. This can be used as a guideline for either the printed or digital portfolio. You design one master page template with all of the common elements positioned where you want

11.32
Graphic designers frequently use QuarkXPress because of its excellent page composition and precision text features.
Design work courtesy of Jennifer Brungart.

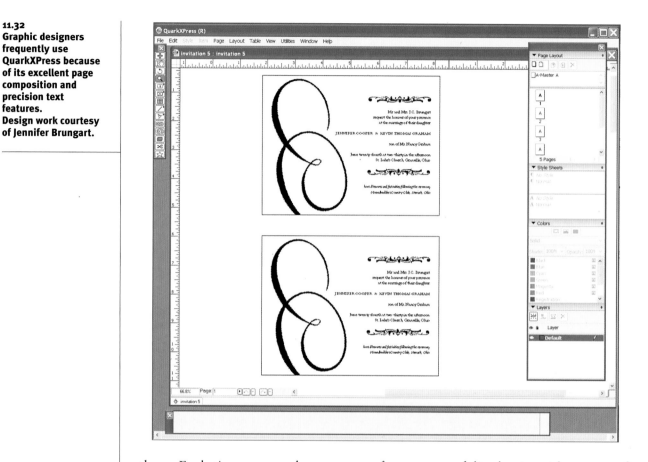

them. Each time you need a new page for your portfolio, begin with a copy of this master template.

Personalize your template. You can use generic templates from web sites or the ones available in software applications to save you time. But generic templates are not useful in the disciplines of architecture, landscape architecture, or interior design because our industries recognize the portfolio itself as a reflection of your personality and design philosophy. *Start* from the generic template and *then* personalize it, as in the layout in Figure 11.33.

Anything you can do to make your portfolio unique will enhance your chances of getting into your preferred degree program or landing that great job. To share your pages with others who might not have the same layout software, you should consider saving your files as Portable Document Format (PDF) files.

PORTABLE DOCUMENT FORMAT FILES

Once you have your digital portfolio pages laid out, you need to present them to others. One ever increasingly popular option is to use PDF files. This is a file format created and viewed with Adobe Acrobat software and works on either platform. It accurately represents the layout, font, and graphics displayed in your document, as in the layout in Figure 11.34.

For example, let's say you create a custom logo and use two fonts in your resume. If you save the file in the word processing software in which you created

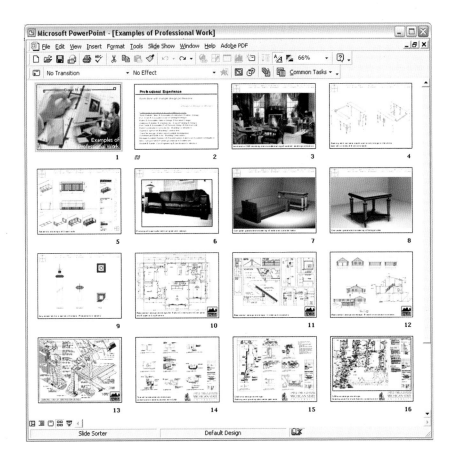

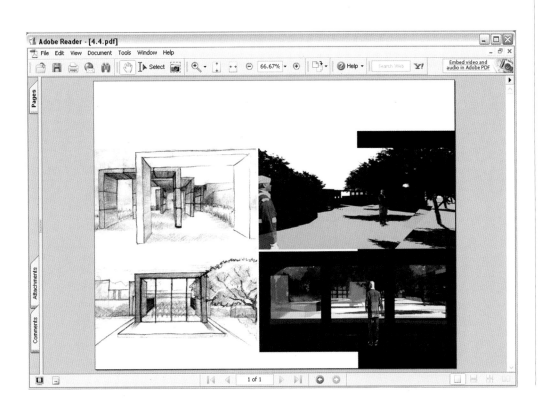

it, you can email it to someone or put it on your web site. But in order to see it, the viewer would need the same software. Even more, they would need to have the same fonts loaded on their computer as you have on yours. Because TrueType fonts available on a Windows platform are not always available on a Macintosh platform, major problems can occur. Acrobat embeds font information directly into your PDF file, leaving your text the way it is and your graphics exactly where you put them. When the document is opened, what you created is exactly what others see.

PDF files have several advantages for presenting your digital portfolio. PDF files are easy to access, have content that can be zoomed larger, can be created from multiple applications, and are stored to CD without difficulty. They also support high-resolution graphics and are secure, which means someone can't manipulate items on each page because the layout is locked in. As great as PDF files can be, they do have a few disadvantages. Like any other file, large PDF files take longer to download and display on the web than simple HTML pages. Special software must be purchased to create PDF files (i.e., Adobe's Acrobat Distiller) and reviewers must have special software to view them (free Adobe Reader).

Creating a PDF File

How do you create a PDF file? PDF files are based on the page layout language originally used for printing to a postscript laser printer. You simply generate the

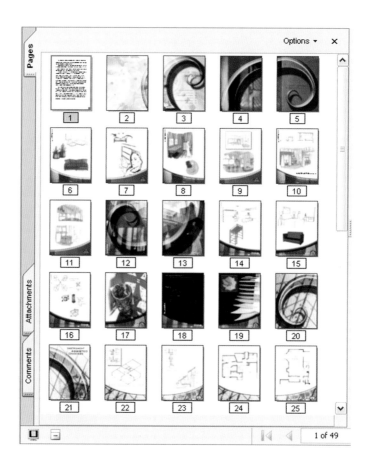

11.35
Merge all of your PDF pages into one document with Adobe Acrobat software. Design work courtesy of Shelby Bogaard.

page layout as desired and print it to the PDF Writer, which is a print driver loaded onto your computer. Instead of pages coming out of a printer, a file will be created with the PDF extension. A nice feature of PDF files is the ability to merge many PDF pages into one master file, like the one shown in Figure 11.35. You can rearrange the pages in any order. After all, no one likes to open 15 separate files. Make it easy for the practitioner to review your work.

A word of caution: Keep in mind the size of the file. One PDF file is more convenient to review than many separate documents. But the file will be large. Keep your PDF file under 1 MB because storage space is often limited on email servers. If you wish to compress your PDF file, use Acrobat's PDF Optimizer feature. This will reduce the file size to something more email and web friendly.

To view a PDF file, you need the free Acrobat Reader plug-in available at Adobe's web site (www.adobe.com). Also check out Adobe's web site for software to convert PDF files to HTML.

PDF Files in Your Portfolio

PDFs have become extremely popular with designers because they are a swift and uncomplicated means for promoting your work (Eisenman 2006). Use the header and footer options to put your name on every single page. This will help the practitioner get them all back together again if they become separated.

Adobe Acrobat now supports insertion into the PDF file of multimedia files, such as embedded motion graphics and videos. All that is required is a mouse-click to launch the animation and the correct software to view it.

Finally, print your PDF file in both color and black and white. How does it look? Is this what you want the practitioners to see when they print it and possibly circulate it around the office? When you photocopy either the color or black-and-white pages, do you lose color value or contrast?

CONCLUSION

As you can tell, there are many additional components in a digital portfolio that can demonstrate your abilities with technology. Define the purpose and audience before investing time and expense into designing motion graphics, animations, videos, narrations, and background music for your digital portfolio. Will the investment pay off? In the next chapter, we will continue our discussion of the digital portfolio by looking at the software applications for presenting your work via laptop, Internet, or on CD.

PRESENTING YOUR PORTFOLIO

12

Digital Portfolio Presentation Formats

Although digital portfolios are not required to get a job or a position in an educational program, they are becoming increasingly popular. What computer-aided design (CAD) was to the drafting table, digital portfolios will be to the future of the interview process. One of the best benefits of having your work in a digital format is flexibility. You can modify projects and presentations so easily. You can devise a whole series of portfolio presentations simply by revising your layouts and reorganizing your portfolio elements.

This chapter provides an overview of the software applications and techniques for presenting your digital portfolio. Consider which presentation style will work best to make your images truly superb. We'll look at presentations on a laptop, on the Internet, and on CD.

But before we proceed, it bears repeating to remember your audience. Not everyone may be as computer savvy as you. A portfolio created with unusual software or that requires an obscure, expensive, or licensed image viewer will limit your potential audience. I know many practitioners and educators who are too busy to download applications just to preview work someone sent them. If it's easy to review, it's more likely people will review it (see Box 12.1).

What hardware and software will interviewers use to view your portfolio? What skills are needed to access it? It is preferable to create the portfolio in software that others probably own and know how to use (i.e., PowerPoint, Internet Explorer, Acrobat Reader).

Regardless of *how* your digital portfolio is presented to others, there are two common modes for viewing it: autoplay, and navigation by clicking on menu options. Autoplay portfolios do not require reviewers to do anything except insert

If a portfolio on CD requires me to download software to review it, I absolutely do not. With the frenzied pace of work and the glut of digital information, professionals most likely will not take the time to download software to review a portfolio. Frankly, sticking the disc in the computer and opening it sometimes seems too time consuming. A brief, succinct, printed "teaser" brochure or postcard should be sent with any CD portfolio.

Carl Matthews
Associate Professor
Interior Design, School of Architecture
University of Texas at Austin
Austin, TX

Box 12.1

a CD. That's it. Anyone can access and review your portfolio content. However, portfolios with autoplay do not allow users to stop and go as they please. The reviewer is led through a predefined, often pretimed, sequence of images and slides, like that in Figure 12.1. This type of portfolio works best if you want your storyboard to be linear. The autoplay function may not work properly so test, test, and retest it before distributing it.

12.1
Pause and play buttons appear on an automated slideshow. This gives the reviewer control over the viewing pace. Design work courtesy of Melissa Zlatow.

Portfolios with freedom of navigation allow reviewers to spend as much or as little time as desired on various parts of your portfolio. The downside is that you have no idea in what order they will review your work. You cannot assume they will see your absolutely best work first. They may see it last. (It's like the practitioner who flips to the last page of your printed portfolio to review that work first.) Again, this is another reason to never include *any* low-quality work in your portfolio!

LAPTOP PRESENTATION

You may have the opportunity to present your digital portfolio on a laptop or personal computer at a job interview (see Figure 12.2). (This is not the case for a school admissions portfolio, which is seldom viewed with the candidate present.) A portfolio presentation on your own laptop gives you maximum control over any technical difficulties. You open your presentation and your fonts, colors, images, and animations look and run exactly as designed.

Never assume the interviewer will have the necessary equipment for you to present your digital portfolio, or that the firm will even approve of this format (see Box 12.2). Plan on taking a laptop with you if at all possible. If you do not own a laptop, rent or borrow one from a friend. Make sure all the necessary programs are available and running properly. You can call ahead and ask the receptionist or the designer if an LCD projector and adequate presentation space will be available. Even if the interviewer says the firm has a computer you can use, take your own. You don't know what type of operating system and software is on that computer. What if your files won't open?

Charge the laptop's battery the night before the interview *and* take its power cord. The last thing you want is to look unorganized by asking your interviewer

12.2
It may be easier to present from a laptop by having the interviewer(s) sit next to you. This way, everyone can see the presentation while you have control of the laptop.

Hard copies are a must. Laptop-only portfolios are not acceptable unless projected (which is not always practical). They are just too hard to see and not very fluid.

Mike Davin
Director of Hospitality Studio
FRCH Design Worldwide
Cincinnati, OH

Box 12.2

to borrow a power cord or mouse. Lastly, when flying to an interview, take the laptop with you as carry-on baggage. This is not the time to check it through as luggage and not see it when you reach your destination. Bringing your own laptop to an interview also means you may be carrying around your *only* computer. If anything happens to it, you may be in more trouble than you care to think about. This is obviously a weighty negative of laptop presentations. Reminder: Back up valuable files on an external drive.

I often travel to conferences to present my research. I try to only bring my presentation on a CD so I don't have to lug a laptop through airport security. Occasionally, I must bring my own laptop. With the laptop comes the power cord, electrical converters (if going overseas), the cable to connect it to an LCD projector, a cordless mouse that doubles as a remote, and extra mouse batteries. I once offered to let a keynote speaker use my laptop so she would not need to travel with hers. (Why should we both suffer?) I helped her load her presentation and get everything set up prior to her speech, including the cordless mouse. About 15 minutes before she was to begin, the mouse stopped responding. Inserting two fresh batteries quickly eliminated a moment of panic. Problem solved. Moral of the story: Come prepared to your presentation.

WEB-BASED PRESENTATION

Another presentation venue is the Internet. If you are a student and are interested in creating a web-based digital portfolio, you are in good company. Seen as a potential job recruitment tool, the Internet is being used by students in many schools to present their work. Firms can conduct candidate searches for open positions and narrow the list of job candidates before even contacting anyone for an interview. This is a major advantage of a web-based portfolio: increased visibility and access to practitioners who might never know you otherwise. Other advantages include the use of multimedia, hyperlinking capabilities, and access on multiple platforms. A web-based portfolio with a flexible layout gives you the ability to update it whenever you want with your latest and greatest designs. As seen in Figure 12.3, a simple user interface with lots of graphics and point-and-click linking makes it easy for even a novice to navigate.

A web site is relatively inexpensive to host, especially after taking into account the increased global exposure your work will get for being available in this format. Because the Internet permits instantaneous communication, an email address on your web site can be clicked immediately, allowing a practitioner to invite you to a job interview. You can even use your digital portfolio *in* an interview—saving you the hassle of transporting a bulky portfolio case through downtown pedestrian traffic.

In opposition, there are several disadvantages, including the accurate representation of quality work and security concerns. First, you lose all the subtleties of design choices that you have in a traditional portfolio, such as paper weight and finish, scale, size, and binding choice. Colors may be altered and lack full impact.

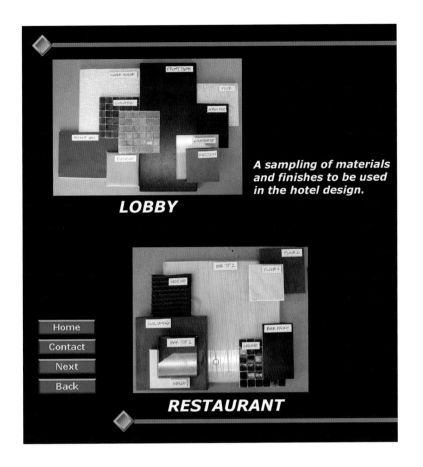

LEFT: 12.3
All of the navigation
options are in one
place on this web site,
making it easy to
interact with.
Design work courtesy
of Shelby Bogaard and
Kristy Harline.

BELOW: 12.4
This technical line
drawing does not
transfer well to digital
media at a larger
scale. The zoomed
image on the right
becomes blurry
and jagged.
Design work courtesy
of Charudatta Joshi.

And the maximum resolution the Internet can transmit is a pathetic 72 dots per inch (dpi). This low image quality cannot convey the subtle information of printed media, such as line weight and fine hand lettering on construction drawings (see Figure 12.4).

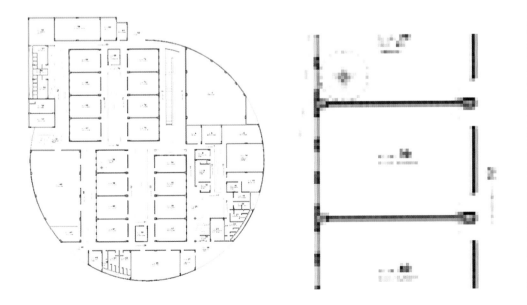

The lack of tactile sensation in a digital portfolio detracts from it. The interior environment consists of various textures to reflect human sensory needs. Our design solutions, as communicated to our clients, should reflect textures specified for the final interior spaces. Digital portfolios capture color and pattern, but lack the ability to offer the client the tactile quality of texture.

Stephanie Clemons, Ph.D.
Professor
Interior, Design, Department of Design and Merchandising,
College of Applied Human Sciences
Colorado State University
Fort Collins, CO

Box 12.3

For our professions, which represent building materials, textiles, and other finishes as small tactile samples, the digital portfolio is at a disadvantage. These materials cannot be accurately represented and experienced on the Internet. Not only are the samples often scanned very small, you obviously lose the tactile sensation (see Box 12.3). One way to resolve this concern is to bring a small material sample board to your interview (as covered in Chapter 4).

Once you put something out on the Internet, it is difficult to keep it to yourself. You may have some proprietary material that you would not want others to take. Be aware that everything on your site is in the public domain. Intellectual property violations are likely. If your work is copyrighted, the copyright notice should be visible. One solution is to put parts of a design project on your web site, but not the entire project. This gives the reviewer enough information to make an informed decision about offering you an interview and gives you enough peace of mind to know your design ideas are not freely floating around cyberspace. A related issue is protecting your privacy (Cole et al. 1999). Because your site is accessible to everyone, limit your personal information to the bare-bones contact information. We'll discuss this in detail shortly.

As a web designer, you would be expected to create the most amazing, engaging web site. But you are not a web designer. You are an architect, interior designer, or landscape architect. You are not expected to have these advanced technology skills. It's great if you do have them through additional education or experience. But it's not an expectation of our professions.

There are a number of items to consider when designing your web site. These include the organization of your information, how a reviewer will navigate or travel around your site, the size and resolution of the reviewer's screen, and the readability of your site. Two factors are critical in the success of your web-based portfolio: organization and navigation. One without the other is fruitless. A well-organized set of projects that cannot easily be accessed is as frustrating as a beautifully designed web site that is haphazardly arranged. Let's talk about the organization of your web site first.

Organization of Your Web Site

There are many ways to organize your web site. It can be organized into categories, by project, or by theme. An easily understood web site has work grouped under major headings, with further layers of information under each heading.

A web-based portfolio consists of a home page and several links to other pages on your site. Besides your design work, you will have a resume page, a place for your contact information, and a gallery of project images. You may have additional pages like an entry splash page and a credits or acknowledgments page to thank those who have assisted you in your work. Similar to a CD with a planned presentation, a web site can be created in a linear fashion to take the viewer through a selection of pages. Or it can be nonlinear, like the branching and star formations discussed in Chapter 5.

Unlike a sequenced portfolio presentation, a web site has multiple pathways and is multidimensional. Viewers have the freedom to jump around to any portion of your web site. There is no need and rarely the desire to read something on the web site from start to finish. You need to anticipate this. You have no control over how someone views your site. Therefore, each portion of each page needs to stand on its own. Each page has to be understood out of context with the other pages. This can be the most challenging aspect of web site design—anticipating the wandering ways of the viewer. It's like wayfinding in a building.

Structure your web site to take advantage of its multimedia and navigation features. Keep the infrastructure flexible—flexible enough to add, delete, or rearrange your web pages. This is known as a maintenance strategy. The larger your web site, the more complicated the task of organizing and managing it will be. This should be in the back of your mind when organizing your content. You can easily be burdened by the time requirement to keep up with your own content.

Once you determine the components and pieces of your web-based portfolio, sketch out its organization. Try drawing an organizational chart or site map in which you group subjects together, but not in a linear fashion. This map will help you recognize where links should be made between your pages. Your site map should illustrate how you group your work together, how that work is split into pages, and how those pages are connected together again. You can draw this map using flowchart software or even sketch it on a series of sticky notes that you rearrange on your wall. Use whatever method suits your working style. Let's begin with the traditional entry point to a web site, the home page.

The Home Page

Start the organization of your web site with the first page, known as the home page. It is the main page and usually the starting point for entry into your digital portfolio (see Figure 12.5). (The splash page, discussed next, is optional.) The home page provides the first impression for your site and for you as a designer (see Box 12.4).

12.5
Imagine you are the reviewer. How will you travel through the site? Plot the organization of your web site in a flow chart.

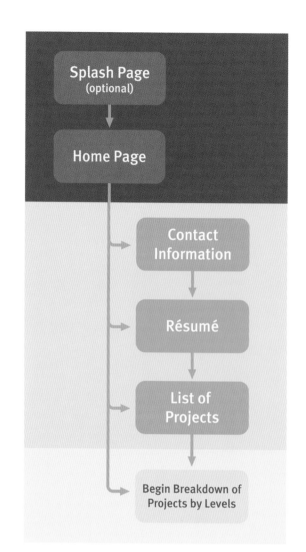

Your home page should tell the visitor what it's all about: that this is your design portfolio and this is your area of design. It should have clear links to your other web pages, only a few images that suit the purpose of your design, and common interface elements, such as navigation buttons and bars.

Without question, first impressions are lasting impressions. We're all strapped for time, and we expect to be wowed by both the quality of the designs *and* the quality of the presentation. The first few pages speak volumes about a candidate's talent, creativity, attention to detail, and overall professionalism.

Nikki Duffner
Corporate Recruiter
Hellmuth, Obsata & Kassabaum
St. Louis, MO

Box 12.4

12.6
Although these two home pages look different, they both have user-friendly links to the designer's resume and portfolio. Design work courtesy of Amol Surve and Paul Hibbard.

As illustrated in Figure 12.6, your home page may contain your contact information, or you can provide a link on this page to another page that contains this information. People finding your portfolio on the web are likely to respond via the web. Make sure your contact information includes your current email, designed as an active link. Also ensure that your email account has enough memory available to receive emails. I often email students' whose mailboxes are full and the email bounces back. If someone interested in interviewing you cannot get in touch with you, how can he hire you?

Keep in mind that having your portfolio available on the Internet makes it accessible to anyone. This is a good thing and a bad thing. Anyone who finds your web site will now have your name and email address. It is important to consider how much information (and what kind of information) you are willing to put on your web site. Therefore, I would recommend you avoid displaying anything intimate on your web site, such as your phone number, mailing address, birth date, or social security, passport, or student identification number. Unfortunately, identity theft is a reality.

Besides your contact information, include your resume for that little bit of extra exposure. Include a place on your home page for a notice indicating the last date on which the site was updated. This helps the viewer know if he is looking at old, outdated material or brand-new work. It's also important to include a link

12.7
Make the link back to your home page easy to find.
Design work courtesy of Paul Hibbard.

back to the home page, as shown in Figure 12.7. Otherwise, a reviewer will need to back out of the site one page at a time. This is tedious and wearisome.

The Splash Page

An optional splash page can be the very first page of your web site, even before the home page. It usually contains some sort of multimedia presentation meant to impress the reviewer, like the one in Figure 12.8. This page must load quickly, in no more than 10 to 15 seconds. Anything longer and you may risk losing your reviewer. Have you ever entered a web site only to wait while it downloaded an animated introduction? Most likely, this mediated spot was created in Flash, the animation software discussed in the last chapter. Or it's an animated vector image called a *Scalable Vector Graphic (SVG)*. SVG is a web graphic format that uses mathematical calculations to represent design. SVG files can be dynamic and interactive if your browser is SVG enabled.

Of course, if you include a splash page, you will want everyone to view it. Not everyone can or does. If you include an animation, have a link to the appropriate plug-in to allow reviewers to download it. Rather than risk them not seeing your video because of formatting obstacles, provide them the option to open your movie in another player (i.e., QuickTime, RealPlayer, or Windows Media Player).

Once considered an amazing feat of design genius, these Flash introductions are now relatively easy to do. With that said, they are time-consuming to download and often provide less information than a well-designed home page. If you must have one of these animated introductions, provide a courtesy Skip Intro link for the reviewers who want to go straight to your portfolio.

A Navigation System

Good navigation through a web site requires some thought and preplanning. The logical progression through your site should be intuitive. How will others move around your site? Can they get back to your home page quickly? After all, when they've seen enough to be impressed, you want them to be able to rapidly find your email address so they can contact you for an interview.

Think of your web site as an information system, like a map. It must be legible, effortlessly understood, easily read, and searchable. People have to find what they're looking for and find it quickly. Good navigation effectively guides the reader through your site. Think of it this way: Your school or city library has a vast amount of information. It has a librarian to help you. Think of your web site navigation as the librarian who helps viewers move around your site.

A navigation system creates smooth movement through the portfolio. In a traditional portfolio, this movement is linear and directed. In a digital portfolio, contents are linked in a network and the reviewer can jump from one page to another (see Figure 12.9). It is not advisable to create a complex web site, especially if reviewers have to navigate a labyrinth to view all your work.

Everyone seems to get caught up in the look of the web site, the color, fonts, graphics, and multimedia bells and whistles, like movies and sound. But your web site is simply an interface, a way for a potential employer to have ready access to your portfolio. Too many options and too much flexibility are sufficient for the reviewer to get lost in your maze of networks. Where am I? What page am I on? Where can I go? How can I get back to where I was a few minutes ago? If reviewers cannot figure out where to go on your site, you can guess where they'll go—the exit!

Give them a sense of place. Give them directions for how to get around your site. As shown in Figure 12.10, a table of contents on your home page is useful, as some reviewers want to get right to certain areas of your work.

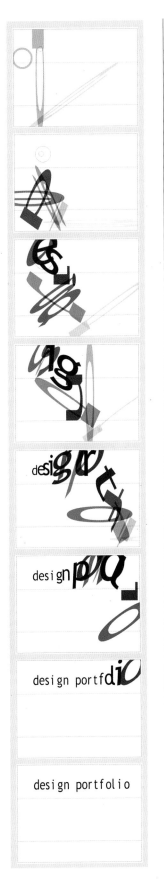

12.8
These screen captures were taken from a designer's Flash animation splash page. In 3 seconds, the words "design portfolio" fly onto the page. Short animations are great for splash pages. Design work courtesy of Manu Juyal.

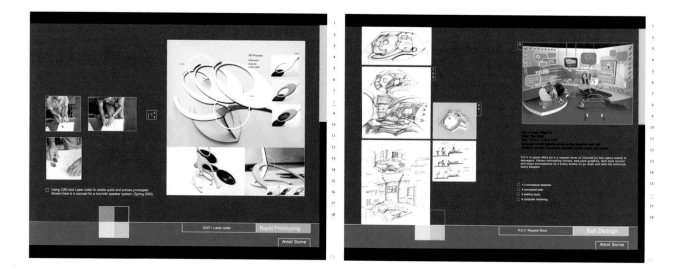

ABOVE: 12.9
Each page of this designer's web-based portfolio is listed numerically. Reviewers can visit pages in sequence, or can freely jump from one page to another. Design work courtesy of Amol Surve.

BELOW: 12.10
This table of contents allows the reviewer to access precisely the type of project she wishes to review. Design work courtesy of Paul Marquez.

It's important to provide guided, controlled navigation through a hierarchy of content. This is known as a *branching navigation system* (see Figure 12.11). Typically, there are three levels of content. The first level lists featured projects and gives a visual sample of what is at that level. In the second level, you go inside each project and display its contents. The third level is optional, where you can access detailed information. While browsing, reviewers can only see the content of one level at a time, thus reducing the chances of getting lost. The major levels may look different, but the tiers within each level should look similar and have common graphic elements.

Navigation Tools

The graphic user interface (GUI) is critical for allowing ease of access. GUI (pronounced *gooey*) is the graphic relationship between the user and the computer.

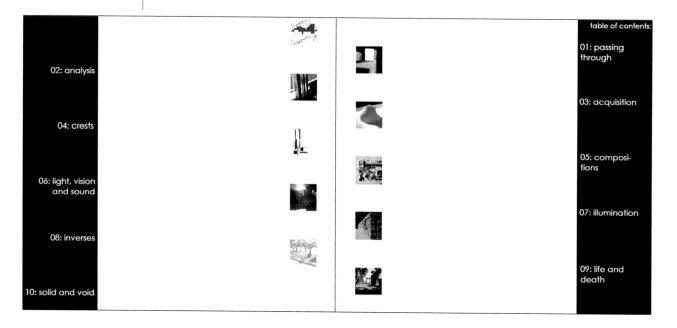

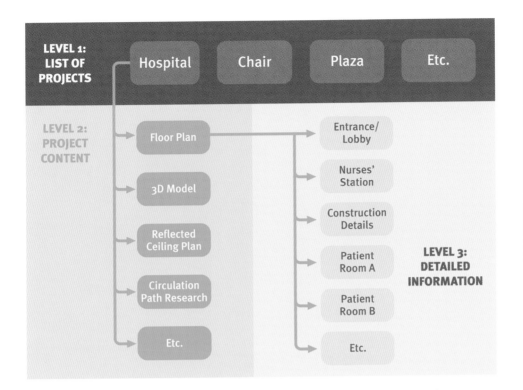

LEFT: **12.11**
A branching navigation has multiple levels, starting with the major project. Within that project, the next level takes you to project content, followed by the last level of detail.

BELOW: **12.12**
As designers, we associate meaning with visual symbols such as arrows. Use icons whenever you can, instead of lines of text.
Design work courtesy of Manu Juyal.

Rather than reading lots of text, the reviewer uses icons, graphics, windows, pop-up menus, scroll bars, and a mouse to click around your web site (i.e., a point-and-click interface). Make your web site clear by means of icons rather than text. For example, arrows like the ones in Figure 12.12 are easier to identify than a text link that says, "Click on this line to go to the next page."

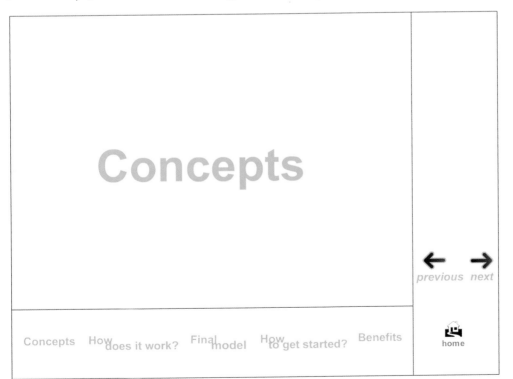

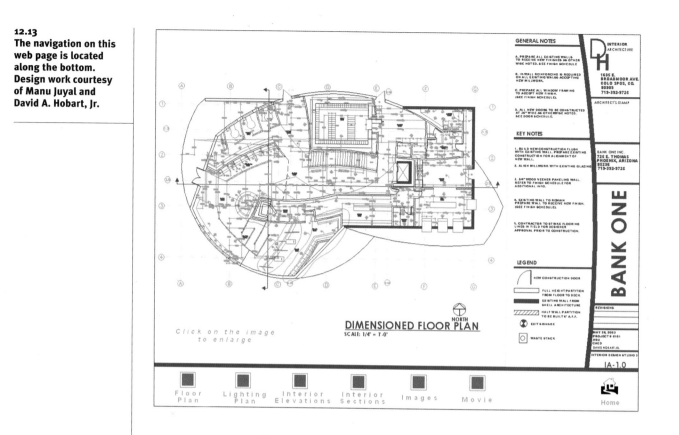

A main part of the user interface within your site includes the navigation graphics, such as buttons, bars, logos, and image maps. A navigation bar is where you keep all the buttons and informational text. You'll usually find these bars along the top or bottom of the page. The navigation bar provides a list of options so the user can choose where to go on your site. In its simplest form, it lists site categories. Keep the navigation bar in the same place on every page, whether at the top, along the side, or the bottom like the one in Figure 12.13. A simple navigation button is a geometric shape, sometimes with shading around the edges to give it a three-dimensional (3-D) appearance. A button represents a link to another page on your site (see Figure 12.14).

Whether using buttons, hot links, or other graphics for your navigation tools, keep them *simple* and consistent throughout the site. The navigation used in Figure 12.15 is simple yet elegant. These tools are *not* to take precedence over your portfolio content. Your biggest design challenge when creating your web site is balance. Too simple an interface is boring and lifeless. A complicated interface is overwhelming and obnoxious. Just because you *can* produce complicated buttons and bars does not mean you should.

Although strictly graphic buttons can be self-explanatory (like an arrow to go to the next page), most buttons work best if there is some text inside to tell the reviewer what they do. Maybe it's a flag of text that pops up if your mouse passes over it. Keep in mind there is no guarantee that everyone who sees these buttons will recognize what they do, and they may not even touch them.

You can create your own buttons in multimedia software like Flash. It's tempting to put snazzy, animated buttons in your web site. These are the buttons that change color when the mouse passes over them. If you have the tenacity to create them, they are more interactive and can help the user recognize that something will happen if they press that button. However, be aware that these buttons result in large files that take up plenty of your web space. There are some users who really want web pages to download quickly. To aid in this endeavor, they sometimes turn off images so pictures on a site do not appear.

Don't get hung up on your buttons. Remember that the goal is your portfolio. Think of your time. You should spend more time on the images of your work than on things like navigation tools. I once had a student in my class who was very bright and very detail-oriented. He was assigned to build a 3-D cabinet in CAD. He was really good with the software and enjoyed it immensely. Too immensely. He spent hours and hours detailing the cabinet, all the way down to 3-D screws. But he never finished his presentation sheets and subsequently failed the project. Your interface components should never be the focus of your web pages.

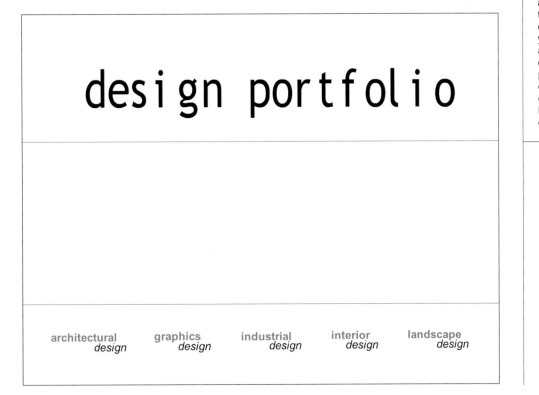

design portfolio

architectural *design*   graphics *design*   industrial *design*   interior *design*   landscape *design*

You say you don't have the time (or desire) to design your own navigation tools? That's OK. Look online for free stuff. Search on the Internet for keywords such as "interface buttons" or "web buttons." You'll get a list of web sites where you can download tools, such as icons, images, fonts, sound effects, buttons, and 3-D objects. Some tools are free; others can be purchased for a nominal fee. (Just make sure to answer honestly if someone asks you if you designed all the navigation on your site.)

Web Color and Resolution

How someone sees your web-based portfolio is dependent on a number of factors, such as screen size and resolution, connection speed, processor speed, depth of monitor color, and the computer platform (Cohen 2000). Although today's monitors can read millions of colors, it does not hurt to use web safe colors. (These are the 216 colors discussed in Chapter 11.) These colors can be coded in HTML because each one has a six-digit number associated with it. HTML code recognizes the number and displays the appropriate color on the viewer's monitor. By sticking to this palette of 216 colors, you are ensured that your web pages will be viewed with the exact colors you want regardless of the computer platform or browser being used.

As we discussed earlier, color can look different on computer monitors than on the printed page. There are also color differences between platforms and web browsers. You would be wise to test your web site on both platforms and in multiple browsers before making the link available to potential employers.

You cannot predict the color settings on someone else's monitor. There are different ways to solve this problem. You could create two sets of images, one for Macintosh users and the other for Windows users. You could embed an ICC color profile in each image. (That's a standardized, cross-platform color profile established by the International Color Consortium.) But let's be realistic. These approaches take time and may be a waste anyway. Strive to have colors on your digital images that closely resemble the original work.

Screen resolution is different on different monitors as users have control over the clarity and quality of their display (see Figure 12.16). The resolution on some monitors may be set to 640 × 480. This is quite different from a higher screen resolution of 1280 × 1024. Your portfolio will look dissimilar on each monitor. Create your web site to look good on the higher resolution screen. It will still look good at a lower resolution.

Let's talk about screen size. Web pages use tables, which are responsible for the vertical and horizontal position of elements, helping your images stay in place. You have control over the size and location of these tables. Be wary of creating visuals that fill a 19-inch or 21-inch monitor. Not everyone has these larger monitors. If you have a graphic image that stretches to the edges of a 19-inch screen, it will be cut off when viewed on a smaller screen. For web sites, you need to consider the scrollbars on the side and bottom. These will cut into your pres-

12.16
Every computer has individual display properties.

entation area. This makes your 800 × 600 space even smaller, so select a resolution of 760 × 410.

Pay attention to the vertical direction as well. Any information you include that runs longer than 600 lines on CD or 410 lines on the web will run off the bottom of the screen (Myers 2005). In order to access it, reviewers must scroll down the page. It's likely they will completely dismiss that information. You would be better off creating graphics for the lowest common denominator, such as the 15-inch screen.

Site Readability

An attractive graphic design and page layout make for good readability. Guidelines for a readable page include the use of a consistent layout, some white or negative space, contrasting elements, and simple, understated elements (Morgan 1996). The same principles of design and organization used in a traditional portfolio hold true for a digital portfolio as well. Remember the discussion of positive and negative space in Chapter 6? Apply the same principle to your web pages. Seek a balance between page elements and the background. Having contrast is good. Negative space gives the eye a place to rest before moving on to the next content area on the page. Like the negative space in Figure 12.17, this is not wasted space.

RIGHT: 12.17
In this balanced layout, the dominant color images on the right command attention, while the white space on the left gives the reviewer a place to rest his eyes. Design work courtesy of Daniel Childers.

BELOW: 12.18
Stare at this vibrant color combination and the page will start to vibrate. A color by itself may look great on the computer monitor, but next to another color, it can actually hurt your eyes! Design work courtesy of Charudatta Joshi.

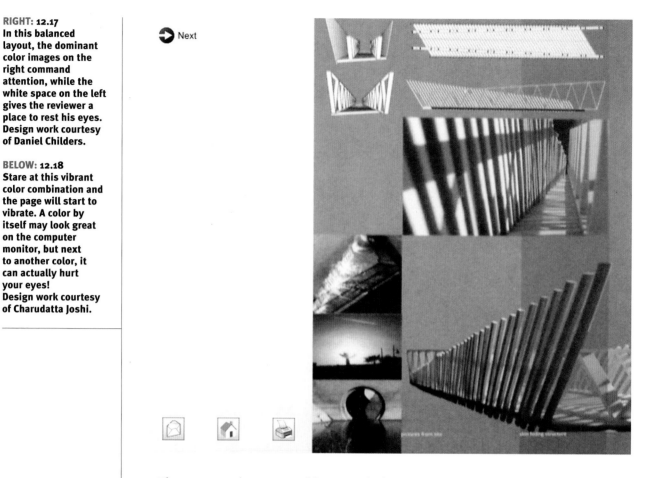

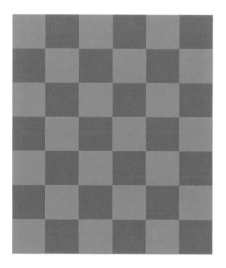

If you created a personal logo, include it on every page of your web site. You never know which page the practitioner will print out and distribute. Multiple pages can be coordinated by referring to the same logo on each page. The white area *around* text and images is negative space. It's tempting to cram as much information on each web page as you can, but this leaves no place for the viewer's eye to rest. If you have lots of information, break it into columns or even separate pages. They're only a link apart and the viewer will be more inclined to go to your other pages if they are uncluttered and a pleasure to review.

As discussed in Chapter 6, colors have a psychological impact on reviewers. For web sites, use only two to three colors total for backgrounds, navigation tools, and text. (Obviously, your project images will have many colors of their own.) Too much color can overstimulate the eye. Recall that some colors are considered "warm" while others are considered "cool." Warm colors will come forward on your web page; cool colors will recede. The use of complementary colors in printed material can be eye-catching. But viewed digitally on a CD or web site, the colors do not focus well. Brilliant hues that have a complementary or near-complementary relationship cause visual vibration (see Figure 12.18).

Box 12.5

Students often ask me, "How many pages should I have in my web-based portfolio?" I wish I could provide a definite answer, but there is no optimal number of web pages for your site. If you have too few pages, a reviewer will think the web site is incomplete or weak. If you have too many, a reviewer must click through countless pages to get to what she wants (see Box 12.5).

Thumbnail Images

A smaller version of a larger graphic can allow reviewers to preview a graphic quickly before deciding to view it at a larger size and in more detail. These are called *thumbnail images*, or just *thumbnails*. These smaller files (such as the ones in Figure 12.19) allow the web page to quickly load.

Some may say that a disadvantage of a web-based portfolio is the necessity to keep graphics small enough to download quickly. Smaller files equals faster downloads, which equals happy reviewers. A thumbnail image smaller than 75 KB will take little time to download. You will not be able to show the viewer fine details in your work at a measly 72 dpi.

12.19
Thumbnail images allow the reviewer to quickly ascertain the contents within each web page.
Design work courtesy of Allison Saunders and Julia Kancius.

building process

final chair

RIGHT: 12.20
Thumbnail images can also be used as icons for the various levels of project information. In level 1, projects are listed. Click on a thumbnail and you are taken to other levels. Design work courtesy of Paul Hibbard.

BELOW: 12.21
This lighting plan is too small to be seen in detail. The web page is set up so that a click on one half will cause it to fill the screen. Design work courtesy of Manu Juyal and David A. Hobart, Jr.

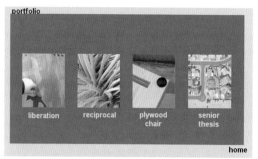

Level 1

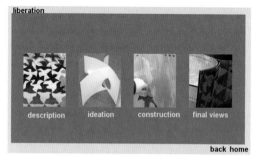

Level 2

Level 3

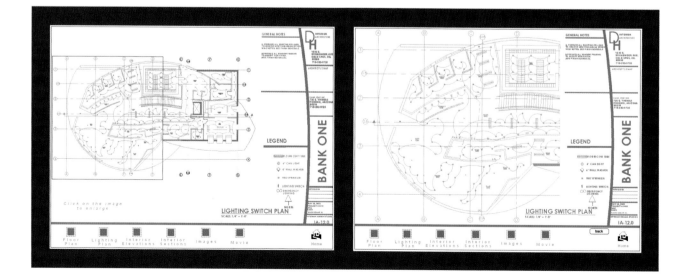

Rather than viewing these thumbnail images as a hindrance, think of them as a great marketing tool, a teaser to entice reviewers to see more of your work. By clicking on them, reviewers can either see a larger detailed version of the same image or be guided to another level of your design project (see Figure 12.20). Thumbnail images greatly help in organizing your online work, too. You can use them on your web site's site map, main directory page, or project sample pages.

Thumbnail images can be created in Photoshop or other image-editing software. It is easiest to save the same image as two separate files, each at a different image size. Try to keep the thumbnails no smaller than an inch. Anything smaller is very difficult to see clearly on a monitor. When creating your web site, you will simply link the two files together. As illustrated in Figure 12.21, you can even have a slightly smaller version of a drawing appear larger within the same web page.

Text on the Web

The appearance of text on your web site is another important consideration. A font selected for your printed portfolio may look stupendous—on paper. It may not be legible on a computer monitor.

Text Legibility

The same principles for having legible text in your printed portfolio (discussed in Chapter 7) are valid for your digital portfolio. There are several additional considerations, such as the use of lowercase letters, inclusion of negative space, color, size and levels of titles, and placement on the page. The goal is to have comprehensible text. What looks great on paper does not always look great onscreen!

Our design professions are unique in their use of stylized typefaces, like that shown in Figure 12.22. Because lettering used in architectural drafting is all capital letters, we are familiar with this style of communication. Nevertheless, avoid using capital lettering for large quantities of text, as this is difficult to read onscreen. Save architectural lettering for the text that accompanies your project images, not the labels and project descriptions you'll type underneath them.

As in your printed portfolio, use no more than two or three fonts. Sure, you can purchase font packages with tens of thousands of fonts. That doesn't mean you need to use all of them in your portfolio! Text on-screen should be slightly larger than you would have it on printed material. If you would use 10-point type for a project description on paper, provide the same project description in 14-point type on your web site. Don't stretch or compress your text too much or it will be difficult to read, even in a larger font. Leave enough white space between lines and paragraphs (called *leading*) to allow easier readability.

Negative space within the font is also a necessity for easy viewing. Even using upper- and lower-case letters (rather than all upper case) puts some white space around the letters and makes them easier to see. Be wary of fonts with vertical strokes spaced closely together, such as the City and Country Blueprint fonts (see Figure 12.23). There is simply not enough space between the letters to clearly read

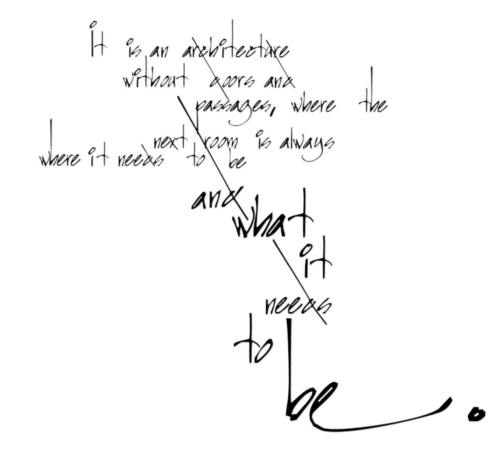

It is an architecture without doors and passages, where the next room is always where it needs to be and what it needs to be.

City Blueprint: illegible

Country Blueprint: illegible

Too thin is illegible!

Wider is legible!

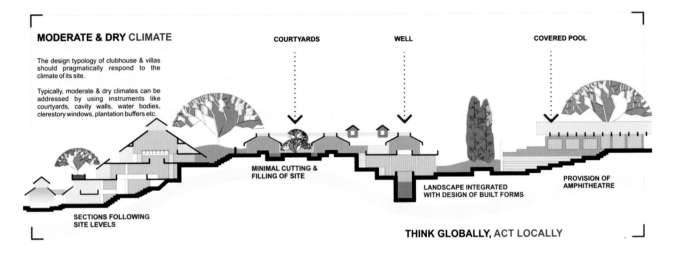

the words they spell unless you stretch them. Also, fonts with thin or narrow elements like the ones in Figure 12.24 will not display well on a monitor because they are only one pixel wide. Instead, select fonts that will cover multiple pixels on a monitor—something broad and bold.

Remember that the monitor is a series of pixels, or squares. That can explain why some text looks horrible on a web site. A pixel cannot be divided because it is the smallest unit on the screen. You cannot have half a pixel with the background color and the other half as part of your text. Therefore, try to avoid script or italicized fonts, as these *must* lean and curve, hitting the pixels in all the wrong places.

Text and its background color should contrast, making it easier to read on a monitor or screen, like the image in Figure 12.25. Titles should stand out from the rest of the text on your web pages. Headings and subheadings allow visual contrast on your web page. As exemplified in Figure 12.26, there are several levels of

ABOVE: 12.25
The dark text in this image is clearly visible on a white or pale background.
Design work courtesy of Charudatta Joshi.

BELOW: 12.26
HTML has several preset levels for the size and type of font.

Heading Level 1

Heading Level 2

Heading Level 3

Heading Level 4

Heading Level 5

12.27
Three levels of text are plenty. The most dominant and visible level should be used for the most important information on your web page, like the project title.

Title Level One is the Largest and Boldest!

Title Level Two is Slightly Smaller and Less Bold!

Title Level Three is Plain, Easy to Read Text!

headings available in HTML, although you probably don't want to use more than three. A title in a larger font than the other text screams importance (see Figure 12.27). If that headline is important to you, use that larger font (rather than CAPS). Also, put it higher on the page, again denoting its importance. Keep titles short and fewer than 75 characters. If a title is too long to fit on someone's 15-inch monitor, it will wrap to the next line (often in a strange manner, too).

Overall, avoid large amounts of text. As in your printed portfolio, your design images should be more powerful on the screen than lines and lines of written description (see Box 12.6). (You will still include text, just not tons of it.) If you must include paragraphs of text, avoid having the text run the entire width of the screen. Instead, break the text into two columns, like a newspaper. This is easier to read on a computer monitor as the eye moves in shorter left-to-right movements (see Figure 12.28).

Placement of your text is essential. Large amounts of text should always be justified at left, like the small amount of text in Figure 12.29. That's what everyone is familiar with. (Unless you're reading a wedding invitation, centered text is just too hard to read.) It's hard enough reading a bulk of text onscreen without having to search for the starting point of each new line. For anything more than three sentences long, use left justification. Titles can be centered or right justified, although again, left justification is the default location. On the whole, your text should not detract from your images. You need to ask yourself what is more important: having a digital portfolio with wildly stylized text or having one with text that is a bit more toned down but far more legible?

Text enhances the visual experience and strengthens the viewer's understanding of the page content. Text must be concise and to the point. A viewer should be able to scan the images and text on a page simultaneously without consciously stopping to read the text. Phrases or bullet points are recommended.

Linda Nelson Johnson
Associate Professor and Assistant Director
Interior Design
Washington State University
Pullman, WA

Box 12.6

Cross-Platform Text

As if text legibility were not enough to contemplate, not all fonts are accessible across platforms, appearing differently on a Windows or Macintosh system. In order for others to view the fonts you have selected, they must have the same ones installed on their computer. If not, the web browser will substitute another font in its place. Just because *you* may have these fonts installed on your computer does not mean everyone else does too. I recall working on a project in graduate school and I selected a stylized font that I had purchased. I emailed a professor my thesis presentation and got a very curt reply that he could not understand my presentation. I wondered why. The next day, he showed me the presentation on his computer. He did not have this special font and his system substituted a symbols

12.29
Left-justified text is easy to read. This portfolio page has just enough text to describe the design while letting the images speak for the designer.
Design work courtesy of Yang Peng.

Product Design   Peng Yang's Portfolio   4

七佰年

Winning Prize 'Amurulte' Furniture Design Competition

seven hundred years

Project Product Design
Client Competition
Date May 2005

Description
This project was my participation work for 'Amurulte' Furniture Design Competition and finally won a winning prize. It inherits the style of Chinese traditional furniture and uses wood broads instead of those precious tree wood. Additionally, compared with traditional Chinese chairs, sitting area is increased and height is lowered in order to follow modern research in human factors.

typeface for the text. So instead of letters and words, he saw pages of complete gibberish. No wonder he was frustrated. When emailing my work to others, I now stick to common fonts that I know others will have on their computer or I email the font necessary to read my work in its true form. Better yet, I create a PDF file that preserves the typeface and layout as they should be.

Besides replacing one font for another, substituting fonts may squish or stretch your text across the page. Lines and paragraphs might even be cut short. Your web pages certainly will appear different. Stick with one of the seven cross-platform fonts shown in Figure 12.30: Arial, Courier, Geneva, Helvetica, Times, Times New Roman, and Verdana. Test your web page on both platforms. The text may adjust slightly but should be similar.

In addition, each platform has a different screen resolution. Windows will display at 96 ppi; Macintosh at 72 ppi. What does this mean? It means you can see smaller text on a Windows computer more clearly than you can on a Macintosh. That's another reason why text on your web site should be a bit larger than your printed portfolio. If you can legibly read your text (without squinting your eyes) on a Macintosh computer with its lower resolution, it should be exceptionally clear on a Windows computer. Therefore, bigger text is better.

Web-Authoring and -Editing Applications

Raster, vector, and layout applications can help you design a site but not build it. For that, you'll need a web-authoring and management program to take care of all the links, pages, animations, sounds, and so on. Admired applications are Macromedia Dreamweaver and Microsoft FrontPage. These applications can help you create, modify, and publish your web pages. Both programs have similar features and capabilities. They all have layout surfaces on which you position and scale your web elements. All can generate web pages by inputting code or using desktop publishing layout modes. You can create static, dynamic, or multimedia elements in your pages and preview them in different web browsers.

These applications can make the task of coding relatively painless by entering information in a Design View, just like you would in a word processor. These applications rely on an interface between the view of your web design and its code, known as WYSIWYG (pronounced wiss-ee-wig). This stands for What You See Is What You Get and refers to a computer's ability to show a document that is being edited more or less exactly the way it will appear in its completed form. These software applications are like desktop publishing software with a relatively simple user interface. As you type in information or place images on the page, the software is writing the HTML code for you.

So what makes them different? Well, the graphic user interfaces are different (i.e., how the software looks and works). FrontPage is similar to other Microsoft Office products and has layout wizards to get you going quickly. Macromedia contributes its own product, Dreamweaver, which works great with Flash, Fireworks, and Director. Not sure which one to use? Try them out by downloading preview versions from the company web sites.

Macromedia Dreamweaver
Macromedia Dreamweaver is an HTML editor that helps you design and develop your web site (see Figure 12.31). Now administered by Adobe Systems, it is available on both Macintosh and Windows platforms. It is an extremely popular web development tool because you can design your pages while the software hides the

Arial

Courier

Geneva

Helvetica

Times

Times New Roman

Verdana

12.30
Not sure if your digital portfolio will be viewed on a Macintosh or a Windows platform? Stick with these seven cross-platform fonts.

12.31
Macromedia Dreamweaver is a web-authoring and -editing application that integrates with other former Macromedia products like Flash and Director.

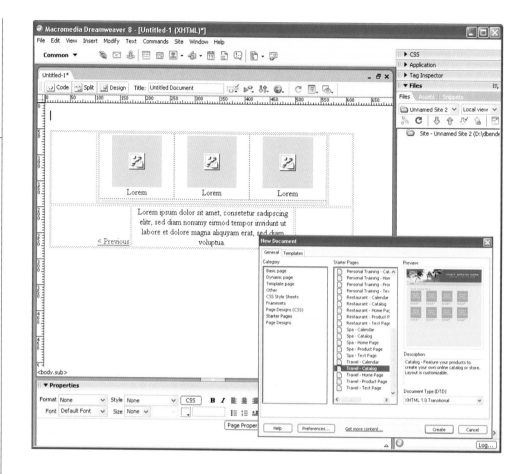

code from sight. It comes with a drag-and-drop user interface to make creating web pages easier. You have the option to work in page layout mode, in code mode, and in a preview mode where you can see your code and the results are shown in a color insert. What's more, it has site management tools to keep your web pages organized. Even a neophyte can design a good-looking web site with this software.

Microsoft FrontPage

Microsoft FrontPage is a web editor and administrative tool that is relatively easy to use (see Figure 12.32). FrontPage features automated web templates that come with the software (for those with little web-authoring experience). Unlike other templates, these create animated buttons for pages you add to the navigation system. FrontPage visually helps you see your site's file structure, is easily integrated with other Microsoft Office products, and automatically changes the links on all your pages when you change the location of a page. FrontPage is no longer being developed by Microsoft, but has been replaced by two products: SharePoint Designer, a web site program based on the Windows SharePoint Service (which offers online publishing of typical file formats), and Expression Web Designer, a similar program that is aimed at web design professionals who wish to develop complex web sites.

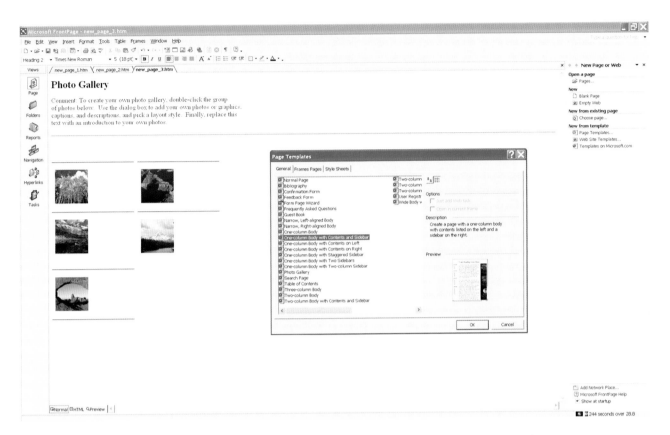

12.32
Microsoft FrontPage
has templates to get
you started designing
your own unique
web site.

Web Templates

You have plenty of work to share with others. You even have a rough layout. Does the technology to implement your web pages hold you back? Use a standard template provided in the web-authoring software, if available. You can always improve on it later as you learn more about HTML and web design. Or look online for portfolio skins, which are ready-to-go web templates in Flash and other applications. Some of these templates are free; others can be purchased. There are hundreds of these templates available to jump-start your web page production.

Access to Your Site

Once you have designed your web site, you will need to get it into the proper format to display it on the Internet. In this section, we'll discuss HTML, linking information, the function of a server, and finally, how a practitioner finds your portfolio on the information superhighway.

Hypertext Markup Language

This is when knowing a little something about HTML comes in handy. The Internet began as a text-only medium whereby one computer could communicate with another using signals sent over a modem. But words were not enough so CompuServe designed the first graphics format (GIF) (Smick et al. 2006). Then HTML became a popular markup language used to circulate information on the web.

Recall from Chapter 8 that HTML stands for Hyptertext Markup Language. It is essentially a language of computer code. Code is what you do not see when you visit a web page. It is the information *behind* the web page that determines how it looks and how it functions. It tells the web browser what information to display on the page, and where. To see the code of any page, select the Source option from your browser's View menu (see Figure 12.33).

This book does not teach HTML coding, as there are plenty of obtainable resources for this purpose (books, web sites, courses, and so on). Know that your web site code must be precisely entered because web browsers are unforgiving. One mistake and the page will not load or it will load with your page all messed up. Names and locations of files must be typed precisely. HTML code is also unforgiving. Whether you are doing the coding yourself or using web-authoring software, be careful when editing code.

HTML allows you to create paths or links between the files stored on your web server. This is a way of organizing bits and pieces of information. A simple kind of link is a hypertext link, a word or phrase that is underlined in your text. A more sophisticated link uses a graphic icon to represent the intended action. When you click on the text or icon, you are moved to the new content. Keep hyperlink colors consistent with the default values everyone is familiar with. An unvisited link will be blue while a link that has been accessed (or visited) will be purple.

A broken link is a link that isn't functioning because the code cannot find the linked file. This happens most often when you move a linked file from one location on your computer to another. Let's say you stored a file somewhere on your

12.33
Hypertext Markup Language, or HTML, source code can be viewed and even copied from any web page by accessing the Source code option from the browser menu.

```
exchange[1] - Notepad

File  Edit  Format  View  Help

<!--Copyright (c) 2000-2003 Microsoft Corporation. All rights
<!--CURRENT FILE== "IE5" "WIN32" frameset -->
<!--CURRENT TEMPLATE == frameset.00000001 -->
<HTML>
<HEAD>
<META HTTP-EQUIV="Content-Type" CONTENT="text/html; CHARSET=ut
<TITLE>Microsoft Outlook Web Access</TITLE>
<BASE href="https://exchange.asu.edu/exchange/dbender1/">
</HEAD>
<SCRIPT language="JavaScript">
var g_iNewWindowWidth = 700;
var g_iNewWindowHeight = 500;
var g_fwarnonLogoff=false;
function warnOnLogoff()
{
if (g_fwarnonLogoff)
alert("To help protect your mailbox from unauthorized access,
}
</SCRIPT>
<FRAMESET border="1" frameborder="1" onUnload="warnOnLogoff()'
<NOFRAMES>
<BODY><P>This page uses frames, but your browser doesn't suppo
</NOFRAMES>
</FRAMESET>
</HTML>
```

computer, like C:\My Documents\titleimage.jpg. When someone visits your web page and clicks on the link for this image, the image will appear in its correct location and layout. Suppose you now feel the need to reorganize your computer files. You move the file to another directory but do not change the link on your web site. Uh-oh. Now if someone visits your web site and clicks on the same link, the image cannot be found because the path is now broken. You have two options: Either put the file back where you had it originally, or retype the HTML path to include the file's new location. You can see why it's important to continually check your web site to ensure that no paths are broken or no files have mysteriously disappeared.

If using the same image from one page to the next, make sure that the web software you are using is not renaming the image. If your personal logo is on every page and you name the file "greatlogo.gif," make sure each page references that file and not "mylogoA.gif, mylogoB.gif" and so on. Otherwise, you could have the same image referenced 17 times with 17 different file names.

What if you make a change to your web page and the next time you look at it, you don't see any changes? Remember that web browsers cache pages so the browser will not have to read its information twice. When you make a change to your own page, your browser does not know this and will continue to pull the original page from cache memory. Use the refresh or reload button to command the browser to retrieve the latest changes.

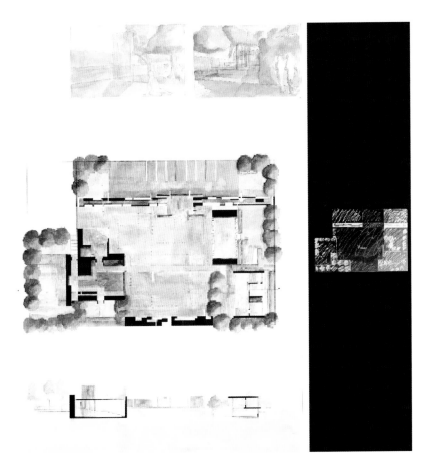

12.34
Save time by turning an entire page layout into one single web page.
Design work courtesy of Paul Marquez.

One way to avoid HTML and web programming is to do your entire page layout in one of these layout applications. Save the whole page as an EPS (Encapsulated Postcript) file. Open it in Photoshop as an RGB file at 72 dpi. Flatten the layers when you save it as a JPEG. You have just turned the entire page into one picture that you can post on your web site, like the one in Figure 12.34. This is a nice shortcut but can be limiting if you want the interactivity in your portfolio that only a web site can provide.

Loading to a Server

Once your site has been constructed on *your* computer, you'll want to put it out there for all to see. You'll need to put all your files on a server, a large storage device where files reside that is accessed whenever someone pulls up that web site. The term *server* can actually refer to the physical hardware of the computer that answers requests from clients, or to the software needed to process these requests. Two digital languages are involved in communication between a web page and its server, HTTP and FTP. Hypertext Transfer Protocol (HTTP) is the location of the web site. Commonly seen at the beginning of a web site address, this protocol requests and retrieves necessary files from the server when someone calls up the site. File Transfer Protocol (FTP) is an Internet service used to upload and download files to directories on a server. FTP tells the server what to do with the files being called up from the server.

Where do you get a server? Most likely, you will not buy one yourself, but will rent space on one to house your files. Many schools provide students with space on the school's server. This is a wonderful benefit while you are enrolled in school. Unfortunately, this privilege is often revoked shortly after graduation. (Different schools have different server policies. Check with your school about continued use of server space after you graduate.)

Consider renting web space from an Internet service provider (ISP). An Internet service provider is a regional or national retail company that supplies Internet service to customers for a monthly fee. There are many on hand, such as America Online, Earthlink, Prodigy, and so on. Search on the Internet for various options. Know approximately how much space you will need in order to accurately compare prices and capabilities of various hosting services.

When acquiring server space from your school or ISP, your site will have a domain name. This is a unique name for your site followed by a period (i.e., a dot) and a classification of the type of site. For example, a web site sponsored by your school will end in .edu, while a commercial (.com), non-profit organization (.org), or government (.gov) site will have a different classification. When contacting others about your site, don't forget to give them the classification at the end.

Test your web-based portfolio before launching it to the public. Provide links to any necessary plug-ins. Determine if your video clips will open in a separate window or be embedded in your web page. Test and retest everything! Test it on both platforms and through different web browsers. Test it on computers with different monitor sizes, storage memory, and Internet connection speeds. Look for font, text, and color problems. Look for links that may be broken or missing. Look at downloaded files for any problems or speed concerns. You can never test your web site enough.

Search and Access

Once you have developed your web-based portfolio, it is time to let others know about it. It is *not* recommended that you send your entire digital portfolio to anyone. If your portfolio has any semblance of decent resolution, the file would be absolutely huge. Instead, email only your web site link. It is much simpler to read a few lines of introduction and then click on a link to view your portfolio online. (We'll talk more about email content in Chapter 14.)

Be conscious of the fact that there may be security concerns in the offices where your audience does business. They may have a firewall in place, which is a system to guard a confidential network from unauthorized outsiders. The system can include hardware and software, as well as monitoring and administrative tools (Cohen 2000). These systems may prevent some practitioners from accessing your site. For example, I was teaching CAD to a group of practitioners in their office on several weekends. Midweek, one of the designers requested some additional instruction. Rather than drive an hour to their office, we tried to videoconference together, connecting our two computers so I could observe his progress onscreen. His office had a firewall in place that absolutely prevented me from connecting with his computer. This is a safety precaution for the firm. Do not be discouraged if a practitioner has some difficulty viewing your digital portfolio. Maybe you'll need to deliver or mail a copy on CD instead.

Practitioners are more likely to visit your site when you give them the web site link directly (via email, letter, phone, or personal contact) than they are by accidentally stumbling across it. But it does happen. How do you get people to find you? Through search engines, such as Google and Yahoo. The search engine will

Google

| **Web** | Images | Video | News | Maps | **more »** |

amol surve portfolio   Search

Web

Amol Surve - Portfolio
Portfolio.
www.public.asu.edu/~asurve/ - 4k - Cached - Similar pages

Amol Surve - Portfolio
HomePage.
www.public.asu.edu/~asurve/Slide1.htm - 9k - Cached - Similar pages
[More results from www.public.asu.edu]

12.35
Tag your web site with as many relevant keywords as possible so it comes up in a search.

hunt through titles, which are listed at the top of a web page. Make your title count by putting your name and the word "portfolio" in it, like the web site shown in Figure 12.35. Additional keywords in your headings can trigger the search to locate your site. What kind of design do you specialize in? Retail, corporate offices, remodeling, home design? What are you good at? CAD, rendering, modeling, drafting, specifications? What words other than design can help people find your web-based portfolio?

A Review of Web-Based Portfolios

In closing, remember that a web-based portfolio has many advantages, such as increased exposure, opportunity to constantly show your latest work, and the inclusion of animation and interactivity. The little things can have the most impact on the usability of your site. Unnecessary glitz and glitter is no substitute for a well-developed site. Yes, these features might be technically impressive, but if they are not user friendly, no one will appreciate them.

Putting your portfolio on the Internet provides a convenient way for anyone to access your material from anywhere in the world. Be culturally sensitive with the material you place on your web site. Your audience is now global. Designers in other countries may misunderstand slang terminology or graphic icons common to your region of the world.

A web-based portfolio can be beneficial for interviewing in other states or countries. A potential employer in another time zone can preview your portfolio at his leisure and then conduct a telephone interview with you, during which you virtually present your work (Novitski 1995). As a design student, you are familiar with making presentations to specific people, such as clients, critics, professors, and other students. With a web-based portfolio, it's difficult to focus a presentation because your audience is unknown (Novitski 1995). You cannot assume that the viewer is familiar with your school's curriculum, the topic of your project, the process you used to create your work, or even local use of building materials and codes.

Keep in mind the speed of Internet connections. How long will a reviewer wait to see your portfolio? How long would you wait? It's easy to get swept up in the color, movement, and sound of your web site. These extras often result in large files. A 1-MB file can take as long as two minutes to download from a web site on a dial-up connection with a 28.8-kbps modem. In today's culture of speed and efficiency, this is really slow. But there are still some people who connect to the Internet using dial-up. Don't exclude them from viewing your designs by having huge web files.

Lastly, your web-based portfolio (and your portfolio in general) is a work in progress. Don't rush to get everything up on your web site at once, overlooking errors and mistakes in the process. Construct and upload your pages one at a time. Take time to put forth a polished site because substandard work does not reflect well on you.

Now you may think, "Great, I'll never be done with this web site." Constant refinement is a *benefit* of a web-based portfolio. Once the structure of your web site is in place, it's simple to switch out a few images here and there to keep your site fresh and alluring. The Internet's greatest strength may be its flexibility and immediacy (Cole et al. 1999). Use of the Internet supports continuous portfolio development, unlike static media on CD, which we will talk about next.

CD AND DVD PRESENTATIONS

You can provide a sample of your work to others on CD. A CD can be mailed or delivered to a school or potential employer as a means of introduction (additional postage is minimal). Or after an interview or site visit, you can leave it with those you met as a reminder of your abilities and talent. Some practitioners like receiving work on CD because they can keep the information stored on their office shelf or in their desk drawer. When you email files, the recipient has to download the information to his or her hard drive, taking up precious computer memory. When more memory is needed, guess what will be deleted first?

A CD has many advantages over a traditional printed portfolio, and even a web-based one. CDs are small, lightweight, portable, and effortless to carry. They provide secure and private storage for your work. Recent reductions in the cost of CD burners make it easier to distribute your work in this universal format. The discs themselves are relatively inexpensive so you can prolifically distribute your portfolio. (Although mini-CDs seem fashionable and trendy, they do not run well and are not widely accepted in industry yet. We'll talk more about mini-CDs in Chapter 14.)

Servers break down occasionally, making your web-based portfolio temporarily unavailable. CDs do not need a server. Therefore, speed is not so important. The only speed considerations with this medium are the drive speed of the disc player, the memory or buffer size, and how quickly the disc can advance to full spin speed. Files on a web site must be small because they take time to download. Files on a CD are viewed faster and can be larger. Most importantly, you can go beyond the normal for dramatic effects, such as virtual reality, 3-D modeling, rendering, animation, and audio or video narratives (Kliment 1998).

A few disadvantages of using CDs to present your portfolio are worth noting. You cannot update a CD portfolio as quickly as a web-based one. Once you burn the data, it's burned. If you find a mistake or wish to add a last minute project, you'll have to create a new layout and burn new CDs. The recording process is slow and labor intensive if you are burning the CDs yourself because you can only do one at a time. CDs can hold much larger files (e.g., rendered images and walk-through movies like those represented in Figure 12.36) than what can be stored on your web site, although these still require some time to load. But this isn't nearly as time consuming as downloading files from the Internet, especially if the practitioner has antiquated technology that limits download capacity (like a dial-up connection). CDs can be convenient because of their size and portability, but they

12.36
These beautifully rendered images look better when viewed at a large enough size to see their details. A CD can hold far more portfolio information than will be downloaded from a web site by the average impatient reviewer.
Design work courtesy of Alexandra C. Ayres, Sally Azer, and Kelly Robinson.

can also get lost and misplaced easily. Lastly, CDs are not tough as nails and can get scratched, damaged, or even shattered if mishandled. They are no more permanent than any other form of plastic media.

If you have decided to distribute your portfolio on CD, plan your content carefully. Many of the same principles for presenting your portfolio on the Internet hold true for one on CD as well. When creating layouts for distribution on CD, 600 × 800 or 760 × 410 are good resolution settings. Considerations such as text size, color, style, and placement affect a CD portfolio. It'll be reviewed on a monitor just like one on the Internet, right? Knowing how colors are displayed on different monitors and different platforms will influence the way your work is viewed.

CD Portfolio Formats

How you format the CD can impede or promote the viewing of your work. It's not a good idea to put a bunch of independent files on the CD because reviewers may not have the same software, or worse, their computer may open the files in the wrong software. For example, when they click on an AutoCAD drawing, the computer might try to open it in Adobe Illustrator. Has something similar ever happened to you? Remember how frustrating it was? A stand-alone presentation is your best option. This means your presentation does not require reviewers to have the original software to experience it. This doesn't mean software is not required. In this format, your work is viewed through players and plug-ins, such as reading PDF files with Acrobat Reader or watching movies with Shockwave. It might be a good idea to include the needed plug-ins on the CD.

One option for a CD portfolio is to take your web-based portfolio and simply burn it to CD. This is known as a browser-based portfolio. This is a great time-saver for you, as you only need to manipulate your digital work once. The HTML files and all other supporting files and images are copied to CD. You must ensure you save all the necessary files, and in the same hierarchy that your HTML code was written. When reviewers put the CD into their computers, they can view your portfolio through a web browser. But it does require reviewers to be connected to the Internet in order to view your work. Hence, downloading large files is a negative consideration.

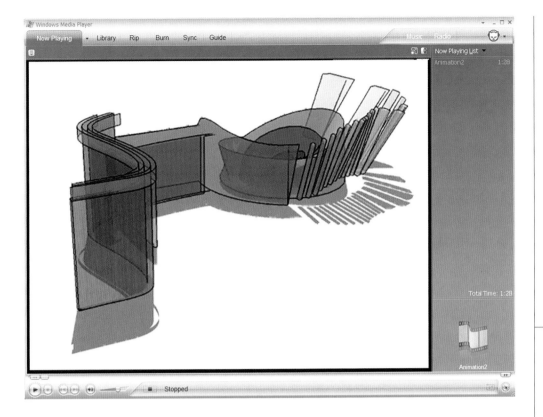

LEFT: 12.37
An animated walkthrough can originate from different software applications and can be used for concept development as well as final presentation. Design work courtesy of Ellie Combs, Jennifer Gozzi, and Elaine Hu.

BELOW: 12.38
When this designer's CD is put into a computer, the autorun file starts an animated splash page sequence. The reviewer need do nothing except sit back and enjoy the presentation. Design work courtesy of Manu Juyal.

To take advantage of what a CD can do, your CD portfolio should be slightly different than the one viewed on the Internet. Otherwise, why wouldn't you just send people to look at your web site? On CD, your digital portfolio can have larger files. You can have longer animated walkthroughs (like the one represented in Figure 12.37), larger image sizes, and a wider variety of materials.

Still, keep in mind that just because a CD can hold gobs of projects does not mean you need to cram it completely full. Why bother? It is very likely a reviewer will either love or hate your work in the first 30 seconds of viewing it. If he loves it, he'll contact you for an interview. If he hates it, your CD goes in the trash. Sometimes "less is more." Show your best work first to entice the viewer onward.

You can also create a CD that starts playing automatically. You've probably heard the terms *autorun* or *autoplay*, which have the same meaning. You put the CD in your computer and certain actions are automatically executed. You don't have to look for software or click on anything—the CD just starts to run. You do this by adding a couple of small files to the root directory of the CD, one of which is an autorun file like the one in Figure 12.38. This file signals the computer that the CD is autorun media. It tells the computer what software to start after the CD is inserted and to begin running your portfolio presentation.

Packaging Your CD

Your CD package will consist of a CD, its label, a case, and possibly an optional mailer insert inside. One of the benefits of the CD portfolio is the case. It can be a CD jewel case or any of the other available paper, vinyl, or plastic sleeves. Carefully design all surfaces of the case (front, back, and inside too). Your name and the word *portfolio* should be the most visible text on your case. If the case has a spine, put a label there as well. (This could be the most visible portion if the practitioner stores the CD on a shelf or stacked with other CDs in a pile because only the side will show, as illustrated in Figure 12.39.)

A CD needs a label. Using a permanent marker to write your name and email on your CD will certainly *not* impress anyone. The CD label should either be burned directly onto the CD with thermal printing, or printed using a CD label kit (Figure 12.40). Thermal printing is a type of inkjet printing that creates the image on the CD using a heated print head instead of printing on paper. It will not smear, is water-resistant, and can be used on your CDs to display a custom design. Check your local CD duplication service for rates on short runs of 100 to 500 discs.

12.39
How will you identify and differentiate your CD portfolio from everyone else's?

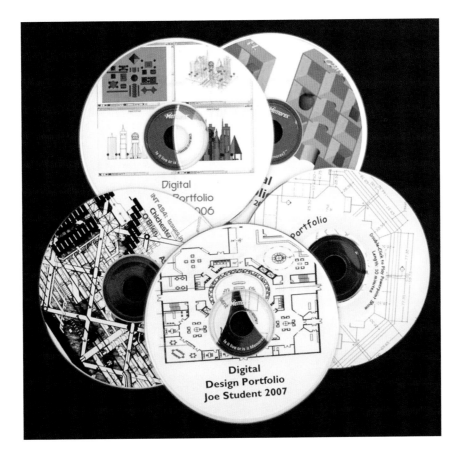

12.40
You can include some of your design work on your CD label. Just make sure your *name* is prominently displayed.

Avoid purchasing CDs that have the label affixed to them already, as they will tear off and eat away at the disc coating. Labels you create with a kit should have the labels precut to the correct size. Position it dead center on the CD, as an askew label will prevent the CD from playing.

Design the label to be graphically consistent with your interviewing items. Get your personal logo, name, and contact information on the label. If the CD becomes separated from your case, it can be matched up later. Keep the text size large enough to be read clearly and in one or two fonts, only. The same rules discussed for using text, color, visual layout, and the design elements and principles in a printed portfolio apply equally well here. This is your introduction to a firm. How much do you want to make a positive impression? A pixellated raster image on the cover with tiny text will *not* get the job done.

KEEPING YOUR DIGITAL PORTFOLIO SIMPLE

Make tradeoffs between what you want and the time you realistically have to get it done. With all the advances in technology, there are so many things you can do with a digital portfolio. But should you? Will adding those cool interactive navigational buttons really enhance your web-based portfolio? Will adding four videos to your digital portfolio help you say more about your designs than a series of really impressive still images? A few small web pages may be better than one

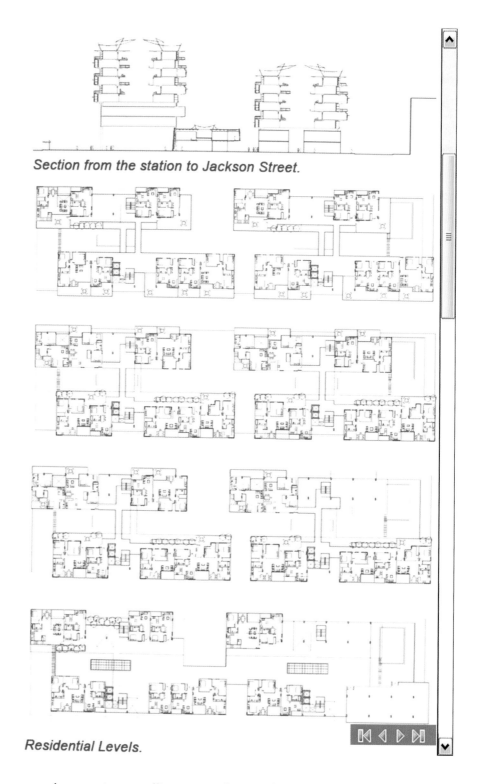

Section from the station to Jackson Street.

Residential Levels.

large one that requires scrolling to see the very bottom (see Figure 12.41). A background of solid color may be a better choice than a fancy textured background. Layout decisions will be influenced by your time (or lack of time). Think about *why* you are doing something. Does it add to your portfolio or detract from it? If it detracts from it, don't do it. Remember, KISS (see Box 12.7).

Box 12.7

It is so tempting to saturate your portfolio with all the bells and whistles, but you want to keep your audience as wide as possible. Never assume everyone has the latest and greatest technology, or that they'll know how to use it. Consider our discussion of baby boomers in Chapter 3. The easier you can make it for the owner or principal of the firm to review your portfolio, the better off you'll be.

CONCLUSION

It is important to maintain a balance between high-end technology such as animation and 3-D environments with traditional 2-D images. Videos, interactivity, and animations in your portfolio should never overpower your design work. Review the advantages and disadvantages of all three presentation formats (laptop, Internet, or CD) before deciding which one is right for you. In Chapter 13, you will critically evaluate your portfolio to determine its strengths and weaknesses. We'll also talk about the importance of peer review to provide external constructive criticism, and how to successfully present your portfolio in a job interview.

13

Evaluating and Presenting Your Portfolio

I n this chapter, we finalize the portfolio process by critically evaluating it. It is helpful to have others evaluate your portfolio as well, offering constructive criticism for its improvement. We then spend time covering the presentation of your portfolio—the payoff for all your hard work and effort.

SELF-EVALUATION

Are you done with your portfolio? Are you sure? Now is the time for a rigorous evaluation of your work. This is a critical part of the development of any presentation material.

If you planned your time well, you should have some time left over before you need to show it in an interview or turn it in for a school review. Put it away and come back to it two or three days later. Look at it again with fresh eyes. Stand back and review it. Close your eyes halfway and see if something in your layout jumps out too much, like the rendering in Figure 13.1. When you close your eyes halfway, they focus not on the color of the object but on the value or intensity. Also look at your work upside-down. This stops your brain from trying to read the text or understand the images. Look at the layout and presentation. Is it balanced on the page? Is there enough or too much negative space? Further ask yourself the questions in Box 13.1. This questionnaire can also be given to a peer who is reviewing the portfolio.

You may notice something that needs to be fixed. This can be on your layout or in one of your projects. Don't think a little flaw will go unnoticed during a review. If you notice it, someone else will too. Fix it.

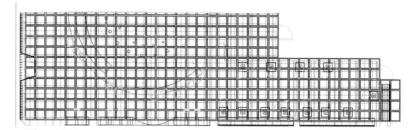

Plan View - Customer entrance at left

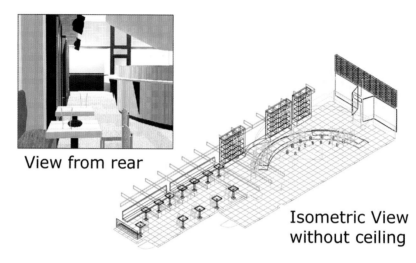

View from rear

Isometric View
without ceiling

A portfolio evaluation checklist will assist you in preparing to show your portfolio at an interview or before sending in to a school review board. Use the checklist provided in Table 13.1 to evaluate your portfolio. Try to think like a professor or practitioner.

PEER REVIEW

As designers, we tend to think that our creativity is exceptional and our designs are perfect. We all dislike a studio critique where the critics don't blissfully enjoy our designs as much as we do. It may be difficult to be constructively critical of your own work, so ask others to help you. Every person has his or her own ideas about what quality and creativity means. Take advantage of this variation in perceptions by seeking feedback from others.

Once you have finished the self-evaluation checklist provided in Table 13.1, have a critical friend or two do the same. Make an additional copy of these pages for them. Who are critical friends? Persons who will look you in the eye and give you an honest answer, whom you trust to tell you the truth. These can be friends, peers, or family members. Ask them what they think of your portfolio and if they have any questions after reviewing it. Ask them what they learned about you by reviewing your portfolio. Encourage them to provide you with constructive feedback and a truthful reaction. You can involve these critical friends at the very beginning of your portfolio process by running your storyboard and table of con-

PORTFOLIO EVALUATION QUESTIONS

- Does your portfolio convey your capabilities?
- Is your best and current work displayed?
- Are you showing some evidence of your design process?
- Are your technology skills unmistakably evident?
- Is your work at the level that shows you can start working as a professional?
- Does your portfolio represent your potential to grow as a designer?
- Does it have a focus and concentration?
- Is it structured and organized?
- Is anything missing?
- Are there clear categories of information?
- Is it easy to read and understand?
- More importantly, will the intended audience understand it?
- Does the linear or nonlinear navigation style succeed?
- Is the portfolio cohesive? Does it hold together?
- Does it need additional revision?
- What is most effective? Least effective?
- What holes are evident in your portfolio?
- What skill sets are not represented?
- For a digital portfolio, ask yourself:
  - Does it crash?
  - Can you view it on multiple platforms?
  - How does it look on different monitors?
  - Are special viewers or software needed?
  - Does it load quickly?
  - Have I backed up all my files in a safe place?

Box 13.1

tents past them, or at the very end, by having them review and evaluate your portfolio when you believe it is complete. The extent of their involvement is only limited to the time they have available to help you and the amount of criticism you can handle.

Besides trusted friends, show your work to others who are knowledgeable about your field, such as classmates, mentors, or professors. Where else can you seek feedback on your portfolio? Does your school offer portfolio workshops through the student chapter of your professional organization? Are there seminars where design practitioners are available to offer feedback on your work? You may need to ask multiple friends and classmates to get a variety of opinions. Seek advice from architects and designers you admire and respect. Is your portfolio exceptional or just adequate? Ask others to review your portfolio, resume, cover letter, and other promotional material as well. This process of seeking external feedback provides you with others' trusted judgment. Their comments may confirm what you know or at least suspect is exceptional and lacking in your work. It is never easy to accept criticism. If you have confidence in the viewpoint of your trusted friends, consider yourself fortunate to get this criticism.

PORTFOLIO CHECKLIST

1 = Not obvious
2 = Minimally obvious
3 = Obvious and of low quality
4 = Obvious and of high quality

Rate the following statements using the scale above.

Organization

The portfolio is structured by theme or content.	
Projects are highlighted with captions.	
There is a clear beginning and end.	

Clarity

Projects signify required technical skills.	
Pieces are good examples of your probable design skill.	
All titles, captions, and project descriptions are readable.	

Creativity

The use of color, font, format, and layout distinguish this portfolio from others.	
The organizing theme or layout is one of a kind.	
Ability to use technology is plainly evident.	

Professional Appearance

The quality of images is suitable to the portfolio's final presentation media.	
Projects are presented in an attractive manner.	
The number of pages or images is appropriate.	

Total your scores from the above. How does your portfolio rate?

37 to 48 points
Your portfolio's content and intent characterizes your advanced perception of your design knowledge and skills. Ideas and projects are strongly related. Your individual point of view is creative and refreshing. The portfolio organization is technically skillful.

25 to 36 points
Your portfolio is on track but not complete. You have a clear understanding of portfolio content and format, but it is not polished yet. Relationships between ideas and selected images are good. The portfolio shows an adequate approach to organization and creativity.

13 to 24 points
Your portfolio contains confirmation of required design skills, but it is not well organized. Ideas and projects have an underdeveloped relationship. Evidence of your design skills is not represented in the images and layout you have selected.

0 to 12 points
Your portfolio needs a lot of work! It needs a unified theme or organization to make it one cohesive object. The individual images need refining, and the layout and organization could be much better.

Table 13.1

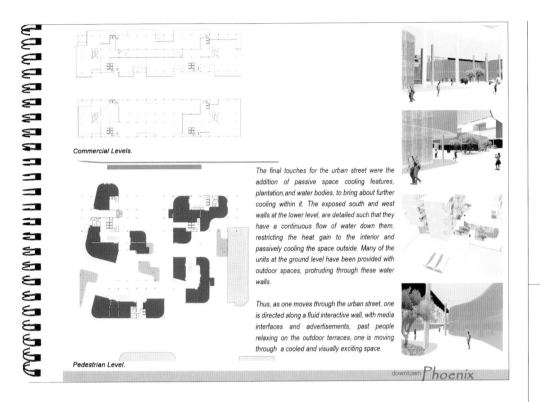

Commercial Levels.

The final touches for the urban street were the addition of passive space cooling features, plantation, and water bodies, to bring about further cooling within it. The exposed south and west walls at the lower level, are detailed such that they have a continuous flow of water down them, restricting the heat gain to the interior and passively cooling the space outside. Many of the units at the ground level have been provided with outdoor spaces, protruding through these water walls.

Thus, as one moves through the urban street, one is directed along a fluid interactive wall, with media interfaces and advertisements, past people relaxing on the outdoor terraces; one is moving through a cooled and visually exciting space.

Pedestrian Level.

downtown *Phoenix*

PRESENTING YOUR PORTFOLIO IN AN INTERVIEW

Our fields are very competitive and very visual. If you have a professional-looking portfolio with excellent samples of your skills and abilities, you increase your chances of beating out the competition and getting the job you want. However, the portfolio will not interview for you or perform for you on the job. It will only

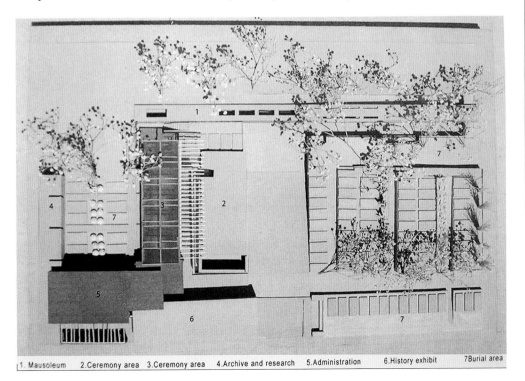

1. Mausoleum   2.Ceremony area   3.Ceremony area   4.Archive and research   5.Administration   6.History exhibit   7 Burial area

get you in the door. The rest is up to you. Now that you have created a fabulous portfolio, you will want to prepare yourself to present it in an interview. Keep your portfolio ready to go at a moment's notice. You never know when you'll get that one key call inviting you to an interview.

Remember that a firm is not hiring a portfolio. It is hiring a person—someone who thinks on his or her feet, solves complex problems, works well with others, and is a valuable asset to the firm. No matter how the portfolio is packaged, it's still about you and your skills. A firm's reputation is on the line whenever it makes a hiring decision. Your portfolio reassures the firm that you are capable of upholding the reputation of the firm and increasing its profit potential.

Preparing Yourself

A few days before your interview, contact the firm and ask if there are any particular portfolio requirements you must adhere to or any application forms you need to fill out. Ask if the interviewer or interviewers want to see your original work at its full size or if smaller sized reproductions are acceptable. Firms will differ in their requirements.

Some architects and designers will insist on seeing printed work or even the original presentation boards (see Box 13.2); they are more experienced at assessing work in its original form. Others are familiar with the capabilities of technology and can evaluate reproductions; they understand that some detail will be lost when you decrease the size of your work and that the tactile features disappear (see Figure 13.4).

What you bring to the interview also depends on the kind of position you are applying for. If you are looking to work in a firm that not only does built work but also develops fabric designs for furniture upholstery, the interviewer will obviously want to see your original material sample boards. On the other hand, if you are applying for an entry-level position as a CAD operator in a large architecture or planning firm, showing your computer-assisted projects will be more beneficial than handcrafted 3-D models. Target your portfolio to the firm and the position. This is a benefit of selecting a portfolio system that allows you to rearrange, add, and subtract individual components.

> **It seems to** be a trend in our industry [to move toward digital portfolios] but I do hope this is not the case. I know from our work that everyone gets really excited to see beautiful hand sketches and creative boards. I do think that there will always be a place for "traditional" methods integrated with digital technology.
>
> Lia Dileonardo, M.Arch, AIA Assoc.
> Principal
> DiLeonardo International, Inc.
> Warwick, RI

Box 13.2

Ask if there will be more than one interviewer. Ensure your portfolio examples are large enough to be seen by all. You can ask if the group would prefer to review your work via a laptop and liquid crystal display (LCD) projector. Bring extra copies of your resume and any other leave-behind items. Remember to make eye contact with everyone around the table while answering their questions.

Show and Tell

At the interview, let the practitioner lead the discussion. The interviewer will notice you have a portfolio case with you when you are first greeted. When the time is right, you will be asked to share your portfolio. Its presentation will naturally fit into the conversation. It is possible that you won't even have time to review your portfolio. Or, the interviewer could be so impressed with you that he doesn't even bother reviewing your work! This is a rare occurrence but it does happen. In this case, the portfolio is used after the interview is done and the position has all ready been secured (Hall 2001).

As the portfolio is a designer's essential communication tool, you will most likely present it. Unless the firm has an available conference room, you may be interviewing in the designer's office (see Figure 13.5). You may need to present your portfolio on top of a desk that is overflowing with stacks of paperwork and rolls of drawings and plots. It can be awkward trying to balance your boards or zippered case in this environment. Practice beforehand with friends. Also, as the practitioner is the one who should be looking at your work, it is likely you will be looking at it upside-down. Know how to present this way.

A past study of design practitioners showed they were

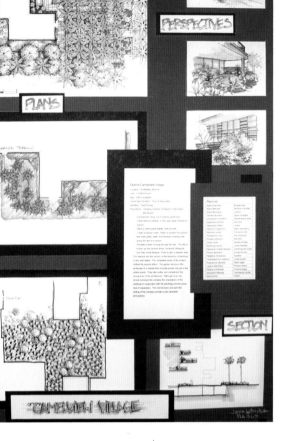

willing to spend approximately 30 minutes reviewing a portfolio (Matthews and Gritzmacher 1984). Although there is no exact amount of time any practitioner will spend reviewing your work, the amount of time in today's offices can be considerably shorter. Designers and architects are busy people. You may only have 10 minutes to present your designs. On the other hand, you may have an hour. Obviously, your work is an indication of your potential success in the firm, so the interviewer will spend as much time as he or she deems necessary.

Like a formal classroom presentation, your portfolio presentation will clearly involve speaking and interpersonal communication skills (see Figure 13.6). You cannot simply flop your portfolio in front of the practitioner and expect him to silently flip through your work. Just as you must persuade a client to buy into a design proposal, you will have to persuade the interviewer to buy into *you*. Practice presenting your portfolio to a friend or classmate. Time yourself. See what questions are raised when you present. Anticipate these same types of questions during your interview and be prepared to have solid professional answers.

With this in mind, be prepared to discuss each piece. After all, this is your portfolio and you are the only one who is intimate with the background of each piece. Most of your presentation will involve flipping through pages in your portfolio book or displaying presentation boards for the interviewer to see. Even though there is some text on Figure 13.7, some explanation is still necessary.

Some practitioners want to get their own hands on your work and go through it at their own pace and at their discretion. Therefore, you may be turning the pages or the interviewer may be turning the pages. If the interviewer wants to turn the pages, by all means, let him control the presentation.

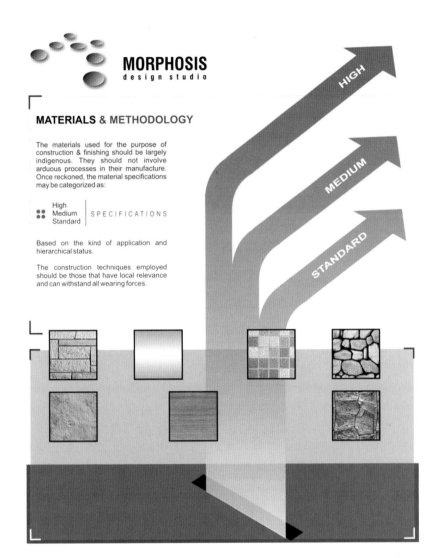

MORPHOSIS
design studio

MATERIALS & METHODOLOGY

The materials used for the purpose of construction & finishing should be largely indigenous. They should not involve arduous processes in their manufacture. Once reckoned, the material specifications may be categorized as:

High
Medium
Standard

SPECIFICATIONS

Based on the kind of application and hierarchical status.

The construction techniques employed should be those that have local relevance and can withstand all wearing forces.

HIGH

MEDIUM

STANDARD

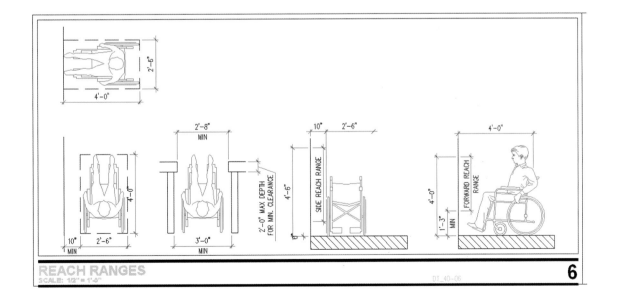

REACH RANGES
SCALE: 1/2" = 1'-0"

6

D1_40-06

Listen for clues from the interviewer as to what he or she wants to know, such as the mechanics of the piece or how you came up with the original idea. The interviewer will recognize a space plan when he sees one so there is no need to say, "This is a space plan." Instead, call out something distinctive, such as the universal design, locations of building systems, or some specific client need that your design met (see Figure 13.8).

Be prepared to explain any and all work in your portfolio (see Figure 13.9). You will likely be asked why you created a design in a certain way. Your skill at articulating your answer will influence the way you are viewed as a designer. Unless you are prepared to discuss a project in depth, do not include it in your portfolio. You never know which project will catch the eye of your interviewer, who then may want to discuss the reasoning behind the solution. If you're not comfortable discussing it, leave it out.

To prepare yourself to present your portfolio in an interview, look at each project and ask yourself these questions:

1. What was my idea?
2. How does this project represent my competence in a design skill?
3. What did this project mean to me?
4. What did I learn as a result of doing this project?
5. Was this the result of a two-day charette? Or a three-month project?
6. How did this project change the way I designed afterward?
7. Why was it important to include *this* project?

If the timed practice of presenting your portfolio took longer than 20 minutes, you are spending too much time commenting on each piece. The solution is *not*

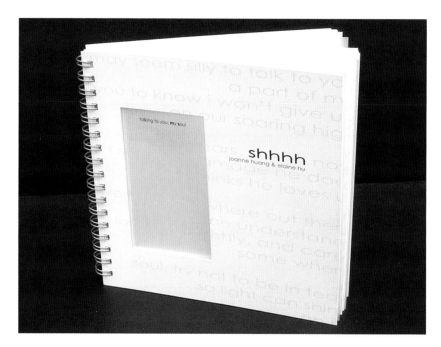

13.9
A concept booklet like this can illustrate the background research and initial design phases of a completed project. Bring it with you and present it if and when requested. Design work courtesy of Elaine Hu and Joanne Huang.

Box 13.3

to talk faster. Rather, shorten your comments or remove some items from your portfolio. It is more likely that the interviewer will cut you off before you have completely gone through your entire portfolio. If he wants you to elaborate on any particular piece, he will ask you to do so (see Box 13.3). (Even more reason to make that first piece absolutely smashing.)

If you have brought along your design journal or sketchbook, refer to it during your interview. Don't start the portfolio presentation with this piece. Remember, it is a supplement to your more important, polished work (see Figure 13.10). It is

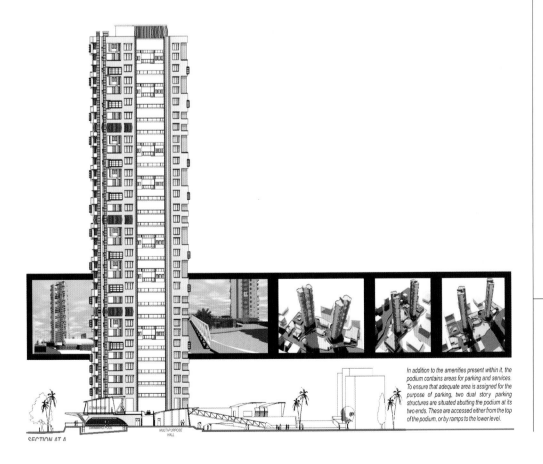

In addition to the amenities present within it, the podium contains areas for parking and services. To ensure that adequate area is assigned for the purpose of parking, two dual story parking structures are situated abutting the podium at its two ends. These are accessed either from the top of the podium, or by ramps to the lower level.

SECTION AT A

13.10
These drawings were created digitally and can be reproduced over and over again in printed format. Design work courtesy of Zubin Shroff, Academy of Architecture, Mumbai.

not the focus of your abilities, but adds depth to your finished products. From reviewing your portfolio, the interviewer will be seeking indications of your work style and habits. Craftsmanship also counts. A sloppy layout, careless mounting, damaged pages, and feebly reproduced digital images all count against you.

When showing your portfolio, pay attention to the interviewer's body language. Is he or she fidgeting or moving around? It may be time to move on to another project. As first impressions of you hold true for first impressions of your work, the first project you show should be your best. If the interviewer is impressed, he or she will pay attention as you show more of your work.

Don't apologize for your work or tell an interviewer how you would have done something differently. Phrases such as "I didn't do as well as I could have," "This was much better until my teammates insisted on changes and ruined it," or "My professor made me do it this way" convey a negative impression. If you make excuses about your work during an interview, the interviewer will wonder if you would do the same thing during a presentation to a paying customer. If you feel like saying something negative about a piece in your portfolio, either rework it so it is acceptable or completely remove it from your portfolio. Also, dismiss any thoughts of telling the interviewer how much time it took you to do the project, the compromises you had to make along the way, the sleep you did not get while meeting the deadline, and how wrong the jury was when they critiqued your work. This is the dialogue of a student and something a practitioner does not care to hear. Keep your description engaging and professional.

Because it is likely the reviewer is not your age, avoid slang terms and cultural references applicable only to your generation. How can you tell if this is the case? Have a person older than you critique your portfolio. Verbally present it to this person. Is anything offensive or open to misunderstanding? The closer you are to your audience in age, the easier it will be to present appropriate information. In all cases, use design terminology common in industry.

Taking Criticism and Subsequent Steps

If the practitioner is critical of any piece in your portfolio, keep smiling (see Box 13.4). Write down the suggestions for improvement. Although you may want to do otherwise, politely thank the interviewer for his or her comments. You may not agree with these comments. You might even throw the comments in the trash as you walk out of the building. But write them down anyway.

Some interviewers may ask you to leave your portfolio behind. If possible, comply with the request. You can easily accommodate the request without difficulty if the portfolio you have with you is a reproduction like the one in Figure 13.11 and you have all the original electronic files. If asked to show more work, get excited. This means that you are being seriously considered for the position. Also, the final hiring decision may be in someone else's hands, and your work needs to stay behind so it can be presented to others. In both scenarios, leaving

The employers want to know if the applicant is "coachable." Have a project that shows development of ideas and processes from initial, raw inspiration through refinement in the portfolio. This can be the basis of a discussion in the interview about how the student responds to critique and might be a unique event of the interview that helps the student stand out as the candidate of choice.

Kenneth R. Brooks, ASLA, APA, RLA
Associate Dean of Academic Affairs
Professor of Landscape Architecture
College of Design
Arizona State University
Tempe, AZ

Box 13.4

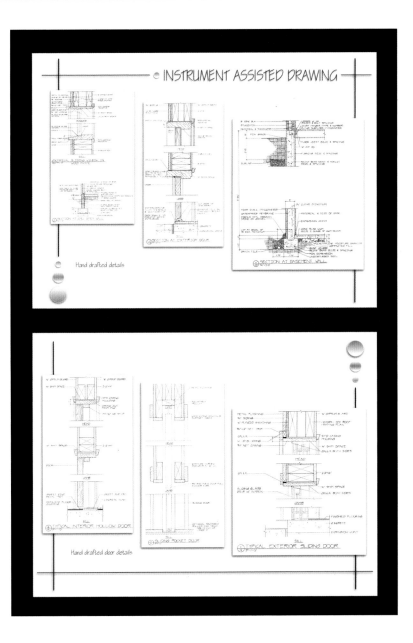

13.11
These two pages of drafted work can be left behind after the interview as a reminder of your abilities as a designer. Design work courtesy of Katie L. Fulton.

your work behind may be essential to obtain the job. Ask when you can come pick it up and definitely remember to go get it.

Finally, your portfolio is only a small indicator of your potential as a designer. It cannot demonstrate all there is about you as a person. The best portfolio does not guarantee getting the job.

Your attitude when presenting your portfolio will positively or negatively influence the interviewer. The principal of a firm had just interviewed someone with the most amazing portfolio. She was very impressed and in awe of the creativity and technical capabilities of the individual. Unfortunately, the woman with the smashing portfolio had a bad attitude. She knew she had a great portfolio. She went into the interview with the attitude of, "What can this firm do for me and my career?" She had an arrogant attitude and subsequently was not hired. Your attitude should be one of, "What can I bring to this firm?" rather than, "What's in it for me?" Yes, you should be confident and self-assured of who you are as a designer when presenting your amazing portfolio. But there is a difference between confidence and arrogance. Therefore, keep in mind that your attitude is a significant factor in the hiring decision.

CONCLUSION

Once you have finished your portfolio, you can see how important it is to take a deep breath, step back, and critically review your own work. Ask others to review it too, like friends, professors, and any practitioners with whom you may have a personal relationship. Practice presenting it to others. What makes sense? What does not? Improve your portfolio to address any appropriate criticism. This will only make your portfolio better. In the next chapter, we will discuss the entire job search and interview process. You may wish to create several additional promotional items, such as a marketing sampler, resume, cover letter, and leave-behind piece.

14

The Interview Process

This chapter explores the entire interview process, whether for an internship or a job. We'll start with a quick discussion of finding an entry-level position through design publications, professional organizations, and personal networking. Some guidelines are provided on how to contact the firm that interests you. You'll need several items to start, including a marketing sampler, resume, cover letter, and personal references. The interview itself can be an anxious experience if you're not prepared. We cover a number of guiding principles for interviewing and achieving maximum success. Last but not least is a discussion about the follow-up to your interview that includes a leave-behind sample of your work, thank-you letter, and information on securing the position. These items are all part of your personal promotion package.

PERSONAL PROMOTION PACKAGE

The portfolio is only one piece of the whole promotional package. You will be admitted into a design program because of your portfolio *and* other elements such as your grade point average and design philosophy. You will be invited for an interview because of your research on the firm, resume, cover letter, references, marketing teaser, contact phone calls, and your personality. It is one whole package (see Box 14.1).

Think of this as personal branding. You may be familiar with the term *branding*, the process a company uses to convey a favorable image for a product that differentiates it from its competition. For example, if you hear the slogan "Just do it," what athletic company do you think of? (Answer: Nike.) If I asked you to visualize the Nike swoosh, what graphic image comes to mind? The same principle applies to your promotional material. You are creating a personal identity. If you have created a personal logo like the one in Figure 14.1, put that icon on *everything* you distribute. Your personal branding could include the fonts you

It may be more time consuming to create both traditional and digital portfolios, but as you create your business package (cover letter, resume, teaser images, and more) both should be part of it. The more tools you have for getting a job will help, as this will help you tailor an interview specifically for firms that are looking for different things. If the firm is into lots of computer renderings and animations, do a PowerPoint off a digital portfolio; if they are into thought process and your design development, show rougher brainstorming sketches in a traditional format. As a student and new professional, stay as flexible as you can because you won't know where and when that best opportunity to find your fit in this profession will come.

Paul Hibbard
Project Designer
Mancini Duffy
New York, NY

Box 14.1

select, a few graphic elements, or the color and texture of the paper you use for all your correspondence. Do whatever you can to distinguish your work from that of other designers.

At some point while searching for a position, you'll need to develop a personal promotion package. This can include any or all of the material listed in Table 14.1. All the material should be linked together through the same color paper, same fonts, and design elements on all items. You may wish to design a small

14.1
A personal logo can create a brand or personal identify for all of your job-search materials.
Logo courtesy of Ellie Combs.

THE COMPLETE INTERVIEW PACKAGE

1	Acceptance letter and envelope
2	Business card
3	Compact disc portfolio
4	Compact disc case
5	Compact disc label
6	Compact disc mailing package
7	Contact email
8	Contact log
9	Cover letter
10	Email with web site link
11	Design philosophy
12	Interview mailing envelope
13	Leave-behind piece
14	Material sample board
15	Personal logo
16	Portfolio case
17	Printed portfolio
18	Promotional postcard
19	References
20	Refusal letter and envelope
21	Resume
22	Sampler
23	Sketchbook
24	Thank-you letter and envelope
25	Web-based portfolio

Table 14.1

special logo that can be put on each piece of correspondence or insert a few decorative elements across the top or along one of the sides. For example, I wouldn't use double lines under my name on my business card but then put three interlocking circles at the bottom of my resume. Why not keep the double line design concept going? It should be one comprehensive package.

FINDING THE RIGHT FIRM

The job search requires persistence and determination. Where you intern or work will depend on your particular area of interest and who you are as a designer. Recall your responses to the questions in Chapter 3. Who you are as a person and a designer will play the most important part in being happy and successful in your career. The opportunities available in your area, the contacts you have made in your profession, and the ties that your school and its alumni have established with firms over the years will also contribute to your victory in locating the right firm. Three avenues for finding an internship or job are prominent. These are design publications and web sites, professional organizations, and personal networking.

Design Publications and Web Sites

Many prominent and successful architecture, planning, and design firms are featured in design periodicals, professional journals, and trade magazines. Make note of the firms and designers who appear often in these publications. Make note of those who are practicing in your area of interest (such as hospitality design or public works). Look for work you admire and see if the firms meet your expectations. Think again about who you are and what gets you excited as a designer. Would you enjoy working with these designers? Does your personal design philosophy and style correlate with that of the firm? Contact the firm for corporate brochures or other marketing materials. If the article provides the firm's web site, check it out.

If you're targeting a large firm (one of the top 100), it's a good bet that their work has been published in one of the popular magazines. Smaller and mid-size firms may be less prevalent in these publications and may be more accessible through online searches. Home and business magazines in your local area may have ads for smaller and residential design firms.

Internet job searching is popular because it's fast, inexpensive, and efficient. Many design firms now have web sites that include valuable information. Make sure that you explore the web for available information. However, don't forget the yellow pages of telephone directories, chamber of commerce listings, and local newspaper advertisements, too.

Professional Organizations

Professional organizations like those listed in Table 14.2 are another excellent source of job-searching information. These professional organizations have a tremendous amount of information on their web sites.

Local chapters in large metropolitan areas are likely to subsidize public lectures, sponsor special events, and post local job listings on their chapter web site. There may be a fee for attending meetings but it is well worth it to get exposed to the organization and its membership. Another avenue to check out is the latest industry awards. Who's won the latest ASLA or ASID competition? What about IIDA and AIA? Are these practitioners and firms that interest you? These award

PROFESSIONAL DESIGN ORGANIZATIONS

AIA	American Institute of Architects	www.aia.org
ASID	American Society of Interior Designers	www.asid.org
ASLA	American Society of Landscape Architects	www.asla.org
IIDA	International Interior Design Association	www.iida.org

Table 14.2

announcements are sometimes linked to the professional organization web site or national organization publication.

Personal Networking

The best way to find the great internships and jobs is by personally networking with practicing designers. Networking is a huge part of our design industry. When a design firm has an opening, its own employees may know someone who is qualified for the job. The firm may forego the time and cost of publicly advertising for the position and collect a pool of applicants through word-of-mouth promotion instead. This makes networking a key component of our professions. Networking with and through others can introduce many opportunities to you.

Networking can be easy or intimidating. Networking comes naturally for some individuals, while others have to work a bit harder. Two tips: (1) remember the person's name by repeating it in the conversation and (2) write down on the back of a business card where you met and the date. When you meet the person again, it'll be easier to recall the name by recalling the context in which you met previously. Networking does take time and energy. But the effort is well worth it when it comes time for you to job hunt.

Making Contacts

There are several ways to make contacts with practitioners in your industry. Conferences, organization meetings, and work-related social events are places where you'll make solid contacts. It's easiest to develop industry contacts during these informal gatherings and get-togethers. This takes much less effort than making an appointment with a complete stranger (see the low-risk interview later in this chapter). If you are currently working in the field, you will undoubtedly run into past interviewers at these events. Definitely reintroduce yourself! Let them know in which firm you are presently employed and the types of projects on which you are working. This is another opportunity to build your professional network. Seldom in today's workforce does an individual stay with the same firm for an extended period of time. The latest statistics show that younger workers stay with an employer for a period three times shorter than older workers (United

States Department of Labor Statistics, 2004). At some point, you *will* be out there again, pounding the pavement for a new position.

From the publications you read, seek out conferences, shows, and other formal meetings. Consider attending one or more of these that are most applicable to your area. Make contacts with the architects and designers there. These may be practitioners who are local to your area. Or maybe the conference is in another state, a state to which you would like to relocate in the coming months. An added bonus to attending these meetings is that you'll be exposed to the latest topics, trends, and techniques in your field. Take advantage of these opportunities. You cannot build a network by sitting at home. You must get involved.

If you are new to your field and attending school, start networking right where you are. Approach one of the upper-division studios to talk to the upperclassmen. One of these graduates may be your future boss. Get to know the students in your program. Get involved in the student chapter of your professional organization. If your school has a senior-to-freshman mentoring program, sign up and participate. Establishing a friendly relationship with other students today will result in contacts when you graduate. Stay in touch with graduating seniors. Again, they are your future colleagues and supervisors.

Other networking contacts include any practitioner who served as a critic or guest lecturer in your classes. If you did not get their business card or contact information, ask your instructor for the information. Seldom is this request denied, as part of an educator's responsibility is to make contacts with industry and to pass those contacts on to others.

If you have access, go through your school's alumni listing. Get in touch with alumni to see how they are enjoying the profession and if they have any advice for you as a student. Ask them if they know of any openings in their firm or other firms. Alumni are usually quite willing to help because they were once in your shoes. They can remember what it was like to search for that first design position.

How to Network

There are several avenues for networking. Attend workshops and public lectures offered at your school or in your area. They don't even have to be sponsored by your discipline. You may be an architect but hear of a public lecture by an interior designer, landscape architect, or engineer. Regardless of who the speaker is, attending it will help broaden your views on a particular topic. Hot trends in one of our fields are usually hot trends in all the others. Remember, the built environment is interconnected. What has an impact on the building itself will have an impact on the interior and exterior as well. Attending these talks will also raise your awareness of who the key players are in your field and in your region of the world. If the topic is so interesting to you that you would enjoy working in that field, follow up with the practitioner in a personal letter. State how expressive and inspiring his or her talk was and how you would like to receive any advice he or she can give. The practitioner may be too busy to answer your letter personally, but it's worth a shot. Who knows? He or she may be so impressed with your resourcefulness that when a job opening occurs and you apply, you may get an interview.

Be more than a casual member in the student chapter of your professional organization. It is better to be actively involved. If you hold a leadership position or are involved in some philanthropic activities organized by this group, this indicates you take an interest above and beyond your schoolwork. This allows you to network with members of a professional organization and is a great way to build up your portfolio. These organizations typically invite student participation in fundraising activities, community service projects, and other volunteer activities. For example, your local chapter may be involved in the design of a new Ronald McDonald or Habitat for Humanity house and site. These experiences can add quality work samples to your portfolio. By including these samples, you again demonstrate to a potential employer that you are an individual who is involved beyond the basics.

An internship experience often leads to employment, either with the firm in which you interned or through contacts made during the internship. When your internship ends and you discontinue your working relationship with the firm, keep in contact with its designers. Let them know how you are doing and when you will be graduating. Although you may not wish to work at this firm upon graduation or they may not have an opening at that time, they can help you expand your network by referring you to other designers, firms, and openings. Work your network!

When you begin looking for a new position, it helps to let other people know of your quest. Let all your existing contacts know when your portfolio is ready and that you are seeking employment. By the time you are looking for your first entry-level job, you should have a mailing list of practitioners. If you've been jotting down names and firms of practitioners who have been involved in your professional organization, critics in your studio classes, guest speakers in your lecture classes, supervisors and colleagues from internships and part-time jobs, and any other practitioner you've ever met, you should have quite a list of contacts.

RESEARCHING THE WORKPLACE

You need to give the same care and attention to determining where you want to work as you do to your friends and significant other. This means researching your future workplace. Research does not mean burying yourself in the library stacks, looking up data and esoteric articles. In its simplest form, doing research means you are gathering information. This can be through web sites, professional affiliations, networking, phone contacts, and personal visits.

Conducting research will help you discover a wealth of information about any firm's design philosophy, former clientele, preferred aesthetics, and corporate way of life (also known as corporate culture). Knowing this information will help you finesse your cover letter and portfolio, while also helping you speak

When researching any workplace, find answers to these questions:

- Who are the decision makers in the firm?
- Who are the principals and CEOs of the firm?
- What does the work of the firm look like?
- What do other practitioners say about this firm? Are they held in high esteem? Or are all their employees jumping ship?
- Do you admire the work of the firm?
- Would you be proud to work for this firm?
- Is there an opportunity for advancement in this firm?
- Is the salary level commensurate with that of other firms in this field?

14.2
Do your research before contacting a firm. These questions may help you get started in your research process.

with confidence in your interview. Although the firm is interviewing you, you are also interviewing it to see if it can offer you the type of experience you wish to have. The more you know about the firm, the more comfortable you will feel in the interview.

Gather information about the company by contacting an accessible company employee such as the receptionist. Even though he or she is not doing the hiring or appointing, this person may be able to provide information about the firm and its employees. Many firms have corporate brochures or marketing packets. Request these products. Smaller firms may have little marketing material, while more mature firms with established clientele have no need to market themselves at all. You should find out things like project goals, fiscal outlook, number of employees, type of organizational structure, number and location of branch offices (if applicable), published projects, and recent design awards and honors. More questions to ask can be found in Figure 14.2.

You need to learn more about the firm and the type of candidates it seeks. Gathering preliminary research about the firm shows the interviewer that you are knowledgeable about the firm and that you are resourceful. If you know nothing or very little about the firm, why would it want to hire you? Brush up on your design terminology and jargon. Read through the latest architecture, interior design, landscape architecture, and other design magazines and journals. What are the hot topics right now? Which designers and firms are the movers and shakers? Being aware of trends and current issues can be an asset in an interview setting.

There's nothing worse than trying to persuade an employer that you are the right person to hire, only to have the company perceive that you know nothing about their operation and that they are one more name on your mailing list. It's worth the time and effort to research each firm before applying for an open position.

TRACKING THE SEARCH

When your list of job prospects grows, managing and scheduling your interviews becomes more intricate. You must be organized. One simple way to track your search progress is with an Excel spreadsheet or table in word processing software. Update this form each time you contact each firm. Contact information could include the items in Figure 14.3.

14.3
Track your job search
with a spreadsheet
that organizes this
type of information for
each firm.

Name of firm _____

Kind of firm and types of projects they do _____

_____

Office address _____

Phone number (with extension) _____

Fax number _____

Email address _____

Web site address _____

Name of contact person and job title (i.e., senior interior designer, human resource
director, etc.) _____

Name of secondary contact (i.e., design assistant, receptionist, administrative
assistant, etc.) _____

Date you mailed your resume and cover letter _____

Names of the files you used for correspondence _____

How you heard of firm (i.e., publication, personal contact, etc.) _____

Interview date or "not accepting interns" _____

Notes section for first impressions, other details, etc. _____

_____

_____

_____

CONTACTING DESIGN FIRMS

The initial contact you make with a practitioner or firm will set the tone for any future relations with that person or company. There are several ways in which to make the initial contact: through a phone call, an email, or a personal site visit. You will continue communicating during the hiring process via phone and email. These forms of indirect contact require the same level of professionalism as personal face-to-face contact. Just because the practitioner cannot see you does not mean he or she is not forming an initial impression of you (good or bad). Increase your chances of making a good impression by following some of the guidelines suggested in this section.

Phone Contact

Most practitioners are extremely busy. They are juggling project deadlines and other professional commitments. Don't be discouraged if you leave a message and they do not immediately call you back. Have some patience. Politely yet persistently call them for an appointment. Remember, every phone call is yet another opportunity to make a first-rate impression.

When you do get the practitioner on the phone, be brief and to the point. Say something like, "Good morning, this is (your name) from (your school or current firm). I mailed my resume to you last week. Have you had an opportunity to review it? I'm very excited about the possibility of working for your firm. When will you be setting up interviews for this position?"

If you are transferred to the practitioners' voice mail, keep your message brief. Give your name first, and then your phone number. Say your number clearly and slowly. After your contact information, briefly explain the reason for your call. You can ask the person to call you back, saying something like, "This is (your name) and I am calling regarding an interview with your firm. I can be reached at (your number). Thank you". There is no guarantee the person will call you back. As a general rule, the person who has the most to gain should initiate the call. That would be *you*.

Some of the practitioners you contact when using your previously established network to locate open positions may have no current openings in their firm. When this happens, thank the practitioner for his time and ask if he knows of any other firms that may be hiring. When you're new to the field, this is an important source of inside information. Nine times out of ten, the practitioner will try to help you by referring you to a friend or colleague. This is how you turn an initial contact that doesn't have an opening into an appointment with a firm that does. This approach allows you to contact the next person by saying, "So-and-so suggested I contact you," and may be more likely to result in an appointment.

Because you may be receiving incoming calls from practitioners, your home answering machine and cell phone voice mail messages should sound professional.

Lastly, smile when talking on the phone. I know this sounds crazy but it really makes a difference. You can actually be "heard" smiling. I knew an administrative assistant who kept a small mirror by her phone. One day, I asked her about it. She replied that it was a visual reminder to smile when answering the phone. Face it— you cannot sound grumpy and distressed when you smile. Your voice should exude confidence and enthusiasm.

Email Contact

Your email address should be as professional as you are. It's sometimes fun to have a cute or sassy email address while you're in school, but these are not acceptable when corresponding with practitioners. With a funny email address, who will take you seriously? Use a school email address if one is available. If necessary, get a second email address from a service provider for professional use only.

Be cautious of what you write in any email. Reread the message before sending it because it is now a permanent record of your correspondence and writing skills. Check your spelling and grammar. Do not rely solely on the spell checker in your software, because it will not catch all grammatical and usage errors.

Check your email frequently. Keep your mailbox under the quota set by your service provider. It is very frustrating to be trying to contact someone only to have the email bounce back because his or her inbox is full. You do not want this to happen when a firm contacts you to come in to interview.

It is tempting to send both your resume and your digital portfolio to a practitioner via email. Unfortunately, there is no guarantee an email system will process the attached files. Files can be quarantined as having a virus, rejected because the size exceeds the maximum message size, or discarded because the recipient's mailbox is full. Emails can also appear as spam. Unless you have told the practitioner to expect your digital portfolio, you risk your email being deleted without a second thought. If you decide to email anything to a practitioner, some words of warning: send only a few pictures at a time, keep file sizes small, and send easy-to-open files like those in PDF format.

The Low-Risk Interview

In the months or even years *before* you need employment, use a networking tool known as the low-risk interview. Contact a designer and ask to meet with him at his office to talk about his work. Call at least a week in advance to make an appointment at a time that his schedule allows. By meeting at his office, you are spending the time traveling, not the practitioner. Going to his office gives you the added bonus of observing the day-to-day activities in the work environment. How can you know whether you'd even like to work at this firm without speaking to someone or seeing how they work?

These discussions are low risk and unthreatening because neither you nor the practitioner has anything to lose. You are not there to interview for a job. The practitioner has made you no promises of hiring. The key to fruitfully scheduling a short meeting is to let the designer know that you are only gathering information and *not* seeking a job. Another helpful tip is to commit to a very short and odd time period, like 9 or 13 minutes. This will certainly get someone's attention because everyone says, "I'd like to talk with you for 10 minutes." Be unusual and get someone's attention. Then stick to your commitment. After being introduced to the designer, ask only two or three key questions about his role in the firm, what his career path was, what he likes best about the firm, what excites him about being a designer, and so on. When your time is up, politely tell him that you only asked for X minutes and make reference to leaving. More than likely, the practitioner will tell you that he can speak with you longer. After all, how flattering for him to have an enraptured audience of one hanging on his every word.

SELF-PROMOTIONAL ITEMS

Self-promotional items you may need to assist in your job search include a business card, a marketing postcard, and a marketing sampler. Whatever you design and distribute to increase your visibility should be part of a deliberate, well-conceived promotional plan, not a series of random mailings and contacts. Make

14.4
This one-of-a-kind business card was created with a laser cutter.
Business card courtesy of Mark Chichester.

sure you include your email and contact number on all correspondence. Every time a practitioner sees something from you, it should look like it came from the same package.

The Business Card

A business card is one way of helping a potential employer remember you long after your initial meeting. Most students think, "I'm only a student so why would I have a business card?" It's yet another opportunity to have your name in front of a potential employer.

Cards work best printed on heavy cardstock. Buy the best you can afford. Decide on either vertical or horizontal layout. The typical size of a business card is 2" × 3½". Anything more than this will not fit inside a wallet, revolving card file, or business card storage case.

One of my former students used a digital laser cutter in a most unique manner (see Figure 14.4). Most students use it to cut scale models and prototypes out of various solid building materials. He used it to cut tiny holes in his business card. Use whatever resources are available to you (and are considered affordable) to stand out from the crowd.

If you choose to create a double-sided card, design the back with a logo, an image of your work, or a highlight of some of your design specialties. Are you experienced at model building or computer animation? Maybe your design work leans toward sustainable and green design, or you have an international flair. You can use the back of the card to list and display this information.

Marketing Postcards

As mentioned earlier, a good way to keep in touch with practitioners you have met over the years is by occasionally mailing them a postcard, to inform them about what you're doing or to thank them again for the time they gave you in the past.

A postcard is preferable over a letter in an envelope because the designer will have to open the envelope. If it's not correspondence he or she is anticipating, it might get thrown in the "I'll get around to it later" pile or worse, in the circular file, which is a polite way of saying trashcan. Design your own postcard at a reasonable price. Try your local office supply store or copy center to create postcards in small quantities. Search online for companies that can create larger quantities.

Just as a newly planted flower needs water to survive, a newly established network must be maintained. Use occasions such as winning a design competition or graduation as a reason to send a postcard to designers you know. When it's time to start interviewing for an entry-level position, you will have contacts that truly remember you because you took the time to remember them.

The Marketing Sampler

Some practitioners feel you can increase your chances of getting an interview if you include with your resume a small and concise sample of your work, like the one in Figure 14.5. This is known as a marketing sampler. Think of the marketing sampler as a portfolio preview. It's also known as a mini-portfolio, a teaser, or a mailer (see Box 14.2).

Quantity is not important, but quality is. After all, this is a *small* sample of your work, not everything you have ever done crammed into a small handout. Make sure that the quality of your drawings represents your best skills and ideas. Use text, images, and graphics similar to those found in your portfolio. That way, when the practitioner sees your portfolio during an interview, it will look familiar. Select projects that have solutions to design problems that are directly relevant to the type of work handled by your potential host firm.

Send a contract design solution to a firm that specializes in contract design; send residential work to a residential firm, and so on. These can be "expensive, time-consuming, and should be used only for targeted firms or known job openings" (Mitton 2004, 210). Keep in mind the cost of mailing this sampler. Unless sent digitally, such efforts can be expensive and time-consuming.

Samples can be odd shapes, sizes, and formats, such as those shown in Figure 14.6. A crisp, color 8.5" × 11" laser print will work fine and should be relatively inexpensive. It is best to reduce the work to a format that can be mailed with your resume and cover letter. Another point about this sampler is to make sure that all reductions are legible. Remember that your potential supervisor may not have your eagle eyes.

You have the option to email the sampler as an attachment. Keep it in a ready-to-read format, such as JPG or PDF. Designers who spend their valuable (and billable) time trying to access your digital sampler and cannot, will be frustrated before they even look at any of your designs. Make your sampler easy to review.

14.5
An 8½" × 11" format folded in half makes an effective marketing sampler.
Sampler courtesy of Jeffrey Lothner.

If a student sent me a one-page printed "teaser," would it influence my decision to grant an interview (assuming it's a good teaser)? I would encourage any student to grasp an opportunity to differentiate him or herself. The typical design process employs graphic communications to aid in conveying ideas. Including a strong representation of one's graphic abilities can certainly influence a candidate's chance of rising to the top of the resume pile.

Janice Carleen Linster, ASID, CID
Principal
Studio Hive, Inc.
Minneapolis, MN

Box 14.2

14.6
A small project book can be used as a marketing sample (before the interview) or a leave-behind piece (after the interview).

Overall, send high-quality work that demonstrates good skills, effective concept development, and attention to detail. A visually appealing sampler will increase your chances of being called for an interview.

The Leave-Behind Piece

Similar to the marketing sampler, create a leave-behind piece. This is a sample of your work that you "leave behind" with the interviewer as a visual reminder of your visit. Also known as a sample sheet, this promotional piece should include your *best* work. Maybe it includes the first or last project you had in your portfolio, or both. This is not the place to feature a new piece of information. You want the interviewer to see your leave-behind sheet and recall that he or she has recently seen that project in your portfolio. It serves to trigger their memory at the end of a long week after they have interviewed several other applicants.

The leave-behind piece should be atypical and represent your exceptional skill and ability. *It should not be the same as your marketing sampler.* If you used one, the interviewer already has this in his or her possession. Include the same contact information on this piece as you have on your resume, because it could become separated from your resume during the interview process.

The leave-behind piece can be unusual in size and shape. It can be a 5" × 7" photograph, a letter-sized photocopy of your work, an ingenious postcard, or a

14.7
A leave-behind book of images will help interviewers remember you. Design work courtesy of Katie L. Fulton and Jennifer Gozzi.

promotional brochure. It can even be printed to a smaller size on stiff cardstock, like the concept book in Figure 14.7.

Similar to the marketing sampler, this works best as an 8½" × 11" color print. This keeps it the same size as your resume and is easy to file. This piece can include some written statements about your design interests, such as sustainability, furniture design, and so on. Make sure whatever you include in writing reflects what you said in your interview. If you never mentioned your interest in furniture design and your entire leave-behind sheet is all about furniture design, the practitioner is going to wonder who he just interviewed and whether this piece was created by the same person.

If you present your digital portfolio on your own laptop during the interview, you could be asked to leave a copy of your entire digital portfolio. When I give a presentation, at least one person in the audience always wants a copy of the file. I now carry a few extra CDs of the presentation to distribute afterward. CDs are inexpensive. Make multiple copies and bring extras with you.

The only negative to this additional promotional piece is the time you'll spend creating it. Yet it is a beneficial form of personal advertising. It is best to leave it with the interviewer rather than mailing it with the thank-you letter. If the interviewer is impressed with you, he or she will want to discuss your potential with colleagues in the firm. This could lead to a second interview or even a job offer.

THE RESUME

The resume is an extremely important aspect of your application for a design position. Written communications have to be well done, to the point, and written in a way that merges straight facts with a promotional approach. Your resume must establish your credibility, yet be exceptional and stimulating. Not only do you have to introduce yourself to prospective employers, you have to arrest the reader's attention, arouse interest, and persuade the reader that you are the person who should ultimately get the job.

Resume Content

As seen in Figure 14.8, you can include numerous items in your resume. Required items include contact information, education, and work experience. Optional information includes an objective, honors and awards (such as design competitions and school scholarships), special skills (such as cultural, lingual, or technology skills), community service and volunteer efforts, and memberships in honor societies and professional organizations.

What you decide to include depends on what you have to offer. For example, you may be a double major in school who hasn't had much time to gain work experience during the school year. The section on education in your resume may be more prominent than that in the resume of someone who is highly involved in extracurricular activities for a professional organization or community service group.

To have an objective or not, that is the question. There is debate among practitioners about whether a career objective should be included at the top of the resume. Some practitioners like you to set the tone for what is to follow; others

14.8
A resume has standard and optional categories. Depending on your level of work experience, you may have more optional information in the first few years in your profession.

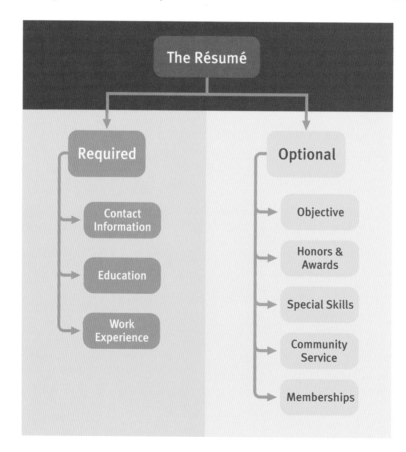

think the space could be better used to provide information on your skills and abilities. An objective statement is intended to help you emphasize your key qualifications for the position, as well as inform the reader of your career goals. It should be one sentence. If you include an objective, tell the employers what you can do and what you are looking for in a job. Avoid generalities by tailoring it to the firm that will get this copy of your resume. A generic objective such as, "To obtain a position in an architecture firm" is not as effective as "To obtain a summer internship allowing me to use my skills in landscape architecture and construction in a large, urban design firm."

In the education section, list your highest degree earned, school, and graduation date. If you are currently in school, put "Expected May 200X" for the graduation date. Don't mention high school or community college certificates and degrees if you have been awarded your bachelor's degree. Include any special educational experience, such as an overseas study program, a minor, or any emphasis area.

Include your grade point average if it is an A– or higher. By the time you head out for your second employment position, your grade point average can disappear from your resume. You can, however, leave a note about graduating with academic honors, such a high honors, best of class, *summa cum laude*, and the like. Check with your school to determine the guidelines for these accolades, as grade point averages for an A may differ from school to school.

A large section of your resume will present your past and current work experience. Even if your work experience is widely divergent with plenty of part-time and summer jobs, list them because employers consider your exposure to *any* work situation important.

There is some debate about whether you should list only jobs related to your design profession or all jobs you've had in the past few years. Definitely include all job experiences related to your design field. Keep in mind other favorable aspects of employment, such as competitiveness, reliability, loyalty, integrity, honor, and ethics. These positive characteristics can be exhibited in any position, even if you're a stocking clerk.

Your work experience includes your internship. Many students think this may not count as work experience if the internship was unpaid or brief. It certainly is work experience so put it on your resume.

Underneath or next to the title of your position (i.e., cashier or design assistant), put the name of the company and its location (i.e., City, State), as not everyone may be familiar with the locations of these firms. The location also tells the reader that you were employed in different parts of the country or world, and thus exposed to different cultures and ways of life.

Next, include a short list of tasks, job activities, and responsibilities you performed in each position. These can be written in complete sentences, although most people appreciate two to four brief statements in bullet form. Use positive action verbs like those in Figure 14.9 to introduce energy into the descriptions. Keep the tense of your verbs consistent. Work experience you have done in the

14.9
Use some of these
action verbs when
describing your work
activities.

Action Verbs

Collected, Combined, Commissioned, Communicated	Chaired, Challenged, Changed, Collaborated	Built, Calculated, Catalogued, Centralized	Assigned, Assisted, Attained, Authorized	Approved, Arranged, Assembled, Assessed	Altered, Analyzed, Appointed, Appraised	Advanced, Advised, Aligned, Allocated	Accomplished, Achieved, Adapted, Administered
Drafted, Drew, Edited, Eliminated	Discovered, Displayed, Distributed, Documented	Devised, Diagnosed, Diagrammed, Directed	Designated, Designed, Determined, Developed	Customized, Decided, Delegated, Demonstrated	Coordinated, Crafted, Created, Critiqued	Consolidated, Constructed, Consulted, Converted	Compiled, Completed, Composed, Computed
Helped, Highlighted, Identified, Illuminated	Graphed, Guided, Handled, Headed	Functioned, Furnished, Gathered, Generated	Figured, Filed, Formulated, Fulfilled	Extended, Fabricated, Facilitated, Fielded	Examined, Exceeded, Expanded, Explained	Enhanced, Equipped, Established, Evaluated	Enabled, Encouraged, Engaged, Engineered
Mapped, Marketed, Maximized, Measured	Led, Located, Maintained, Managed	Joined, Launched, Learned, Lectured	Introduced, Invented, Inventoried, Investigated	Installed, Instituted, Instructed, Integrated	Initiated, Innovated, Inspected, Inspired	Improvised, Increased, Influenced, Informed	Illustrated, Imagined, Implemented, Improved
Proposed, Provided, Pursued, Quantified	Prioritized, Processed, Produced, Projected	Positioned, Prepared, Presented, Preserved	Perfected, Performed, Photographed, Planned	Organized, Overhauled, Oversaw, Participated	Notified, Obtained, Operated, Ordered	Modified, Monitored, Multiplied, Navigated	Merged, Minimized, Modeled, Modernized
Simplified, Sketched, Solved, Specified	Selected, Separated, Served, Shaped	Reviewed, Revised, Scheduled, Searched	Researched, Reshaped, Responded, Restructured	Reorganized, Repaired, Replaced, Represented	Regulated, Remodeled, Rendered, Renovated	Received, Recognized, Recommended, Recorded	Quoted, Rated, Rearranged, Reassembled
Widened, Witnessed, Worked, Wrote	Verified, Visited, Volunteered, Weighed	Updated, Upgraded, Utilized, Validated	Transformed, Transported, Troubleshot, Undertook	Targeted, Tightened, Trained, Transferred	Supplied, Supported, Surveyed, Synchronized	Succeeded, Suggested, Summarized, Supervised	Started, Strengthened, Structured, Studied

past should use action verbs in the past tense (e.g., coordinated, developed, managed). Work you are currently doing should be described in the present tense (e.g., coordinating, developing, managing). One word to avoid overusing: design!

Why list routine tasks that everyone can do, like answering the phone, attending staff meetings, or making photocopies? You may have done these tasks but surely you had more responsibilities. List more sophisticated work such as developing a filing system, creating computer-based presentations, and attending client meetings. Choose your words carefully. Large firms may scan resumes into an electronic database. That way, they can search for keywords (such as AutoCAD, sketching, or hospitality design) to narrow the interview field. Use the correct lingo and buzzwords in your profession.

Incorporate dates of employment to show a steady employment record. If there is a gap in your employment history, be prepared to explain why. Be honest. Maybe you were taking additional classes. Maybe you took time off for personal reasons. Whatever the reason, you should not be asked by an interviewer to go into detail about why there is a gap, but you should be prepared to offer a short explanation. Likewise, if you were working during school or held simultaneous jobs, make sure this is apparent from the dates.

Do you have any special skills? Did you live overseas for part of your life or can you fluently speak a second language? Any unusual exposure to diverse cultures and ways of life can tell prospective employers that you have a global awareness that others may not possess. Special skills could include a mastery of technology, as indicated by a list of the software you know. This is a helpful section for newer architects and designers. (Recall our discussion in Chapter 3 on Generation Y.) If you can, find out which software applications are used by the firm. This information is sometimes provided under the photos on the firm's web site, in captions that list the software used to produce the image. You can also call the firm directly. If you are familiar with these applications, emphasize them in your resume.

Honors and awards would add selling points to your resume. Did you receive a school scholarship? Were you selected to receive an award from your school or professional organization? Was your work selected for an exhibit or gallery display?

Including community service and volunteer activities is a good idea if you have little work experience. Be careful to not prejudice the reader. For example, if you went on a church mission's trip to Haiti, be sensitive to its relevance to your professional development. If you helped build a church or some homes during that trip, this would relate to design. Maybe you volunteered to take pledge calls for a particular political candidate. The choice is up to you if you want to put items on your resume related to religion, political affiliation, or sexual orientation.

Include a listing of any professional organizations or honor societies of which you are a member. These could include church groups, fraternities or sororities, or national organizations in which you are active. If you were the chairperson of a fundraising event or held a leadership position in the student chapter of your professional organization, definitely make note of this.

One statement that tends to end up at the bottom of many resumes is a mention of work, educational, and personal references. Another is a similar statement about your portfolio. There is no need to include the line "References available upon request" or "Portfolio available upon request" at the bottom of your resume. It is an expectation in our design fields that you will bring these items when you interview.

Check and recheck for spelling errors. Do not rely on your computer's spell-checking feature. The software will not catch simple grammatical errors (such as "here" versus "hear"). Be careful of spelling mistakes in titles. If they are in capital letters, your software's spell checker may skip right over them. If you are not willing to perfect a document as important as your own resume, a prospective employer will wonder how careful you will be in the work you do for the firm. Double-, triple-, quadruple-check your resume for errors!

Ask yourself, "If I received this resume, would I interview me?" If your answer is no, then you need to fine-tune this one-page promotion. After all, this is your sales pitch to get the position. A poorly written resume says, "I have difficulty summarizing my strengths and experiences." If you can't handle this, the firm will wonder if you have the knack to communicate and focus.

Resume Format

The format or look of your resume says a good deal about you. Although what is *in* the resume is more important than how it looks, a well-designed resume will at least get read. How can you get someone to acknowledge the *contents* of the resume if the appearance is sloppy, hard to read, and poorly structured? The overall appearance of your resume says as much about you as the information you place in it.

There is no single prescribed format. If there were, every resume would look the same. The only consistent instruction regarding a resume is to keep it to a *single* page. Your goal is to elaborate on your skills and experience in an interview. In your resume, you want to come across as an individual with unique qualities, to stand out above your competitors. Many credible books have been written on resume format. Seek out these sources in the library, at local bookstores, or at your school's career center.

We in the design fields can bend the rules of resume-writing a bit, infusing our resumes with subtle design elements and style. Since your resume is a creative resume, you have some leeway in the design. It must include all the components of a traditional resume, yet be done in a creative manner. This doesn't mean that you have free rein and can go overboard with fluffy graphics and a poorly developed layout. You cannot use the excuse of a creative resume to cover for an unstructured, sloppy format.

Use only letter-size paper. Many firms photocopy and file resumes in a standard filing system. This is not a wedding invitation. Smaller or odd sizes will either get misplaced or destroyed. Use high-quality paper that is acid-free, 100 percent cotton, and 24-pound weight. The color and texture of paper you choose for your resume may set you apart from others. This is not to say that you should choose such a bright eye-catching color that you cannot read it without your eyes watering. Think about things like, "What will this look like when faxed?" or, "Will this paper copy well and the text still be legible?" Print one resume on the colored paper and make a black-and-white copy to ensure it copies well.

Avoid printing close to the edges of the paper. Leave margins big enough for an interviewer to use in jotting notes while talking to you on the phone or during your interview. Do not use distracting borders that draw attention away from the important skills and activities listed in your resume. Your choice of font is important and should be the same as that used in your cover letter. Resist the urge to use fancy or bizarre typefaces. If it's difficult to read, there's a good chance it won't be. Also, the resume may go online so choose standard fonts for Windows and Macintosh platforms. What's more, consider how these strange typefaces will look after copied two or three times. Put a personal logo that you have designed on here, too. The logo can tie together all your correspondence, such as resume, cover letter, business card, portfolio, and so on. It's not a requirement but an option you can use to make your items stand out from the rest.

Contact information should be listed at the top or along the side of the page. Use a larger or bolder typeface for your name so it stands out from everything else. Besides your full name, include your mailing and email addresses, and home and cell phone numbers. Make it easy to find. If applicable, include both your current home address and permanent home address (if away during the school year). You never know if a rejection this year may result in a phone call in the middle of next year, when you've changed locations.

Traditionally, there are two formats for listing your work experience: chronological and functional. The chronological resume, as shown in Figure 14.10, is the most widely used format. It lists your work experience by date, starting with the most recent job and going backward (i.e., reverse chronological). A problem with the chronological resume is its focus on what you have done, rather than what you can do. If you lack work experience and are just starting out, a chronological resume can look quite bare. In this case, you would be better off using a functional resume until you have enough job experience to bulk up a chronological resume. A functional resume, as shown in Figure 14.11, is more of a listing of your talents and proficiency. Any experience you have can be organized into categories by areas of specialization. However, it is more difficult to write and the reader cannot easily determine your contributions to past employers.

A third format combines both the chronological and functional resumes together (see Figure 14.12). This is a particularly good choice of format when your work experience is in a similar area. Say, for instance, you have held three or four positions as wait staff in various restaurants. The tasks would be similar, so repeating them as separate bullet points under each job would be redundant. Instead, list the positions held in chronological order (with appropriate dates) and then list the composite skills and abilities below that.

Street Address | Phone
City State Zip | Email

Star Designer

Objective

To obtain more experience in hospitality design.

Education

Arizona State University   **Expected Graduation: May 2008**
Interior Design
GPA: 3.6 / 4.0

Study Abroad
Arizona State University: *Design in Context*
Summer Session Italy and Switzerland   **Summer 2006**
Summer Session France and Spain   **Summer 2005**

Work Experience

My Big Fat Greek Restaurant   **July 2006–Present**
Server
- Assisted with customer's food and wine selection.
- Learned how to provide customers with the best restaurant experience.

Imagine That Architecture   **March, 2006**
Assistant
- Arranged displays of furniture and accessories.
- Worked with customers to select furniture and accessories to meet their needs.

Goldie's Sports Café   **May–October, 2005**
Server
- Assisted in a team to provide high quality customer service.
- Performed various tasks i.e. running food, bussing tables, and serving.

Luxury in Living   **January–February, 2006**
(A trade show of famous Italian designs)
Assistant
- Managed and provided information on Italian designs.
- Hosted V.I.P. opening event for the exhibit.

Organizations and Honors

ASU Deans List   **Present**

IIDA Member Student Chapter   **Present**

All State Jazz Choir   **2003–2004**

Street Address
City State Zip

Phone
Email

Star Designer

Objective

To obtain more experience in hospitality design.

Experience

Hospitality

- Two years experience in serving.
- Developed a reputation for excellent customer service by:
  ...assisting with customer's food and wine selection;
  ...creating a personal relationship with the customer.
- Operated in a team with other servers to create the best restaurant experience.
- Performed various tasks i.e. seating customers, serving, expediting food, and bussing tables.

Design

- Skilled at evaluating options in design and generating functional solutions.
- Developed skills in rendering, perspective drawing, and hand drafting.
- Trained and familiar with design software: AutoCAD, Photoshop, Illustrator, InDesign, and FormZ.
- Experienced in design overseas from two study abroad trips to France/Spain and Italy/Switzerland through the Arizona State University Design College.

Organizations

IIDA member

Arizona State University Dean's List

Education

Arizona State University
Interior Design
Expected Graduation: May 2008
GPA: 3.6 / 4.0

14.11
If you have less work experience, consider a functional resume, which focuses on your abilities and skills. Resume courtesy of Shelby Bogaard.

LISA BROOME

Address, Phone Number, and Email Address

OBJECTIVE

I am pursuing a creative position that will allow me to use my passion for research, based in cultural issues and ecological sustainability, to assist in product opportunities and development.

EDUCATION

Master of Science in Design, concentration Industrial Design
Arizona State University, 2006, Fall 2004 - Present 4.0/4.0

Bachelor of Science in Industrial Design
Georgia Institute of Technology, 2004
Certificates of Study: Marketing and Psychology
Graduated with High Honors

ABILITIES

Design
Effectively use research from the field to identify new and relevent product opportunities
Strong product ideation skills
Distill large amounts of data into actionable product insights

Work Ethic
Dependable and self-motivated when accepting new responsibilities
Efficiently learn skills and processes to adapt to changing situations

Communication
A strong capability for expression visually and verbally
Capacity for listening well in order to disseminate information and solve problems

Technical
Proficient in Adobe Photoshop, Illustrator, InDesign, QuarkXpress, Ashlar Cobalt
Proficient in 3D rendering with Alias Wavefront, Form Z
Proficient in MS Word, Excel, PowerPoint
Photography (digital, 35 mm, b&w dark room experience)
Knowledge of materials and processes for constructing 3D models

EXPERIENCE

Arizona State University, Teaching Assistant: Fall 2004 - Present
College of Design, Industrial and Interior Design Departments
Classes Taught: Design Principles (1 semester)
Classes Assisted: Design Awareness (2 semesters), Design Hist. II (1 semester)

Huie Design, Inc., Environmental Graphic Design Intern: Summer 2002 -Spring 2004
130 Krog St. NE Ste. C, Atlanta, Ga 30307
Schematic planning, wayfinding, information hierarchy, business operations
Clients: Arden's Garden, Weaver and Woodbury, TVS Architects

Mason and Sons Woodworking and Construction, Internship: Summer 2001
4880 Macon Hwy. P.O. Box 247, Bishop, Ga
Site planning, hand drafting of residential lots/homes
Clients: Athens Historical Society, home owners

ACTIVITIES &
AWARDS

IDSA, Industrial Designers Society of America
GSCD, Graduate Students in the College of Design
ASU President's Honor Roll, 2004-2006
Education Assistant for the IDSA Western District Conference, Spring 2006
MSD Travel Grant 2005
Accepted to present research at By Design Conference, Toronto, Canada 2005
Technology Assistant for DED Conference, Doctoral Education in Design, Summer 2005
Earl & Ellen Davis Scholarship, 2005-2006
Volunteer Work: Techwood Tutorial Project, Habitat for Humanity, LHAC

References and portfolio provided upon request

14.12
Many resumes are hybrids between chronological and functional resumes. Resume courtesy of Lisa Broome.

Packaging and Mailing Your Resume

How you package and send your resume *does* make a difference. To send a grouping of items, such as your resume, cover letter, references, and sampler, you might consider designing a package to contain them (see Figure 14.13).

Carefully follow mailing regulations and consider this cost when designing the package. Also think about how the recipient will open the package and review the documents inside. Although you may design this package to be returned to you, the recipient has no responsibility to do so. That's why this package should only include quality photocopies of your work.

Steer clear of mass mailings! The average response rate of mass mailing a resume is between one and three percent. Be strategic about who you contact. Don't buy mailing labels from your professional organization to blanket the entire population of firms. Suppliers and businesses buy these labels to solicit their goods. The labels are quickly recognized by practitioners as a mass mailing and are often discarded before even opening the envelope. For that reason, hand or laser print addresses directly onto the envelopes. Another item to consider is your return address. Shun cute labels with flowers, cartoon characters, or other whimsical designs.

Avoid folding or stapling your resume. This can cause problems when the practitioner wishes to photocopy it. Use 10" × 12" envelopes that are color-coordinated with the paper used for your other items. It's not much more expensive to mail your resume this way.

Lastly, increase the chances that your resume will be read by strategically planning *when* you send it. Try to time it so your resume arrives at the firm in the middle of the week. Mondays are hectic, and Fridays are usually when the backlog of mail is quickly (and severely) sorted.

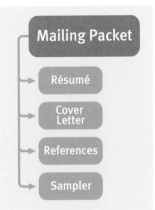

14.13
A creative mailing packet can contain all your introductory interviewing material and make a positive impression, too.

Digital Resume

You may be thinking, "This is so old-fashioned. Why not just email my resume to the firm?" A printed resume that is designed for electronic distribution is known as a digital resume. This form of resume is not yet fully accepted in the workplace. It's becoming a popular format as more and more firms use electronic communication in their daily operations. But it's not quite there yet. Only send your resume via email if requested to do so.

If a practitioner asks you to email your resume, you have a couple of choices. You can cut and paste the resume into the body of your email message, rather than sending it as an attachment. This ensures that the recipient gets the resume, which might otherwise be stripped off by an email server if provided as an attachment. If you insert your resume in the body of your text, the layout will look nothing like your original resume. You cannot use bullets or special symbols because they don't always transfer in emails. The same goes for unusual fonts, fancy formatting, and special logos or graphics.

The second option is to save your resume as a PDF file. Mention the type of file you've attached in the email itself, as well as how to access it. It doesn't hurt to include a link to enable the recipient to download the free Reader software. Send a test email to yourself to ensure it works. In either case, always send the resume with a brief note in the body of the email. This would be similar to what you have in your cover letter. In addition, include your contact information in the email so if the file does not transfer completely or will not open, the receiver can contact you to resend it or send it in another format.

Regardless of what you put in your resume, how you format it, or how you get it into the hands of the intended reviewer, your resume must be factual yet stylish. Your resume must be so impressive that it does not get overlooked. Moreover, your resume will be around long after you and your portfolio have left an interview. It must continue to positively represent your skills and capabilities. Take the time to do it right. You'll be glad you did.

THE COVER LETTER

Whenever you fax, email, send, or deliver your resume in person to a firm in search of an internship or job, you must include a cover letter. The purpose of the cover letter is to introduce you to a prospective employer. The content should complement, not duplicate, the detailed information in your resume. Mention a couple of skills you are really good at without restating your entire resume. This is a waste of the reviewer's time. A cover letter usually consists of three or four paragraphs on one page. By being brief and concise, you exhibit business shrewdness and professionalism.

The cover letter tells why you are the best-qualified candidate for the job. Our design industries are competitive. The jobs are out there but so is the competition. What skills and personality traits can you highlight to make you stand out from the rest? Multidimensional people are appreciated in any job situation. You are more than a designer who is efficient and professional. Your letter must convey your personality and your well-meaning intentions of benefiting the firm and its employees. Your letter should reflect individuality, without appearing familiar, cute, humorous, or overly confident. You are writing to a stranger about a subject that is serious to you both. Be serious yet enthusiastic. Make your letter so appetizing that the reader can't wait to turn the page and get to your resume.

Cover Letter Content

Whenever possible, address your letter to a specific person by name and title. A receptionist at the firm can give you this information. Salutations such as "To whom it may concern" or "To the senior designer" will not be taken seriously. It's like getting mail that is addressed to Occupant. Do you give those letters much attention?

There is a successful format for your letter, as illustrated in the sample letter in Figure 14.14. In the initial paragraph, state the reason for writing. It's important to clearly state which job you are applying for, because large firms often have mul-

Date

Your name
Street address
City, State, Zip
Phone number
Email address

Mr. Smith
Senior Project Manager
XYZ Design Firm
1234 Long Street
City, State, Zip

Dear Mr. Smith,

I am enthusiastically applying for an internship position with XYZ Design Firm. I am familiar with your work in hospitality design (as depicted in the recent issue of *Architectural Digest*) and am impressed with the innovation and originality of your work. I recently met several of your designers at the May IIDA "Canines in Crisis" fundraiser. They impressed on me their enthusiasm and joy at working in your firm. Yours is the type of firm in which I can thrive. I believe I can be a valuable asset to your group.

I feel that it is essential for me to sustain a realistic point of view while pursing a degree in interior design from ABC University. Therefore, I am proud to be financing my entire education through various work experiences. Last summer, I worked as an assistant to architect John Doe in St. Louis. I developed a cataloging system for material samples, met with clients, drafted construction details, and did various office tasks as requested. Because of the knowledge gained in this position, I feel I can make a direct and immediate contribution to XYZ.

The enclosed resume provides more details of my work experience and technology skills. I have also enclosed a sample of my work in computer-aided rendering and three-dimensional model making. These two skills are mentioned on your firm's website and are only two of the many skills I can offer your firm.

I believe I would make an exceptional addition to your winning team. I will be contacting you on May 18 to discuss the possibility of an interview. Thank you for taking time out of your busy schedule. I look forward to speaking with you.

Sincerely,

Joe Designer (with signature above)

Enclosure

14.14
The format of this sample letter has proved to be very successful.

tiple job openings advertised at the same time. Are you applying for an internship? Entry-level designer? Senior project manager? Be very clear in that first paragraph. If you are looking for an internship but the designer reading your letter thinks you are applying for the entry-level position, you won't have the necessary credentials for that position and your resume will end up in the trash.

Tell how you became aware of the firm in the first paragraph. Indicate from which resource you learned of the company's work (news media, professor, employment service, journal, friend, and so on). If you reviewed work done by the firm in person or saw a project featured in a trade magazine, that's a nice thing to add to your cover letter. State how you saw its design of X facility in X city, published in X magazine, and how it's the kind of work that you love, and so forth. Did you network with some of the firm's designers at a recent industry event? Did a friend intern there last year and recommend you for this position? This is where your earlier research will pay off.

It is important to target each firm individually. A letter that is not relevant to that firm shows you did not care enough to research the firm. A form letter speaks volumes. It says, "I'm not really interested in your firm enough to spend time getting to know who you are." You can have generic parts of your letter, which can be cut and pasted. But some sentences must relate specifically to the target firm.

The bulk of your letter should focus on what you can provide the firm, not the other way around. In the second paragraph, focus on your skills and how they relate to the position. What skills do you possess that can aid their operation? How can what you know meet their needs? What can you bring to them that someone else could not? Explain how your academic background or work experience makes you a qualified candidate for the position. Use key words that draw the reader's attention. Focus on *them* and what you can offer, not what you anticipate from the firm or the fact that you need this job.

The third paragraph is often the shortest. Refer the reviewer to the enclosed resume, which summarizes your unique qualifications, training, and experiences. Ask if the reviewer desires additional information or references. Also draw attention to the sample of your work, if included.

In the final paragraph, close your communication by taking the initiative and asking the reviewer for a response. Be bold and request an interview. What's the worst that can happen? (He or she says no. Big deal.) If the firm is located a great distance from you (out of state or overseas), request a telephone interview. Pick a day about 7 to 10 days after the date on your cover letter to contact the recipient. State in the closing sentence something like, "I will be contacting you the week of February X to discuss the possibility of an interview." (Definitely call when you say you will.) Lastly, thank the reviewer for his or her time. Be sincere.

Cover Letter Format

You are a designer. You are also required to have good communication and writing skills. The arrangement of your cover letter is significant. It should be neat and pleasurable to read. It should flow well and be succinct. With only three or four paragraphs, brevity is appreciated. Avoid these common cover letter mistakes:

1. Generic salutation
2. Letter is too short . . . or too long
3. Full of clichés and buzzwords
4. Grammar and spelling mistakes
5. Feeble attempt at humor
6. Misuse of words
7. Over-the-top sentences

A letter's sloppy appearance implies a lack of skill with word processing software. If your communication skills are deficient or English is not your first language, seek assistance from a campus or library writing center, or other literacy organization.

As with the resume, print the cover letter neatly on 8½" × 11" white (or other color) bond or high-quality paper. Keep it clean and free of errors. Print only on a laser or high-resolution ink-jet printer. If using color, remember that the firm may photocopy your materials and make sure that colors will copy well. Do not staple the cover letter to the resume. Let it stay loose. Put it in the same large envelope with everything else.

Put the word Enclosure (or Enc.) at the bottom under your typed name to indicate that an enclosure is included (that would be your resume, references, and marketing sampler). Many people forget to follow this simple business procedure. In conclusion, think of the cover letter as an alluring preview, a teaser if you will. You want potential employers to eagerly turn to your resume.

REFERENCES AND LETTERS OF RECOMMENDATION

It is standard business practice to have individuals who are familiar with your education, work ethic, and personality provide a reference for you. These individuals must be aware of your creative ability, design capability, and the way you work, individually and with others. Three references are typical; four are acceptable. Your list should be varied. Typical lists will include one past or present instructor and two previous or current employers (see Figure 14.15).

Be strategic about who you select to be a reference. Who is most familiar with your work? Who can be enthusiastic on your behalf? The reference can be in the form of a written letter of recommendation, an email letter, or even a phone call. The most common form is a letter. This letter must be personable. It must demonstrate that the writer really knows you and your abilities as a designer and future employee. It will be helpful to the writer to have the most recent copy of your resume and to have a few ideas about what area they should focus on when writing. For example, when a student I know well asks me to write a letter of recommendation, I ask for a resume and also a few topics. It would not make sense

14.15
Your reference list
should use the same
font, size, title, and
design elements or
personal logo as your
resume and cover
letter.

□ ———— YOUR NAME ———— □

REFERENCES

Your Address and Phone Number

email: list here   website: list here

Name, Credentials (i.e., Ph.D., MFA, MD, AIA, etc.)   Phone number
Title   Email
Company
Address
City, State, Zip

Name, Credentials   Phone number
Title   Email
Company
Address
City, State, Zip

Name, Credentials   Phone number
Title   Email
Company
Address
City, State, Zip

Name, Credentials   Phone number
Title   Email
Company
Address
City, State, Zip

for me and two other references to all say the same things about you. Should I focus on your creative potential, your work ethic as illustrated in class participation, or your enthusiasm and motivation?

A letter of reference or a recommendation only holds weight if the person writing it says something positive and holds a position of respect and credibility. A letter from your Uncle Joe saying you are a nice person holds far less weight than a letter written by your past employer saying you were a dependable, conscientious employee. Letters from your studio instructor are the most valuable type of academic reference. This person has seen you develop a design from start to finish as well as interact with colleagues, clients, and critics. Thus, his or her recommendation will be much more relevant to prospective employers than a letter from an instructor from a lecture course.

For design students with little work experience, a character reference is acceptable. This is a person who can vouch for your character, work ethic, disposition, and personality. It should not be a relative. This person should be someone who knows you well enough to speak (or write) on your behalf but would not appear biased in your favor, like your mother or Aunt Jane. This person can be someone you know from your volunteer experiences, your involvement in a professional organization, or your extracurricular academic experiences.

Design a separate reference page that is identical in appearance to your resume. Use the same paper, font, logo, and layout. You should list your most recent employer as the first reference, unless you are still employed and your current employer is not aware you are looking for another position. (That would make for an uncomfortable situation for both your current and potential employers.) Your educational reference would come second. Not listing any of your past employers or any of your instructors raises too many questions. The third and possibly fourth references can be an employer, an educator, or a personal reference. A reference from a past employer holds more weight than a letter from your studio instructor. True, the professor has witnessed your creativity under severe stress and project deadlines. But the employer has seen you in a work setting and can attest to whether you were a benefit (i.e., profitable) to the firm.

Include your references with your resume. If someone is interested in hiring you, they may call your references before they offer you an interview. Or they might not call your references at all. I've experienced both situations. I've interviewed and was hired without a single contact made to my references. I've also interviewed and had the interviewer call all of my references immediately.

When asking others to be a reference for you, ask if they would be willing to write you a letter of recommendation (or receive a phone call) when needed. Avoid using a generic form reference letter that is addressed "To whom it may concern." These are usually not very specific to your skills in light of the position you are seeking. It makes a better impression to name the person who will be reading it. Doing so also emphasizes to the reader that the letter is current.

Lastly, you must tell your references that they are on your reference list. Maybe you asked your supervisor six months ago. He might have forgotten. Remind your references that you are interviewing and for what position. Keeping in touch on a regular basis with all of your academic and professional contacts is essential to effective networking.

THE INTERVIEW

Once you have targeted the firm, sent your resume packet, and followed up, you can anticipate having an interview with the firm. An interview is a structured conversation between two or more people. Representatives of the firm will ask you specific questions to ascertain your personality and skills as a designer. This is a way for the firm to gather information about you and your opinions about various topics and events. An interview is more of a formal consultation or meeting than a casual conversation. Interviews can be conducted in person, over the phone, by email, or even with teleconferencing. If you live in close proximity to the firm, your interview will be in person. On average, a good first interview will last 30 to 60 minutes, although it can extend longer if you are invited to meet other designers and tour the office.

Before the Interview

The interview process actually begins when a firm contacts you, either by phone or email, and offers you an interview. Call back within 24 hours if possible. Time is of the essence. In the two days it may take you to respond, someone else might be offered your interview slot or even the job.

By all means, if you have already accepted another position or have changed your mind about interviewing with the firm, contact them and politely ask to be removed from the applicant pool. It is quite unprofessional to not respond and blow off an interview request. Failing to cancel an interview once you have accepted another position not only tarnishes your reputation but that of your classmates and your academic program. This is especially true for internships, as many firms are committed to your school and repeatedly hire interns year after year.

Preparing for the Interview

Have your calendar in front of you when you contact the firm to set up an interview. Be willing to shift your schedule to accommodate theirs. Get accurate directions to the interview location. Most likely, it will be in the design office. Sometimes it may be at your school or a local coffee shop or café.

Call the day before the interview to confirm the interview time. You'll probably talk to a secretary or receptionist. Get the correct spelling, title, and pronunciation of the interviewer or interviewers. Verify the location and other travel details such as parking or construction in the area.

Be on time. Be prepared for traffic or construction on your way to the interview. Being 10 to 15 minutes early is acceptable. It is better to be early than to be late. If you are late, apologize, explain why, and do not bring it up again.

When you enter the firm, greet the receptionist with a smile and introduce yourself. You may have had previous contact with this person so now he or she

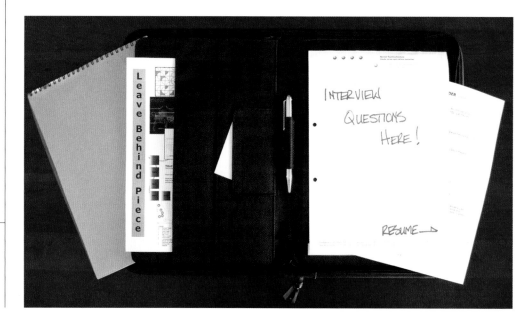

14.16
Adequately prepare for your interview and come looking professional and organized.

can put your name with your face. Tell him or her that you are here for an appointment with Mr. So-and-So. Ask where you can wait. If offered something to drink, choose water. Coffee and tea are diuretics and will dry out your mouth.

The receptionist who initially greets you is very important in an office and should not be overlooked. The person in this position is the gatekeeper to the office beyond. Always treat this person with respect and courtesy. You are making an impression on this person as well. He or she often breaks ties when two individuals are vying for the same position (i.e., "She was nicer on the phone to me than he was").

Come prepared (see Figure 14.16). Bring extra copies of your resume and references (clean, neat, and unfolded) and a nice pen or mechanical pencil. Lastly, *turn off your cell phone* before you walk in the door.

Dressing for the Interview

Table 14.3 lists several stages for a typical interview. It begins with the first impression you make on the interviewer. Generally speaking, you have between 10 seconds and 4 minutes to make a positive first impression. If you look and act like a professional, you will be treated like a professional. You should be overdressed for the interview, not underdressed. Whatever clothing you choose should convey an image of assurance, capability, and professionalism. Your appearance should impress on the interviewers that you are serious, while your portfolio will convince them of your talent.

During the Interview

When the practitioner approaches you in the waiting area, you will need to stand up and shake his or her hand. You may have to juggle a coat, umbrella, purse, briefcase, and portfolio case. Have everything on the left side of you so your right hand is free. Then pick up extra items with your right hand before you are escorted into the interview room.

Most likely, one person will interview you. Occasionally, you will interview with two designers or as many as six or seven. This is known as a team or group interview. Everyone has a role to play, whether asking questions or simply watching your body language. Every person asks a question or two and has their own opportunity to assess the candidate. Under some circumstances, the questions asked and the way they are asked must adhere to equal opportunity hiring procedures. For each candidate, the same person must ask the same question in the same manner and tone of voice. This ensures all candidates are provided an equivalent hiring process. Some of the team may never ask you a question but may stare at you the whole time, observing your nonverbal behavior.

Do not sit down until offered a chair. When you sit, sit up straight. It's best to sit on the edge of your seat and not even let your back touch the back of the chair. Your posture will be very upright. This seating stance indicates an eagerness and willingness in your nature because you are leaning forward a bit. You will be less tempted to completely relax and slouch. Instead, you will exude confidence and energy.

STAGES OF A TYPICAL INTERVIEW

	INTERVIEW TOPICS	INTERVIEWER EXPECTATIONS
First Impression	Initial greeting Small talk about the weather, traffic, mutual acquaintances, etc.	Firm handshake Good eye contact, smiling Business attire Good manners, at ease, poised
Education	Reasons for choosing your school and major Value of your degree Effort required to achieve grades Courses enjoyed the most and the least Toughest design problems Reaction to professors and critics	Intellectual abilities Breadth and depth of knowledge Ability to relate course work to career goals Willingness to work hard Ability to cope with complex problems Willingness to take criticism from others
Work Experience	Types of jobs held and why you took them Level of responsibility Relations with coworkers Duties liked the most/least	High energy level, enthusiasm Ability to be self-directed and motivated Ability to work well with others; interpersonal skills
Honors and Activities	Role in athletic, community, social, and extracurricular activities Hobbies, cultural interests Deans list, scholarships, high GPA	Diversity of interests Awareness of the world outside of college Desire to excel to the highest level
Type of Work Desired	Successes and failures Skills and deficiencies Short- and long-term objectives; career aspirations Interest in this design firm	Realistic knowledge of strengths and weaknesses Awareness of opportunities Career-oriented rather than job-oriented Knowledge of the firm and its design work
Responsibilities	Where you might fit What would you do in this position Who would supervise you Current and future projects	Informed and relevant questions Willingness to take direction and action Desire to learn from others Interest in design firm
Conclusion	Explanation of next step in interview process Cordial farewell	Attention to information as a sign of continued interest Another firm handshake and smile

Table 14.3

An area of the interview that is often overlooked is the time between introducing yourself and when the serious questions start. This initial time of pleasant chitchat should not be overlooked. Your personality is being assessed. The interviewer is watching how you interact with others. Can you be a team player? Rarely is any design in the built environment the result of individual effort. Almost everything is completed as a team of professionals. How you get the job done when working with others is as important as your ability to get it done.

The first question of an interview is seldom a hard-hitting one (like what your design weaknesses are or why you left your last job) but an icebreaker question intended to put everyone at ease and to get you talking. It may be, "Tell me about yourself" or, "What influenced you to be a designer?" Have an answer that focuses on more recent events in your life that have influenced your design decision-making abilities.

Numerous books have been written about interviewing, and they contain hundreds and hundreds of potential interview questions. It is worth reviewing these resources. Some common questions are: Why do you want to work for us? What are your strengths? Your weaknesses? What can you do for us that the other candidates cannot? Where do you see yourself in five years? Why should we hire you?

Make eye contact! When you look someone in the eye, whether it's at an interview or in everyday life, you are telling the person that he or she has your complete and undivided attention. When you shift your eyes all over the place, it sends a message that you would prefer not to speak with this person. You may be nervous, which is common and expected. Tell the interviewer, "I'm a bit nervous." He or she will understand because we've all been in the interviewee's seat before.

Think positive and be confident. Nothing conveys a lack of self-confidence more than a weak handshake, shaky voice, restless hands, or wandering eyes. *Relax*. Nonverbal communication is as important as what comes out of your mouth at an interview. Your body language may tell others more about you than what you say. For example, smiling and a firm handshake show you are confident. Having eye contact with your interviewer is a sign of self-confidence and trustworthiness.

If a question is unclear, ask the interviewer to rephrase the question. There is nothing wrong with saying, "I don't understand the question. Would you rephrase it please?" Likewise, if you don't know an answer, say so. Never try to fake it. You'll end up with egg on your face. Also, stay away from hot topics, such as sex, religion, and politics unless very relevant, such as when interviewing on an election day or for a firm that does a lot of work for the government.

Are you the type of person who sits back and listens to others? Interviewing is not a spectator sport. You'll need to talk. Or are you the type who talks nonstop? If so, take a moment to listen to your interviewer. Truly listening does not mean you're "hearing" what the other person is saying while thinking of your reply. It means you are "listening" and paying attention, using eye contact, and not interrupting. Answer the questions as well as you can, while keeping your responses brief and to the point. Emphasize your strengths and remember that the interviewer is looking for inherent personal energy and enthusiasm.

One of the most difficult aspects of interviewing (or public speaking for that matter) is to control your use of slang expressions. People tend to sprinkle their speech with the expression "you know." Other slang expressions include "like," "uh," "yep," and "um." Record yourself sometime, then listen to which expressions you use most frequently. You will be more conscious of your language from that point on.

Most importantly, show your interest in the firm and your enthusiasm for the position. The energy you project will be reciprocated. An enthusiastic tone of voice is infectious. Remember to breathe. Remember to smile. Remember to laugh if your interviewer has a good sense of humor. (You might want to laugh at his jokes even if he does not have a good sense of humor.)

A good interview is nothing more than a conversation between two people. You're sharing information and discussing common interests. Toward the end of the interview, the interviewer will ask you if you have any questions. You should come prepared with a short list of intelligent questions to ask at this time. Have them neatly typed or written legibly on paper or note card. (Pulling out a napkin from the local restaurant with the questions scrawled on them in purple marker will not make a favorable impression.) Meaningful questions can focus on details about the firm, the training process, or other job-related concerns. Another good set of questions involves performance evaluations. Don't be hesitant to ask the interviewer, "How often will I be formally evaluated?" or, "How can I receive feedback?" This shows how serious you are and that you are open to criticism from others. A good approach is to get the designer talking about himself or herself. Notice that the following winning questions are all phrased positively. This is a wonderful way to end an interview, on an extremely positive note.

1. What do you think gives your firm the competitive advantage over other firms?
2. Why do you enjoy working here so much?
3. Can you describe a typical day here in the office?
4. What makes the culture of this office so exciting?
5. Why do you think your firm is so successful?
6. What path did your career take?

Be focused and concise. Know *why* you are at the interview. When it's time to wrap things up, you will notice your interviewers gathering their papers, pushing their chairs back, and so on. Summarize key points you want them to remember when you leave. This is the time to emphasize how interested you are in working with them and why you are the best match for the position. Be enthusiastic. Be excited. Be animated and eager. Job offers are lost because applicants seem indifferent. Leave on a positive note!

Multiple Interviews
For positions with heavy responsibility, several interviews may be necessary. The first interview often acts as a screening procedure to narrow the field of intervie-

wees. It's the interviewer's first opportunity to meet you and assess your skills and personality. At this point, the interviewer can see if you are qualified for the job and if you really want it. It would be in your best interest to be eager and enthusiastic about the position. Your second interview, or the job itself, is hanging in the balance.

Depending on the position and the applicant pool, a firm may select an individual after the first round of interviews. A second interview seldom occurs when the job posting is for an internship or a part-time job. The investment in hiring someone is much greater for a full-time position, especially one in management or leadership. These second interviews are longer, typically involve more than one interviewer or interviewing session, and are more detailed and in-depth.

Although some people get their first job on their first interview, they are an exception to the rule. Plan on having interviews at several different firms. With this in mind, a few rejections here and there will not throw you into despair. The more attention you've given to researching and targeting the firms, the higher your odds are of being offered a position.

Workplace Culture

Fitting in. We hear these words all the time. The potential you have to fit in to the culture and social structure of the firm is important. If you adequately researched the firm, you should have a good idea whether you will fit in.

As you will spend plenty of time with your coworkers, they will form your at-work family. Therefore, you are asking the other designers to invite you into their close-knit group. The interviewer will be looking for indications that you are similar enough to your future coworkers to maintain peace in the office environment, yet individual enough to bring something special to the group. Your conversation with the interviewer is a narration as much about the quality of your work as it is about your qualities as a person who will fit in.

Another evaluation being made is your ability to pleasantly converse in a social setting. Much of what we do as interior designers, landscape architects, and architects is social in nature. We meet with clients. We meet with contractors. We meet with vendors and suppliers. We also meet with other practitioners. Many of these meetings are in social settings, like building openings, professional organization social gatherings, client parties, office parties, and so on. Will you represent the firm well in these social settings?

After the Interview

Before you leave the interview, find out when you can call the interviewer to follow up. You can ask when a decision will be made about filling the position. There are other candidates to interview and discussions to be had among the firm's employees. When you stand up after the interview, shake the interviewer's hand one more time (or all of them if it's a group interview).

Recording Your Impressions

As soon as you can after the interview, write down some notes. Do this in the car or on the bus or subway before you head home or back to school, while your memory is fresh. Make notes about job responsibilities, salary (if discussed), hours of operation, and other pertinent facts. Acknowledge your feelings. Do you think you can work with these people? Is there some underlying tension you didn't like? Were you comfortable with the designers? What was your initial reaction to the office and the interviewer(s)? Did the work they discussed sound interesting to you? If you have several interviews in a two- or three-week period, the more notes you make now about the firm, the people, the office, and so on, the easier it will be to recall your interview during follow-up phone calls.

The Thank-You Letter

It is common courtesy to follow the interview with a formal thank-you letter. It should be short and professional, yet warm and personable. This is also another opportunity to promote yourself and remind the firm how right you are for its open position.

What do you write in your letter? First of all, thank the interviewer for his or her time. That's the main reason for the letter. You can then use the rest of the letter to promote yourself, as demonstrated in Figure 14.17.

Point out something unique and positive about your experience interviewing with them, possibly something about the office environment or the projects of the firm. Make a few positive statements about yourself and your qualifications for the job. End by thanking the practitioner again and asking for an action on the firm's behalf, such as contacting you soon.

Not surprisingly, the thank-you letter should coordinate in paper, font, and format with your resume and cover letter. Use a standard business format with your contact information at the top and the interviewer's contact information next. A newer trend is to write your thank-you on a cool postcard. It is more memorable than a letter and more likely to actually be read.

Should you send the thank-you by postal mail or email? It depends on whether you think time is of the essence. Most likely, a traditional thank-you letter is appropriate. However, if the interviewer stated that you were the last person to be interviewed and the decision would be made shortly, it may be in your best interest to email your thank-you note. You want to put your name and another positive reminder of yourself in front of the interviewer's eyes once more before the final decision is made.

If you were interviewed by a group of practitioners, send each one a separate letter. Don't just change the name; change a point or two within the body of the letter, too. The structure of your thank-you letter can be generic. But mention something specific and particular about the interview. Verify the correct titles and spellings of all persons who interviewed you.

Date

Your name
Street address
City, State, Zip
Phone number
Email address

Ms. Smith
Senior Project Manager
XYZ Design Firm
1234 Long Street
City, State, Zip

Dear Ms. Smith,

I would like to thank you for taking the time to meet with me to discuss the designer position at XYZ Design Firm. I was quite impressed with the projects your firm creates and the quality of the designs. I am certain my creative abilities and technical skills will fit the needs of your firm. I value the time you spent speaking to me. As our discussion has given me more insight into your work, I am even more energized about the prospect of working with you and your design team. I feel I would be a meaningful asset to XYZ.

Again, thank you for your time. I look forward to hearing from you soon.

Sincerely,

Susan Designer (with signature above)

14.17
The thank-you letter is another opportunity to remind the interviewer of how perfect you are for the job!

14.18
If you need to enclose something in the envelope with your letter, call attention to it in the letter.

Date

Your name
Street address
City, State, Zip
Phone number
Email address

Mr. Smith
Senior Project Manager
XYZ Design Firm
1234 Long Street
City, State, Zip

Dear Mr. Smith,

Thank you very much for the opportunity to interview yesterday for the position of design intern. It was a delight speaking with you and learning more about XYZ Design Firm.

I would like to reiterate my sincere interest in working for XYZ Design Firm. My education in interior design and my work experience at ABC Design Group will enable me to be a productive member of your design team.

In our discussion, you mentioned that construction details are a typical part of your design projects. Although I did not have a detail such as this in my portfolio, I am enclosing an example now to show you my ability to produce these drawings.

Thank you for your consideration. I look forward to hearing from you soon regarding my position in XYZ Design Firm.

Sincerely,

Chris Designer (with signature above)

Enclosure

Were you asked to send something to the firm after the interview? Occasionally, an interviewer will look for a particular skill or skill set in your portfolio. If you did not include that skill but have a sample at home, tell the interviewer you will send a copy shortly. Include it in the envelope with your thank-you letter and state in the letter that you did remember to follow up (see Figure 14.18).

Many jobs have been won with a thank-you letter because it indicates respect, attention to detail, and professional courtesy. The interviewer will expect you to send this letter promptly. If you do not, your chances of getting the position will decrease. Believe me, the practitioner will notice if you *don't* send a thank-you letter.

SECURING THE JOB

Now that you have done your best in the interview, presented what you believe to be the best portfolio in the world, and sent a gracious thank-you letter, it's time to sit back and wait. Admittedly, no one likes this part of the job-hunting process. No one likes waiting to hear back from a firm. It's difficult to say when the firm will make a decision because you do not know how many other candidates are interviewing.

Some decisions take more time. If practitioners say they will contact you in a few days and they do not, don't be upset. These are busy professionals. Most likely, they are still interested in talking to you but have not had the time. Don't write them off. It is perfectly acceptable for you to call the firm about 7 to 10 days after your interview. Politely ask if a decision has been made regarding the position.

If no decision has been made, wait patiently. And keep pursuing other opportunities. There are no guarantees that you will get a job for which you have interviewed. You want to open as many doors as possible. Keep networking and contacting designers about open positions.

At the interview, the interviewer may be so impressed with your work, your attitude, and your personality that you are offered the job right there on the spot. Wow! This happens but is not common practice. Most firms will seriously consider multiple candidates for the same position. If the process is taking longer than usual, you may need to remind the interviewer that you still exist by sending a short and polite email or postcard. Ask if the firm has made a decision yet. Some jobs aren't filled for months. You need to keep your name in front of the interviewer without being labeled as a pest or annoyance.

When the firm decides you are *the* one, you'll be contacted and offered the position. If you decide to accept, work out all the details with the firm. The firm may send you a letter of agreement, which is a document that details your job responsibilities, salary, dates of employment, perquisites and benefits, and other conditions of employment. It typically needs to be signed and returned to the employer before you begin working. It would be wise to read this letter carefully and clarify any discrepancies before signing.

Consider that once you have made a commitment, it is your professional duty to send an acceptance letter. This letter simply states that you agree to the conditions of the offer and that you are excited about working for the firm. If you are offered a position that you choose not to accept, you can verbally decline the offer. But it is also common practice to send the firm a refusal letter, clarifying the reasons why you have chosen not to accept the position. This is known as graciously declining without burning bridges. Before you wrap up your search process, contact any other firms to which you have applied to cancel any upcoming interviews.

CONCLUSION

This chapter shows that the interview process has many components, from knowing how and where to even begin the job search, to gathering all the materials you'll need, to succeeding in the interview itself. Refer again to Table 14.1. Which of these 25 items will you need to secure a job? You may not need all of them. The key is to impress the practitioners with your design work, your organization, and most importantly, during the interview, with your knowledge, focus, and personality. The next chapter talks about caring for your portfolio and describes how to always keep it current and ready to go for that next job interview.

15

Continuing Your Portfolio

Once your portfolio is complete, you need to continually care for it and update it. It is never done. We also talk in this chapter about how to handle less-than-positive criticism about your portfolio and the job search process. Knowing how to go through these tough times with a winning attitude and a willingness to alter your portfolio or its presentation can mean the difference between success and failure.

CARING FOR YOUR PORTFOLIO

Now that the traditional and digital formats of your portfolio are done, you need to continually care for your portfolio. Keep it clean, current, and properly stored and insured. You have just spent considerable time, effort, and expense to create a beautiful and functional portfolio that reflects who you are as a designer. Keep it clean. Periodically wipe your portfolio case with a damp cloth. Clean out any extraneous material found inside, such as gum wrappers, coins, pieces of torn paper, and so on. Erase any stray marks on your projects. Replace any pages that are torn, scratched, or damaged. Keep it looking as professional as the image it should convey.

Deterioration Over Time

It would be nice if your portfolio stayed perfect. The paper would be perfect, the case would be perfect, the CDs would be perfect, and so on. The reality is that your work will become damaged over time. Glues lift, prints fade, mounted work bubbles up, and presentation boards curve. Store your work with care. Even digital work is not safe from the effects of age. Inks and toner fade, and the paper is just as unstable. Even the best printout with the best ink on the best paper will fade with time. Some printer inks may even chemically react with the plastic sleeves in your portfolio. The solution is to periodically check your portfolio. When something begins to deteriorate, fix it immediately. Don't leave it sitting on a shelf collecting dust until the night before a major job interview.

Digital Storage

Store your digital work on your computer's hard drive and keep several backup copies on CD or an external hard drive. Always put a date on your backups and a short description of what's on them. Like paper and other materials, digital material will deteriorate over time. Every couple of years, recopy your digital files. Remember that as technology becomes cheaper, better, and faster, memory devices and storage systems will improve. Suppose you had stored your early work on 5¼" floppy disks. Today you probably wouldn't be able to access any of the material because it's unlikely you could even find a computer that could read those disks. They were quickly replaced by 3.5" disks, then Zip disks, Jaz disks, CDs, and now DVDs and USB drives. Therefore, it's possible that the CD you store your files on today will not be accessible five years from now. If the storage device becomes antiquated, you'll never pull up those files again. Continually copy your portfolio material to newer storage devices when they become available and you feel it is economically feasible.

Physical Storage

Store your portfolio and its case in a dark, cool place away from any heat sources. Wrap it in plastic to keep it free of dust and odor. You probably don't want to store your work in your closet next to all of your athletic shoes, or in your kitchen pantry by the garbage can. The smell of cigarette smoke can turn off some interviewers. If you have your portfolio in this type of environment, air it outside or in another setting for a couple days prior to an interview. Do not put an air freshener inside your case as it is too fragrant.

Place your work on a shelf high above the floor with nothing placed on top of it. Make sure your storage area is safe from floods and mildew. Anticipate all consequences.

The backup copies of your digital work should be stored in the same cool, dry location. Keep your backup copies in totally different locations. For example, I take an occasional backup CD of my home computer files to my office and vice versa. If there is ever an unfortunate disaster at either location, I will at least have something recent to work from again.

Insurance

Now that you have invested countless hours and money into your finished portfolio, you will want to protect it. In most instances, nothing will happen to your portfolio. You'll use it for interview after interview without any damage to your work. It doesn't hurt, though, to insure your portfolio from theft, fire, and water damage with an insurance company. Keep a record of your expenses, as some companies may request verification that it really cost as much as you claim. Unfortunately, you cannot get reimbursed for your time and effort. Photograph it, too, because you will need physical proof of your portfolio's existence before you will be reimbursed. Keep these photographs in a safe place, preferably far away from your portfolio. Think about it. If your portfolio is lost in a fire and you stored the photographs of it in the same case, those photographs would also be destroyed. When shipping your portfolio, insure it with the shipping company for the full value of the portfolio itself and its case. If it is lost or damaged, your job search process has just been delayed. If you have a policy on your portfolio, it may not be covered when you send it somewhere or travel with it. Check these details with your insurance provider.

CONTINUALLY UPDATING YOUR PORTFOLIO

After you have consumed all this information, you may think that you are done with your portfolio. Sorry. Your portfolio is never finished. As you finesse your technical skills and expand your creative avenues, these changes should be represented in your portfolio. Whether a traditional printed portfolio or a digital one on CD or the web, it should be continually updated to reflect your most recent work.

You might wonder, "Why should I update my portfolio? I've gotten into graduate school or I've landed a prestigious job. I don't need my portfolio anymore." This would seem like a logical time to carefully store your portfolio in your closet where it can sit collecting dust. Don't allow this to happen. It's great to celebrate for a while because you deserve it. You obviously created a stunning personal promotional package that knocked the socks off of your professors or current employer.

Continue to collect and organize material for your portfolio. A good time to freshen up your portfolio is at the end of any school or work projects. Check with your firm about including samples of its work. (See copyright concerns in Chapter 5.) Occasionally, select new pieces from your files and purge old pieces from your portfolio. Don't add more without subtracting your older, less polished work. Once you have a system in place for organizing your projects, your portfolio will almost maintain itself.

There is ongoing pressure for lifelong learning in our design professions. Portfolios are perceived as a way of recording ongoing learning achievement. Don't think of updating as completely abandoning all that you have done so far. To update means to keep it current and fresh, not to undergo a major overhaul. Admittedly, there is never a perfect time to update your work. You're a busy person. You have deadlines to meet and a personal life, too. But you have to keep your portfolio current and ready to show on a moment's notice. You never know when a fabulous opportunity will come knocking on your door, such as a promotion, job change, design competition, or speaking engagement at your alma mater or a professional organization event. With current portfolio material, you have a wealth of pieces to use for these opportunities.

A digital portfolio has some special needs and must be updated more frequently than the printed version. Because we are so used to instant change in our society, a web site that never changes is stagnant and stale. You want visitors to your site to see your most current work. A great time to update it is every time new software comes on the market, which is about every 12 to 18 months. Each newer version brings with it new opportunities for creative expression. Not only might you find something that will make your portfolio even better, but you'll stay knowledgeable about the latest software applications, too.

You might not have the time for a complete overhaul or redesign of your web site, but you can make some fairly effortless changes to freshen it up. Since the home page is the first page your visitors see, it is worth it to make a noticeable change on this page every once in awhile (Prociuk 2005a). A good way to freshen your site is to liven up your home page with a slightly altered style. Try a different color scheme or add another color, nothing too wild or far offset from the rest of your site. Alter the font type or style, such as italic or bold. This can produce subtle differences in look and appearance. Adding a section and link that says, "What's New" on your home page will allow returning visitors to see the newest additions without having to search through all the pages. You can either put all your new work on one new page, or scatter the newer images throughout your site. Either way, make it easy for the user to find your new work. Your portfolio should never stagnate or become stale. Your portfolio is a journey, not a destination.

DEALING WITH REJECTION

Depressing as it might sound, prepare for some rejection. Your inquiry regarding a firm's open position may be one of hundreds, even thousands it receives. If you question this, think of how many educational programs exist that require students to have a summer internship or will graduate students in the design fields at the same time as you. If you receive a rejection letter, do not think you've struck out and the game is over. It is imperative that you keep trying!

If you don't get the job or get admitted into a degree program, seek feedback. Find out what the reviewers have to say about your work and how they rated your portfolio. There is nothing wrong with calling the interviewer one last time to thank him or her for taking the time to interview you. Then ask if he or she has any advice to improve your chances of success in future interviews. Was there something in the portfolio that could be improved? Was there a skill set not represented? Was it your work experience or education that prevented you from getting the job? If you ask with a sincere attitude and do not interrupt with rebuttal, you should get a reasonable explanation. Take the criticism with a grain of salt and critically review your portfolio. If a project needs to be reworked, alter it to better match the audience. Ask for advice from your classmates, your school's recent alumni, professors, and practitioners.

Keep everything in perspective. A job rejection is not a personal offense. Maybe you didn't fit the job description or you just were not the best candidate for the job. It's tempting to lash out at the designer or firm. A person's criticism of your portfolio is that person's opinion. It is not fact; it is only an opinion. As more and more practitioners review your portfolio, you will hear a balance of positive and negative comments. The same unappealing remark repeated a few times is a good indication that something in the portfolio needs to either be removed or reworked. If a reviewer just doesn't like the color of a rendered perspective, it is his or her personal opinion. Think of this advice as a way to improve your presentation and not a personal attack on you as an emerging professional.

Job rejections are likely, especially for internships as this is your first time venturing into the profession. If you didn't get the internship, ask why. Ask the interviewer, "If you were me, how would you correct this or what would you do differently?" You never know, you may get another chance. Firms will expand when work is flowing and will contract when times are tough. If business is good, internship openings are plentiful. When the economy is bad, internships are usually the first to be cut, even if the position is unpaid. (Even an unpaid internship will require the time of a paid employee to train and supervise an intern.) A firm that has no openings today may have openings tomorrow. Firms invest in young designers because these are the professional designers of tomorrow.

Be patient. Even when you have followed every lead, had a number of interviews, and networked until your feet were about to fall off, it still may take a few months to find that perfect position. If something's in your way, you've got to go around it. Know what you want and then go after it. The professions of the built environment can provide wonderful and diverse careers to any who seek them. The best advice I can give is to love what you do. If you do, you will persevere. Stay optimistic. Keep going. Do not quit.

CONCLUSION

I would like to reiterate that there is no *one* correct way to design a portfolio. There is no magic formula to present a portfolio, either. Your portfolio and the process you use to create it are as unique as you and your designs. The methods and suggestions presented in this book represent successful techniques. I hope these have been helpful to you. Keep in mind that even a successful portfolio will not result in immediate fame and fortune. Be realistic in your expectations.

As mentioned before, finishing your portfolio does not mean you are done. This is not a race where you cross the finish line. You will continually improve your skills and proficiency, and these need to be represented in your portfolio. The hardest part of creating a portfolio is starting one. Once you have started one and are comfortable with the format, future projects and commissions can be added with little effort or stress. But you cannot add to something that doesn't exist. So roll up your sleeves and dig in.

As you grow in your knowledge of design, newer projects will replace older ones. As painful as it may be, you will need to discard some projects. It's easy to be protective of your past work. But you cannot move forward if you are holding on to the past.

Your voyage through portfolio production will require a vast amount of energy, time, reflection, and learning. You will feel at times very frustrated and at other times, simply elated with yourself. This voyage will tie together knowledge and skills learned in the past, your present abilities, and those incidents yet to come. You will push yourself beyond what you know and believe as a designer. All of this will be reflected in a portfolio of which you are extremely proud!

Appendix: Web Sites

Adobe Acrobat
www.adobe.com/products/acrobat/
Adobe After Effects
www.adobe.com/products/aftereffects/
Adobe Flash
www.adobe.com/products/flash/
Adobe Flash Player
www.adobe.com/downloads/
Adobe Illustrator
www.adobe.com/products/illustrator/
Adobe ImageReady
www.adobe.com/products/creativesuite/
Adobe InDesign
www.adobe.com/products/indesign/
Adobe Photoshop
www.adobe.com/products/photoshop/
Adobe Photoshop Album
www.adobe.com/products/
photoshopalbum
Adobe Premiere and Premiere Pro
www.adobe.com/products/premiere/
Adobe Reader
www.adobe.com/products/reader/
Adobe Shockwave Player
www.adobe.com/downloads/
American Institute of Architects
www.aia.org

American Society of Interior Designers
www.asid.org
American Society of Landscape Architects
www.asla.org
Apple Final Cut Pro
www.apple.com/finalcutstudio/
finalcutpro/
Apple Macintosh
www.apple.com/macosx/leopard/
Apple Motion
www.apple.com/finalcutstudio/motion/
Apple QuickTime
www.apple.com/quicktime/
Architectural Registration Examination
(ARE) www.ncarb.org
Autodesk 3D Studio Max
www.autodesk.com/3dsmax
Autodesk 3D Studio Viz
www.autodesk.com/viz
Autodesk AutoCAD
www.autodesk.com/autocad
Autodesk Discreet Combustion
http://usa.autodesk.com
Autodesk Revit
www.autodesk.com/revit
Auto-des-sys FormZ www.formz.com

BurnatOnce
www.burnatonce.net/downloads/
CorelDraw Graphics Suite
www.corel.com
Corel PhotoPaint www.corel.com
Council for Interior Design Accreditation
(CIDA) www.accredit-id.org
Council of Landscape Architectural
Registration Boards www.clarb.org
Digital Smart Digital Audio Editor
www.audioeditor.us/dae/
Easy CD Creator www.roxio.com
E-Book Systems Flip Album Pro
www.flipalbum.com
Extensis Portfolio www.extensis.com
Google Sketchup www.sketchup.com
Graphisoft ArchiCAD www.graphisoft.com
International Interior Design Association
www.iida.org
Landscape Architect Registration
Examination (LARE) www.clarb.org
Landscape Architectural Accreditation
Board (LAAB) www.asla.org
Letraset StudioTac Adhesive
www.letraset.com
Macromedia Director
www.adobe.com/products/director/
Macromedia Dreamweaver
www.adobe.com/products/dreamweaver/
Macromedia Fireworks
www.adobe.com/products/fireworks/
Microsoft Expression Interactive Designer
www.microsoft.com/expression/

Microsoft FrontPage
office.microsoft.com/en-us/frontpage/
Microsoft Office Products
office.microsoft.com
Microsoft Publisher
office.microsoft.com/en-us/publisher/
Microsoft Windows
www.microsoft.com/windows/
Microsoft Windows Media Player
www.microsoft.com/windows/
windowsmedia/
National Architecture Accreditation Board
(NAAB) www.naab.org
National Council for Interior Design
Qualification Examination (NCIDQ)
www.ncidq.org
NCH Express Burn www.nch.com.au/burn/
Panavue Image Assembler
www.panavue.com
Portfolios and Art Cases
www.portfolios-and-art-cases.com
QuarkXPress www.quark.com
RealPlayer www.real.com/
RealViz Stitcher www.realviz.com
RMBSoft Sound Edit Pro
www.rmbsoft.com
RT Innovations Portfolio Cases
www.rtinnovations.com
SmartDraw www.smartdraw.com
Sony Sound Forge
www.sonycreativesoftware.com
United States Copyright Office
www.copyright.gov

References

Baron, C. 2004. *Designing a digital port-folio*. Indianapolis, IN: New Riders.

Barrett, H. 1998. Strategic questions: What to consider when planning for electronic portfolios. *Learning and Leading with Technology* 26 (2): 6–13. Retrieved November 4, 2003 from http://electronicportfolios.org/portfolios/LLTOct98.html.

———. 2000. Create your own electronic portfolio: Using off-the-shelf software to showcase your own or student work. *Learning and Leading with Technology* 27 (7): 14–21. Retrieved November 4, 2003 from http://www.iste.org/LL/27/7/14b/index.cfm.

Bender, D. 2003. Online CEUs—what's stopping us? *Interiors & Sources* 10 (4): 104–6.

Berryman, G. 1994. *Designing creative port-folios*. Menlo Park, CA: Crisp.

Black, A. L., and L. Waxman. 2000. Keeping pace with the technology of practice. *ISDesignet*, October. Retrieved April 9, 2003 from http://www.isdesignet.com/magazine/Oct'00/idec.html.

Brown, C. E. 2005a. Optimizing images for the web—part I. Pointafter.com. Retrieved December 19, 2005 from http://www.pointafter.com/Archives/n10108.htm

———. 2005b. Optimizing images for the web—part III. Pointafter.com. Retrieved December 19, 2005 from http://www.pointafter.com/Archives/n10110.htm

Clemons, S. A., and J. McCullough. 1989. Attitudes of interior designers toward CADD and CADD education. *Journal of Interior Design Education and Research* 15 (2): 29–34.

Cohen, J. 2000. *Communication and design with the Internet*. New York: W. W. Norton.

Cole, D. J., C. W. Ryan, B. Mathies, and R. Clemens. 1999. Electronic portfolios: Applications in student assessment. In *Selected papers from the 10th International Conference on College Teaching and Learning*, ed. J. A. Chambers, 33–40. Jacksonville, FL: Florida Community College.

Merriam-Webster Online. 2006. Portfolio definition. Retrieved September 3, 2006 from http://www.m-w.com/.

Dye, B. 2002. Glossary of wireless terms. Retrieved August 25, 2006 from http://www.braddye.com/glossary.html.

Eisenman, S. 2006. *Building design portfolios: Innovative concepts for presenting your work.* Gloucester, MA: Rockport.

Fegette, S. 2006. Tips for rookie video producers. Adobe Design Center. Retrieved August 22, 2006 from http://www.adobe.com/designcenter/dialogbox/rookie_video/.

General Electric. 2005. Learn about light. Retrieved August 10, 2006 from http://www.gelighting.com/na/home_lighting/products/education/.

Hall, S. 2001. From trainee graduates to graduate trainees: Towards an illumination of the teaching of professional practice on design degrees. In *Proceedings of the International Conference on Design and Technology Educational Research and Curriculum Development,* 36–40. Leicestershire, UK: Loughborough Univ. Retrieved November 2, 2003, from www.lboro.ac.uk/idater/.

Heath, M., and S. Cockerham. 2001. Electronic portfolios for faculty development. Paper presented at the 6th Annual Mid-South Instructional Technology Conference, April 2001. Retrieved September 26, 2003 from http://www.mtsu.edu/~itconf/proceed01/index.html.

Hungerland, E. C., and B. Hungerland. 2002. *Marketing your creative portfolio.* Englewood Cliffs, NJ: Prentice-Hall.

Karpati, A., A. Zempleni, N. D. Verhelst, N. H. Velduijzen, and D. W. Schonau. 1998. Expert agreement in judging art projects: A myth or reality? *Studies in Educational Evaluation* 24 (4): 385–404.

Kilbane, C. R., and N. B. Milman. 2003. *The digital teaching portfolio handbook.* Boston, MA: Pearson Education.

Kliment, S. A. 1998. *Writing for design professionals.* New York: W. W. Norton.

Lankes, A. M. 1995. Electronic portfolios: A new idea in assessment. ERIC Digest: Clearinghouse on information and technology. EDO-IR-95-9.

Leeman-Conley, M. 1999. The how and the why of electronic portfolios in higher education. Paper presented at the 1999 Technology in Education International Conference and Exposition. Retrieved September 18, 2003 from http://www.promedia.net/users/conley/papers/TechEd99.html.

Linton, H. 2003. *Portfolio design,* 3rd ed. New York: W. W. Norton.

Marjanovic, I., R. K. Ruedi, and L. Lokko. 2003. *The portfolio: An architectural student's handbook.* Oxford, England: Architectural Press.

Marquand, E. 1994. *How to prepare your portfolio: A guide for students and professionals,* 3rd ed. New York: Art Direction Book Co.

Matthews, J., and J. Gritzmacher. 1984. Preferred content and format for portfolios and review criteria. *Journal of Interior Design Educators and Research* 10 (2): 28–31.

McHugh, S. 2005a. Raw file format. Retrieved March 20, 2006 from http://www.cambridgecolour.com/tutorials/RAW-file-format.htm.

———. 2005b. Digital image interpolation. Retrieved March 20, 2006 from http://www.cambridgeincolour.com/tutorials/image-interpolation.htm.

_____. 2005c. Image resizing for the web and email. Retrieved March 20, 2006 from http://www.cambridgeincolour.com/tutorials/image-resize-for-web.htm.

McKenna, A. T. 2000. *Digital portfolio.* New York: Rockport.

Merriam-Webster OnLine Dictionary. 2006. Portfolio definition. Retrieved September 3, 2006 from http://www.m-w.com/dictionary/portfolio.

Mitton, M. 2004. *Interior design visual presentation.* New York: Wiley.

Morgan, E. L. 1996, November 15. Design elements for great web pages: Readability, browsability, searchability plus assistance. Retrieved December 19, 2005 from http://www.lib.ncsu.edu/staff/morgan/design/design.pdf.

Myers, D. R. 2005. *The graphic designer's guide to portfolio design.* Hoboken, NJ: Wiley.

Nayyar, S. 2001. Inside the mind of gen Y. *American Demographics* 23 (9): 6.

NCES. 2002. Teaching undergraduates in U.S. postsecondary institutions: Fall 1998. U.S. Dept. of Education, National Center for Education Statistics. Retrieved December 12, 2005 from http://nces.ed.gov/pubs2002/2002209.pdf.

Nielson, K. J., and D. A. Taylor. 2002. *Interiors: An introduction,* 3rd ed. New York: McGraw-Hill.

Novitski, B. J. 1995. Students weave a computer web. *Progressive Architecture* 76: 39–40.

Oblinger, D. 2003. Boomers, gen-Xers, and millennials: Understanding the new students. *Educause Review* 38 (4): 37–47.

Pablo, J. 1999. Harnessing the potential of on-line continuing education. *Interiors & Sources* 77 (7): 166–7.

Paul, P. 2001. Getting inside gen Y. *American Demographics* 23 (9): 42–9.

Penston, G. 2006. *Adobe Creative Suite 2 how-tos: 100 essential techniques.* Berkeley, CA: Adobe Press.

Pitrowski, C. 2004. *Becoming an interior designer.* Hoboken, NJ: Wiley.

Pressman, A. 1997. *Professional practice 101.* New York: Wiley.

Prociuk, G. 2005a. Five simple changes guaranteed to freshen up your website. Pointafter.com. Retrieved December 19, 2005 from http://www.pointafter.com/Archives/n10212.htm.

_____. 2005b. 20 do's and don'ts of web usability. Pointafter.com. Retrieved December 19, 2005 from http://www.pointafter.com/Archives/n10204.htm.

Reznikoff, S. C. 1989. *Specifications for commercial interiors.* New York: Whitney Library of Design.

Romaniello, S. 2003. *The perfect digital portfolio.* New York: Ava.

Scher, P. 1992. *The graphic design portfolio: How to make a good one.* New York: Watson-Guptill.

Seguin, M. 1991. *The perfect portfolio for artists and writers: How to put together a creative "book" that sells.* Hawthorne, NJ: Career Press.

Smick, M., P. S. Burke, F. Meza, S. Moniz, C. Rose, and S. Smith. 2006. *Using Adobe Creative Suite 2.* Indianapolis, IN: Que.

Tain, L. 2003. *Portfolio presentation for fashion designers,* 3rd ed. New York: Fairchild.

Talarico, W. 2003. Say hello to generation Y. Retrieved February 9, 2004 from http://www.steelcase.com/en/pdf/knowledgepapers/GenY.pdf.

Testerman, J. K., and H. D. Hall. 2000–2001. The electronic portfolio: A means of preparing leaders for application of technology in education.

Journal of Educational Technology Systems 29 (3): 199–206.

United States Copyright Office. 2006. Copyright office basics. Retrieved October 9, 2006 from http://www.copyright.gov/.

United States Department of Labor Statistics. 2004. Employee tenure in 2004. News release 04-1829. Retrieved February 27, 2006 from http://www.bls.gov/opub/mlr/2004/10/lmir.htm.

Univ. of Wisconsin–Madison. 2003. Learning technology & distance education. E-portfolio feasibility study: Executive summary. Madison, WI: Author. Retrieved September 19, 2003, from http://wiscinfo.doit.wisc.edu/ltde/ORFI/eportfolio/executive.htm.

Vistek Ltd. 2006. Imaging and photographic terminology database. Retrieved August 30, 2006 from http://www.vistek.ca/glossary/.

Wood, J. 2004. Open minds and a sense of adventure: How teachers of art and design approach technology. *International Journal of Art and Design Education* 23 (2): 179–91.

Credits

Note: Uncredited images in the book are courtesy of the author.

Chapter 1

Figure 1.1: Courtesy of Michael Barnfield

Figure 1.2: Courtesy of Alexandra C. Ayres, Sally Azer, and Kelly Robinson

Figure 1.3: Courtesy of Jeffrey Prince

Figure 1.7: Courtesy of Yang Peng

Figure 1.8: Courtesy of Jeremy M. Gates

Figure 1.9: Courtesy of Amol Surve

Figure 1.10: Courtesy of Mat Wingate

Figure 1.11: Courtesy of Daniel Childers

Chapter 2

Figure 2.1: Courtesy of Allison Saunders

Figure 2.2: Courtesy of Elaine Hu

Figure 2.3: Courtesy of Jennifer Walls

Figure 2.4: Courtesy of Yuki Ueji

Figure 2.5: Courtesy of Shrikar Bhave

Figure 2.6: Courtesy of Stuart Braiman

Figure 2.8: Courtesy of Emily K. Callaghan

Figure 2.9: Courtesy of David M. Solnick

Figure 2.10: Courtesy of Zubin Shroff

Figure 2.11: Courtesy of Shelby Bogaard

Figure 2.12: Courtesy of Amy Oditt

Figure 2.13: Courtesy of Charudatta Joshi

Figure 2.14: Courtesy of Alexandra C. Ayres; Sally Azer; Kelly Robinson

Chapter 3

Figure 3.1: Courtesy of Cindy Louie

Figure 3.2: Courtesy of Erin Dinno

Figure 3.3: Courtesy of Rachel K. Dankert

Figure 3.4: Courtesy of Katie L. Fulton; Jennifer Gozzi

Figure 3.5: Courtesy of Charudatta Joshi

Figure 3.6: Courtesy of Jeffrey Prince

Figure 3.7: Courtesy of Mat Wingate

Figure 3.8: Courtesy of Daniel Childers

Figure 3.9: Courtesy of Alexandra C. Ayres; Sally Azer; Kelly Robinson

Figure 3.10: Courtesy of Elaine Hu

Figure 3.11: Courtesy of Charudatta Joshi; Kim H. Nguyen

Chapter 4

Figure 4.1: Courtesy of Daniel Childers

Figure 4.2: Courtesy of Jeffrey Lothner

Figure 4.3: Courtesy of Ellen Barten

Figure 4.4: Courtesy of Aaron J. Kulik

Figure 4.5: Courtesy of Ashley Delph

Figure 4.6: Courtesy of Charudatta Joshi

Figure 4.7: Courtesy of Jeremy M. Gates

Figure 4.8: Courtesy of Lauren Maitha;
Ellen Barten

Figure 4.9: Courtesy of Elaine Hu

Figure 4.10: Courtesy of Jeffrey Prince

Figure 4.11: Courtesy of Stephanie Fanger

Figure 4.12: Courtesy of Rachel K. Dankert

Figure 4.13: Courtesy of Stephanie Fanger

Figure 4.15: Courtesy of Ashley Delph

Figure 4.16: Courtesy of Jeffrey Prince

Figure 4.18: Courtesy of Jeffrey Prince

Figure 4.19: Courtesy of Sally Azer;
Joanie Liebelt

Figure 4.21: Courtesy of Shrikar Bhave

Figure 4.22: Courtesy of Han Yoon Lee;
Shelby Bogaard; Tracy Franson

Figure 4.23: Courtesy of Paul Marquez

Figure 4.24: Courtesy of Brian WinThant
Tong

Figure 4.25: Courtesy of Lisa Perrone;
Cindy Louie; Kristy Harline

Figure 4.27: Courtesy of Shelby Bogaard

Figure 4.28: Courtesy of Melissa Zlatow

Figure 4.29: Courtesy of Shrikar Bhave

Figure 4.31: Courtesy of Paul Marquez

Figure 4.32: Courtesy of Karina Mutiara
Dharmazi

Figure 4.33: Courtesy of Lauren Maitha;
Joanne Huang

Chapter 5

Figure 5.1: Courtesy of Zubin Shroff

Figure 5.3: Courtesy of Aaron J. Kulik

Figure 5.4: Courtesy of Aaron J. Kulik

Figure 5.5: Courtesy of Aaron J. Kulik

Figure 5.6: Courtesy of Aaron J. Kulik

Figure 5.9: Courtesy of Aaron J. Kulik

Figure 5.10: Courtesy of Shelby Bogaard

Figure 5.11: Courtesy of Jeffrey Lothner

Figure 5.12: Courtesy of Liisa Taylor

Figure 5.13: Courtesy of Daniel Childers

Figure 5.16: Courtesy of Alexandra C.
Ayres; Sally Azer; Kelly Robinson

Figure 5.17: Courtesy of Liisa Taylor

Figure 5.18: Courtesy of Jeffrey Lothner

Chapter 6

Figure 6.1: Courtesy of Zubin Shroff

Figure 6.3: Courtesy of Aaron J. Kulik

Figure 6.4: Courtesy of Alexandra C. Ayres;
Sally Azer; Kelly Robinson

Figure 6.6: Courtesy of Aaron J. Kulik

Figure 6.7: Courtesy of Christy Phifer

Figure 6.9: Courtesy of Aaron J. Kulik

Figure 6.10: Courtesy of Christy Phifer

Figure 6.11: Courtesy of Allison Saunders;
Pamela Stradling

Figure 6.13: Courtesy of Aaron J. Kulik

Figure 6.14: Courtesy of Han Yoon Lee

Figure 6.16: Courtesy of Katie L. Fulton;
Jennifer Gozzi

Figure 6.17: Courtesy of Julia Kancius,
Lindsay Miller, Amy Oditt

Figure 6.18: Courtesy of Aaron J. Kulik

Figure 6.21: Courtesy of Aaron J. Kulik

Figure 6.22: Courtesy of Katie L. Fulton

Figure 6.24: Courtesy of William Iadevaia

Figure 6.26: Courtesy of Aaron J. Kulik

Figure 6.28: Courtesy of Aaron J. Kulik

Figure 6.29: Courtesy of Jon Vredevoogd

Figure 6.30: Courtesy of Jeffrey Prince

Figure 6.31: Courtesy of Zubin Shroff; Karl
    Mascarenhas; Adel Bagli; Karl Wadia;
    Academy of Architecture, Mumbai
Figure 6.33: Courtesy of Daniel Childers
Figure 6.34: Courtesy of Paul Marquez
Figure 6.35: Courtesy of Paul Marquez
Figure 6.36: Courtesy of Alexandra C.
    Ayres; Sally Azer; Kelly Robinson
Figure 6.38: Courtesy of Shrikar Bhave
Figure 6.39: Courtesy of Aaron J. Kulik
Figure 6.41: Courtesy of Amol Surve
Figure 6.42: Courtesy of Aaron J. Kulik

Chapter 7

Figure 7.2: Courtesy of Megan Williams;
    Zsavay Andrews
Figure 7.5: Courtesy of Han Yoon Lee
Figure 7.7: Courtesy of John Milander
Figure 7.9: Courtesy of Lauren Maitha;
    Lindsay Miller
Figure 7.10: Courtesy of Aaron J. Kulik
Figure 7.11: Courtesy of Shelby Bogaard
Figure 7.12: Courtesy of Carol Kleihauer
Figure 7.13: Courtesy of Tess Parker
Figure 7.14: Courtesy of Jeffrey Prince
Figure 7.15: Courtesy of Charudatta Joshi
Figure 7.16: Courtesy of Paul Marquez
Figure 7.17: Courtesy of Shrikar Bhave
Figure 7.18: Courtesy of Yang Peng
Figure 7.19: Courtesy of Alexandra C.
    Ayres; Sally Azer; Kelly Robinson
Figure 7.20: Courtesy of Liisa Taylor
Figure 7.22: Courtesy of Zubin Shroff
Figure 7.23: Courtesy of Amol Surve
Figure 7.24: Courtesy of Cindy Louie
Figure 7.25: Courtesy of Jeffrey Lothner
Figure 7.26: Courtesy of Hayley Johnson
Figure 7.28: Courtesy of Daniel Childers
Figure 7.29: Courtesy of Aaron J. Kulik

Figure 7.34: Courtesy of Jeremy M. Gates
Figure 7.37: Courtesy of Elaine Hu
Figure 7.38: Courtesy of Jeremy M. Gates
Figure 7.39: Courtesy of Lauren Maitha;
    Lindsay Miller
Figure 7.40: Courtesy of Julia Kancius;
    Allison Saunders
Figure 7.41: Courtesy of Ellen Barten
Figure 7.46: Courtesy of Stuart Braiman
Figure 7.47: Courtesy of Charudatta Joshi
Figure 7.48: Courtesy of Julian Sin

Chapter 9

Figure 9.1: Courtesy of Aaron J. Kulik
Figure 9.2: Courtesy of Aaron J. Kulik
Figure 9.5: Courtesy of Aaron J. Kulik
Figure 9.7: Courtesy of Aaron J. Kulik,
    Dick & Fritsche Design Group
Figure 9.8: Courtesy of Rachel K. Dankert
Figure 9.11: Courtesy of Aaron J. Kulik,
    Dick & Fritsche Design Group
Figure 9.15: Courtesy of Alexandra C.
    Ayres; Sally Azer; Kelly Robinson

Chapter 10

Figure 10.1: Courtesy of David A. Hobart Jr.
Figure 10.3: Courtesy of Jeffrey Lothner
Figure 10.4: Courtesy of Elaine Hu
Figure 10.6: Courtesy of Ashley Delph
Figure 10.7: Courtesy of Anca Muresan
Figure 10.8: Courtesy of Elaine Hu;
    Joanne Huang
Figure 10.9: Courtesy of Paul Hibbard
Figure 10.10: Courtesy of Liisa Taylor
Figure 10.11: Courtesy of Allison Saunders
Figure 10.12a: Courtesy of Allison Saunders;
    Julia Kancius

Figure 10.12b: Courtesy of Lindsay Miller;
   Lauren Maitha
Figure 10.13: Courtesy of Shana D. Payne
Figure 10.14a: Courtesy of Chelsea
   Harwood; Pamela Stradling
Figure 10.14b: Courtesy of Elaine Hu;
   Joanne Huang
Figure 10.15: Courtesy of Elaine Hu
Figure 10.17: Courtesy of Mat Wingate
Figure 10.19: Courtesy of Stacey Smith
Figure 10.20: Courtesy of Stephanie Fanger
Figure 10.22: Courtesy of Julian Sin;
   Amy Oditt
Figure 10.29: Courtesy of Paul Hibbard
Figure 10.31: Courtesy of Shelby Bogaard
Figure 10.35: Courtesy of Liisa Taylor
Figure 10.42: Courtesy of Aaron J. Kulik

Chapter 11

Figure 11.1: Courtesy of Paul Marquez
Figure 11.2: Courtesy of Charudatti Joshi
Figure 11.3: Courtesy of Alexandra C.
   Ayres; Sally Azer; Kelly Robinson
Figure 11.4: Courtesy of Daniel Childers
Figure 11.5: Courtesy of Zubin Shroff
Figure 11.7: Courtesy of William Iadevaia
Figure 11.12: Courtesy of Manu Juyal
Figure 11.14: Courtesy of Zubin Shroff
Figure 11.15: Courtesy of Paul Hibbard
Figure 11.16: Courtesy of Eric Cylwik
Figure 11.17: Courtesy of Katie Crestin;
   Alexis Raterman
Figure 11.18: Courtesy of Eric Cylwik
Figure 11.22: Courtesy of Manu Juyal;
   David A. Hobart Jr.
Figure 11.23: Courtesy of Rachel K. Dankert
Figure 11.29: Courtesy of Paul Marquez

Figure 11.32: Courtesy of Jennifer Brungart
Figure 11.34: Courtesy of Daniel Childers
Figure 11.35: Courtesy of Shelby Bogaard

Chapter 12

Figure 12.1: Courtesy of Melissa Zlatow
Figure 12.2: Courtesy of Charudatta Joshi;
   Shrikar Bhave
Figure 12.3: Courtesy of Shelby Bogaard;
   Kristy Harline
Figure 12.4: Courtesy of Charudatta Joshi
Figure 12.6: Courtesy of Amol Surve;
   Paul Hibbard
Figure 12.7: Courtesy of Paul Hibbard
Figure 12.8: Courtesy of Manu Juyal
Figure 12.9: Courtesy of Amol Surve
Figure 12.10: Courtesy of Paul Marquez
Figure 12.12: Courtesy of Manu Juyal
Figure 12.13: Courtesy of Manu Juyal;
   David A. Hobart Jr.
Figure 12.15: Courtesy of Manu Juyal
Figure 12.17: Courtesy of Daniel Childers
Figure 12.18: Courtesy of Charudatta Joshi
Figure 12.19: Courtesy of Allison Saunders;
   Julia Kancius
Figure 12.20: Courtesy of Paul Hibbard
Figure 12.21: Courtesy of Manu Juyal;
   David A. Hobart Jr.
Figure 12.22: Courtesy of Charudatta Joshi
Figure 12.25: Courtesy of Charudatta Joshi
Figure 12.29: Courtesy of Yang Peng
Figure 12.34: Courtesy of Paul Marquez
Figure 12.36: Courtesy of Alexandra C.
   Ayres; Sally Azer; Kelly Robinson
Figure 12.37: Courtesy of Eleanor Combs;
   Jennifer Gozzi; Elaine Hu

Figure 12.38: Courtesy of Manu Juyal

Figure 12.41:   Courtesy of Zubin Shroff

Chapter 13

Figure 13.2: Courtesy of Zubin Shroff

Figure 13.3: Courtesy of Liisa Taylor

Figure 13.4: Courtesy of Jeffrey Lothner

Figure 13.7: Courtesy of Charudatta Joshi

Figure 13.8: Courtesy of Alexandra C. Ayres; Sally Azer; Kelly Robinson

Figure 13.9: Courtesy of Elaine Hu; Joanne Huang

Figure 13.10: Courtesy of Zubin Shroff; Academy of Architecture, Mumbai

Figure 13.11: Courtesy of Katie L. Fulton

Chapter 14

Figure 14.1: Courtesy of Ellie Combs

Figure 14.4: Courtesy of Mark Chichester

Figure 14.5: Courtesy of Jeffrey Lothner

Figure 14.7: Courtesy of Katie L. Fulton; Jennifer Gozzi

Figure 14.10: Courtesy of Shelby Bogaard

Figure 14.11: Courtesy of Shelby Bogaard

Figure 14.12: Courtesy of Lisa M. L. Broome

Index